THE JUGGLER

Also by Warren F. Kimball _____

"The Most Unsordid Act": Lend-Lease, 1939–1941 (1969)

Franklin D. Roosevelt and the World Crisis, 1937–1945 (ed.) (1973)

Swords or Ploughshares? The Morgenthau Plan for Defeated Nazi Germany, 1943–1946 (1976)

American Diplomacy in the Twentieth Century (ed.) (1980)

Churchill & Roosevelt: The Complete Correspondence, 1939–1945 (3 vols., edited with commentaries) (1984)

THE JUGGLER

FRANKLIN ROOSEVELT AS WARTIME STATESMAN

Warren F. Kimball

PRINCETON UNIVERSITY PRESS   PRINCETON, NEW JERSEY

Library of Congress Cataloging-in-Publication Data

Kimball, Warren F.
The juggler : Franklin Roosevelt as wartime statesman /
Warren F. Kimball.
p.   cm.
Includes bibliographical references and index.
ISBN 0-691-04787-1 (cloth)   ISBN 0-691-03730-2 (paperback)
1. Roosevelt, Franklin D. (Franklin Delano), 1882–1945.
2. World War, 1939–1945—Diplomatic history.   3. United States—
Foreign relations—1933–1945.   I. Title.
E807.K48   1991
940.53'2273—dc20   90-43562

This book has been composed in Linotron Sabon

Princeton University Press books are printed
on acid-free paper and meet the guidelines
for permanence and durability of the Committee
on Production Guidelines for Book Longevity
of the Council on Library Resources

Printed in the United States of America

First Princeton paperback printing, 1994

10   9   8   7   6   5   4

For Four Friends _____

CHARLES C. ALEXANDER

LAWRENCE J. FLINK

LLOYD C. GARDNER

DANIEL B. HOWELL

Contents

List of Illustrations _____

Everything's Under Control.

Preface

IT ALL looked so easy. In the aftermath of publishing the Churchill-Roosevelt correspondence, I had written a number of papers on aspects of American foreign policy during World War II. Instead of submitting those essays to various journals, I thought it would be nice, and less complicated, to put them all together. But by placing them between one set of covers, what looked easy suddenly got hard. The essays were developed at different times for different audiences and had no organizing theme, other than American diplomacy during the Second World War. Colonialism, a thread that runs through a number of the essays, demanded separate treatment. Just calling it a book, even a book of essays, imposed a new discipline on the material. As one friend put it: "Why is it FDR the 'juggler' and not FDR the bumbler?"

I have rewritten all the new essays, trying to focus them on the personal foreign policy of Franklin Roosevelt, particularly the assumptions that underlay that policy. In the case of the two previously published essays, they are reprinted as they originally appeared (typos are corrected), but I have included addenda to point out how they illustrate Roosevelt's foreign policy. Only you, the reader, can determine whether I have managed to bring the disparate essays under control and, in the process, shed some light on "the juggler."

What unity does exist is due largely to the prodding and coaxing of three very good friends and colleagues: Lloyd C. Gardner of Rutgers University; David Reynolds of Christ's College, Cambridge; and Charles C. Alexander of Ohio University. Not only did they suffer through many of the early drafts of the essays when they were first written, but they ploughed through them all again when they took on the form of a book. Likewise, John A. Thompson of St. Catherine's College, Cambridge, read an early draft of the entire manuscript and made valuable suggestions that were crucial to its reorganization. Walter LaFeber of Cornell University also tried to rescue me from a number of opaque arguments and inconsistencies. My frequent failure to heed their advice only reinforces what they already knew about my stubbornness. In addition, the specific essays were read by others whom I have thanked in the notes. I continue to marvel at my good fortune to be in a profession with so many members who cheerfully give of their time and talent with no reward beyond this kind of pat on the back.

I owe a special debt of gratitude to Fred Pollock, coauthor of the essay on Roosevelt and colonialism ("In Search of Monsters to Destroy"), for taking time out from his very busy life to do the bulk of the research and drafting of that chapter, and to comment on others. That he is willing, even eager, to do that kind of work only illustrates the seductiveness of history.

As ever, the Director of the Franklin D. Roosevelt Library, William R. Emerson, and his entire staff have earned special thanks. Although these essays were built on research done for the Churchill-Roosevelt correspondence, FDR Library personnel continued to provide superb support and a friendly atmosphere within which to do research. The Presidential Libraries comprise a unique and invaluable system, and the FDR Library deserves praise and credit for establishing the benchmarks.

The British—Scots, Welsh, and English—offered atmosphere and opportunities crucial to my work. The librarians and archivists at the British Public Record Office (Kew, England) and the British Library of Economics and Political Science (London School of Economics, London) were most helpful. Most of the rewriting and additional research was done while I was Pitt Professor of American History at the University of Cambridge (Corpus Christi College), England. My thanks go to that University, and particularly its History Faculty, to the Master and Fellows of Corpus Christi College, and to my own university administration at Rutgers, for making it possible for me to accept that post. It was a unique and valuable opportunity to write and to interact with a different community of scholars.

A word on photography as history. Photographs reflect only an instant of truth and often mask the context of that history. These illustrations have been selected and captioned to reflect my interpretations of Roosevelt and the history of his foreign policy. To do that, I have used a number of candid shots taken with fixed-focus reflex cameras. The resulting photography is often "soft" and fuzzy—but historical clarity is what matters.

But nothing is more important than the support, praise, criticism, and love of my wife, Jackie. She has heard these essays delivered at least twice: once while I paced the living room, and again before the intended audience. Each time she reacted with an enthusiasm and interest that buoyed my spirits.

15 June 1990

THE JUGGLER

The Faces of FDR.

Introduction _____

On Diplomatic History and FDR

A NUMBER of scholars, even some trained in diplomatic history, have argued that traditional studies of American foreign policy and diplomacy have little if anything new or worth saying about the development and character of the American nation. Some of these complaints reflect a proper concern that historians of American foreign relations tend to be too parochial and Washington-centered—that we are all just frustrated secretaries of state. That is borne out by those diplomatic historians who, themselves, have dismissed much of their colleagues' work for the ultimate irrelevance—its failure to provide a guide for current and future foreign policymakers. Other reproaches are first cousins to the widespread contempt for what is called political history. But there are defenders. Historian William Leuchtenburg, sounding a call for political history to become respectable again, made a passing comment on diplomatic history: "We know better now," he wrote, "than to isolate diplomacy from domestic currents, but still have to test [the] hypothesis—[that] 'The role of the State in domestic affairs tends to be replicated in its foreign policies.' "[1]

I would turn that around to argue that foreign affairs likewise tend to create domestic policies. For example, jealousy and fear of Soviet power and growth are more than just an extension of the domestic side of our political economy. Similarly, Franklin Roosevelt's response to Nazism was more than just the externalization of the New Deal, even if he saw New Deal–type programs as the solution to most of the world's ills, promising that "if war does come we will make it a New Deal war."[2] What unites foreign and domestic affairs is nationalism—Americanism, if you will—the intellectual and emotional force that is a fundamental link between the state and the society, and a fundamental link between social and political history.

Examining these links is a way historians of American foreign policy and diplomacy can contribute to a better understanding of how and why Americans have become what they are. So-called diplomatic history can and does help us to understand ourselves and our society, for we are not merely inward looking, isolated animals, acting without reference to the external world. The assumptions by which we operate include assumptions about the rest of the world and how we should relate to it. And, to invoke the pragmatism of William James, our understanding of those assumptions needs constant reexamination.

Foreign policy is best understood by analyzing it at three levels—tactics, or actual diplomacy; strategy, or what we usually call foreign policy; and assumptions, or concepts—the unspoken but fundamental starting point for the tactics and strategy. The most challenging and yet rewarding task that faces historians of American foreign policy is to identify and explain the givens, the assumptions that are so hard to identify—for because they are assumed, policymakers see less need to discuss or defend them.[3] Of course we cannot understand and appreciate assumptions without evidence, and new evidence oftentimes stimulates new insights about assumptions. The broad structure of a foreign policy may be comprehended by the public documentation, but the nuance and context of that policy, or rather those policies, requires more.[4]

That is particularly true when strong leaders impose, or try to impose, their own conceptions and values on the nations they govern. Roosevelt's consistency, shrouded as it was in rhetoric and tactical maneuverings, is striking. His sense of purpose reminds one of the pronouncement of critic/essayist George Steiner, that true greatness requires an all-engrossing, immature, and selfish sense of purpose. Historians and contemporaries have long agreed on Roosevelt's immaturity and selfishness. His assumptions gave him the sense of purpose.[5]

Focusing on the attitude and policies of a single person, even the president of so powerful a nation as the United States of America threatens to distort the broader thrust of history, although an argument can be made for FDR being representative of mainstream American thinking. But in any event, there is the practical aspect of presidential power. As Justice George Sutherland commented on a United States Supreme Court decision relating to presidential authority in foreign affairs:

> It is quite apparent that if, in the maintenance of our international relations, embarrassment—perhaps serious embarrassment—is to be avoided and success for our aims achieved, congressional legislation, which is to be made effective through negotiation and inquiry within the international field, must often accord to the President a degree of discretion and freedom from statutory restriction which would not be admissable were domestic affairs alone involved.[6]

Whatever one thinks of Sutherland's remarks or the growth of presidential power during the twentieth century, much of what came to be labeled the "imperial" presidency developed while Franklin Roosevelt was in office.[7] At the same time, Roosevelt's "competitive" administrative style, wherein different officials and agencies seemed to have responsibility for the same tasks and policies, often worked to make him the referee and thus concentrate power in the White House.[8]

One of the characteristics of Franklin Roosevelt's long presidency was his emphasis on personal diplomacy, both in his use of personal contacts and in his desire to shape the broad, long-term direction of American foreign relations to meet his own criteria. Nevertheless, Roosevelt's subordinates never received broad, sweeping guidance about his goals—apparently because Roosevelt himself had not developed his thoughts in any logical manner. His style seemed better suited for nineteenth-century diplomacy, when a handful of diplomats could be personally tutored and led in the direction a president wanted.[9] Still, just as he put his personal stamp on the New Deal at home, so he tried to imprint American policy abroad with his own ideas—for better, and for worse. Oscar Wilde once argued that "it is personalities, not principles that move the age." But those personalities have principles.

All of which leads to the wartime diplomacy of Franklin Roosevelt.

"I never let my right hand know what my left hand does."

I

The "Juggler": The Foreign Policy of Franklin Roosevelt

> You know I am a juggler, and I never let my
> right hand know what my left hand does. . . . I
> may have one policy for Europe and one dia-
> metrically opposite for North and South Amer-
> ica. I may be entirely inconsistent, and further-
> more I am perfectly willing to mislead and tell
> untruths if it will help win the war.
> *(Franklin D. Roosevelt, 15 May 1942[1])*

SO MUCH FOR the old canard that President Franklin Roosevelt had no
foreign policy and merely reacted to day-by-day events. By his own admission, he was disingenuous, deceptive, and devious; but he had a policy. Unfortunately—or perhaps fortunately for those of us who have
made a career and a living out of studying the sly squire of Hyde Park—
Roosevelt did not then go on to describe just what those inconsistent and
diametrically opposite policies really were. In this instance, however, we
can perhaps take him at his word, since he had no idea that historians
would ever know what he said.[2]

But that does not solve the dilemma posed by the ancient Cretan philosopher, Epimenides, who observed, "all Cretans are liars," and then,
we must assume, left the scene with his listeners scratching their heads.[3]
It was a performance Roosevelt would have appreciated. That dilemma
of trust is insoluble for Roosevelt if we take him strictly at his word,
however tempting that may be. But there is an alternative that may not
confront whether or not Cretans are liars, but will help us to understand
Roosevelt's foreign policies. His self-analysis suggests that the assump-

Portions of this paper and the essay titled "The 'Juggler' " were delivered as "Roosevelt
and Churchill: Reflections on the Politics of the 'Good War,' " Rutgers-Newark Faculty of
Arts and Sciences Distinguished Lecture, 4 April 1988. I am indebted to the Rutgers University Institute on Conflict Resolution and Peace Studies for a fellowship in the spring of 1988
that enabled me to work on those essays as well as for the perceptive comments and suggestions of the other fellows. My thanks to Christopher Thorne, of the School of European
Studies at the University of Sussex, for his perceptive and valuable comments.

tions that underpinned and shaped his foreign policy can be discerned, but only if we concentrate on broad, long-term issues and actions. His tactics and strategies may often have seemed at variance with each other and with those assumptions we can identify. But fundamental assumptions often require tactical and strategic backing and filling; one step back in order to take two steps forward, as it were. Crisis management, firefighting, the immediate requirements of specific questions and answers, always take precedence. "Quick-fix" solutions that all too often merely paper over the cracks have a seductive appeal to leaders looking to escape criticism and controversy. Roosevelt was no exception. But tactics and strategies change with the situation; assumptions remain constant, always pulling policy in their direction whenever the noise of other forces dies down. The danger in emphasizing assumptions is the temptation to manufacture a mechanical, static Roosevelt, boring ahead relentlessly toward a set of clear, defined goals. Nothing could be further from the truth. Roosevelt reacted, shifted, rethought, and recalculated.

Frequently his apparently different and opposing strategies—"I never let my right hand know what my left hand does"—betrayed a refusal or inability to think about problems in a structured way. Roosevelt often simply muddled through, sweeping obstacles under the rug in the hope that they would go away in time. But to stop there is to miss the broader consistency that shaped his policies—his assumptions.

Some of those assumptions came out of the American values he shared with most other members of society. Some came out of his reformist, New Deal experiences. But there were important personal characteristics of style and attitude as well. One was his extraordinary optimism. From the outset of his presidency, he exuded confidence in his ability to lead America through the Great Depression, an aura of optimism that was an integral part of the solution. That positive attitude carried on into the war as well. Time and again, Roosevelt pushed for greater efforts, set higher goals, and acted with the "jaunty conviction that people can do more than they think possible if they have to," to use one historian's apt phrase.[4] In hindsight, his apparently whimsical and arbitrary decisions on production followed a consistent pattern. Demands for greatly increased aircraft output (1938), more aid to Britain (1940–41), immediate delivery of aid to the Soviet Union (1941), and massive increases in both tank and ship production (1942), were not only achieved, but helped stimulate the overall U.S. war production miracle. One can almost hear the old man chuckling to himself, "Some whimsy!"

His debonair administrative style drove people to distraction, but there was a method to his madness.[5] Consistency may be the hobgoblin of small minds, but it is a hobgoblin rarely associated with Franklin Roosevelt. Nevertheless, whatever the source of his assumptions, they aimed his policies in a detectable and consistent direction. Determining that direction is the challenge.

Roosevelt's personal involvement in policy was often, for much of the war, channeled through his closest adviser and aide, Harry Hopkins—a man who shared or accepted most of the President's assumptions. Hopkins had come to the administration through involvement in New Deal domestic programs, but once the war began, acted as what would now be a combination of White House Chief of Staff and National Security Adviser to the President. Then, following the Teheran Conference in December 1943, Hopkins moved out of the White House where he had lived for three and one-half years to set up housekeeping in a Georgetown apartment with his wife of seventeen months. Roosevelt professed not to understand the explanation that a chronic, debilitating liver ailment required more rest than the White House atmosphere permitted. On New Year's Day 1944, Hopkins felt ill, left a group of friends, and went upstairs to rest. He was out of commission until July 1944, by which time Roosevelt had become used to operating without his alter ego. Hopkins' influence had depended on two factors; his remarkably close personal relationship with the President, and his overall awareness of almost everything that went on in the White House, something that was still possible in the Roosevelt era. Despite the enormous growth of the Federal Government during the New Deal, the White House bureaucracy was relatively small and manageable compared to the burgeoning monster that exists today.[6] Loyalty was something Roosevelt expected, but it was often a one-way street, and Hopkins' departure from the White House moved him outside the "family" the President wanted around him. That, combined with having lost touch with events, changed Hopkins' role. He retained a good deal of influence with the President, but no longer acted as Roosevelt's surrogate.[7]

There is a thread of irony that connects the three great twentieth-century "liberal-progressive" American presidents—Woodrow Wilson, Franklin Roosevelt, and Lyndon Johnson. Each was first elected as a vigorous domestic reformer; each made his reputation, for good or ill, by his conduct of a war—or rather, by his conduct of war and peace. That is, perhaps, least accurate for Roosevelt and unfair to all three men, each of whom made pivotal contributions to American liberal reform at home. Yet the progressive reforms of Wilson, FDR's New Deal, and the civil rights/Great Society successes of Johnson, all seem to take second place behind their successes and failures as wartime leaders. Those connections need further exploration, but suffice it to say that war and liberal reform became connected in one way or another.[8]

Franklin Roosevelt began his career in national politics as Assistant Secretary of the Navy during World War I. Not surprisingly, he tended to ape the exuberant, interventionist nationalism of his cousin, ex-President Theodore Roosevelt. Again like his cousin, he was a staunch and loyal partisan. But as a member of the Hudson Valley gentry, he was comfortable with the farm-oriented progressivism of the Democratic Party. Despite that "gentleman farmer" pose, during the Great Depression, FDR would almost single-handedly broaden the party's voter base to include urban residents and ethnic minorities.

That "progressivism," with its implied optimism about human nature, informed Roosevelt's foreign as well as his domestic policies. Never an ideologue, but always a believer in the "American way of life," he tried to combine humane reform with practical, workable politics. When asked to identify his greatest accomplishment, he said it was saving American capitalism, that combination of free enterprise and individual rights that, to him, characterized the society. He gently criticized the United States for failing to pay sufficient attention to broader social concerns, but always argued for personal initiative and responsibility.[9] In an atmosphere of crisis, he set the nation on the path toward centralization and over-reliance on the national government and particularly on the president, but that was not his intention. Accused by contemporaries of being radical, he repeatedly tried to work with a balanced budget, and tried to avoid any long-term system of relief payments, arguing for the dignity of work. Like any successful modern American politician, he was sensitive to the pressures of the ballot box. He made unsavory compromises and appointments, avoided controversy, and moved with caution in the public arena. But privately, out of the glare of congressional and press scrutiny, Roosevelt moved with consistency and broad purpose, even while experimenting with various and superficially contradictory solutions. It was a confusing presidency—it was a confusing time.

Roosevelt began his thirteen-year presidency, the longest in American history, in an atmosphere of national crisis. The Great Depression threatened the unity of American society like nothing since the Civil War. Foreign affairs played no part in his election in 1932, for the domestic collapse preoccupied Americans.[10] But the world would not be ignored. Adolf Hitler gained power in Germany at almost the same time that Roosevelt became president. In Japan, the early 1930s saw a parochial, ultranationalistic army faction take control of the government. Mussolini, already in power in Italy, was planning expansion into North Africa and across the Adriatic Sea, even as FDR took the presidential oath of office for the first of four terms. Whatever the interaction of domestic crisis, economic dislocation, and international rivalries, the United States was constantly involved.

Throughout the 1930s the world was preoccupied by economic chaos, even while Europe and Asia were threatened by expansionistic nationalism. Roosevelt and the United States faced that same set of conflicting concerns, only from a peculiarly American point of view. The experience of making peace after World War I had convinced many Americans that Europe was incapable of breaking the cycle of warfare over frontiers and empires that had plagued it for centuries. President Woodrow Wilson had proposed dramatic reforms, but European leaders had rejected reform and concentrated on geopolitical security, reparations, and revenge. Although the United States did not retreat into some sort of cocoon in the 1920s, its leadership on the international stage was inclined toward independent, unilateral actions.

There were striking exceptions. The Washington Conference of 1922 created a Rube Goldberg, jury-rigged system of international cooperation in the Pacific. Elsewhere, the United States cooperated with the League of Nations in its nonpolitical activities, and even gave quiet support to efforts to solve smaller political disputes. With the Locarno Agreement seeming to promise an end to German revanchism, the outlawing of war in the Kellogg-Briand Peace Pact of 1928 is better seen as an expression of optimism than as the silly, jejune "international kiss" of later critics.

By the time Roosevelt became president in March 1933, that bubble of belief had been burst. Japanese use of naked force in Manchuria had forced the world to realize that its dream had collapsed. Dream-breakers are never popular, so little wonder that the Japanese, who saw themselves as doing only what the Europeans had done for a century or more in China, were condemned internationally. Hypocrisy, cried the Japanese. We've changed, answered the Europeans. Americans shared the sense of disillusion, but saw no way to prevent such violence except with the same violence. The Great Depression did not create American unilateralism or its distaste for Europe's politics, it only provided another justification.

The internal crisis Roosevelt faced in 1933 dominated his attention, but not exclusively. He rejected a plan, inherited from his predecessor, Herbert Hoover, for stabilization of European currencies because he decided, for the wrong reasons, that it would not work. He extended diplomatic recognition to the Soviet Union, despite domestic opposition, because it simply made sense to accept the fact that the Soviet government ruled the country, and besides, it might serve to restrain Japan and even stimulate a bit of Soviet-American trade. As Mussolini moved into Ethiopia, and both Germany and Italy got involved in the Spanish Civil War, the American Congress moved to segregate the United States from the crisis that was developing. Superficially, those efforts spoke of "isolating" America from Europe's conflicts. But beneath that rhetoric was the reality that the best the world's banker could do was postpone the inevitable. Privately, Roosevelt told the Europeans that the United States would support whatever steps they took to quarantine and limit the conflicts—parallel policy was the phrase used by the State Department. The United States would not lead in Europe, for after all that role had been rejected by the Europeans in 1919. When reporters wanted to know why stories from London kept asking, "Why doesn't the United States suggest something?" Roosevelt retorted, "Why should we be doing the suggesting?" But the Americans would work with the European democracies if those nations took the bit in their teeth. As the situation deteriorated, Roosevelt moved closer and closer to Britain and France. When Neville Chamberlain opted for appeasement, Roosevelt went along, although he commented privately that if a police chief makes a deal with gangsters that prevents crime, he "will be called a great man." But if the gangsters break their word, "the Chief of Police will go to jail." The President thought that Chamberlain seemed to be "taking very long chances."[11]

The collapse of appeasement, and the inability and/or unwillingness of the British and Soviet governments to work together to restrain Hitler, culminated in a Nazi-Soviet Pact and a German invasion of Poland. Britain, embarrassed and angry, had to resist with force, or risk the destruction of any belief that they were "a serious actor on the international stage." Both public opinion and international credibility demanded, and got, a declaration of war on Germany.[12] The French, frightened by the thought of war with Hitler but even more frightened by the thought of not having Britain as an ally, followed suit.

Roosevelt formally declared American neutrality, as law and politics required, but for the next two and one-third years, he consistently worked to insure that Britain would not fall to the German military threat. Initially, that meant the small though significant step of modifying existing American laws, particularly the neutrality legislation, to permit the British and French to buy war goods from the United States. The sudden and unexpected collapse of France in May–June 1940 shocked Roosevelt into providing more extensive aid to Britain in anticipation of a German invasion of the British Isles. A swap of American destroyers for leases on British bases in the Western Hemisphere not only enhanced American security, but was a major psychological step in getting the United States and Britain "all mixed up together" in the public (and congressional) mind. Lend-lease—an obvious declaration of economic warfare—came next, with Anglo-American naval planning, American convoying of merchant ships, and an extension of United States naval patrols far out into the Atlantic soon to follow. Whatever Roosevelt's role in each specific step, the entire process took the course he set. To the British, it was a slow, torturous road; for Roosevelt, it was a road he hoped would lead to the containment of Hitler, the survival of Britain, and the elimination of any need for large-scale American intervention. Yet whatever the President's wishful hopes, he consistently expanded America's role as the German threat increased—even to the point of publicly promising aid to the Soviet Union when it was attacked by Hitler in June 1941.

Simultaneously in the Pacific, Roosevelt followed an increasingly hard and unyielding line against Japanese expansion. That he used the Pacific crisis as a "back door" to the war against Hitler is debatable, although by late 1941 there was a sense of inevitability in the White House about war with Japan. Had the Japanese avoided any attack on American territory while continuing to expand into Southeast Asia, Roosevelt would have faced an awkward political decision, but the timing and extent of United States participation in the war was decided by the Japanese bombing of Pearl Harbor on 7 December 1941 and the seemingly gratuitous German declaration of war three days later.[13] Whatever Roosevelt's intentions, once the United States entered the war his wartime policies and postwar goals shifted dramatically. Active participation meant a chance for active leadership, and that was an opportunity not to be lost.

There is something curious about the romanticized American vision of World War II. Author Studs Terkel has, with irony, sarcasm, and perception, written of the Second World War as the "Good War." Why is that? What is there about the Second World War that makes it one Americans are so comfortable with? And should they be so comfortable? There are a half-dozen solid monographs proving that the United States, and Europe for that matter, did not go to war to save Jews or anyone else from the Holocaust or enslavement. Dislike of Nazism played a role, but that was only part of the picture.[14] Men, women, and children on both, or rather all, sides died by the millions in senseless and inhumane ways— from slave labor camps and mass executions, to the firebombings of Tokyo and Dresden, to the London "blitz," to the atomic bombs.

In fact, it wasn't a "Good War"[15]; it was just a war, even if the elimination of Hitler and the specter of Nazism was a necessity and a blessing. To understand that reality, we need to understand the foreign policy of Franklin Roosevelt—what is best called his Americanism, his desire to create a liberal world. But what does that mean?

In this case, the problem is Franklin Roosevelt himself. There are few if any surprises left about his tactics, that is, his diplomacy. The archives in Moscow surely contain some fascinating and unexpected data on Soviet actions and reactions to American policy, but the record of what FDR actually did is, for the most part, complete.[16]

FDR's strategy is another matter. In fact, there are many who have denied that he had any strategy at all. That is the thrust of arguments by early so-called "court" historians like William Langer and S. Everett Gleason who, writing in the decade after World War II and with "isolationism" as the villain, sought to defend Roosevelt's actions by picturing him as one who only reacted to events, one whose foreign policy was akin to flying by the seat of the pants. After all, they imply, if Hitler and the Japanese were clearly aggressors, then why debate the issue of whether or not the President lied? The United States had done the right thing—there was no need to dig any deeper. Whether or not those deceptions were part of a clear foreign policy was never answered. A. Whitney Griswold, writing earlier in 1938, likewise found Roosevelt merely an opportunist, labeling the President's policy in East Asia "The '24-Hour' Policy."[17] That characterization was shared by many who worked with Roosevelt. A puzzled Secretary of War, Henry Stimson, wrote:

> His mind does not follow easily a consecutive chain of thought but he is full of stories and incidents and hops about in his discussions from suggestion to suggestion and it is very much like chasing a vagrant beam of sunshine around a vacant room.[18]

Anthony Eden complained in 1943 that he felt more comfortable in Stalin's Kremlin than the Roosevelt White House. At least in Russia they meant business, while in Washington all was "confusion and woolliness"—a phrase perhaps lifted from the British ambassador in Washington, Lord Halifax (who was a bit woolly himself), who claimed dealing with the Americans was "like hitting wads of cotton wool."[19] Yet Eden and others in Britain feared in August 1941 that "F.D.R. means to keep out of the war and dictate the peace if he can," and others expressed doubt that "F.D.R. believes much or at all in his democratic slogans."[20] Which was he—confused and woolly, or a Machiavellian manipulator?

Perhaps he was neither, but rather a prisoner of public opinion, a domestic politician out of his depth—an image popular with historians. Certainly he was ever-aware of those forces, as elected officials must be. "Circumscribed by what he knew to be the mood of Congress and the American public," in dealing with international affairs he adjusted his tactics and strategy, but not his assumptions.[21] He understood the public's need and desire for instant gratification, and he often massaged that need. Yet, in talking of the postwar world, he spoke in terms of twenty, thirty, and fifty years. His insistence on the confidentiality of discussions indicates his desire to manage the news lest his efforts to head in the direction of fundamental goals be crippled by the need to compromise at the tactical and strategic level. Yet he argued that "pitiless publicity" and "free ports of information" would preserve and extend freedom and reform.[22] It was a balancing act that could not and did not always work.

But perhaps he was open to being manipulated—not because of a politician's opportunistic reverence for public opinion, but because, by 1943, he was a sick and dying man whose deteriorating health made him easy prey for an imperialistic Winston Churchill or a ruthless Joseph Stalin. Comments on his health are found in many of the memoirs of the day. One of Churchill's aides believed that Roosevelt's illnesses and weakness "led to a costly enfeeblement of Anglo-American liaison at the highest level," a charge echoed by others.[23] There is no question that Roosevelt suffered from a number of maladies, serious and less so. He experienced intermittent bouts of forgetfulness because of an insufficient blood supply to the brain (the medical phrase is secondary metabolic encephalopathy) caused by a combination of high blood pressure, congestive heart failure, anemia, and congestion in his lungs. Although those episodes became frequent after mid-1943, even then they were very brief—usually lasting less than a minute. The President may have missed a few words during such incidents, but the settlements in Eastern Europe or East Asia were not made in a few words. Moreover, those settlements followed lines he had persistently pursued, or been forced to accept. However much Roosevelt's illness made him drowsy and forgetful, that is not the same as lacking a consistent foreign policy.[24]

The oft-repeated claim that Roosevelt's wartime foreign policy was essentially a function of military strategy is plausible, but only at a level that focuses on immediate geopolitical issues, ignoring or muting assumptions and ideas. Military realities evidently shaped certain decisions—the role of the Red Army is the most obvious example—but General George Marshall's description of discussions among the American military chiefs of staff suggests deeper priorities: "We discussed political things more than anything else. . . . But we were careful, exceedingly careful, never to discuss them with the British, and from that they took the count that we didn't observe these things at all."[25]

That is not to dismiss or belittle the importance of Roosevelt's interventions into global and regional military strategy, but rather to put them in perspective. Military strategy was always crucial; after all, how can one shape the peace until one wins the war? But that is a far cry from arguing that "in lieu of a policy, most political decisions were dictated by military necessity."[26] If that is shorthand for saying that the Red Army's occupation of Eastern Europe critically limited Roosevelt's options, fine. But it leads to the belief that the President had no broad policies and simply reacted to the situations that confronted him. Roosevelt made decisions on a number of occasions that changed military strategy or went against the advice of his military advisers.[27] Those were, almost by definition, political decisions. And those decisions were shaped by his assumptions and broad political strategies.

The most obvious example is the President's insistence on providing aid to the Soviet Union in 1941, in the face of almost unanimous military opinion that the Red Army would be defeated and Soviet resistance would collapse.[a] It was a decision reminiscent of his demands for aid to Britain in 1940 and 1941, even while many military and political leaders were arguing for building America's defenses first. When he overruled

[a] See below, " 'They Don't Come Out Where You Expect': Roosevelt Reacts to the German-Soviet War, 1941."

General Marshall and the War Department in the summer of 1942 to insist on the invasion of North Africa, politics not military considerations were Roosevelt's reasons. With a Second Front in Europe eighteen to twenty-four months away, the Anglo-Americans could not afford to leave the Soviet Union as the only power militarily engaged against Germany. Moreover, if American forces did not get into action against the Germans—Hopkins referred to the need to "bloody" American forces—Roosevelt knew that pressure would build for him to concentrate on the Pacific War against Japan. A few months later at the Casablanca Conference, Roosevelt's actions further illustrated the political nature of the North African campaign.[b] Politics, not military considerations, were also at the root of the President's willingness at the Teheran Conference to let Stalin change Anglo-American strategy by asking for Anglo-American assistance in the Aegean/Balkans area, thus delaying the invasion of northern France.[c] Time and again at conferences ostensibly dedicated to military strategy, politics carried the day. That was true for Anglo-American relations as well as for the Soviet Union. Anticolonialism and a fear of getting sucked into defending British interests was a constant concern, as American reluctance to let the British military get involved in the Pacific Ocean campaign demonstrates. American concern about colonialism and the desire to be dominant in the Pacific after the war caused Churchill's repeated offers of naval assistance to fall on deaf ears. Roosevelt's musings about an Anglo-American imperium had ended at Casablanca, to be replaced by his deep concern about the role of the Soviet Union after the war. His decision to retain the atom bomb as an exclusive Anglo-American monopoly not only suggests a lingering comfortableness with the British, but reveals the limits of his willingness to be candid with the Soviet Union. Unlike Churchill who, the story goes, when surprised coming out of the tub by Roosevelt, commented that the Prime Minister of Great Britain has nothing to hide from the President, apparently the Americans did have some things to hide from the Soviets.[28]

Even in cases where the President went along with military advice, he did not simply give in; rather, it was a back-and-forth process in which he accepted the advice the military chiefs had tailored to fit what they thought he would accept.[29] That is why his reversal of the chiefs of staff over the North African invasion is so striking—Roosevelt had to put his foot down in a public way. His decision at the Second Cairo Conference in 1943 to scrap plans for an invasion of Burma (codenamed BUCCANEER), despite Marshall's angry objections, was political in the sense that Roosevelt had become convinced that Chinese leader Chiang Kai-shek was both ineffective and independent-minded, a combination that would

---

[b] See below, "Casablanca: The End of Imperial Romance."
[c] See below, " 'The Family Circle': Roosevelt's Vision of the Postwar World."

require the United States to be China's sponsor and guardian for some time after the war.[d] The President's refusal to adopt Churchill's political arguments for an attack against Germany through northeastern Italy and the Balkans—the soft underbelly approach; or an all-out race to beat the Soviets to Berlin or Prague, were based on his political strategy, even if they had support from most American and many British military advisers.[30] As for Roosevelt's "concessions" to Stalin in East Asia (given at Yalta), those were also political, despite the general consensus in Washington that Soviet armies would be needed in the war against Japan. A restoration of what Stalin claimed were historic Russian boundaries was a means of getting the Soviets to participate in the world system envisaged at Teheran. (Boundaries seemed so unimportant to Roosevelt and to many Americans, who failed to draw the parallel between irredentist issues in Europe and Asia, and Mexican muttering that the American Southwest was legitimately theirs). At the same time, the East Asian arrangement would promote postwar stability by insuring that the Soviets would not support the Chinese communists. What so often seemed spontaneous was rarely so. The United States did not enter the war in order to reshape the world, but once in the war, that conception of world reform was the assumption that guided Roosevelt's actions.

Even those who argue that Roosevelt changed his policy toward the Soviet Union later in the war and became a convinced Cold Warrior make a case for his having a very real foreign policy—even if events forced him to change it. To illustrate: Franklin Roosevelt has been praised (or condemned) ever since World War II for refusing (or failing) to treat the Soviet Union as an enemy during the latter stages of the war. When, in the late 1950s, William A. Williams suggested that Roosevelt was little different in his political economy from other American presidents, readers reacted with anger and scorn. In 1967, when Arthur Schlesinger, Jr., representing a far different perspective, gingerly advanced the thesis that FDR was, by late 1944, aware of and working to neutralize Soviet expansionism, most were unconvinced. But finally, when Walter LaFeber from the left and Norman Podhoretz from the neoconservative right both argued the same thing—albeit from a very different set of premises—we had to look anew at Franklin Roosevelt's policies and, more important, his assumptions.[31] My analysis leaves me convinced that FDR never abandoned his commitment to avoid creating a confrontational world, but either way the argument is for conscious policy, not haphazard hipshooting.

Nor is it enough to say that Roosevelt acted out of intuition (that "ominous word," wrote one British official). Perhaps Isaiah Berlin was closer to the mark when he wrote of Roosevelt's "half-conscious premonitory

[d] See below, ' 'In Search of Monsters to Destroy.' "

awareness of the coming shape of society."[32] Few people, and fewer political leaders, are systematic thinkers, although Roosevelt's aversion to
such efforts were stronger than most. What Berlin called FDR's "awareness" imbued his actions, but that implies an implausible degree of
empty-headedness, unless awareness is equated with assumptions.

George Kennan, whose brief contacts with Roosevelt during World
War II left him convinced that the President operated out of sheer whim
and fancy, drew a far different conclusion thirty years later. "I have the
impression," he wrote, "that in major instances he [FDR] influenced public opinion less through the power of his own words than through the
quiet shaping, in a manner conducive to his own purposes, of the environ-
mental factors, the external factors, in which the formulation of wartime
policy had to proceed." Kennan went on to damn Roosevelt's foreign
policy as that of "a very superficial man, ignorant, dilettantish, severely
limited in intellectual horizon." But the point remains—Roosevelt did
have a foreign policy—or at least a set of consistent assumptions that
shaped his reactions and policies.[33]

Initially, Roosevelt's harshest critics were those historians and contemporaries who accused him of conniving to enter the war on the side of
Britain. They attributed to him a clear and consistent foreign policy, even
while they condemned him in bitter, ad hominem terms for consciously
deceiving the American Congress and public.[34] But as East-West tensions
intensified in the postwar era, those condemnations seemed irrelevant as
Winston Churchill, accused of conniving with Roosevelt to bring the
United States into the Second World War, became a hero in the new
struggle against the threat of communism and the growing power of the
Soviet Union.[35] Now, critics charged Roosevelt with having appeased the
Soviets from the outset of the war, culminating in a "sell-out" of Eastern
Europe, China, and Western security at the Yalta Conference.[36] Even
though such critics often accused him of being foolish and naive rather
than Machiavellian, their condemnation was of his consistency in offer-
ing Stalin concessions in the foolish hope of gaining the cooperation of
the Soviet Union in the postwar world. As Senator Robert Taft put it:
"Our policy seems to have been based on the delightful theory that Mr.
Stalin in the end will turn out to have an angelic nature and do of his own
accord the things which we should have insisted on at the beginning." But
Taft agreed there was a "theory."[37]

Whatever the run-up, Franklin Roosevelt's thinking on international
affairs matured during and because of World War II. The war demanded
policies; not only to deal with immediate military strategy and geopolitical problems that go with wartime coalitions, but also because the war
presented an opportunity for long-range reform. And reform appealed to
the optimistic progressive in Roosevelt. FDR had never wanted war in

order to play international reformer, anymore than he wanted the Great Depression in order to have the New Deal, or Wilson wanted World War I in order to embark on an international crusade. But wars create new situations. Nations never actually fight a war for the same reasons that they begin or enter the conflict. The United States entered World War II in part because of the failure of a policy of deterrence in the Pacific, in part because a Europe dominated by an aggressive, hostile Hitlerian Germany threatened the political, social, and economic welfare of the United States.

But once in the war, Roosevelt's perspective shifted, particularly as victory against Germany became more certain. He remained deeply concerned that Germany might start another war, and advocated draconian measures to prevent that from happening. Disarmament, de-Nazification, and dismemberment remained the essence of his policy for postwar Germany.[38] But he also became convinced that America's future welfare was not independent of others. The President sought to set the world on a new, or at least somewhat different, path. It was, of course, just another chapter in the age-old debate over change versus constancy as the fundamental nature of the universe. Human nature does not change, argue realists from Augustine to John Adams to Kissinger, and relations between nations only reflect that nature. The best we can do is to understand our faults and flaws and try to construct systems that mitigate their effect. On the contrary, insist the humanists, from Pelagius to Jefferson to George Lucas, human society can and has developed and improved, even with its imperfections. To assume we cannot change is to give in to the "dark side," to surrender to what William James called a kind of Oriental fatalism. But Roosevelt had no interest in that or any other philosophical debate. As was his nature, he seemed to try to halve the difference. But what is striking is the consistency with which his assumed ideals asserted themselves. He did not seek the "golden mean," but rather used compromise as a means to his ends.

Studying Roosevelt, particularly his foreign policy, can be "like peering into a kaleidoscope," but only if we never take it apart.[39] Twist the end off that toy, and what seemed a random display, created by the outside force of spinning the tube, suddenly has internal logic.

But perhaps we should listen to the voice of the Juggler himself. . . .

The Architects of Aid to Russia—Roosevelt and Hopkins at Hyde Park.

II

"They Don't Come Out Where You Expect": Roosevelt Reacts to the German-Soviet War, 1941

> Their Government seems to me quite baf-
> fling. . . . I suppose it is rather like a disorderly
> line of beaters out shooting; they do put the
> rabbits out of the bracken, but they don't come
> out where you expect.[1]
> *Lord Halifax (on the Roosevelt Administration)*

IN THE TELEVISION adaptation of Herman Wouk's novel, *The Winds of War*, the omnipresent fictional hero, U.S. Navy Captain "Pug" Henry, is a member of an American delegation sent in the autumn of 1941 to assess Soviet military capabilities and supply requirements. During the course of a dinner at the Kremlin, a Hollywood caricature of a Soviet admiral offers a double-edged toast. Raising his glass, the admiral praises the American navy, which he says he knows will acquit itself bravely once the United States abandons its policy of letting others fight its war and joins the struggle against Hitler. Captain Henry, an unlikely combination of Solomon, Shakespeare, and Machiavelli, responds by standing the accusation on its head. Toasting Stalin, the American salutes the Soviet leader's shrewdness in postponing war with Germany until the USSR had time to prepare. So it was, he continues, with the United States; once America was similarly prepared for war it too would enter the fray.

Fiction distorts fact, but sometimes in the process arrives at a curious sort of truth. Americans were no more prepared, psychologically or militarily, for war in 1941 than were their Soviet counterparts. The Soviet

This is a significantly revised version of a paper presented at the 1st Symposium of the Soviet-American Project on the History of World War II, Moscow, USSR, 21–23 Oct. 1986 (sponsored by the American Council of Learned Societies/International Research & Exchanges Board, and the Soviet Academy of Sciences). A much abridged version was published in the Soviet Union as "Crisis Diplomacy, June–December 1941," *Annual Studies of America, 1988*, G. N. Sevost'ianov, ed. (Moscow: Publishing House "Nauka," 1988), pp. 127–45 [in Russian], and in *Soviet-U.S. Relations, 1933–1942* [Grigory Sevost'ianov, ed.] (Moscow: Progress Publishers, 1989), pp. 53–71.

Union did not declare war on Germany, it responded to an attack. The United States did not declare war on Germany—or Japan—it responded to an attack.[2] Both nations saw Hitler's defeat as benefiting their own interests; both nations seemed quite willing to let western Europe, primarily Britain, do their fighting for them in 1940–41. Whatever the other distortions of this quite lightweight piece of television fiction, it does catch the essence of Soviet-American relations in the summer of 1941.

On 22 July 1941, Germany launched its attack on the Soviet Union— Operation BARBAROSSA. Just three days later, Franklin Roosevelt's closest adviser, Harry Hopkins, cabled the President to suggest a mission to Moscow. Hopkins wanted to fly to the Soviet Union to meet with Soviet Premier Joseph Stalin, using a recently opened air route from Invergordon in Scotland, around Norway's North Cape, and on to Archangel in northern Russia. Roosevelt's approval came within twenty-four hours. There were no instructions for Hopkins, only assent. A message for Stalin that followed contained encouragement and promises of aid to the Soviet Union, but no guidelines or advice for Hopkins.[3]

What did Roosevelt hope to achieve with what seemed a spur-of-the-moment authorization for a vague, unstructured visit? Where was the careful agenda such meetings normally demand? Is this a classic example of the President's reputed habit of conducting diplomacy by impulse, by whim and fancy? Perhaps. But Roosevelt's image of impulsiveness usually masked a consistent pattern, and Hopkins' trip to the Kremlin was no exception. The President's intuitive assessment of Soviet capabilities was, as things turned out, more accurate than that of most of his intelligence, military, and political advisers. It was an insight of crucial importance for the war.

Americans, Britons, and Soviets were compelled to join forces against Germany out of national interest and expediency. Ideological perceptions shaped, to a degree, how each of those nations defined national interest, but so did more practical assessments of military strategy, logistics, and geography. Immediate geopolitical questions, particularly ones regarding the Soviet Union's ability and willingness to resist the Germans, tended to obscure the longer-term issue of Soviet-American relations. But historical perspective suggests that what happens in periods of crisis diplomacy frequently, almost invariably, affects and even defines the long-term, postcrisis relations between states. How then, did Roosevelt's diplomacy in that crisis period from June through December 1941 shape Soviet-American relations thereafter? Was it, as some Soviet historians have claimed, simply a matter of "trying to prolong the war in order to weaken the USSR"?[4] Or were there other, less anti-Soviet concepts and concerns that underlay American policy?

Since early in 1941, both British and American intelligence had received increasing indications that Hitler planned to attack the Soviet Union. The British hesitated in passing the information to Moscow. Part of that hesitation was because they believed, with a bit of national conceit, that the Germans had spread rumors of an eastward move as a prelude to the more important invasion of Great Britain. But British analysts also thought that there was no need for such an attack since the Soviet Union would invariably cave in to German demands. Moreover, they feared that Stalin and his advisers would interpret any British warnings as a ploy designed to lure the Soviet Union into a provocation that would destroy its treaty with Germany. Eventually, in early April 1941, the warning was passed on, but Soviet histories as well as reports from Sir Stafford Cripps, the British ambassador in Moscow at the time, indicate that the Soviet Government chose to treat the information just as London had feared.[5] The American ambassador to the Soviet Union, Laurence Steinhardt, similarly cautioned that such warnings would be seen as "an attempt to drive a wedge between the Soviet Union and Germany," but Under Secretary of State Sumner Welles, a close confidant of the President, early in March 1941 passed on the information to the Soviet ambassador in Washington, Konstantin Umansky. By late April/early May, newspapers in both London and New York speculated about a German move into Soviet-held territory.[6]

Warnings of an impending German attack reached Moscow from Soviet sources as well. Their intelligence apparatus in Germany may have been less active during the period of the Nazi-Soviet Pact, but reports did arrive from other agents, particularly Richard Sorge in Japan. One Soviet diplomat in Berlin in 1941 has written of "regularly transmitting" the alarming signals back to Moscow starting as early as March of that year. Nikita Khrushchev, in his famous secret speech to the 1956 Communist Party Congress, likewise referred to reports of the German threat coming "from our own military and diplomatic sources." Stalin's disbelief of both foreign and Soviet sources may be explained by reports that, the day before the German offensive, he received intelligence assessments concluding that warnings of a German attack were mere disinformation ploys by the West.[7]

More important than warnings to Stalin about BARBAROSSA, given his disregard of such information, was the effect that foreknowledge of the impending German thrust eastward had on the Lend-Lease Act. During the congressional debate in January 1941 over that legislation, opponents of the bill attempted to add amendments that would limit lend-lease to Great Britain and Ireland unless Congress added other nations by name. Eventually, an amendment was introduced specifically excluding the Soviet Union. In each case, the amendments were defeated, although the vote was along party lines. It is difficult to find any specific statements about aid to Russia made by Roosevelt prior to the passage of the Lend-Lease Act. Nevertheless, the President's insistence that the legislation not contain any restrictions, when added to strong indications of German plans to attack Soviet positions, is more than just suggestive—it demonstrates his instinctive awareness of the importance of the Soviet Union in the overall international equation.[8]

There is a parallel between Soviet actions and those of the United States in the months immediately preceding the Japanese attack on Pearl Harbor, even with the vast differences created by geography and domestic political considerations. Both Roosevelt and Stalin tried to delay what they, or at least their advisers, thought was the inevitable conflict. In the United States, military leaders warned that their nation was ill-prepared for war and that they should "put off hostilities with Japan as long as possible," hoping "to tide the situation over for the next several months."[9] Thus, Roosevelt left the U.S. Pacific Fleet at Hawaii—much more vulnerable to attack than he or his naval staff ever imagined. As for Stalin, according to one Soviet history:

> [He] mistakenly assumed that Hitler would not risk violating the non-aggression treaty unless he were given a pretext for doing so.
>
> Right up till the last moment Stalin considered it inexpedient to bring the troops . . . into a state of full combat readiness. The leadership of the People's Commissariat for Defence at that time shares responsibility with Stalin for this and for the defects in the general preparations for defence.[10]

The parallel breaks down quickly after that. American leaders assumed that a policy of deterrence, particularly in the form of the Pacific Fleet and what American military leaders proclaimed the new super-weapon, the B-17 "Flying Fortress" bombers, would halt Japanese expansion.[11] Soviet leaders, on the other hand, adopted a policy of appeasement, however temporary.

The initial reaction of officials in the Roosevelt administration to the German attack reflected their preoccupation with the threat to Great Britain. British Ambassador Lord Halifax reported after a talk with Roosevelt that "the time that we had been thus able to gain had made the President feel much more hopeful than he did a [few?] weeks ago."[12] Others were more worried. For over a year, Roosevelt and his aides had worked, against substantial domestic opposition, to expand its aid-to-Britain effort. The first reaction of Harry Hopkins was colored by fears that the Russo-German war would lend strength to the arguments of military men and so-called isolationists who wanted to "arm America rather than England." Perhaps tongue in cheek he credited the aid-to-Britain program with forcing Hitler to turn "to the left."[13] Two of Roosevelt's major Cabinet officers, Secretary of War Henry Stimson and Secretary of the Navy Frank Knox, thinking the Soviet Union would be defeated before year's end, likewise recommended that the United States take advantage of German preoccupation with the Russian front to increase naval support to Britain.[14]

There were those whose responses captured the intensity of the suspicion and emotion that existed between the two nations. Ambassador Steinhardt offered an image of unredeemable bestiality and savagery in a message to Secretary of State Cordell Hull sent only five days before the German attack:

> My observation of the psychology of the individuals who are conducting Soviet foreign policy has . . . convinced me . . . that it is not possible to create "international good will" with them . . . and that they are not affected by ethical or moral considerations, nor guided by the relationships which are customary between individuals of culture and breeding. Their psychology recognizes only firmness, power and force, and reflects primitive instincts and reactions that are entirely devoid of the restraints of civilization. . . . Concessions . . . have been received . . . with marked suspicion and . . . as evidence of weakness.

Yet, in the same message, Steinhardt claimed that while the Soviet government disliked Britain, it had "great respect for the United States."[15] Much similar advice flowed into Washington, solicited and unsolicited, recommending caution and even distrust in dealing with Moscow. William Bullitt, who had soured on the Soviets after serving as the first U.S. ambassador to that government, predicted a quick Soviet collapse and warned "that Communists in the United States are just as dangerous enemies as ever."[16]

Ideology in the guise of practicality reared its head when, two days after the German attack, George Kennan, a young State Department Russian expert, sat at a desk in the American embassy in Berlin and wrote a personal note to his friend, Loy Henderson, then with the Division of European Affairs in the State Department. Twenty-five years later, when Kennan wrote his memoirs, he proudly included the note. His comments combined moralizing with expediency. He warned against following Churchill's lead in extending "moral support" to the Soviet Union "as an associate in the defense of democracy." To do so, Kennan argued, would cause the United States to identify itself

> with the Russian destruction of the Baltic states, with the attack against Finnish independence, with the partitioning of Poland and Rumania, with the crushing of religion throughout Eastern Europe, and with the domestic policy of a regime which is widely feared and detested throughout this part of the world. . . .

In every border country concerned, from Scandinavia—including Norway and
Sweden—to the Black Sea, Russia is generally more feared than Germany. . . .

Such a view would not preclude the extension of material aid wherever
called for by our own self-interest. It would, however, preclude anything which
might identify us politically or ideologically with the Russian war effort. In
short, it seems to me that Soviet Russia could more soundly be regarded as
a 'fellow traveler' in the accepted Moscow sense, rather than as a political
associate.[17]

Such condemnations of Soviet immorality, had they been adopted as
American policy, could have only reinforced Russian fears that Britain
and the United States would do in 1941/1942 what the USSR itself had
done in 1939: strike a peace with Hitler while the German army was
engaged on the opposite front.

American suspicions were heightened by Soviet actions. The Soviets
seemed not to have changed their political agenda—an agenda that most
Americans found unpalatable. Among some American officials, Wilsonian ideals of self-determination still prevailed; for others, fear of Bolshevism—itself a label that triggered an image of radical violence—colored
all their thinking about the Soviet Union. Either way, an issue like independence for the Baltic states, for example, became a matter of principle
for Americans and a litmus test of Soviet intentions for many U.S. government officials. Thus, only a week after the German attack, American suspicions were confirmed when Soviet Ambassador Umansky asked for recognition of his government's incorporation (or reincorporation) of the
Baltic States into the Soviet Union. Regardless of whose arguments were
right or wrong, just or unjust, realistic or unrealistic, it was a diplomatic
blunder to raise the issue at a time when Soviet-American relations were
undergoing a major reassessment. Umansky tried to create a pleasant atmosphere for his proposal ("a little restaurant in the country close to
Washington"), but his guest, the same Loy Henderson to whom Kennan
had written, told the Russian diplomat that "there were divergencies of
principle which it did not seem possible to bridge at the present time."
When Umansky angrily labeled Baltic State government-in-exile officials
"Nazis, pro-German, dishonest, hypocritical, [and] slimy," Henderson
flatly refused to discuss the matter any further.[18]

The question of the Baltic States even involved the President, for it
threatened his policy of avoiding territorial settlements until after the
war. Rumors that the British were willing to accede to Soviet demands for
recognition of their sovereignty over the Baltic states prompted Roosevelt to comment to Churchill in July 1941 that "the plebescite was on
the whole one of the few successful outcomes of the Versailles Treaty."
A month later, at the Atlantic Conference (the first of the Churchill-

Roosevelt meetings), the Americans expanded on that theme by insisting that postwar territorial arrangements would have the consent of the peoples involved. Churchill quickly exempted the British Empire, and Stalin did the same for the Baltic area.[19] But that still left the matter of plebiscites in general, and the Baltic States in particular, unresolved.

In addition to such issues of substance, the game of diplomatic tit-for-tat, which had marred Soviet-American relations throughout the 1930s, continued unabated, as it has for over half a century. Granted, it was tightly isolated in the name of the joint war effort, but there is a historical *déjà vu* about a protest on 30 June, only one week after the outbreak of the Soviet-German war, from the Soviet ambassador in Washington about "limited freedom of movement" in the United States for Soviet officials. The State Department's response was equally unimaginative, arguing that "such action had been forced upon us by discrimination against American officials in Moscow."[20]

The initial response of American diplomats to the German attack on Soviet forces is hardly surprising. Churchill and Roosevelt had agreed in mid-June to extend aid to the Soviet Union once war broke out, but those promises from the President were immediately circumscribed by words that made clear the primacy of aid to England.[21] At the same time, a number of American officials warned that Soviet agents in the Western Hemisphere should be kept under surveillance since Russia's policy of friendship toward the United States was based solely on expediency and could change at any time. After all, as one State Department memo put it, "the Stalin Government might again come to an agreement with Germany."[22] Such fears were given apparent substance in late August when reports reached Washington that the Soviet ambassador in London, Ivan Maisky, had warned that his government would negotiate with Hitler unless the United States joined the war and a second front was launched. Stalin seemed to second that threat when he told Churchill that without a second front plus certain supplies, the Soviet Union might be unable to conduct "active operations" for a long period of time.[23] But most threatening of all from a Soviet point of view was the belief that the Germans would achieve a quick, overwhelming victory in Russia.[24]

That latter issue created serious problems. British and American pessimism in 1941 about Soviet chances of survival was a product of a combination of factors: the obvious weakness of leadership in the Soviet military following the purges, the Red Army's inept performance in the Winter War against Finland, previous German military successes, the carryover of distrust and antagonism toward the Soviet Union that had been immensely heightened by the Nazi-Soviet Pact, and the Soviet refusal to share, even in small ways, knowledge about their military situation. Stalin was imprisoned by the same dilemma that had preoccupied

Churchill since September 1939; how to strike that delicate balance between a portrait of need so as to justify aid, while not painting the kind of
dismal picture that might convince the Americans that the Soviet Union
would collapse. After all, Churchill himself had decided in May of 1940
not to throw good money after bad and held back on further British aid
to France. If, in fact, the Red Army's ability to resist would have been
evident to foreign observers then the Soviet decision for secrecy was a
serious mistake. Such unwillingness to share information not only hampered logistical planning but also reinforced the latent suspicion of the
Soviet Union that so many Americans brought with them.[25] But the capability of the Soviet Army to hold out was not so apparent. During the
summer and early autumn, even Soviet generals believed Moscow would
fall, as the testimony of foreign ambassadors in Moscow demonstrates.
Keeping the Americans and British away from the front may have been
more than wise, it may have been necessary. But it was an early and provocative step away from the kind of cooperation and sharing that would
characterize the Anglo-American relationship.

Even though the U.S. State Department and British Foreign Office
were already busy debating issues that would become postwar problems
in relations with the Soviet Union,[26] both Roosevelt and Churchill
were strangely silent about the German-Soviet war in their usually all-
encompassing correspondence. On the eve of the war, the Prime Minister,
knowing that operation BARBAROSSA was due to begin any day, observed
that Hitler was wrong to think that "capitalist and right-wing sympa-
thies" would be with Germany. Instead, commented Churchill, we "will
go all out to help Russia." A facade of humor did not hide the sharp edge
to the remark made by "Jock" Colville, the Prime Minister's Private Secretary, after hearing the promise: "I [Colville] said that for him, the arch
anti-Communist, this was bowing down in the House of Rimmon."
Churchill's now famous reply put ideology in the perspective of crisis—
"If Hitler invaded Hell he [Churchill] would at least make a favourable
reference to the Devil." There is a certain irony in Churchill's treatment
of Soviet actions in 1939 as a sort of "Eastern Front" against Germany,
and Stalin's desire to see Hitler bogged down in wars in western and
southern Europe—thus leaving the Soviet Union alone.[27]

But the ideological issue continued to bother many British leaders.
When Duff Cooper, the Minister of Information, asked Walter Citrine of
the Trades Union Congress to put together a speech saying that an alliance with the Soviet Union was in "the cause of all free people," Citrine
responded that the USSR was not fighting for any principles cherished by
Great Britain.[28] That summed up the feeling of many. The tone of
Churchill's private and even public messages was never "Russia must survive," but rather "Russia must resist as long as possible—for that will

help England survive." And what else should a national statesman say? Neither Stalin nor any other Soviet leader had argued that Britain's survival was "essential" to the USSR. In fact, they had acted in precisely the opposite manner by signing the pact with Nazi Germany. Perhaps Soviet leaders saw no other choice in 1939, or perhaps Stalin could not resist the dangerous gamble for territory over security, but that does not change the fact that the treaty facilitated, if not guaranteed, a German attack on Western Europe.[29]

Neither Roosevelt nor Churchill made any direct mention to the other of the Soviet Union or the Russian campaign until after their meeting off Newfoundland early in August, six weeks after the German attack. For that entire period, their correspondence centered on logistics and the naval situation in the Atlantic. It was almost as if the President had taken the advice of Stimson and Knox.[30] Even when Roosevelt complained to Churchill about rumors of British postwar commitments to various "racial groups" in the Balkans, the President did not draw the obvious conclusion about the tensions such promises posed for Soviet-British relations.[31]

For both Roosevelt and Churchill, it was a time for waiting. Hasty decisions and promises would not change the course of events in Russia. Even Soviet officials indirectly accepted that an immediate second front was unlikely, if not unrealistic.[32] During a brief private talk with British General Hastings Ismay in late September 1941, Stalin himself admitted that "he quite understood why we [Gt. Britain] could not at the moment establish a Western Front."[33] That left the Soviets with their requests for supplies—requests that were couched in the language of understandable panic and fear, giving them the tone of demands.

For the British, requests for assistance posed a dilemma. Rejecting a second front was easy, and proposals for sending armed forces to fight in the Soviet Union were never practical, given worldwide British commitments. Even more serious thinking about sending troops and/or aircraft to the Caucasus had the purpose of defending the Middle East, not aiding the Soviets.[34] Promising all possible logistical aid to the Soviet Union cost little. But actually sharing war supplies with them was a vastly different matter. The British War Office and Chiefs of Staff were uniformly pessimistic about Soviet military chances and assumed that, if the Germans pushed the Red Army east of the Urals, effective Soviet resistance would end. To agree to any long-term sharing of supplies made no sense, an argument ironically similar to that made by the American military about aid to Britain back in June 1940.[35] Still, if the Americans insisted, then the British had to work with the U.S. or risk being left holding an empty bag, or at least a less full one. Throughout 1941 and on into early 1942, Churchill and his advisers invariably found reasons to restrict aid to Rus-

sia in order to use it elsewhere, often in the Middle East, but those arguments usually were rejected by the Americans.[36] Only rarely during the
war did Churchill permit an open dispute to develop with Roosevelt—
and those instances were ones that triggered emotional responses, like
India and Greece. Aid to Russia, particularly in this early phase of the
war, was not such an emotional issue. Churchill's promise to aid the Soviets was, from all outward appearances, made in good faith. But with
Churchill, bombast was strongest when he was least able, or willing, to
deliver. As delivery dates drew near, some more immediate problem—a
German threat in North Africa, the fear of a Soviet collapse in the Caucasus, the continued expansion of Japan—always took priority. British
officials worried that Churchill's "sentimental and florid" style would
"have the worst effect on Stalin who will think guff no substitute for
guns." Anthony Eden complained that "it is . . . entirely due to him
[Churchill] that we cannot now do more for Soviet Russia. . . . P.M. and
Chiefs of Staff are entirely negative—no effort is being made to help Russia elsewhere." As late as October of that year, Churchill still spoke of the
Soviet Union as a liability; he would send supplies, but British forces
would go no further than the Middle East.[37]

In Washington, the tone of early discussions between Umansky and
State Department officials, particularly Sumner Welles, was one of doubt,
delay, distrust, and disingenuousness. Americans doubted that the Soviet
Union could survive the German attack; they looked to delay sending aid
lest it be wasted (the fall of France was an ever-present memory); and they
distrusted long-term Soviet intentions (there were repeated references to
the Nazi-Soviet Pact, to the activities in the United States of Soviet agents,
and to suspicious requests from Soviet officials for secret military technology).[38] Nevertheless, like the Soviet Union, the United States government had to make its decision based upon self-interest. As Welles put it on
June 23:

> Neither kind of imposed overlordship [Nazi or Soviet] can have, or will have,
> any support or any sway in the mode of life, or in the system of Government,
> of the American people.
>   But the immediate issue that presents itself . . . is whether the plan for univer-
> sal conquest, . . . which Hitler is now desperately trying to carry out, is to be
> successfully halted and defeated. . . . It is the issue . . . which most directly
> involves . . . the security of the New World in which we live. . . . [A]ny defense
> against Hitlerism . . . will therefore rebound to the benefit of our own defense
> and security.[39]

But, as was often the case, Roosevelt took a view different from that of
the bureaucrats. He had long been inclined to view the Soviet Union's
policies as more nationalist than communist, more practical than ideological. That inclination had prompted him to reject Bullitt's arguments and

to listen instead to Joseph Davies, who had succeeded Bullitt as ambassador in Moscow. The Nazi-Soviet Pact and, to a lesser degree, even the Soviet attack on Finland in November 1939, which outraged the President, were interpreted by the White House as prompted more by Soviet fears of German aggression than communist expansion.[40]

When the Germans attacked the Soviet Union in 1941, Roosevelt chose not to apply the neutrality legislation since that would have cut off trade with Russia, but that was a far cry from providing effective assistance.[41] Before he could propose to a dubious Congress and public a policy of long-term aid to the Soviets, he needed to do more than state the obvious; do more than just appeal to national self-interest. The Gallup Poll found that, in the days immediately after the German attack, Americans looked upon the Soviet Union more favorably than on Nazi Germany. But that did not eliminate a general distaste for the Russians, nor did it allay concern that aid to Moscow would not only be wasted but would take away from American preparedness. As a result, most Americans opposed giving the kind of aid to the Soviet Union that had been extended to Britain.[42] Roosevelt needed more information to determine just what aid would help, but he also needed the kind of public gathering of information that would create an image of expertise; an image of a wise and informed leader acting on the best and most recently obtained facts. That image and information was to come from two missions to Moscow—that of Harry Hopkins in late July, and that of Averell Harriman in October.[43]

As the President's closest and most trusted adviser, Hopkins had moved from domestic to international politics as that became the area of crisis. When Roosevelt decided that someone should discuss the American aid program, as well as broad strategy with Churchill in the light of the German attack on the Soviet Union, Hopkins was the logical emissary. No record has surfaced of the lengthy White House discussions between Roosevelt and Hopkins on the evening of 11 July, but five days later Hopkins arrived in Scotland aboard a lend-lease bomber. Churchill, "never one to overlook a glimmer" of hope, as Robert Sherwood put it, may have seemed to Hopkins a bit more optimistic by then about Russia's ability to prolong the war, but the bulk of their discussions apparently centered on the naval war in the Atlantic, preparations for a Churchill-Roosevelt meeting off Newfoundland, and, most important of all to the British, the issue of strategy in the Middle East. Hopkins summed up the American position succinctly on that latter issue when he told Churchill and his generals that "there are now grave doubts as to whether it is wise for you to go any further in that region." Putting the cart before the horse, the British responded that the imminent collapse of Soviet resistance made it imperative that the Middle East be strengthened.[44] It was the first in a war-long series of disagreements between Britain and the United States over policy in that part of the world.

There are few references to aiding the Soviet Union in the British or American records of Hopkins' visit to England, but British slowness in following-up Churchill's promise of aid was indirectly highlighted in a speech given by Hopkins over the BBC. Although the bulk of the talk concerned American aid to Britain, it closed with a pointed reference to the President's recognition

> of the magnificent fight which the people of Russia are putting up against the diabolic legions of barbarism and blackness. As your Prime Minister said a month ago today on this same program "Anyone who fights against Fascism is our ally and our friend." We in America feel that too and any aid which we can give to either China or Russia will be given—and immediately.[45]

Perhaps the speech rang a warning bell in Churchill's mind, for he met with Hopkins immediately afterward and, while they walked on the lawn at Chequers, told the American "in minutest detail of the efforts that Britain was making and planned to make to bring aid to Russia. He talked with his usual vigor and eloquence," Hopkins recalled, and stressed "the importance of Russia in the battle against Hitler."[46]

Churchill seized the opportunity to strengthen the image of Anglo-American alliance by inviting Hopkins to attend some cabinet meetings, an unusual move that brought a tart "this is rather absurd" comment from Alexander Cadogan. Hopkins' first visit to the cabinet came immediately after he arrived on 17 July, "looking more dead than alive." Four days later he attended a full cabinet meeting. But his formal attendance was all an elaborate charade. After a carefully structured discussion that said everything the British thought Hopkins (and Roosevelt) wanted to hear, the six-item prepared agenda was completed. Churchill rumbled that Hopkins might prefer to leave since they were only going to go over some domestic issues, and Hugh Dalton then ushered the President's personal representative out of the room. Once the American was safely out of the precinct, the cabinet session resumed to discuss the sensitive matter of the United States and the Far East.[47] Duff Cooper, instructed by Churchill to inform the press of Hopkins' presence in Cabinet, shrewdly realized that Roosevelt's critics in the United States would see it as "another device for ensnaring America into the war." No press announcement was made, despite Churchill's testy minute: "It was a pity not to state the fact as I desired. None of these arguments appeals to me."[48]

A trip to Moscow was a logical idea for Hopkins. At his own suggestion he had been the President's eyes and ears in England back in early 1941. Now Hopkins made a similar proposal.[49] As he put it in his message to Roosevelt:

> I have a feeling that everything possible should be done to make certain the Russians maintain a *permanent* front even though they be defeated in this im-

mediate battle. . . . I think it would be worth doing by a direct communication from you through a personal envoy. . . . Stalin would then know . . . that we mean business on a *long term* supply job.[50]

Hopkins traveled as an expert in supply matters, but the gist of his message to Roosevelt was political; the Soviet Union should be made part of a permanent wartime coalition against Hitler, not just propped up to provide Britain with a brief respite. More significant, the message assumes a similar attitude on the part of the President, an indication that the mission to Moscow, or at least a policy of long-term support for the Soviet Union, had been discussed before Hopkins left Washington. The absence of any record or recollection of extensive discussions between Hopkins and Roosevelt on how to respond to the entry of the Soviet Union into the war is, itself, suspect. Despite military predictions that Soviet resistance would quickly collapse (the War Department estimated "a possible maximum of three months"), the broad implications of the new situation demanded discussion. Yet the only subject mentioned in Robert Sherwood's one-sentence summary of "the long talk" between Hopkins and Roosevelt on 11 July, was the extension of American naval patrols to include Iceland. Two days later, the Presidential adviser was on his way to England.

Roosevelt did send Hopkins a message for Stalin. The words related to Soviet supply requirements—particularly ones that could "reach Russia within the next three months." But the unmistakable implication was more than that, for the President spoke also of "a great amount of materiel" that would be available *after* that critical three-month period. In other words, if the Soviet Union stayed in the war, large–scale American aid would be forthcoming.[51] Given the tenor of Hopkins' statements in London and his subsequent reports from Moscow, it is clear that he and Roosevelt were looking for evidence needed to create a political atmosphere within the administration that would permit the extension of American aid to Russia. That was the impression of British Ambassador Stafford Cripps during his first meeting with Hopkins in Moscow. As the ambassador noted in his diary, the President, according to Hopkins, was "all out to help all he could even if the Army and Navy authorities in America did not like it."[52]

Roosevelt's actions at home, just as Hopkins was about to depart from Moscow and before he passed on any detailed report, fit the pattern. When Treasury Secretary Henry Morgenthau reported that Soviet officials were getting the run-around, the President angrily ordered Stimson on 1 August to "get the planes right off with a bang next week." According to a gleeful Morgenthau, Stimson "looked thoroughly miserable." Although Roosevelt admitted such early aid was being sent "in order to help their [Soviet] morale," he indicated his commitment to an effective, long-term aid program by stating he would "put one of the best administrators in charge." The next day, in one of those infrequent but memorable moments of command, he ordered: "Use a heavy hand—act as a burr under the saddle and get things moving. . . . Step on it!" He continued to put on the pressure, writing to Stimson that quantities of munitions be supplied "immediately" to the Russians. Granted, what Roosevelt demanded be sent to the Soviet Union would (should, according to Stimson and his generals) have gone to rebuild American military strength or to Great Britain. But Roosevelt did more than merely tell the British that their needs would be reconsidered, given Soviet requirements. He did more than merely mortgage planned output. He set a production bench mark that no one thought realistic for American war production— yet U.S. industry would exceed those goals by 1943.[53]

Roosevelt's predisposition to aid the Soviet Union fit his grand strategy in 1941. Even though he had moved closer and closer to accepting the inevitability of American entry into the war, the President still hoped, however wishfully, to avoid sending American soldiers to fight in Europe, despite Churchill's persistent, if indirect, entreaties.[54] When military assessments pointed out that only the Red Army could achieve victory over Hitler in a land war, aid to the Soviet Union became a presidential priority.[55] Churchill himself recognized that Soviet involvement could diminish or at least delay the chances of full American entry into the war, a scenario that threatened all of the Prime Minister's plans. Shortly after the Atlantic Conference—the Churchill-Roosevelt meeting held aboard warships anchored in Placentia Bay, Newfoundland—he presented another pessimistic picture of the Soviet military situation, connecting such comments with pleas for the United States to join the fray.[56]

Whether to obtain information, justification, or for public consumption, Roosevelt immediately agreed to Hopkins' proposal to fly to Russia. The American left London on 27 July for Scotland and the long, cold flight over the Arctic, wearing one of Winston Churchill's gray Homburgs, and carrying a diplomatic visa hastily handwritten by the Soviet ambassador in London (which no one examined). On the four-hour flight from Archangel to Moscow, Hopkins was struck by the vast forests that seemed to him to pose an almost impenetrable barrier to German tanks, but that was about the only chance he had to assess the military situation in person. His talks with Stalin, Molotov, and other Soviet officials provided no surprises. The Soviets seemed to hate Hitler, appeared determined to resist, and made requests for the kind of production equipment and raw materials that indicated their own faith in being able to fight a prolonged war against the Germans.[57] Ambassador Steinhardt, hardly a friend of the Soviets, was openly surprised at the warm, gracious reception for Hopkins and "unusual attention" he received in the press. "He [Hopkins] was received promptly by Stalin who granted him very extended interviews and discussed with a frankness unparalleled in my knowledge . . . the subject of his mission and the Soviet position." During a German air raid (which did not destroy Moscow buildings like "matchsticks," despite some earlier predictions), Hopkins and Steinhardt were assigned a bomb shelter. The disgruntled ambassador observed that never before had a shelter been placed at his disposal, bringing a hearty laugh from Hopkins.[58]

Hopkins found some things he did not like. He was no Lincoln Steffens, seeing the Soviet state as the next stage in world social development. Stalin's intimidation of subordinates frustrated attempts by Hopkins or anyone else to gain anything useful from discussions with other Soviet officials. One Soviet general, when asked if his forces needed tanks and antitank guns, responded, "I am not empowered to say." In his recommendation to Roosevelt for a nuts-and-bolts supply conference in the autumn, Hopkins insisted that the meeting had to be in Moscow since "no-one—and I underline that—in Russia other than Mr. Stalin gives any information whatever to any foreigner." Hopkins also wrote that his visit to Moscow drove home "the difference between democracy and dictatorship."[59]

But such negatives were hardly a surprise, and unlikely to change the policy Roosevelt and Hopkins had agreed upon weeks earlier. Perhaps if the presidential emissary had found an atmosphere of gloom and doom in the Soviet capital, things would have been different. But Hopkins' only message from Moscow contained the words the President expected: "I have had two long and satisfactory talks with Stalin and will communicate personally to you the messages he is sending. I would like to tell you now, however, that I feel ever so confident about this front. The morale of the population is exceptionally good. There is unbounded determination to win."[60] Hopkins assessed the will to fight, an intangible that a frightened Steinhardt, eager to flee the German attack on Moscow, and American military leaders, insulated and isolated in the United States, could not appreciate. Despair and fear of defeat are contagious in an army and a government, and are difficult if not impossible to hide—though perhaps if Hopkins had arrived a week later the atmosphere would have been different following the German victory in the Smolensk area.[61] Nevertheless, what Hopkins found in Moscow was not so much a vision of victory by the Red Army, but a determination to fight on, even if Moscow were taken. Time and again, Stalin promised to continue the struggle using the industrial resources that lay east of the capital city. What Hopkins concluded was that aid to Russia was a good bet. Like most other leaders, east and west, he saw the war through the spectrum of his own nation's interests, and prolonging the war on the Russian front clearly met that criterion. Hopkins carefully evaded all suggestions for a formal Soviet-American alliance, for that would have raised impossible political issues at home. After all, the Roosevelt administration had not gone that far for Great Britain, and the Soviet Union was viewed with far greater suspicion and distaste by almost all Americans. That the Soviets even brought up such ideas suggests their remarkable naivete about the United States.

Hopkins' extensive reports to Roosevelt on the Moscow talks were taken from notes that were not written up until later—perhaps not until after the Atlantic Conference.[62] That makes a conversation between FDR and his son, Elliott, held before Hopkins' return, another indication that Roosevelt had made up his mind to provide large-scale aid to the Soviets before the Hopkins mission ever began. The President commented that the British would be concerned about the diversion of supplies to the Soviets, and went on to complain:

> "I know already how much faith the P.M. has in Russia's ability to stay in the war." He snapped his fingers to indicate zero.
> "I take it you have more faith than that."
> "Harry Hopkins has more. He's able to convince me."[63]

A surprising conclusion to draw on the basis of only one brief, predictably optimistic message from Hopkins.

Nor did the question of aid to the Soviet Union take up much time at the Atlantic Conference. For the most part, the Soviet-German war was discussed in terms of the effect it would have in the Pacific. The conflict guaranteed that the Soviet Union could not challenge Japanese expansion, and there was the danger that Japan would seize the opportunity and move into Soviet territory. But whatever the context of discussions about the war between Germany and the USSR, Roosevelt did not seek advice and counsel from the British about whether or not to aid the Soviets. Robert Sherwood has stated that Hopkins' encouraging reports assured agreement on aid to Russia; certainly no one argued with Churchill when he supported Hopkins' recommendation for a conference in Moscow to discuss the details. But the President had made his decision even before the evidence was in.[64]

Following the Atlantic Conference, Roosevelt boarded his train in Portland, Maine, for the ride back to Washington. He was joined by one "Adelai" Stevenson, then a special assistant to the Secretary of the Navy. Stevenson, who had pursued the presidential train in a small aircraft, brought a secret report from the usual "reliable source" that Hitler and Stalin were negotiating. "I don't believe it," Roosevelt remarked. "I'm not worried at all. Are you worried Adlai?" Stevenson, who would be the presidential candidate of Roosevelt's Democratic Party in 1952 and 1956, muttered that he guessed not, and left.[65] Perhaps the President was whistling in the dark, but his commitment was clear.

In a small footnote to the Hopkins mission, British Ambassador Cripps tried to use the American emissary to jolt Churchill and the British Cabinet out of their policy of promises without action. Cripps was convinced that "we must consider the question of help to Russia not as merely sparing to a partner or an ally what we feel we can spare but rather as the point upon which we should concentrate all the supplies that we can raise because that is at the moment the weakest point of the enemy and therefore our best chance of success." It was hardly difficult to get an already convinced Hopkins to agree.[66]

For Soviet-American relations, the period of crisis diplomacy was over, although the Hopkins mission was not the final word. The Anglo-American supply mission that Hopkins had suggested arrived in Moscow in late September 1941. Led by Harriman for the United States and Lord Beaverbrook for the British, it built on the policy Roosevelt had adopted back in July. Specific requirements were defined, and a long-term program of aid developed. Harriman's formal report to Roosevelt repeated what he had already passed on less formally and in person: "Russia can make very effective use of the latest types of American equipment and that *Russia will continue to fight even in retreat.*"[67] The role of the Soviet Union against Germany seemed so important to U.S. Army intelligence that, early in October, it labeled "foolhardy" any concessions to the Japanese that would permit that nation to turn its forces away from the war in China and attack Siberia. The Army War Plans Division agreed.[68] By mid-October, Roosevelt had directed General Marshall to give precedence to delivery of supplies to Russia over any other defense aid shipments. Two weeks later Congress again rejected attempts to prohibit Lend-Lease aid to Russia. The next day the President moved away from the nickel-and-dime approach to funding Soviet supply requirements by promising to make arrangements to pay for up to one billion dollars' worth of goods through the Lend-Lease Act. Within a week, the President formally instructed the Lend-Lease administrator, Edward Stettinius, that the defense of the Soviet Union "is vital to the defense of the United States," thereby making the USSR eligible for the transfer of defense materiel under the terms of the Lend-Lease Act.[69]

By the end of 1941, the basic pattern had emerged. Neither Britain nor the United States was willing to provide aid to the Soviets at a level that would jeopardize their own security, but for the remainder of the war, Roosevelt saw his goals advanced by pushing for more assistance, while Churchill, with a different set of interests to protect, consistently held back.

One thing this episode makes clear is that it is impossible to write about this stage in the development of the Soviet-American coalition without discussing, in some detail, British reactions and policies. That is, in part, because a Soviet-American coalition in World War II never existed; it was always an Anglo-Soviet-American association. Americans may have had their own intellectual and cultural perceptions of the Soviet Union, but American foreign policy was greatly affected by British needs, requests, and suggestions, particularly in the period 1939–1942. Roosevelt developed his own foreign policy toward the Soviet Union, but often that was, as in other situations, in reaction to British moves. The issue of aid to the Soviet Union in 1941, with all the overtones of Anglo-American tension that it raised, foreshadowed the acrimony that would develop between London and Washington over the issue of a Second Front.

At one level, Roosevelt's decision to aid the Soviets was designed to boost their morale, something akin to the President's blithe habit of challenging people by establishing seemingly unreachable goals. But at a deeper level, that aid program was always political. At no time in 1941 did Roosevelt or Hopkins claim that American aid would play any significant role in the battle for Moscow. Quite the contrary. They admitted that little aid could reach the Russians until after that campaign was decided. Similarly during the war, Roosevelt treated the aid-to-Russia program more as a matter of "good faith" than for its value to the Soviet war effort. One careful historian has estimated that value: "The more than $10 billion worth of equipment and supplies sent to the Soviet Union did represent only a small percentage of Russian production—best estimates set the figure at 10 or 11 percent," even though "arms, industrial equipment, raw materials, and food filled critical gaps in Russian output and allowed Soviet industry to concentrate on production of items for which it was best suited."[70] But whatever the actual value of lend-lease to the Soviet Union, Roosevelt had bigger things in mind.

All of the suspicions, excuses, complaints, apologies, and breast-beating about Allied aid to the USSR in the period from 22 June 1941 through mid-1942 cannot disguise a cardinal military fact—the battle of Moscow was won by the Soviet Union, though it was nip and tuck. The Soviets seized every military and logistic advantage they could find: factories relocated in the mountains east of Moscow; abundant reserves of manpower; surprising (at least to the outside world, and especially to the Germans) air strength; shorter lines of communication; the dispersal of German strength created by a long front in the east as well as the need to police conquered areas from France to the Ukraine; partisan activities; and what limited Allied aid could arrive before the battle. German overoptimism plus Hitler's personal timetable, which ran ahead of that of his generals and his economic planners, left a German Army ill-prepared for an extended campaign or for the premature onset of the fall rains and winter snows. Soviet forces used the Russian climate to good advantage— but that came only after two months of bitter resistance that kept the Germans out of Moscow before the weather turned. Soviet leaders may have wavered and prepared for compromise, retreat, and even defeat. But the Soviet soldiers held on. Thus, all of the recriminations about Allied aid during that first year of the Russian front are quite beside the point. Even without the crisis of supply caused by the Japanese attack on the United States, American and British aid to Russia in that twelve-month period could only be a gesture and a hint of things to come, and all the parties knew it.[71]

The significance of the Hopkins mission goes far beyond the President's decision to provide short-term aid to the Soviet Union. Moreover, emphasis on the realities of power and nationalism (geopolitics, as it were) in the conduct of US-USSR relations should not obscure the impact of personalities and personal emotions. Franklin Roosevelt assumed, out of intuition more than evidence, that the Soviet Union would be an active power in the postwar world, though his assessment of the extent of that role steadily grew during the war, as did everyone else's. Whatever the reaction of others to the growth of Soviet power, Roosevelt concluded that the forced cooperation of World War II should provide a building block for cooperation in the postwar era. Yet, would that policy have been possible had Harry Hopkins, or someone else, not provided testimony Roosevelt needed in the summer of 1941 in order to justify a promise of aid to Russia?

Roosevelt has been routinely criticized for his excessive concern for congressional and public opinion, but in 1941 he took the tougher road, going against the thrust of opinion within and without his administration by promising both aid and legitimacy to the Soviet Union. The Hopkins and Harriman missions permitted Franklin Roosevelt to treat the Soviet Union as an ally worth supporting, not an enemy or weak house of cards about to fall. His early commitment to aid is evidence of Roosevelt's sense, more instinctive than reasoned, of the Soviet Union's potential as a postwar power—a striking display of savvy for a President whom many have claimed flew by the seat of the pants when it came to foreign policy.

This fit a pattern in Roosevelt's foreign policy. After all, he had initiated diplomatic recognition of the Soviet Union back in 1933. He never shared the anger and sense of betrayal that Ambassador William Bullitt expressed when the Soviet Union continued its propaganda activities in the United States, in violation of the spirit of the recognition agreement. Even the President's anger about the Nazi-Soviet Pact was muted. He was one of those who predicted the short life of that agreement, warning Stalin early that month that Hitler "would turn on Russia" once France was defeated. FDR's conduct during the Russo-Finnish "Winter War" further suggests his sense that the Soviet Union would become a major player on the world scene. Despite his personal anger and disgust with Soviet actions, and intense public and congressional pressure to take strong measures to provide moral if not real aid to the underdog Finns, Roosevelt avoided any formal break in diplomatic relations with the Soviet Union, settling for vague denunciations of the Russians as aggressors.[72] Such shrewd caution does not reveal any prescient awareness of where the Soviet Union would be in 1945, but it does place Franklin Roosevelt further in the direction of accepting the Soviet Union as a "legitimate" great power than the western European nations were willing to go. Military requirements dominated his immediate thinking, but the peace that would follow was never far behind.

The President's actions in the summer and fall of 1941 also demonstrate his conviction that Britain could not and should not be the broker for Soviet-American relations. It was an attitude that would shape much of his later wartime diplomacy.[73]

Roosevelt's decision to aid the Soviet Union was made with only hope and intuition to guide him. His short-term assessment of geopolitics temporarily overshadowed his commitment to American ideals and institutions and his belief that they could work for the world—his Americanism. That commitment would become apparent when he and Stalin finally met at Teheran in December 1943. But in the summer and fall of 1941, the substance that mattered was Roosevelt's willingness to equate American survival with that of the Soviet Union; an equation that Stalin could understand.

Roosevelt's approach had little if any immediate effect on Stalin's attitude. Promises could always be broken, as Stalin knew, and survival required more than gestures and promises. As the situation worsened in the autumn, Stalin played a double game. His fears of an overwhelming German victory, which would threaten both the Soviet state and his personal rule, apparently prompted him to use a Bulgarian go-between to make a peace offer to Hitler. Following the Bolshevik Revolution during the First World War, Lenin had ceded Soviet territory to Germany in the Brest-Litovsk Treaty of 1918 in order to gain time to consolidate his authority at home. In November 1941, with the Germans at the gates of Moscow, Stalin offered eastern Poland, the Ukraine, and the Baltic states if only the Germans would stop their advance. Hitler, smelling victory, ignored the offer, and that peace never came, leaving Stalin no choice but to throw his lot in with the western capitalists.[74]

To argue that the Soviets appreciated Roosevelt's promise of aid, to suggest that the commitment was seen by the Soviets as a major step toward the legitimization of the Soviet state in Western eyes, is not to argue that such gratitude is a primary determinant in Soviet foreign policy. But even though Stalin hedged his bets and tried to negotiate with the Germans in November 1941, Roosevelt's public pledge was an impressive, even comforting event for the Soviet leaders and people (insofar as they knew about it). The promise came at a time when the very existence of the Soviet state and even the Russian nation-empire was at stake. Both Stalin and Roosevelt knew that Germany posed no immediate threat to the United States. Both understood that little if any American aid could arrive before the battle of Moscow was decided. But had the President not made such assurances and then insisted that the machinery of aid go into high gear, then his policy of cooperation would likely never have been born.

Without access to Soviet documents, we cannot assess the true reaction of Stalin and his advisers to Roosevelt's initiative. Moreover, whatever effect Roosevelt's decision had on wartime relations with the Soviet Union was submerged in all the events that followed. But that opening move was not forgotten in the Soviet Union. Had Roosevelt not acted as he did in 1941, his wartime policy of trying to make collaboration the basis for peacetime unity, even as carefully hedged as it was, would not have been possible.[75] Regardless of how one evaluates that policy, all can agree that without that window of trust and cooperation—based as it had to be on mutual self-interest, expediency, and a common enemy—the postwar world would have been different, and perhaps even more frightening. Later, as *glas'nost* developed in the Soviet Union, Roosevelt's cooperative approach, which began with his reaction to the outbreak of the German-Soviet War, provided a rationale for Kremlin arguments that ideology did not prevent great power cooperation, especially in time of crisis.[76]

Despite Roosevelt's early agreement that he would join Churchill in welcoming the Soviet Union as an ally against Hitler, there was no reason to suspect that the President would end up trying to create a close, stable relationship with Stalin. After all, public opinion in the United States remained suspicious of Soviet intentions. But Roosevelt ignored that. On the flimsiest of evidence that the Soviet Union would continue to fight, and perhaps survive, he sent supplies that Britain had expected to receive. At first glance, that decision seems but a variation on Pascal's wager—the United States had little to lose. But there was more to it than that. At no time did Roosevelt spell out to anyone, probably not even to himself, where his instincts were taking him. But the implications of his decisions are clear. It would be two years before he faced up to the reality of the changing world situation—the growth of Soviet power and the relative decline of Britain's role. Nonetheless, as Halifax ruefully realized, even in 1941 the Americans, in particular Franklin Roosevelt, had not "come out where you expect."

"It is the furthest thing from my mind . . . to trade . . . imperial preference . . . for Lend-Lease." Caption is from a Roosevelt to Churchill telegram: Kimball, *Churchill & Roosevelt*, I, R-105.

III

Lend-Lease and the Open Door:
The Temptation of British Opulence,
1937–1942

ALTHOUGH Great Britain usually stands condemned as an imperialist rather than a victim of imperialism, historians have recently begun to examine the question of whether the economic imperialism of the United States challenged Britain and her empire, particularly during the era of World War II. Some dismiss the idea as relatively unimportant; others claim that primarily economic motivations determined American policy toward Great Britain before, during, and after the war.[1] William Appleman Williams has written that "the issue is not how bad or evil Americans were, but rather the far more profound and human theme of their tragic inability to realize their desire for peace and freedom so long as they declined to modify seriously the principles of possessive individualism that lie at the heart of capitalism."[2] Whether capitalism is the only contemporary economic and political system characterized by such principles is not the question; the problem is, was "possessive individualism" at the heart of America's policies toward Great Britain?

Few would quarrel with the claim of many historians that the expansion of foreign markets is and has been a basic policy of the United States government. Such agreement, however, does not eliminate arguments over the priorities, the means, and the degree of consistency of such policies. Often, the disagreement boils down to one question: did economic goals determine the government's assessment of national security or was economic welfare merely one of the many elements which policymakers considered in determining national goals?

Such a question becomes most difficult to answer during a time of great national crisis such as the one that faced the United States in the late

Originally published in *Political Science Quarterly* 86 (June 1971), pp. 232–59. I wish to express my gratitude to the Penrose Foundation of the American Philosophical Society for a grant which enabled me to do the research for this essay. I am also grateful to Professors Charles Alexander, Alfred Eckes, Willard Gatewood, Robert Griffith, D. E. Harrell, George Herring, Bradford Perkins, Gaddis Smith, and J. Chal Vinson for their perceptive comments which I have all too often ignored, at my own risk. I read a shorter version of this paper at the meeting of the Organization of American Historians in Los Angeles, 17 April 1970.

1930s. When a country's national security is apparently threatened, short-term strategic considerations usually dominate policy. In fact, most students of American policies during the Second World War have criticized the Roosevelt administration for failing to develop realistic long-term postwar plans.

Up to now, my research has left me convinced that in the 1930s American foreign policy toward Britain sprang from just such considerations of national security and a strong sense of the community of interest between the two countries. The Lend-Lease Act of March 1941 contained no provisions which could be termed "imperialistic"; rather, President Franklin Roosevelt and the Treasury Department officials who wrote the bill left repayment clauses purposely vague in order to avoid the kind of war debts problem that occurred after World War I. A direct and unencumbered grant to an ally fighting America's war was politically unfeasible, although Treasury Secretary Henry Morgenthau, Jr., proposed just that. But under lend-lease, repayment was left completely to the discretion of the President. Some American policymakers, particularly Secretary of State Cordell Hull and other top State Department personnel, demanded that Britain repay lend-lease aid and post collateral besides, but Roosevelt steadfastly refused to support such proposals before the passage of the act. There is no doubt that the temptation arose to take advantage of Britain's wartime plight, but in the case of the Lend-Lease Act, American policymakers resisted that temptation. Instead, while presenting the bill to the public as a swap, the administration chose to extend an indirect subsidy, not out of any lofty altruism, but out of an awareness that Hitler was also America's enemy and that a happy ally is one who believes that the war will be worth winning.[3] The question remains, however, was the Lend-Lease Act typical of American economic foreign policy or an exception resulting from the intensity of the crisis in Europe?

The broad outlines of America's economic foreign policy in the late 1930s are well known. Secretary of State Cordell Hull dominated policy making in that sphere, with occasional excursions in the arena of international finance by Secretary Morgenthau and the Treasury Department— excursions which the State Department invariably resented. As a number of historians have demonstrated, Hull saw economic interdependence, as defined by the United States, as the only sure way to peace.[4] Hull put it clearly in a speech in November 1938 to the National Foreign Trade Convention:

> I know that without expansion of international trade, based upon fair dealing and equal treatment for all, there can be no stability and security either within or among nations. . . . I know that the withdrawal by a nation from orderly trade relations with the rest of the world inevitably leads to regimentation of all phases of national life, to the suppression of human rights, and all too fre-

quently to preparations for war and a provocative attitude toward other nations.[5]

Although he occasionally faced reversals from President Roosevelt and others, these were largely reversals in tactics rather than in broad policy. Not only did Roosevelt generally agree with Hull, but, as memoirs such as those by Frances Perkins and Robert Sherwood make clear, FDR disliked worrying about economic matters, being much more comfortable in the world of politics and power. Hull's long-term views were ably supported by his subordinates in the State Department; Francis B. Sayre, the assistant secretary for economic affairs; his successor, Henry Grady; and Harry Hawkins, the head of the Division of Commercial Policy and Trade Agreements, echoed Hull's sentiments precisely, both in public and in private. Herbert Feis, the Department's special adviser for economic affairs, frequently chided the others for impractical proposals, but he strongly supported Hull's economic programs without completely succumbing to the secretary's simplistic faith in them as a cure-all for world problems.

Hull's policies are comprehensible only if one understands his definitions of terms. Although he frequently spoke of freer trade and liberal economics, he really meant equal commercial opportunity—what Williams calls the Open Door. Hull was too shrewd a politician to propound true free trade, though he occasionally condemned the extreme protectionism of the Hawley-Smoot tariff. What some British historians have called "the imperialism of free trade" might better be labeled the "imperialism of equality," for to open certain previously closed doors would obviously mean American capital could dominate that marketplace, whether Hull realized it or not.[6] Hull favored primarily equality of opportunity and the elimination of discriminatory trade practices—equality of treatment being far more important to him than a mere lowering of trade barriers. Equal access for all to raw materials had similar importance for him. He repeatedly asserted that one of Hitler's original goals was to attain nondiscriminatory access to the raw materials necessary for Germany's economic prosperity, and Hull clearly believed that the raw materials of the colonial empires should be made available to the industrial nations of the world. That such access would provide a distinct economic advantage for a nation which could buy in large quantities was of no concern; the inequality of equal competition was a nicety either lost on Hull or ignored by him. His condemnation of economic nationalism extended also to the international money market; he advocated the elimination of any restrictions designed to limit the outflow of gold.[7]

Some basic notions held by the administration regarding Britain's economic wealth and her empire stand out clearly. Secretary of State Hull regularly denounced the preferential tariffs established by Great Britain and her empire in the 1932 Ottawa Agreements and sought their elimination.[8] But he had more in mind than that one limited objective. In February 1937, Hull protested with suspicious forcefulness to the Canadian minister in Washington that "neither I nor my country would . . . weaken a single link in the British Empire." With characteristic piety, he declaimed that "it was not for a moment in my mind or in the mind of my Government to bring the slightest pressure to bear on any portion of the British Empire with respect to the problem of Empire preference." Yet in a not-so-veiled threat, Hull asserted that progress toward peace would be determined by Britain's movement away from economic nationalism.[9] With England desperately trying to establish a political entente against Germany and with an Anglo-American trade agreement under negotiation, there was no mistaking the implication of Hull's remark. Nor was that an isolated instance. Hull had earlier told Walter Runciman, president of the British Board of Trade, that Britain's violations of the principle of commercial equality and her economic nationalism made "normal economic relations between nations" impossible. "It is utterly hopeless," he had warned, "to contemplate the restoration of the many normal and worthwhile international relationships, political, economic, moral or peace, unless the economic approach to existing problems and conditions is vigorously pursued under the leadership of our two countries."[10]

Hull's prime concern remained the threat of German expansion, but he obviously was tempted to use the mounting crisis as a lever against British Empire preference systems. In January 1937, he told Sir Ronald Lindsay, the British ambassador in Washington, that "the complete closing up of the Empire like an oyster shell" came at a most inopportune time, since Congress was deluged with demands for stronger neutrality laws.[11] Hiding behind alleged public sentiment was a device that Roosevelt and Hull used consistently during the prewar years to justify their own policies.

No American government official ever stood up and crassly proclaimed that a major goal of the nation's foreign policy should be the acquisition of Britain's empire. Such blatant colonialism did not tempt Americans in the 1930s. Yet to speak of healthy competition was to reaffirm an American tradition—if not a human instinct—even if the truth was that such competition would be healthiest for the United States. Not surprisingly, much attention focused on the biggest prizes, and in 1937 one seemed to be the British Empire. The Department of Commerce reported that at the end of 1936, British overseas investments had a nominal value of over £3.75 billion and estimates were that Great Britain in some areas would attain new heights of prosperity unequaled since 1914. More impressive was the return from Britain's overseas investments, which came close to offsetting her unfavorable balance of trade.[12]

This image of British wealth, combined with an opportunity to drive a hard and profitable bargain, continually tempted the leaders of the American government.[13] Yet to present economic expansion as the key motive affecting Anglo-American affairs in the late 1930s would be patently absurd. The more emotional issues of the depression and the fear of war almost invariably took precedence. In 1937, however, when "cash and carry" knocked the first hole in America's neutrality wall, economic needs played a role. Trade with belligerents was not provocative after all, so long as such trade did not include arms and was on a strictly cash basis. As the congressional debate and newspaper accounts show, the neutrality legislation of 1937 was prompted by a wish to maintain or increase trade with Britain as well as by considerations of national security. The British had proven most reluctant to negotiate any Anglo-American trade agreement based on a diminishing of the imperial preference system since, from their point of view, such a trade treaty would be primarily aimed at creating a political entente; and most of the British Cabinet did not believe such a pact would bind the United States to assist politically.[14] Given that political situation and the firm American belief that economic nationalism would prevent the establishment of world peace, it is easier to understand why the Americans began to raise the ante in 1937. By the close of that year, political events in Europe and Asia had made Britain far more dependent upon American support. "Cash and carry" was a public announcement that the United States planned to capitalize on that dependence. Promoting peace and profit simultaneously was an appealing policy.

As the political situation in Europe deteriorated, American leaders spoke more frequently about providing England with war materials, and with increasing regularity, the terms for such aid included settlements which would effect permanent changes in Anglo-American economic relations. During the height of the 1938 Czechoslovakian crisis, Roosevelt told his cabinet that the United States would prosper economically even if Europe went to war. Gold from the European nations had already begun to arrive in America for probable use in purchasing war goods (even before the 1939 revision of the neutrality legislation permitting the sale of war goods to belligerents). The President expected Britain and France to confiscate American securities owned by their nationals as exchange for war materials. Yet Roosevelt also claimed that the ability of the British and French to purchase munitions in large amounts had been severely underestimated. A few days later the President told the cabinet that British private investments in the United States probably totaled nearly $7 billion and again referred to Britain's plan to sell her American investments. While the Department of Commerce and the Federal Reserve Board estimated British investments at less than one-third of FDR's figure, the image of British opulence persisted.[15]

The outbreak of war in September 1939 quickly complicated British-American economic relations. Although the British immediately instituted wartime restrictions on dollar expenditures, with the German occupation of Western Europe guns became more important than bank balances. Neutrality legislation and the Johnson Debt-Default Act limited British purchases to a cash basis, and a financial crisis quickly developed. Ultimately, that crisis was resolved in a spirit of mutual friendship and self-interest by the Lend-Lease Act, but not without numerous references to the more mundane matters of British wealth and American economic interests.

The most sensible suggested solution to Britain's dollar shortage in the pre–Pearl Harbor period was that American firms, or the government, accept sterling in lieu of dollars, an arrangement which the Canadians had made and generally referred to as the "sterling overdraft." The idea was never seriously discussed within the Roosevelt administration, and though there is no evidence to demonstrate why it was so casually rejected, the effect was to guarantee Britain's indebtedness to the United States.[16]

As the intensity of the war increased, so did American pressure on the United Kingdom to force the sale of privately owned British investments in the United States. Henry Morgenthau, with ardent support from Hull and other cabinet members, advised English officials to sell such direct investments in America as Shell Oil, Lever Brothers, and Brown & Williamson Tobacco in order to gain both dollar assets and American goodwill. The Treasury Secretary said that 1940 was no time to worry about postwar economic problems, although he deemed it his responsibility to see that England fulfilled her contracts. The rhetoric continued until after the passage of the Lend-Lease Act and portended a classic example of economic imperialism. Yet in fact, only one major British-owned direct investment in the United States, the American Viscose Company, was sold under pressure, and that was clearly part of the legislative strategy surrounding the congressional fight over lend-lease. The potential economic benefits intrigued the American government, but such gains were put aside for the time being in favor of the more immediate requirements of American national security.[17]

Once the Lend-Lease Act became law, the temptation to use it as a means of obtaining economic concessions from Britain—concessions which would promote economic multilateralism as well as directly and indirectly benefit American economic expansion—became too great to resist. Harry Hopkins had assured Churchill in February 1941 that American demands for data on British financial sacrifices were not part of a general government attitude, but necessary because of the ignorance of the American public.[18] The American refusal, however, to help Britain pay for the war materials she had ordered during the first three months of 1941—just before lend-lease took effect—belied Hopkins' assurances. In fact, the dispute over those so-called "old commitments" acted as a strong warning to the British that America would continue to insist on the artificial separation between political alliance and profit-motivated economic policy.

In what proved to be the key theme of later negotiations over the Lend-Lease Master Agreement, British officials in March 1941 predicted that their nation might have to restrict its postwar import surplus because of a falloff in foreign exchange earnings and would then have to establish controls over exports and foreign exchange. The State Department condemned the suggestion as an "artificial" diversion of trade that struck at the heart of Hull's program. But for all of Britain's complaints and gentle threats, they would not be able to say no to the United States.[19]

Fortunately for the British, Morgenthau and the Treasury Department dealt with the financial problems connected with lend-lease. Although they invariably drove a hard bargain, Morgenthau and his staff were clearly far more interested in combating Hitler's Germany than in using American aid as a knife to open that oyster shell, the empire. Not so for Cordell Hull and the State Department policymakers.[20]

Hull never accepted the fact that Britain could be short of dollars while still operating a vast colonial and economic empire. Throughout 1941 he and his staff sought the joint goals of security against Nazism and access to Britain's opulent empire. Although he failed to convince the President that Britain should post $2 or $3 billion of collateral in conjunction with the lend-lease program, he continued to work on the assumption that Britain possessed $18 billion in imperial wealth.[21] The concept of using lend-lease as a lever to force Britain to eliminate the imperial preference system and extend the Open Door to America throughout the empire was not openly discussed in the State Department before the passage of the Lend-Lease Act, but the Department quickly made up for lost time afterward.

In a book published shortly before the negotiation of the Master Lend-Lease Agreement, economist William Culbertson, an ardent and unabashed booster of Hull's economic policies, wrote: "Since the accounts under the lend-lease acts can never be balanced by shipments in kind or in gold, it seems to me that the British Empire should, at the very least, extend to American trade and finance the equality to which they are entitled under the basic principle of sound commercial policy."[22] That statement might have been written by Hull himself.

Roosevelt initially assigned Morgenthau and the Treasury Department the task of expeditiously negotiating a quid pro quo with Britain for immediate transfers of war materials, and he also instructed Morgenthau to work on a general agreement to cover lend-lease.[23] The choice of the phrase "quid pro quo" could have been mere chance, but, intended or not, it set the tone for the negotiations. Many Americans, including Henry Morgenthau, saw Britain's fight against Hitler as just compensation for lend-lease. Even FDR had officially labeled it America's last chance to avoid war. Nevertheless, the pressure of the largely Republican opposition, the promises made before Congress during the lend-lease hearings, the belief that world peace and liberal economics were inseparable, and, one suspects, the ever-present American desire to make a good deal, all combined to set the stage for a series of protracted and bitter negotiations. Instead of an honest subsidy for an ally admittedly fighting America's war, the Roosevelt administration continually asked the question, "What have you done for me—lately?" Like most governments, the Roosevelt administration seems to have followed policies which, if not precisely contradictory, were mutually incompatible. At one and the same time the American government tried with material aid to buoy up an ally's spirit and will to resist, used that same aid as a means of coercing that ally into long-term economic concessions which would hopefully promote peace, and also tried to obtain immediate economic benefits for the United States. One historian recently suggested that instead of "what have you done for me lately?" a better way to phrase the Roosevelt administration's question would be "what have you been planning for the more liberal postwar world which this war is, ultimately, all about?" That was the broad issue as Cordell Hull saw it, but the quid pro quo discussed by Congress and Roosevelt referred to far more immediate and tangible matters.[24]

Though Roosevelt indicated he did not want any specific mention of money, the Treasury Department showed a remarkable lack of imagination in drafting the lend-lease agreement. Treating the agreement as a contract, Treasury officials thought in terms of balance sheets and running accounts. Since the President had cautioned against allowing Hull to "get his nose out of joint," Morgenthau instructed his staff to discuss the various proposed drafts with the State Department, mainly with Dean Acheson, who had joined the department as assistant secretary in February 1941.[25] The difference in approach between the two departments was striking. Late in April, Morgenthau sent Hull the latest Treasury proposal for a lend-lease agreement. Reflecting Morgenthau's belief in a strong executive and more specifically his admiration for Roosevelt, the draft left the basic settlement to the discretion of the President. As one Treasury official put it: it was unlikely that another Coolidge would come along. Nevertheless, the draft did call for replacement of defense articles with an equivalent amount of similar items and established the guideline that such

American aid to Britain as agricultural goods, services, and defense information, should be compensated for by equivalent amounts of tin, rubber, jute, and other empire products. Postwar economic relationships received no mention, despite the prevailing State Department views. As of mid-May the Treasury draft was still under discussion, but Hull and his cohorts had different plans well underway.[26]

As soon as the question of negotiating an overall lend-lease settlement came up in mid-March, advocates of economic liberalism saw their golden opportunity. J. Pierrepont Moffat, always eager to be in on the action, returned to Washington in late March from his ambassadorial post in Ottawa "to preach the gospel that unless we availed ourselves of the present situation to obtain a commitment from the members of the British Empire to modify the Ottawa Agreements after the war, we would ultimately be virtually shut out of our Dominion markets," but, he continued in his diary, "much to my delight I found that people had begun to think along these lines." His simultaneous urging that as compensation for lend-lease aid, the United States accept British assets in Latin America and receive clear title to some Pacific islands jointly claimed by Britain and America indicates a strong concern for more immediate economic benefits as well.[27] That Roosevelt never accepted such a narrow definition of quid pro quo only demonstrates his broader and more mature sense of what was best for America's economic future.

In addition to the discussion over lend-lease, growing Anglo-American cooperation had created a number of troublesome economic problems. In hopes of negotiating an amicable settlement of these questions, the British government dispatched John Maynard Keynes in May 1941 to the United States as a representative of the British Treasury.[28] Although from the outset Keynes angered American officials with his talk of Britain's having to resort to postwar economic and monetary controls, American planners were already working on the assumption that Britain's postwar economic position would force her to adopt currency controls and discriminatory trade systems. As early as 8 April 1941, a State Department draft of a lend-lease agreement had called for "the abolition of Imperial preferences on specific products of interest to the United States." Unlike the Treasury Department drafts, the State Department version dealt with postwar economic policy and dismissed compensation in kind for the actual lend-lease materials.[29] It also expressed concern about American access to empire raw materials.[30] Keynes may have induced the State Department drafters to be more specific, for on 22 May, less than two weeks after he arrived, another draft agreement appeared—this time calling for specific promises by Britain to eliminate any special trade agreements which limited American trade.[31] In essence, Keynes forced the Americans to show their hand. Even more important was Roosevelt's decision on 16 May to give the State Department the assignment of working out the overall lend-lease arrangement with Great Britain. Although the Treasury Department still acted as a consultant, the initiative now lay with State. Morgenthau soon lost interest in playing second fiddle, telling his staff to "let the damn thing go." This assured victory for the State Department approach, that the United States should write off virtually all lend-lease aid to Britain in return for a broad economic commitment.[32]

Keynes' goals were quite simple. Foreseeing an economically prostrate England after the war, he advocated monetary controls, imperial prefer-ences, and other forms of economic nationalism as temporary but neces-sary means of maintaining any real degree of economic freedom for Brit-ain. Americans, used to careful deference and fulsome praise of their benevolence and altruism, reacted in a predictable fashion; Morgenthau and Harry Hopkins thought Keynes should go back to England before he did some real harm, and the anger he stimulated in the Department of State was only thinly disguised.[33]

The State Department's position was not consciously cynical, but rather was based on a fervent belief in the justness and efficacy of the American form of economic liberalism. A small but typical example of the administration's inability to perceive its own double standard was the reaction of Navy Secretary Frank Knox and Morgenthau to a rumor—later proved false—that Britain was keeping books on any defense infor-mation it gave to the United States with the aim of settling accounts after the war. Morgenthau called such actions "bad bull" and claimed that keeping accounts on information would only cause the two countries to withhold such data; yet at the same time the Treasury Department draft of a master lend-lease agreement called for Britain to repay the United States for defense information with raw materials.[34]

By the end of May, Acheson had worked out a detailed draft agreement embodying the two major State Department goals. First, British payment of a quid pro quo should not curtail the supply of dollars Britain had available to purchase American exports; second, the master agreement would be used as a means of gaining active British support for certain basic American economic and political policies. In return for an English commitment to drop discriminatory economic systems, the United States would cancel the major portion of the lend-lease debt.[35]

The Treasury Department, and even a few people in the State Depart-ment like Herbert Feis, opposed such openly coercive use of the agree-ment. They protested what one critic termed the State Department's "mil-lennial blueprint," but Morgenthau refused to carry the fight any further. Though he labeled the State Department draft a "Hermaphrodite," he felt surgery was useless:

As far as I am concerned, I am licked in the State Department. . . . Every time the President asks me to do something, Mr. Hull goes into a sulk and gets mad. . . . I am through being the President's whipping boy on the foreign affairs stuff. . . . Let the President of the United States tell Mr. Hull what kind of document he wants.[36]

During June and July, the State Department drew up numerous drafts and redrafts, incorporating the demand that Britain eliminate her discriminatory trade practices in return for lend-lease. In numerous talks with Lord Halifax, the British ambassador, and with Keynes, Roosevelt remained vague and seemingly sympathetic to the British arguments. His occasional memos to the State Department characteristically expressed a willingness to postpone forcing such concessions out of the United Kingdom; but he never disagreed with the State Department's basic goal.[37] What little guidance Keynes received from Churchill was ambiguous; while ostensibly supporting "broad economic collaboration," the Prime Minister rejected the creation of any machinery to achieve that end. Keynes complained about "the lunatic proposals of Mr. Hull," but he was powerless to alter them.[38]

By the end of July, Keynes had accomplished most of his assignments. After long and occasionally heated bargaining, he and the Treasury officials completed an arrangement that permitted Britain to build up her dollar and gold balances to $600 million, the figure agreed upon as the minimum needed for Britain to service various empire dollar requirements.[39] But Keynes left the United States without any real accord on a lend-lease master agreement. The real stumbling block continued to be article VII of the American draft. Though this was to be only a temporary agreement, since the final terms could not be determined until the end of the war, it set certain basic conditions as part of the final agreement. The specific phrase the British balked at read: "The terms and conditions upon which the United Kingdom receives defense aid . . . shall provide against discrimination in either the United States or the United Kingdom against the importation of any product originating in the other country."[40] The clause struck directly at the imperial preference system, a fact Acheson acknowledged. Keynes protested that England could not sign such a pact without a full-fledged imperial conference, since the dominions were not bound by British decisions. In addition, the banning of monetary controls—which the article apparently accomplished—envisaged a return to a gold-exchange standard for international trade, a move which would obviously work to Britain's disadvantage in a postwar world where America had all the gold. Keynes was careful not to charge the United States with exploiting Britain's crisis, although he evidently believed it.[41] While Keynes fully realized that England's postwar economic and political future lay in cooperation with the United States, he wanted partnership, not colonial status for the British.

For the remainder of the summer of 1941, economic relations between the two countries centered on the Atlantic Conference and the issuance by Britain of a White Paper dealing with the use of lend-lease goods. The United States tried to write a nondiscrimination clause into the Atlantic Charter, but Roosevelt's desire for a speedy and public Anglo-American accord prompted him to acquiesce to Churchill's insertion of the phrase "with due respect for our existing obligations," which preserved imperial preference. Hull feared that the British would interpret this as a surrender, but he could not obtain a clarifying statement from Roosevelt to refute either that impression or the views that Keynes had presented during his Washington visit.[42]

The appearance of the British White Paper of 10 September 1941 provided another instance of American inability or refusal to understand British problems. Issued under intense American pressure, the document was primarily aimed at convincing Congress and the American public that lend-lease aid was not being used to help Britain to compete with the United States in world markets. The American negotiators, however, particularly Hull and the ambassador in London, John Winant, took the White Paper most seriously. The State Department repeatedly referred to various complaints from American business firms about the reexporting of lend-lease goods by Britain and simultaneously displayed very real concern for protecting American markets, particularly those in the dominions and areas where Britain had dominated trade before the war. As one official British historian characterized the White Paper: "Taken literally, its provisions would have constituted an outrageously rigid control of British exports." Once again, the United Kingdom had to swallow its pride and trust in American goodwill, for immediate political necessity outweighed long-term economic considerations.[43]

Hull, obviously eager to seize upon this small victory, cabled Winant instructions to prod some sort of response out of the British regarding the lend-lease master agreement draft which Keynes had brought to London in late July.[44] Apparently on the recommendation of Herbert Feis, the economic adviser in the State Department, Hull had refrained from instructing Winant to get the British government publicly to assure the world that point four of the Atlantic Charter (the one referring to postwar economic affairs) was "more than an empty promise."[45] Now a lend-lease master agreement offered a promising vehicle for that same goal. The relationship between the White Paper and the negotiation of a master agreement is seen even more clearly in the minutes of the Committee on Foreign Trade Problems with the British Empire Arising out of Lend-Lease. That hybrid mouthful, composed of representatives from the Tariff Commission, the Departments of State, Commerce, and Treasury, plus the OPM and the OEM, which administered lend-lease, met in September and concluded that "the Lend-Lease Act was destined to become an increasingly dominant factor in our trade relations with the British Empire." It saw a need to protect American export trade into that empire. It recommended that the White Paper be officially extended to all the British dominions plus India and the colonial empire as necessary. In short, via the White Paper's restrictions on exporting, American trade would be protected—and expanded. The State Department concurred, and ultimately such agreements were made.[46]

On 30 September, Winant cabled Hull personally to recommend strongly that the United States insist on the nondiscrimination clauses which were in the American draft of 28 July. He told Hull that he believed such concessions would be supported by a majority in Parliament and that there would probably be no better opportunity to press the issue.[47] British Ambassador Lord Halifax told Acheson that Britain hoped to substitute more general terminology for the American language, which called for the elimination of preferential and discriminatory systems. Acheson warned that the United States would not support such a change and clearly feared the English were procrastinating. Since various members of Congress had expressed impatience at the failure of the administration to negotiate a quid pro quo for lend-lease, the need to turn to Congress for frequent lend-lease appropriations made delay out of the question.[48] Halifax told Welles that the British government was split on the question of article VII, and he passed on the intriguing, if highly doubtful, information that Churchill supported the American position.[49]

While impatiently awaiting the promised British redraft of the lend-lease master, Harry Hawkins, chief of the State Department's Division of Commercial Treaties and Agreements, sent Acheson a new proposal for rewording article VII. Hawkins, whose position made him the "careerist" with whom Acheson had to work, emphasized the need to get quick tentative approval from some British representative in Washington so that the British would not think of again sending Keynes to continue the negotiations. Keynes' "well-known obstinacy" would, according to Hawkins, make any agreement on article VII unlikely. He too wanted to revise article VII, but unlike the British, Hawkins recommended making it even more specific, particularly in view of the principles espoused in the Atlantic Charter. As he bluntly put it: "Our object should be to use the lend-lease agreement to obtain commitments of real value to us [both]." For the United States, since compensation was required by law, the halting of empire preferences would settle accounts. He casually dismissed British arguments that American preferential arrangements, such as those with Cuba, should also be outlawed by noting that British agreements of that type were far bigger and more important than those of the United States. He was willing to promise lower tariffs on British goods, but advised that the American negotiators hold out for mutual renunciation of bilateral trade agreements and a promise from Britain to abolish the Ottawa system.[50]

The long-promised British redraft finally arrived on 17 October. Halifax explained that British reluctance to agree to the American draft stemmed from political opposition within the Conservative Party plus the unwillingness to accept a unilateral obligation which Britain might not be able to carry out. As expected, the British version contained a weak and ambiguous commitment to avoid discrimination and generally to work to achieve the economic principles of the Atlantic Charter. In short, it promised goodwill and further discussions, but no concrete concessions.[51]

Halifax's plea for understanding concerning Britain's political problem evoked some sympathy within the State Department. Essentially, the Americans refused substantive modifications but were willing to accept procedural changes dictated by British political needs. The result was a new American draft which committed both nations to the "elimination of all forms of discriminatory treatment in international commerce and to the reduction of tariffs and other trade barriers."[52] The difference in language changed nothing. Britain had to promise to "eliminate" discrimination, while the State Department merely genuflected toward tariff reduction, knowing that Congress would have the last say.

One of the drafters of the original American proposal, John Hickerson, the assistant chief of the European Division in the State Department, typified the prevailing distrust of British motives and promises when he wrote Acheson that "now is the time to obtain commitments from the British Government in regard to postwar policy." Though willing to leave out any specific mention of eliminating the preference system and any payments or monetary clearing agreements, he warned that he would not approve the draft unless an oral statement—reduced in writing to avoid mistakes—to that effect were attached.[53] A ludicrous example of diplomatic motion without movement.

Convinced that Britain had no choice but to accept, and heartened by the erroneous belief that the British Treasury alone insisted on an independent British economic policy, the United States presented by early December a version acceptable to the President and the State Department; it was not at all new. Halifax responded with a notable lack of enthusiasm, but Acheson warned that with a new lend-lease appropriation request about to go to the Congress, Roosevelt needed concrete action as soon as possible. Hull, reaffirming the need for haste, insisted that his demand for economic cooperation on America's terms was proper, rational, and just. Blithely he claimed that America imposed the same obligations on itself as on Great Britain. The proposed agreement promised to provide the best method for solving Britain's postwar economic problems. Hull's overview received a strong second from his special assistant and chief speechwriter, Leo Pasvolsky. As Acheson later put it: "He wrote Hull's principle speech," for regardless of the subject or purpose, any speech by the secretary of state usually turned into a plea for economic liberalism. In a fifty-seven-page memo sent to Hull in mid-December, Pasvolsky captured the emotion and conviction of the State Department viewpoint—an attitude which the entire Roosevelt administration echoed, though with somewhat less passion. Convinced that Britain's reluctance to accept article VII indicated "a definite antagonism" toward the policies which the United States regarded "as indispensable to economic progress," Pasvolsky prescribed the standard American cure for economic problems—increase foreign trade. Bilateral balancing of funds, imperial preference systems, and other forms of economic nationalism would be only short-term palliatives. Unconsciously viewing Britain as an integrated element within the American economy, Hull and most American policymakers assumed that what had worked for the United States would work for the United Kingdom.[54]

After Pearl Harbor, the military crisis both nations faced in Asia as well as wrangling over domestic policies in England combined to suspend negotiations on the master lend-lease agreement during most of December. While the American government awaited the British response, an amusing and instructive incident occurred in Washington. Late in November, Dean Acheson had received an invitation to a black-tie dinner of the Business Advisory Council for the Department of Commerce. Included was a copy of a paper to be read by a member of the Council, Professor William Y. Elliott. Elliott viewed lend-lease as a means of underwriting the colonial empires of Europe and asserted that in doing so, the United States should insure that the assets of those empires accrued to America as payment for such assistance. He demanded that the United States "get the British and their allies 'hooked' securely to an agreement before we have . . . given away all our bargaining counters. . . . Only sentimentality would prevent our . . . demanding a fair return for the enormous sacrifices which we will have undertaken to save these empires." Inconceivable as such words were after the Battle of Britain and the course of events in Europe, they had a broad appeal in the United States.

Acheson handled the incident with a combination of patrician and Machiavellian styles. He arranged for the Council to obtain a distinguished speaker who would be available only on the night of the dinner. A few days later the Business Advisory Council informed him that the previous program had been canceled so that Lord Halifax could address the group. Yet in the resulting correspondence between Feis, Stettinius, and Acheson, none ever criticized the substance of the Elliott paper—only its timing.[55]

Churchill's aid was needed to get the lend-lease agreement moving off dead center. A British official suggested that Roosevelt bring up the subject in talks then being held with the Prime Minister in Washington, but Churchill proved unwilling to discuss it. Roosevelt supported Hull's contention that it would be better to strike out article VII entirely rather than accept any further dilution of the prohibition against discriminatory trade practices and passed this information on to the British government. On 3 February 1942, the State Department learned that the British continued to delay settlement because they assumed the President and Morgenthau were indifferent to the proposed agreement and that it was merely Hull's personal fetish. Within twenty-four hours, Roosevelt cabled a personal message to Churchill in which he expressed his strong support for the existing draft and warned that further delay would only harm British as well as American interests.[56]

This brought on one last British attempt to avoid having to "barter Empire preference in exchange for money and goods." British Foreign Secretary Anthony Eden suggested a series of notes to accompany the lend-lease agreement. Essentially, the British objected to the American use of the term "discrimination," and warned that any changes in economic relations between the United Kingdom and the Commonwealth would require Commonwealth approval. The notes cautioned that Great Britain could not commit herself to abstaining from economic and monetary controls until her postwar status was known. The British were pleading domestic political necessity, which should have been a familiar refrain to the American policymakers, but in reality the English were understandably reluctant to open the empire door.[57]

The State Department refused to back down. Acheson and Feis told Halifax that although the United States did not believe article VII committed the British to a unilateral abrogation of the Ottawa Agreements and similar arrangements, the elimination of such discriminatory practices was to be a key item for discussion during the talks provided for in that article. Churchill tried a political ploy with Ambassador Winant when, on 9 February, he remarked that even though he did not believe imperial preferences were of any real value, three-fourths of the cabinet opposed making the elimination of such preferences part of the lend-lease settlement. The last word went to Roosevelt. In an overly solicitous cable, the President asserted to Churchill that the United States had never even considered swapping imperial preference for lend-lease. Roosevelt commented that the proposed notes which the British wanted to accompany the interim master agreement gave the impression that discussion of imperial preference was to be specifically excluded from talks on postwar economic policy. FDR self-righteously claimed that all the United States wanted was "a bold, forthright, and comprehensive discussion" so as to create a "world where men shall really be free economically as well as politically." Given such a grand view, Roosevelt's conviction "that nothing should not be excluded from those discussions" was completely logical. With the exception of perfunctory approval from the dominions, nothing remained but formal British acquiescence to the agreement and its call for "the elimination of all forms of discriminatory treatment in international commerce."[58]

Although American leaders grasped the potential leverage created by British dependence upon the United States, they did not consistently use that leverage between 1937 and 1941. Before the actual outbreak of war, the American government could not resort to obvious coercion, fearing that the Chamberlain ministry would seek a modus vivendi with Germany. Between 1939 and 1941, the formulation of American economic policy rested primarily with Morgenthau and the Treasury Department, which thought essentially about restraining Nazism and pacifying public opinion. After June 1941, however, once Hull and the State Department took over American policy, Great Britain had to stand and deliver. Like most Americans, Roosevelt unquestioningly agreed with the expansionistic goals of Hull's economic program. Yet whether he fully realized what methods he endorsed when he assigned the State Department the task of working out the master lend-lease agreement is highly debatable, though he gave Hull support when the negotiations stalled. Still, the impression left by the documents is that in this case Franklin Roosevelt did not lead, but followed.

That Hull and other American leaders vastly exaggerated the importance of Britain's imperial preference system is obvious, but it is not the key point. The fact was that the determinants of American policy during the negotiation of the Lend-Lease Master Agreement were the American vision of British opulence, the persistence of the Wilsonian concept of the interdependence of peace and liberal economic systems, and the political necessity of striking a good bargain—all in sharp contrast to the factors that stimulated the passage of the Lend-Lease Act itself. Even assuming the best of motives—the creation of a peaceful, prosperous world—the negotiation of the Master Lend-Lease Agreement found the United States remarkably willing and even eager to destroy what it believed to be a cornerstone of Great Britain's empire, the empire of an ally. Granted, imperial preference systems were an anachronism which did not deserve the attention they got. Granted, no conspiracy to exploit Britain existed. Rather, the Roosevelt administration, fearing the English would renew the policies which had supposedly led to depression and war, saw its proposals as a means of saving Great Britain from herself. Nevertheless, American leaders were perfectly willing in this case to use economic and political pressure to obtain British compliance with their view of how the world's economy should be structured. The negotiations surrounding the Lend-Lease Act indicated a basic American respect for the sovereignty and national pride of the British, while those leading to the Master Lend-Lease Agreement found United States officials far more eager to remake other nations in the American image. Clearly Hull's displacing Morgenthau as the prime formulator of economic foreign policy played a key role in this change, but that leaves unanswered the broader question—how great a role did world economic reform play in the formulation of America's postwar planning during the Second World War? One thing is certain, historians can no longer dismiss that question as irrelevant.

1990 Addendum to "Lend-Lease and the Open Door"

Although the bulk of the U.S. sources on the Lend-Lease Master Agreement negotiations were available when the research for this essay was done in 1969–70, the British diplomatic archives were not opened to the public until a few years later. On a trip to the Public Record office in 1973, and occasionally thereafter, I looked at the British materials to see if there was anything in them that would change either the history or the interpretation I presented. I found nothing. Were I to completely rewrite the piece, I would integrate that new evidence, which would only add to my argument, not change it.[59]

One small piece of additional evidence about the continuing American crusade: James Meade, an official in the Economic Section of the British Cabinet Office and later a Nobel Prize winner for economics, wrote in his diary on 27 November 1943, that American officials kept trying to explain that the elimination of Imperial Preference "politically" was "of the utmost importance."[60] As Christopher Thorne, Wm. Roger Louis, and Alan P. Dobson have demonstrated, American opposition to Imperial Preference may have been more symbolic than real, but the United States kept at it until late in the war when negotiations like the Bretton Woods agreements made the issue moot.[61]

The tale tells us a great deal about Franklin Roosevelt. His decision to replace Morgenthau with Hull in the Lend-Lease Master Agreement negotiations with Britain appears, at first glance, to be another example of

---

The historiographical comments and notes in the original essay will seem dated, but to change them would distort the atmosphere that existed when the piece was written.

the President's haphazard management style. But upon reflection, it is clear that while Roosevelt's decision may have been opaque, it was far from haphazard. Hull reflected the President's thinking about the economic structure of the postwar world, and Britain seemed the greatest barrier to those plans. To Americans of the Cold War generations, Britain-as-villain seems misguided and peculiar, at best. But to Americans of Franklin Roosevelt's generation, Britain epitomized much of what was wrong with the world.[62] Closed colonial systems created the jealousies and rivalries that had brought on the First World War, and Roosevelt and his advisers saw the same thing happening in the 1930s. Even a cursory glance at the speeches and memoranda of Cordell Hull, Adolf Berle, and even Henry Morgenthau, Jr., drives that point home. From the very outset of the war, Roosevelt was thinking of the structure of the postwar world. Dr. Win-the-War replaced Dr. New Deal only in the most limited sense. Certainly the war effort had to take precedence over further New Deal reform. But that evades and postpones the question of the postwar world—which seems to be exactly what Roosevelt wanted the press and the public to think he was doing.

The Anglo-American World: Roosevelt and Churchill at Casablanca, surrounded by their Chiefs of Staff.

IV

Casablanca: The End of Imperial Romance

"This will be, only incidentally, a book about
the war. It is designed, more importantly, to
shed some light on the peace."[1]

THIS IS an essay, not a book, but other than that, Elliott Roosevelt's remark bespeaks well my purpose, and as well that of Franklin Roosevelt
and Winston Churchill when they met at Casablanca in January 1943.
For the President and the Prime Minister, and their nations, that conference marked the end of an era—and the beginning of a new age.[2]

To start with, a few thoughts on perspective. First of all, the villains
during World War II, at least as far as Franklin Roosevelt was concerned,
were the Germans and the Japanese—and anyone who was on their side.
Winston Churchill and the British were not the enemy, nor were Joseph
Stalin and the Russians, nor even Charles de Gaulle and the French. Second, Roosevelt and Churchill assumed that, at the end of the war, Germany and Japan would be defeated—unconditional surrender was not a
policy proclamation, it was an assumption.[3] Finally, Roosevelt and
Churchill each had a vision, a conception of how the postwar world
should and would look. To view Franklin Roosevelt as a leader with
nothing in mind but the defeat of Germany flies in the face of evidence
and logic. And certainly no one would argue that Winston Churchill was
without plans for the future.

Those three things put together, it becomes possible to look at wartime
politics from the perspective of Churchill and Roosevelt, politics shaped
by a realization that the postwar world would be constructed by and with
friends and allies whose ideas differed. Roosevelt had a conscious, structured foreign policy, even if there was an enormous gap between concept
and implementation. It was based on his experience and background, not
merely on reactions to public opinion or domestic politics. Roosevelt, an
early disciple of his cousin Theodore's "New Nationalism," later sought

Earlier versions of this paper were presented at the Winston S. Churchill Symposium at
Westminster College, Fulton, Missouri, 24 April 1986, and at the University of Kentucky,
2 Nov. 1986. In addition to the helpful comments received on those occasions, I am most
grateful to Arthur L. Funk, Mark Stoler, and Raymond G. O'Connor for their valuable
suggestions.

to modify and accommodate the broad ideas of Woodrow Wilson to the practical realities of international relations. Like Wilson, Roosevelt saw Americanism as a third force that offered an alternative to old and new, to reactionaries and radicals. Those ideas (not to be confused with idealism) shaped his policies toward his wartime allies, for those allies would become his postwar partners. It is impossible to turn Franklin Roosevelt into a simple cold warrior, given his consistent position that colonialism, not communism, was the -ism that most threatened postwar peace and stability. As Averell Harriman put it:

> Roosevelt and Churchill did not march to the same drumbeat. . . . Roosevelt enjoyed thinking aloud on the tremendous changes he saw ahead—the end of colonial empires and the rise of newly independent nations across the sweep of Africa and Asia. . . . I think he had a belief that his prestige, both personally and as President of the United States, was so great that he could influence the trend.[4]

And it is impossible to understand the Roosevelt foreign policy without appreciating the wartime tensions that existed between Great Britain and the United States—between Churchill and Roosevelt—for the President saw those tensions as one of the major formative forces in the postwar world.[a] That belief may have been stronger in the earlier stages of the war, but it never left him.

Roosevelt's perception of British policies was shaped or at least refined during the war, and much of that shaping came as a result of the President's contact with Winston Churchill. What follows is a look at one segment of that shaping, a segment that seems, in hindsight, to have marked the end of one era and the beginning of another.

Winston Spencer Churchill has become a near mythical figure in American history. His personal characteristics—a reputed love of drink, his skills as a raconteur, his absolute devotion to living by Pacific Standard Time (one staff member at 10 Downing Street spoke of Churchill's late meetings as "the Midnight Follies"[5])—these and like characteristics make up the bigger-than-life image that has become Winston Churchill. But all of that is for his various biographers. Perhaps a description by playwright Robert Sherwood, a speechwriter in the Roosevelt White House during World War II and the author in 1948 of *Roosevelt and Hopkins: An Intimate History*, best captures the American picture of the Churchill style:

[a] Examples of such tension, which coexisted within the most remarkable wartime entente in modern history, are found throughout these essays. Most striking are those relating to the economic system that would emerge after the war (see "Lend-Lease and the Open Door: The Temptation of British Opulence"), and the decolonization of the British Empire (see " 'In Search of Monsters to Destroy' ").

Churchill always seemed to be at his Command Post on the precarious beach-head and the guns were continually blazing in his conversation; wherever he was, there was the battlefront. Churchill was getting full steam up along about ten o'clock in the evening; often after his harassed staff had struggled to bed about 2:00 or 3:00 a.m. they would be routed out. Churchill's consumption of alcohol continued at quite regular intervals through most of his waking hours without visible effect. He was really Olympian in his capacity. Churchill loved to have gay and amusing company at the dinner table. Churchill could talk for an hour or more and hold any audience spellbound. Here was one who certainly knew his stuff, who could recite fact and figure and chapter and verse, and in superb English prose.[6]

What interests historians, however, particularly those who study Anglo-American relations during World War II, are the perceptions of Winston Churchill held by Franklin Roosevelt and his circle of advisers. Those perceptions went a long way toward determining American policy regarding Great Britain and her empire.

An underlying American conviction during the war was that Winston Churchill himself made British foreign policy. Roosevelt remarked long-ingly that he wished he had Churchill's freedom of action, although the President did comment at Yalta that the Prime Minister had to keep in mind that there was a tough Parliamentary election coming up.[7] In January 1941, when Harry Hopkins was told that "Churchill is the British War Cabinet, and no one else matters," Roosevelt's closest adviser re-acted sourly: "I suppose Churchill is convinced that he's the greatest man in the world!"[8] Later that same month, following their first meeting, Hopkins described the Prime Minister as "a rotund—smiling—red faced, gentleman. . . [with] a clear eye and a mushy voice."[9] Hopkins' sarcasm was soon replaced by grudging admiration. There is a striking picture of Hopkins staggering back to his room one cold January night in London after listening to Churchill until two in the morning, dropping into a chair and muttering, "Jesus Christ! What a man!"[10] Sherwood, whose book remains the best study of Anglo-American relations during World War II, offered a view of Churchill that massaged most American prejudices:

It is a matter of sacred tradition that, when an American statesman and a Brit-ish statesman meet, the former will be plain, blunt, down to earth, ingenuous to a fault, while the latter will be sly, subtle, devious and eventually trium-phant. In the cases of Roosevelt and Churchill, this formula was somewhat confused. If either of them could be called a student of Machiavelli, it was Roosevelt; if either was a bull in a china shop, it was Churchill. . . . Roosevelt soon learned how pertinacious the Prime Minister could be in pursuance of a purpose. Churchill's admirers could call him "tenacious, indomitable," and his detractors could describe him as "obstinate, obdurate, dogged, mulish, pigheaded." Probably both factions could agree on the word "stubborn," which may be flattering or derogatory. In any case, it was this quality which, at times, made him extremely tiresome to deal with and, at other times—and especially times of most awful adversity—made him great.[11]

That portrait of Churchill, written shortly after the war by someone whose views were shaped in large measure by his relationship with both Roosevelt and Hopkins, would seem an accurate reflection of American perceptions. But that is a word-picture of the Churchill style. What about the Churchill foreign policy?

Again, we have a ready-made set of images. There are two that dominate. First, that of Winston Churchill, defender of the British Empire. Edward Stettinius recalled how Roosevelt himself once put it:

> When the president told Churchill that China does not want Indochina, Churchill replied, "Nonsense!" The president had said to him, "Winston, this is something which you just are not able to understand. You have 400 years of acquisitive instinct in your blood and you just don't understand how a country might not want to acquire land somewhere if they can get it. A new period has opened in the world's history, and you will have to adjust to it." The president then said that the British would take land anywhere in the world even if it were only a rock or a sand bar.[12]

Now, Churchill may have been right, and FDR was not above taking a Pacific sand bar or two himself, but it is the American image of Churchill that concerns us.[13]

The second image, related to the first, combined Churchill the conniver with Churchill the Old-World politician seeking to play Katy-bar-the-door to change, since change would threaten Britain's position in the world and the position of his class in Britain. What Churchill called tradition, Americans saw as reaction or at least a dangerous dedication to the world of Queen Victoria. Averell Harriman claimed that Roosevelt saw Churchill as "pretty much a nineteenth-century colonialist," and Churchill himself once commented, "In the White House, I'm taken for a Victorian Tory." That image cropped up as well in Whitehall, where one official complained, "With Roosevelt straining to put the British Empire into liquidation and Winston pulling in the opposite direction to put it back to pre–Boer War, we are in danger of losing both the Old and the New World."[14] There was, therefore, a tendency on the part of the Americans to assume that each of Churchill's military proposals masked a reactionary political goal. As General Dwight Eisenhower put it in January 1943:

> I am not so incredibly naive that I do not realize that Britishers instinctively approach every military problem from the viewpoint of the Empire, just as we

approach them from the viewpoint of American interest. One of the constant sources of danger to us in this war is the temptation to regard as our first enemy the partner that must work with us in defeating the real enemy.[15]

Clausewitz would have smiled, for American suspicions betrayed their own hopes.[16]

Those hopes, too much assumptions to be plans, were well expressed in the disarmingly vague phrases of the Atlantic Charter when it stated that the United States and the United Kingdom "respect the right of all peoples to choose the form of government under which they will live; and that they wish to see sovereign rights and self-government restored to those who have been forcibly deprived of them." Churchill may have exempted the French—and British—empires from that requirement, but Roosevelt did not.[17] General Charles de Gaulle, the proud and perceptive leader of the Free French, understood well what Roosevelt was about. Summoned by Churchill, at Roosevelt's behest, to the Casablanca Conference, the Free French leader declined to talk in what he called "the atmosphere of an exalted Allied forum,"[18] but he eventually had no choice. As the Frenchman expected, the President lectured and hectored him, calling France "a little child unable to look out and fend for itself and that, in such a case, a court would appoint a trustee to do the necessary." There was little question who constituted the court. As for the job of trustee, despite the President's apparent commitment to designate General Henri Giraud as France's wartime steward, Roosevelt instead carefully divided the assignment among those Frenchmen who exercised actual control—de Gaulle in places like Reunion and Madagascar, Vichy loyalist Admiral Georges Robert over French possessions in the Western Hemisphere, while Giraud's charge was restricted to French North Africa; all this in the name of the sovereignty of the French people. The specific argument between the President and de Gaulle was over who should lead the French, but Roosevelt went on to make clear that the French Empire was part of the discussion. As the President put it, once the war was over, "victorious France could once again assert the political sovereignty which was hers over her homeland and her empire. At such a time . . . by the use of the democratic processes inherent throughout France and its empire, political differences would be resolved." As the American recorder at that meeting delicately put it, "de Gaulle, with some show of cordiality withdrew."[19]

The connection between British and French colonies was clear to all. Even with the routine caveat that Elliott Roosevelt's memoir, *As He Saw It*, is factually unreliable (though I am not convinced it is much more unreliable than most memoirs, including Mr. Churchill's), the President's son captured the flavor of his father's arguments: "They're all interrelated [said FDR]. If one [colony] gets its freedom, the others will get ideas.

That's why Winston is so anxious to keep de Gaulle in his corner. De Gaulle isn't any more interested in seeing a colonial empire disappear than Churchill is."[20]

Colonialism was not the only aspect of Churchill's Victorian image. His apparent support for preferential trade within the British Empire appeared to Americans as just the sort of policy that caused war, and his willingness to make territorial agreements without regard for the wishes of the inhabitants of the places concerned—the Baltic states is one example—reinforced American beliefs that he was another European power politician. After all, American leaders remained firm in their conviction that World War II was primarily the result of a failure in leadership on the part of the liberal nations in Europe. Even Cordell Hull and Roosevelt, both of whom assailed American isolationists in bitter terms, placed the blame for Hitler and Mussolini on the Europeans who had rejected Wilsonian principles and opted for narrow, selfish policies which made it possible for the United States to reject the Versailles Treaty. Churchill likewise condemned the weak European leadership between the wars, which fit his image in America as the best of wartime partners. But the Prime Minister did not share their critique of the peace settlement, and the Americans worried openly that Churchill was not suited for peacemaking.[21]

But that negative image was balanced by the other Churchill that American leaders saw. The stirring speeches, the indomitable courage, the appealing combination of childishness and sophistication, all helped offset American cynicism about Europe. It is difficult to distrust someone deeply who is invariably described as "cherubic." But most important of all were his repeated, emotional depictions of the Anglo-American unity of culture, history, and purpose—his calls for a true entente between Great Britain (Churchill would have added The Empire) and the United States. It was hard not to feel close to a man who, in April 1941 for example, could so eloquently refer to his cousins across the Atlantic:

> For while the tired waves, vainly breaking,
> Seem here no painful inch to gain,
> Far back, through creeks and inlets making,
> Comes silent, flooding in the main.
> And not by eastern windows only,
> When daylight comes, comes in the light;
> In front the sun climbs slow, how slowly!
> But westward, look, the land is bright.[22]

In January 1943, the strength of the light from both east and west seemed about equal. The Casablanca Conference marks the beginning of an era, for it came immediately after the successful invasion of French

North Africa by both British and United States ground forces. The Americans had arrived (this time to stay) and were finally fighting Hitler's army; Europe would never be the same. But it is more illuminating to look at Casablanca as an end rather than a beginning. The conference was the last time that Winston Churchill and Franklin Roosevelt could sit down and romantically treat the war, and the world, as an Anglo-American affair. It was the last time that the two men could either dismiss, underestimate, or ignore the new forces and powers that World War II was bringing into being—ghosts that haunted the talks and that would bring about the end of the Churchill-Roosevelt romance as well.[23]

That sense of shared control was created, in part, by the relatively equal contribution to the war then being made by the two nations. Although Great Britain had more ground forces facing the enemy—a situation that would not change until the Normandy invasion—the bulk of supplies and war materials came from the United States. Once U.S. troops had engaged the Germans, a psychological barrier had been overcome, for it no longer seemed a case of paying Britain to fight America's battles. Aware of their dependence upon each other, Churchill and Roosevelt, and the British and American Chiefs of Staff, all came to Casablanca in mid-January 1943 to persuade, cooperate, and compromise—not to demand, threaten, and insist.

The context for what I have called the "End of Romance" is the issues that dominated the Casablanca Conference. But part of that context is also geographical and aesthetic—and evocative of the colonial world of the nineteenth century. Shimmering white villas of the Anfa suburb where the conferees stayed, bustling brown and black servants, the sharp contrast between the world Roosevelt and Churchill brought with them and the one they found (even if the flight to Casablanca was the first time an American president had flown while in office); all helped create a storybook atmosphere that rested in the past, not the future. Kenneth Pendar, a State Department representative in Marrakech, and host to Churchill and Roosevelt immediately after the Casablanca talks, described Roosevelt's reaction to a taste of the Arabian, or Moroccan, nights: "When I reached the *salon* at eight, the President had left his wheel-chair, and was alone, stretched out on one of the couches at the far end. . . . As I came up to him, he put out his hand to me, and said with an engaging smile: 'I am the Pasha, you may kiss my hand.' "[24] A fascinating image—the President as Pasha.

In historical hindsight, the talks had significance in three areas: first, the strategic decisions, ostensibly strictly military, but clearly more than that. Second, what proved to be an unsuccessful attempt to choose a leader for the Free French. Third, the unconditional surrender proclamation.

All the time, lurking in the background to everything that went on were twin ghosts—one hidden in the attic, the other a cause of more open concern and tension. The ghost in the attic was the Soviet Empire, that huge reservoir of latent political energy that observers from Toqueville to the British Foreign Office predicted would, some day, be a dominant force in Europe and the world. The downstairs ghost for the Casablanca conferees was nationalism and its opposite number, colonial empires.

Ironically, the relative unimportance of the Casablanca Conference for Anglo-Soviet-American relations is largely Stalin's fault. Roosevelt tried from the outset to make the Casablanca Conference a Churchill-Roosevelt-Stalin meeting, but to no avail. In fact, the President suggested the idea to Stalin a few days before even mentioning it to Churchill. But for reasons that remain unverified and more than a bit curious, Stalin made excuses. Ostensibly, the press of military events in the Soviet Union made it impossible for him to leave. Churchill and Roosevelt accepted that at face value, but suspected that Stalin cared little about Anglo-American problems and wanted only to discuss the Second Front—something that they knew the North African invasion had already postponed, though for how long remained uncertain. Whatever Stalin's reasons—and we have only his official statements to guide us—had the Soviet leader been present at Casablanca, the entire thrust of the conference would surely have been different.[25]

The fact of Soviet power would eventually help destroy the mirage of an Anglo-American world, but at Casablanca, Churchill and Roosevelt still could not foresee the situation that would develop. Earlier in the war, the two had been concerned primarily with encouraging the Russians to hold out against the Germans.[26] By January 1943, the Anglo-Americans were confident about the Soviet Union's survival, but were beginning to worry that Stalin would stop there and not pursue a full victory, leaving Hitler astride most of Europe and able to concentrate his forces against Britain and the United States. Renewed rumors to that effect had reached the State Department shortly before the Casablanca meeting.[27] That the Red Army's victory at Stalingrad would be a military turning point in the war was not at all clear to Churchill or Roosevelt, or to their advisers. A telegram from Stalin to Churchill stating that the Red Army was finishing off the surrounded German forces confirmed that things were going well, but, at the same time, British intelligence complained about the lack of information from the Russian front, and the only mention of the Stalingrad campaign during the Casablanca meeting showed no awareness of its significance. Moreover, while at Casablanca, Churchill did not have access to his precious "boxes," the decrypts of German high command messages—the famous ENIGMA or ULTRA intercepts.[28] No one at the Anfa compound realized that the German surrender at Stalingrad, which would come two weeks later at the end of January, would virtually end Germany's ability to wage an offensive war in Russia.[29] Nor is there the slightest hint that anyone guessed at the degree to which the Soviets would be able to take the offensive a year later. Thus, Churchill and Roosevelt could continue to think in terms of an Anglo-American world. Nonetheless, as the unconditional surrender announcement would demonstrate, the ghost in the attic could not be forgotten—or ignored.

As for the downstairs ghost, the two-faced Janus of colonialism and nationalism, perhaps the most striking image is that of the gutted hulk of the French battleship, *Jean Bart*, lying half-sunk in the harbor at Casablanca, in full view of the arriving dignitaries. The damaged vessel served as a metaphor for empire, both French and British. Despite what seemed mortal damage, enough of the outer shell remained to tempt the owners into trying to refloat the ship.[30] Take, for example, Roosevelt's dispute in 1942 with Churchill over independence for India. The argument is well documented, and was not forgotten by either man, but at Casablanca that issue and others like it were dealt with only indirectly, as part of the maneuvering over the selection of a French leader—maneuvering that was, at least in part, created by de Gaulle's insistence on the restoration of the French Empire.[31] The specific comments about the growing strength of nationalism throughout the world that are attributed to the President by his son, Elliott, may not have been uttered at Casablanca, but there is little doubt that they reflected Franklin Roosevelt's thinking.

It was an issue not joined, but the President made sure that Churchill got the message. Without attributing to Roosevelt some kind of Machiavellian scheme, a dinner meeting with the Sultan of Morocco and Churchill during the Casablanca talks was no accident, nor were the talks about Morocco's future between Harry Hopkins and the Sultan's adviser. Neither was it mere accident that while the Casablanca talks took place, FDR's personal emissary, William Phillips, was in India trying to arrange some sort of British pledge of independence for the subcontinent. Roosevelt did not plan for the two to coincide, but his campaign to convince the British, the French, and the other European nations of the folly of colonialism continued, unabated, throughout the war.[32] Churchill claimed that the President avoided direct confrontation on the issue after their exchanges of 1942 over India, but that was not the case. Not only did the American leader, time and again, send personal representatives to one or another part of the world to preach the message, but during the 1944 Quebec Conference, the two men discussed the Phillips mission at some length.[33] Roosevelt expressed surprise at how radical William Phillips had become after experiencing British colonialism in India, but he was also pleased by his envoy's reactions. As the President put it, "He [Phillips] has been there fairly long now and has his feet on the ground."[34]

The most striking illustration of the President's attitude on colonialism during the Casablanca meetings came during his dinner talks with Moroccan officials. Regardless of the details, all sources make clear that Roosevelt, with what Hopkins called a "glum" Churchill sitting at the table, indicated his sympathy and support for Moroccan independence, including expressions of hope for expanded U.S.-Moroccan economic cooperation. Some of that may have been part of FDR's well-documented antipathy to France and the French Empire but, as Churchill immediately grasped, it was part of a broader attitude. Harold Macmillan quipped that some of Churchill's sulkiness may have been prompted by the absence of alcoholic beverages, a gesture to the Sultan's Islamic practices. But Macmillan, who found the dinner "a curious and impolitic manoeuvre, . . . felt sure that he [Churchill] regarded the President's action as 'deliberately provocative.' " After all, talk about "colonial aspirations" and the "approaching end of 'imperialism' " had obvious meaning for Britain as well as for France.[35] De Gaulle later dismissed Roosevelt's purpose as sheer greed, rhetorically asking the Sultan, "When President Roosevelt jingled the marvels of independence before your Majesty at Anfa, what did he offer you beyond the cash and a place among his customers?"[36] But the Frenchman failed to grasp American fears that colonialism would spark renewed tension and war.

As for the basic strategic decisions taken at Casablanca, they are clear. On the assumption that the Germans would be pushed out of North Africa sometime in the spring of 1943, the Anglo-Americans would:

1. attack Sicily with the aim of "knocking" Italy out of the war (in hindsight, a combination of a decision and a goal that guaranteed an invasion of the Italian mainland from North Africa);
2. create a planning command (COSSAC) for the cross-Channel invasion, and continue the buildup of supplies and forces in England (BOLERO) preparatory to that invasion, probably in 1944 (though Churchill, fearing that the Pacific would be given priority, kept insisting that a small invasion [codenamed HADRIAN] of the Cotentin Peninsula [Cherbourg] and the Channel Islands, could take place in the fall of 1943);
3. attack in Burma in order to open the Burma Road supply line to China.

At the same time, they would continue to prosecute vigorously the war against Germany, especially the strategic bombing campaign and the suppression of U-boat activity; and they agreed to continue supply convoys to the Soviet Union, despite General Marshall's blunt contention that the Allies should not accept heavy losses "simply to keep Mr. Stalin pla-

cated." This remark perhaps reflected Marshall's anger and frustration at
the postponement of the cross-Channel invasion, for he surely realized
that allaying Stalin's suspicions was a fundamental part of Roosevelt's
strategy.[37]

In each case, despite heated debate, Anglo-American agreement predominated. General George Marshall, Chief of Staff of the U.S. Army and
Roosevelt's most trusted military adviser, tried his best to make a large-
scale, cross-Channel attack the top priority, even pretending again to support a shift of assets to the Pacific so as to gain support from the British,
who tended to panic at that thought. But long before the Casablanca
Conference, Roosevelt had suggested a move into Sicily and even the Italian mainland from North Africa, and Churchill had already been thinking
along the same lines.[38] The American military chiefs were themselves unable to agree on alternatives, leaving Roosevelt to follow his own inclinations. But those inclinations—which were to continue direct fighting
against Germany—were political more than military. His decision for the
North African invasion, taken over Marshall's objections, had been motivated by the need to promote and preserve Anglo-American alliance. At
Casablanca, Roosevelt accepted some, though not all, of the British proposals for a number of reasons. First, the attack on Sicily made military
sense, given the commitment of resources already made in that theater of
operations. Second, it promised continuing action as opposed to a long
wait for the buildup required for an invasion of northwestern France, and
action was what both the Soviets and the American public wanted. Third,
if British hopes were fulfilled, it might make a massive cross-Channel invasion safer and easier, though not unnecessary.

As a result, the lengthy military debate served largely to confirm what
the two leaders already thought best. The British also bruited about the
idea of a campaign in the Aegean Sea, but that was quickly dismissed by
the Americans, publicly as unfeasible and privately as another case of the
British putting imperial interests ahead of good military thinking, as well
as a move that could cause an Anglo-Soviet confrontation in southeast
Europe.[39]

The Mediterranean campaign was approved only on the condition that
it not interfere further with the buildup for a delayed cross-Channel attack in 1944. That invasion had already been deferred by TORCH, the
landings in North Africa, and the Americans insisted that what would
become OVERLORD should not be pushed back beyond early 1944. But the
cross-Channel attack was more than just a military plan. The ghost in the
attic had been demanding a major second front since 1941, and everyone
wanted to keep the Soviet Union reasonably happy. After all, Stalin had
tried to set the agenda for the Casablanca meeting, despite his absence, by

sending Roosevelt a thinly veiled challenge: "My colleagues are upset by
the fact that the operations in North Africa have come to a standstill and,
I gather, for a long time, too. Would you care to comment on the matter?"[40] Even if an Italian campaign succeeded beyond Churchill's wildest
dreams, it could never substitute for the major second front promised to
Stalin. The U.S. Joint Chiefs reluctantly admitted that operations in the
Mediterranean were the best they could do for the Russians in 1943.
Harry Hopkins called the effort in that area "feeble," while Roosevelt
recognized that fact even before the Casablanca Conference, proposing
that General Marshall go to Moscow after the talks to assure Stalin that
"the United Nations were to continue on until they reach Berlin, and that
their only terms were to be unconditional surrender."[41] But despite a
sense of uneasiness, particularly on Roosevelt's part, about Soviet reactions, the Casablanca meetings remained an Anglo-American affair.

The agreement to conduct operations in Burma turned out to be of less
significance, although it is worth noting that the Americans had no interest in Burma itself. It was, after all, part of the British Empire, even
though the flirtation with Japan by Burmese nationalists during the war
seems to have convinced Roosevelt that Burma might be an exception to
his insistence that colonial empire was a dangerous anachronism. His letter to Churchill relates these sentiments in no uncertain terms: "I have
never liked Burma or the Burmese! And you people must have had a terri-
ble time with them for the last fifty years. . . . I wish you could put the
whole bunch of them into a frying pan with a wall around it and let them
stew in their own juice."[42] The Americans had no interest in a campaign
to liberate Southeast Asia, particularly since Roosevelt suspected that the
British objective was to recapture part of the empire rather than defeat
Japan. For the United States, the campaign was designed to open the
Burma Road in order to keep supplies flowing to China—a military mission for Marshall, and a political one for the President.[43]

From the point of view of military strategy, the talks went a long way
toward meeting British hopes and plans, although the agreements were
far from a complete victory for Churchill and his military chiefs. For
Roosevelt, the politics of strategy were more important than the strategy
itself—unless his advisers could agree that he was wrong.

But there was straight politics at Casablanca as well. The issue of
choosing a leader for the Free French, those French forces who had rejected the Vichy government and were actively fighting the Germans, was
much more than just a decision for the short term. It promised to be of
long-term influence in determining the postwar structure of France.
Roosevelt consistently held up the goal of democracy—a code word for
Americanization, as de Gaulle saw it. The Frenchman recognized that the

President, to quote de Gaulle, "meant the peace to be an American peace, convinced that he must be the one to dictate its structure, that the states which had been overrun should be subject to his judgment, and that France in particular should recognize him as its savior and its arbiter."[44] Since de Gaulle expressed equally deep fears that the British would seize the opportunity offered by the war to replace French influence, it is clear that he surmised that an Anglo-American entente was operating—at least at Casablanca.[45] And perhaps it was. As Churchill cabled to British Foreign Secretary Anthony Eden when de Gaulle proved reluctant to comply with a summons to come to Casablanca: "The man must be mad to jeopardize the whole future of the relations of his movement with the United States. . . . If in his phantasy of egotism he rejects the chance now offered I shall feel that his removal from the headship of the Free French Movement is essential to the further support of this movement by H.M.G."[46]

One British official historian called the Casablanca discussions on the future of the government of France a "short-term problem of politics."[47] But it was much more than that. It was a major chapter in the war-long debate over the nature and leadership of the postwar world. Although Anglo-American harmony won out at Casablanca, the story is a familiar one. Roosevelt, aggravated by someone who refused to act like a supplicant, sought an alternative. Perhaps it is not surprising that the Americans should settle on Henri Giraud, a French general who was so anti-British that he refused to travel on an English vessel and had to be duped into thinking his transportation from the Riviera to Gibraltar, the HMS *Seraph*, was an American submarine.[48] Even so, the language used by both President and Prime Minister to describe the French imbroglio carried the connotation of cooperation between the Anglo-Americans: "I take it [the President wrote] that your bride and my bridegroom have not yet started throwing the crockery. I trust the marriage will be consummated."[49] The issue of selecting a French leader had a Gilbert and Sullivan finale, as the haughty de Gaulle and the equally haughty Giraud (French historian Henri Michel compared them to a pair of monarchs) were conned and cajoled into shaking hands before the clicking cameras of the press corps.[50] Choreography by Churchill and Roosevelt, the Anglo-Americans.

But the reality of the affair was anything but comic opera. At its core, it was an early round in the Anglo-American struggle over the future of colonialism. It was also, in an ironic way, an apparent barrier to American participation in postwar Europe. Had Roosevelt's man, Giraud, ended up as France's political leader, the President would have felt obligated to support that government. But de Gaulle's dominance reinforced

Roosevelt's reluctance to move in the direction of involvement in the postwar affairs of metropolitan France, even if the President had other reasons for being cautious.[51]

The Unconditional Surrender declaration is best known for the debate over whether or not it prolonged the war by strengthening the German will to resist because of the threat of a harsh, unyielding settlement. Churchill also created somewhat of a controversy when, after the war, he indicated that he had been surprised when Roosevelt announced to the press that the only terms available to the Axis were unconditional surrender.[52]

It also illustrates one of Roosevelt's curious and most intensely held sociological assumptions—that German character had been "Prussianized," necessitating a complete revamping of that society. That made unconditional surrender even more necessary, and was the assumption that, in Roosevelt's case, justified the Morgenthau Plan. What better way to remake a people than to dismember their political institutions, and simultaneously move them out of the industrial age into contact with their honest, peaceful, Jeffersonian agrarian roots?[53]

But the proclamation is more important for what it tells us about the assumptions that underlay alliance politics in World War II. It was much more than merely (as one historian has called it) "a word of encouragement and exhortation addressed by companions to each other at a turning point on a journey still to be long and arduous."[54] It is best understood at three levels. First, as an agreement to achieve the utter defeat of Germany—there would be no "stab in the back" legend this time around. Second, as a promise to the USSR that the Anglo-Americans would fight to the end and not negotiate with Germany, a promise which carried the hope that Stalin would reciprocate.[55] Roosevelt and Churchill did not want the so-called Darlan deal, which had the appearance of negotiations with a Nazi-sympathizer, to set a dangerous precedent, even though the Soviet leader had agreed that the arrangement was practical though unsavory.[56] More important, Churchill and Roosevelt were made uneasy and a bit embarrassed by the invidious comparison between Soviet military successes and the failure of Allied forces to push the Germans into the Mediterranean in the "two to three weeks" originally predicted by General Marshall.[57] Last, the unconditional surrender policy demonstrated Roosevelt and Churchill's belief that the war would present the Anglo-Americans with something akin to a tabula rasa. Unconditional surrender would clear the decks insofar as Germany was concerned (the Morgenthau Plan suggests the same thinking), while Russia would be too devastated by war to challenge British and American leadership.[58] Unconditional surrender may have been, at one level, a commitment to the

Soviet Union, but it also should be seen as a major foreign policy statement made by the Anglo-Americans without consulting or even advising
Stalin. A decision to pursue a noncompromise peace was more than a
military decision. It posited the destruction of Germany as a major European power and worked from the premise that the Anglo-Americans
could run the postwar show. Keeping the Russians happy is not the same
as seeing the Soviet Union as a partner in or rival to Anglo-American
predominance. Churchill and Roosevelt did not share, in early 1943, the
Cold War sentiments later expressed by one British official historian:

> Political warfare specialists might have quoted Sun Tzu's advice, about leaving
> one's enemy a golden bridge for retreat. . . . There was no opportunity for such
> counsels to be heard at Casablanca. Had it been otherwise, the Allied leaders
> might have reflected a little more deeply on the question, whether total victory
> is necessarily the surest foundation for a lasting peace.[59]

There was some fuzzy thinking on the part of Roosevelt and Churchill.
The Anglo-Americans assumed the postwar devastation of the Soviet
Union, while they simultaneously believed that only the Soviet Army
could defeat Germany in a way that could make unconditional surrender
possible—whatever the claims for strategic bombing offered by the U.S.
Army Air Force.[60] Perhaps Churchill and Roosevelt counted on a Pyrrhic
victory, but the contradictions in the images of both a victorious and a
devastated Soviet Union apparently escaped them. Ironically, Stalin accepted but never embraced unconditional surrender, openly questioning
its wisdom on a number of occasions.[61]

But that was not the issue at Casablanca. For the Prime Minister and
the President, the Soviet ghost remained in the attic and their romantic
notion of an Anglo-American world still held sway. Dwight Eisenhower
later described the hubris that enveloped Churchill during the war: "He
had the enjoyable feeling that he and our President were sitting on some
Olympian platform with respect to the rest of the world, and directing
world affairs from that point of vantage."[62] It was a seductive vision that
Roosevelt shared—at least for a little while.

For a multitude of reasons, Churchill and Roosevelt should not have
succumbed to the temptation to dream of a pax Anglo-Americana. Both
men recognized that Hitler's actions would probably create a fundamental change in Europe's structure. Roosevelt had, early on, recognized that
the Soviet Union would be a major player in the postwar world, and
Churchill worried about Bolshevism moving westward. Moreover, there
were fundamental tensions and differing goals within the Anglo-American association as well: the American critique of colonialism; arguments
over military strategy; suspicion on the part of New Dealers about the

influence of monied interests in The City (London's equivalent of Wall
Street); the sheer weight of growing American economic and military
power; disagreements over fundamental issues of economic policy; and
differing conceptions and perceptions of international relationships. The
raw power applied by the Americans in the negotiation of the Master
Lend-Lease Agreement should have made Churchill aware that his hopes
for an Anglo-American economic bloc were in vain.[63] More important,
he should have realized that the Americans, and Roosevelt, would use
that muscle again.

But there were also factors that allowed and enhanced the illusion. At
the time of Casablanca, the extraordinary offensive success of the Red
Army remained in the future; the Stalingrad victory was as yet unappre-
ciated. The Anglo-American war effort was still a joint partnership—
British forces in the field were greater in number, but the Americans had
finally arrived. They were agreed on the need to invade Europe, even if the
scale and location of that invasion would later be a source of dispute.
They were agreed that postwar Anglo-American cooperation was necessary. At the same time, the style of the relationship between the two men
nurtured the daydream. Churchill's oft-repeated claims that he was the
President's "ardent and active Lieutenant" and Roosevelt's avoidance of
direct confrontation with the Prime Minister were typical.[64] Both worked
at the personal touch. When the two journeyed to Marrakech after the
talks, Churchill, who planned to stay on, promised to paint Roosevelt a
picture of the Atlas Mountains—an example of the "easy intimacy" described by Robert Sherwood.[65]

Churchill seems to have left the conference with that sense of Anglo-
American control intact. He reported to Roosevelt on post-Casablanca
talks with Turkish leaders (a vain attempt to enlist that nation to the
allied side) in phrases that betrayed the Prime Minister's feelings: "Great
Britain will certainly do her utmost to organize a coalition of resistance to
any act of aggression committed by any power; it is believed that the
United States will cooperate . . . and even possibly take the lead of the
world."[66]

Harold Macmillan's sarcastic and colorful description of the Casablanca Conference captures the atmosphere of Anglo-American imperium that enveloped the talks:

> About two to three miles outside Casablanca is a curious kind of settlement
> [Anfa] consisting of rich villas belonging to Moroccan millionaires, centering
> around a three-storey hotel with about 50–100 bedrooms and appropriate
> dining-rooms and lounges. The dining-room is on top, and from it is a most
> wonderful view of the Atlantic on the one side and the hills and mountains
> of Morocco on the other. Eighteen of these villas were taken over at short

notice. . . . A wire fence of immense strength and solidity was constructed . . .
and this formed a kind of Roman camp. . . . The whole spirit of the camp was
dominated by the knowledge that two men [Churchill and Roosevelt] were
there who rarely appeared in public, but whose presence behind the scenes was
always felt. . . . I christened the two personalities the Emperor of the East and
the Emperor of the West, and indeed it was rather like a meeting of the later
period of the Roman Empire.

The two Emperors met usually late at night and disported themselves and
discussed matters with their own generals and with each other's generals. And
there was a curious mixture of holiday and business in these extraordinarily
oriental and fascinating surroundings.

The Emperor of the East's villa was guarded by marines, but otherwise
things were fairly simple. His curious routine of spending the greater part of the
day in bed and all the night up made it a little trying for his staff. . . . He ate and
drank enormously all the time, settling huge problems, played bagatelle and
bezique by the hour, and generally enjoyed himself. . . .

The Emperor of the West's villa was difficult of access. If you approached it
by night searchlights were thrown upon you, and a horde of what I believe are
called G-men, mostly retired Chicago gangsters, drew revolvers and covered
you. With difficulty you could get access and then everything was easy. The
court favourites, Averell Harriman and Harry Hopkins were in attendance. . . .
There was a lot of bezique, an enormous quantity of highballs, talk by the hour,
and a general atmosphere of goodwill.

But Macmillan too sensed the ghost in the attic:

The only sad thing about it was that the Russians could not attend. If we had
had the Red Emperor as well, it would have made the thing perfect.[67]

The spirit of Casablanca did not last. De Gaulle soon gained ascen-
dancy over Giraud, forcing the issue of a joint Anglo-American policy
regarding both France-in-Europe and the French Empire sooner than either Churchill or Roosevelt wished. The Giraud–de Gaulle dispute was so
open and obvious that the Germans mocked the famous handshake. The
German cartoon, here reprinted, summed up the situation succinctly.[68]
Soviet victories in 1943, at Stalingrad and later at Kursk, guaranteed that
the Red Army would move into most of eastern and central Europe,
bringing that ghost out of the attic and into direct competition with the
Anglo-Americans. Moreover, the stubborn and unexpected German defense of Tunisia virtually assured the failure of the Italian campaign—
that is, if speed was a part of success. Within a few months after the
Casablanca talks, the American military had concluded that they had
been duped into a Mediterranean strategy, and the British worried that,
once again, the Americans were trying to give "pride of place to the war

IN CASABLANCA

Vergeblicher Kreuzungsversuch (Unsuccessful Attempt at Crossbreeding)

in the Far East." Roosevelt wavered a bit, but stuck with the agreed upon strategies. Nonetheless, the mood had changed. By the late spring of 1943, the President was trying secretly to arrange private talks between himself and Stalin, and the Anglo-American relationship soon became less and less a partnership.[69]

During a White House party bringing in the New Year of 1943, only two weeks before the start of the Casablanca Conference, Franklin

Roosevelt relaxed by watching a motion picture that was to become a classic—Ingrid Bergman and Humphrey Bogart in *Casablanca*.[70] The film's message was clear: war threatened romance. But there was another message for Churchill, had he been there to see it: what romance remained was only for the Americans; the British were nowhere to be found.

"The world will be mighty lucky if it gets 50% of what it seeks."

V

"The Family Circle": Roosevelt's Vision of the Postwar World

He said he wished to welcome the new members to the family circle and tell them that meetings of this character were conducted as between friends with complete frankness on all sides with nothing that was to be said to be made public. He added that he was confident that this meeting would be successful and that our three great nations would not only work in close cooperation for the prosecution of the war but would also remain in close touch for generations to come.

(*Franklin Roosevelt opening the First Plenary Session of the Teheran Conference, 28 Nov. 1943*)[1]

The balance of power which it is the interest of Great Britain and ourselves to seek is the balance between an integrated Europe . . . and the Soviet Union. We shall never again have as much influence on Great Britain and the Soviet Union as we have today. Today they are dependent on us for their lives. We are the lady bountiful. They are the beggars. . . . Our bargaining position will be hopeless after the defeat of Germany; . . . While it is still good, I think, you should invite Stalin to visit you. . . . Wilson thought that his power lay in his moral authority. In those tragic days of 1919, he awoke to the appalling fact that his power had been the physical power of the United States to fill the desperate physical needs of the Allies, . . . There is only one guarantee that the Red Army will not cross into Europe—the prior arrival of American and British armies in the eastern frontiers of Europe.

To win the peace at the close of this war will be at least as difficult as to win the war.

(*William Bullitt letter to Roosevelt, 29 Jan. 1943*)[2]

Mr. Eden then suggested that we pass to the consideration of Russia. He said that in talking yesterday with the President on this subject the President had asked him if he thought there was anything in the Bullitt thesis that the Soviet Government was determined to dominate all of Europe by force of arms or by force of communist propaganda.

(*Memorandum of conversation, by Under Secretary of State Sumner Welles, 16 March 1943*)[3]

WHAT an extraordinary dilemma! How does an American president create the atmosphere of a "family circle," welcoming as an equal a still-feared, self-professed revolutionary, while simultaneously using economic and military coercion to insure the good behavior of that prodigal son? Equals are not subjected to discipline like children, yet Bullitt's advice (which epitomized a growing measure of similar advice from other personal advisers, not to mention the more ominous warnings of State Department career officers[4]) argued for just that approach. Presidents do not voluntarily relinquish an international position of strength, yet Franklin Roosevelt's dream of turning the wartime coalition into a peacetime "family circle" relied upon convincing the Soviets that their interests were not threatened, despite American economic and military strength. That meant convincing Soviet leader Joseph Stalin that Roosevelt could lead the United States, and that the United States could lead the Western nations. It also meant taking both negative and positive steps to convince and reassure the Soviet Union that it could trust the President—and that the President could trust the Soviets.

Which posed another dilemma: how could Stalin be reassured without threatening Roosevelt's leadership at home and in Europe? Privately, Roosevelt could admit the rueful reality of Red Army occupation and Soviet influence in Eastern Europe.[5] But to promise Stalin the Baltic States would bring howls of protest and accusations of sell-out in Congress and the press. To accept publicly Soviet domination of Eastern Europe—particularly Poland—the realities of military occupation to the contrary notwithstanding, would bring a firestorm at home and abroad. Most problematical of all, how could he share the secret of atomic energy—for weapons and for peaceful uses—with Stalin? Roosevelt and his aides called their domestic opponents "isolationists," but that word was misleading. What Roosevelt had to fight at home was unilateralism, the American urge to go it alone in the event that others did not accept American demands. Across the Atlantic, the growth of Soviet political and military power combined with Moscow's soft-pedaling of revolutionary rhetoric, threatened to turn some Europeans toward Moscow instead of Washington. French leader Charles de Gaulle would move in that direction in 1944, and even British Prime Minister Winston Churchill later sought a geopolitical accommodation. If the United States rejected formal cooperation with Europe, as it did in 1919, the Europeans could be forced to look eastward—hardly the postwar reaction hoped for by American planners or, for that matter, by Winston Churchill.

An earlier version of this paper was presented at the 3d Symposium of the Soviet-American Project on the History of World War II, Moscow, USSR, 18–20 Oct. 1988 (sponsored by the American Council of Learned Societies/International Research & Exchanges Board, and the Soviet Academy of Sciences). I am grateful to Lloyd Gardner, Bill Bullitt's greatest fan, for suggesting my straw man.

Even before the President's conception of the postwar order was laid out at the October 1943 conference of British, American, and Soviet foreign ministers in Moscow by Secretary of State Cordell Hull, and then at Teheran by Roosevelt himself, FDR had sketched out some basics. During his first meeting with Churchill in August 1941, Roosevelt suggested that Great Britain and the United States should "police" the world for a transitional period, after which an international organization might be possible. That twosome was soon widened to include the Soviet Union and China. Early in 1942, Roosevelt spoke vaguely of the Four Policemen; then, during Soviet Foreign Minister V. Molotov's trip to Washington that May, the President stated flatly that "the United States, England, and Russia and perhaps China should police the world and enforce disarmament by inspection." When Molotov wondered if that was a "final and considered judgment," Roosevelt said it was. Pressed by the Russian about the role of other large states, the President expressed concern that too many "policemen" might start fighting among themselves, and vaguely proposed that other friendly nations could be "nominally" part of the system. Roosevelt never changed that fundamental outline that combined great power with the disarming of other nations; and he never reconciled the dilemma implied by Molotov's questions—how could that system be established without using force to impose it on friendly states?[6] When Roosevelt threw out the idea of international trusteeships for "many islands and colonial possessions which ought, for our own safr.y, be taken away from weak nations," Molotov replied that Stalin had already expressed full agreement with the Four Policemen idea, and would most likely support the trusteeship concept as well.

Along with those musings on political structure for Molotov's benefit, Roosevelt lightly touched on a scheme for a second set of postwar settlements, in this case arrangements for economic reconstruction. Just as he had done when he announced the Lend-Lease program, the President tried to avoid what he had then called "the silly, foolish old dollar sign," by offering "a new thought based on old experience." It was beautifully simple—repayment of loans should be for the principal only, and over the long term. No interest would be charged. Any investment bankers listening in the wings would have sighed with relief when Roosevelt restricted that alarming notion to loans advanced during the war. But when presidential adviser Harry Hopkins whispered that it might be a good time to bring up the idea of a "special postwar fund" under international control, Roosevelt said nothing, and the subject changed.[7]

Thus, by mid-1942, much of Roosevelt's plan for the postwar political system was on the table. The great powers would act as "guarantors" of the peace, colonial empires would be disbanded, postwar reconstruction would be capitalized, and the rest of the world would be disarmed (one British record quoted Roosevelt once saying, "The smaller powers might

have rifles, but nothing more dangerous."). Molotov commented dryly
that it would all rest on the actions of the Big Four—and then returned to
what he considered the issue at hand, the Second Front. But despite the
immediate pressures of the war, Roosevelt did not forget his postwar
scheme. In December 1942, he told Canadian Prime Minister Mackenzie
King about the "big policemen, who would be the four powers," and a
few days later instructed American military chiefs to draw up plans for an
international police force.[8]

By the time British Foreign Secretary Anthony Eden visited Washington in March 1943, the President had refined but not altered his thinking.
As Eden reported to Churchill:

> The first point raised by the President was the structure of the United Nations
> organization after the war. The general idea is that there should be three organ-
> izations. The first would be a general assembly at which all the United Nations
> would be represented. This assembly would only meet about once a year . . . to
> blow off steam. At the other end of the scale would be an executive committee
> composed of representatives of the Four Powers. This body would take all the
> more important decisions and wield police powers of the United Nations. In
> between would be an advisory council . . . of the Four Powers and of, say, six
> or eight other representatives. . . . This council would meet from time to time
> as might be required to settle any international questions that might be brought
> before it.[9]

Nor was Roosevelt the only proponent of the policeman notion. His bitter opponent in the 1932 election, Herbert Hoover, claimed that his in-
vestigations of American public opinion indicated that most accepted the
creation of a postwar Anglo-American police force.[10]

Even in such a cursory summary, Roosevelt's dilemma was clear: peace
and peacekeeping depended upon the Great Powers, but who was to
watch the watchers? How were the Big Four to keep from breaking the
peace themselves? He could safely assume a high degree of British cooperation, particularly given Churchill's open espousal of a postwar entente
between the two nations, and America's emergence as the senior partner
in the relationship. Roosevelt recognized China's potential, commenting
that it was far better to have them "as friends rather than as a potential
source of trouble." Moreover, the President's scheme required an Asian
replacement in the region for Japanese power.[a] But in the immediate postwar world, a weak and disorganized China would be under American
tutelage—even if Chiang Kai-shek was an increasingly unwilling pupil.[11]
The problem was the Soviet Union. Eden put his finger on the quandary:

---

[a] This is discussed extensively in " 'In Search of Monsters to Destroy,' " elsewhere in this
collection.

"The big question which rightly dominated Roosevelt's mind was whether it was possible to work with Russia now and after the war."[12]

Roosevelt's misgivings prompted him to hedge his bets. The classic example is the secret decision made with Churchill in August 1943 not to share the atomic secret with the Soviets—or anyone else. A few months earlier, Churchill's science adviser, Lord Cherwell, had told the Americans that Britain viewed the bomb primarily as a means of restraining the Soviet Union after the war. Whether or not Roosevelt accepted that argument, he did not try to persuade Churchill otherwise.[13] Once again, Roosevelt had succumbed to the temptation of an Anglo-American condominium over the world—perhaps the only time that daydream reappeared after the Casablanca Conference. Whatever the President's motives, the decision must have helped undermine his efforts to create an atmosphere of trust between himself and Stalin. The Soviet leader knew by early 1942 of the atomic bomb research program—the Manhattan Project—and such knowledge must have raised doubts about Anglo-American good faith. We do not know if Stalin fully comprehended the revolutionary significance of the new weapon. He took a personal interest in Soviet atomic bomb research, but at the same time his scientists assured him that development of such a weapon would take ten to twenty years. After all, a number of American military experts tended to see it as nothing more than just a bigger bang. Roosevelt's military Chief of Staff, Admiral William Leahy, later scoffed to Truman that "the bomb will never go off, and I speak as an expert in explosives."[14] Yet, if the Americans were skeptical of the bomb's utility, why not share the secret with the Soviets and promote a sense of trust? Even if Stalin's appreciation of the bomb's potential was just as benighted, Anglo-American refusal even to mention the project could only reinforce his suspicions of Western designs since it fit into a larger pattern of Anglo-American reluctance to share information, particularly regarding intelligence, technology, and specific military plans. It may have been just an opportunity lost, but if Stalin somehow grasped the real nature of the bomb, then Roosevelt's dream of a "family circle" was doomed from the start.[15]

Which brings us back to William Bullitt's unadorned geopolitical prescription; confront the Soviet Union with British and American military and economic strength. No wonder Roosevelt was inconsistent and vague on detail. Such maneuvers were not simply evidence of his refusal to think systematically. They were much more a result of the dilemmas he faced.

Of course the Bullitt memo is an either/or fallacy. In language that later Cold Warriors would admire and emulate, he posited either the unlikely prospect of a converted Stalin ("a conversion as striking as the conversion of Saul on the Road to Damascus" is the way Bullitt put it), or a sly, shrewd, scheming Stalin who created the illusion of future cooperation in order to lure the Anglo-Americans into giving away their position of strength. The President rejected both extremes, but understood what Bullitt proposed—confrontation and conversion-by-coercion of the Soviet Union into a liberal economic and political democracy. Roosevelt agreed with the ultimate goal, but was unconvinced about the tactics, despite his curiosity about Eden's reaction to the specter of Soviet expansionism.[16] According to Bullitt's recollection, during a three-hour conversation the President continued to hold to the naive view that Stalin was not the "Caucasian bandit" described by the former ambassador. If anything, Bullitt's account suggests that his arguments made Roosevelt even more determined to avoid a premature showdown with the Soviets.[17]

Bullitt followed up with two strongly worded letters. Taken together, they were a call for a declaration of what we now call the Cold War. He proposed that Roosevelt shift the primary United States effort to the war against Japan unless the British and Soviets agreed to fight the Japanese and to accept American plans for the invasion of Europe—plans based on the premise that "our political objectives require the establishment of British and American forces in the Balkans and eastern and central Europe." Foreshadowing what would come about, Bullitt insisted that "the first step toward preventing Soviet domination of Europe is the creation of a British-American line in Eastern Europe. The second is the setting up of democratic governments behind our lines and the prevention of communist revolts."[18] By the time Bullitt's two letters arrived, he had become persona non grata in the White House. But the President's predicament did not disappear with Bullitt. Shortly before the Teheran Conference, a British official commented about the ongoing debate in Washington: was the Soviet Union expansionist, and if so, was that expansionism driven by communism or nationalism?[19] It was a debate that would continue for decades.

And where did Franklin Roosevelt come down in that debate? As is so frequently the case, the best evidence of his reaction is in what he did, not what he said. What follows is part of the story of how Franklin Roosevelt tried in late 1943 to resolve his dilemmas and realize his dreams.

On 11 November 1943, at 9:30 p.m. Washington time, President Franklin Delano Roosevelt left the White House for Cairo, Egypt, and then the Iranian capital, Teheran—a round-trip journey of 17,442 miles taken by a man whose physical infirmities made travel difficult, and air travel dangerous.[20] He did not go that vast distance in the pre–jet plane era in order to deal with the kinds of issues that had been handled by correspondence or by his subordinates since the outbreak of World War II. Military strategy at all levels was important, but such issues were for generals and admirals; presidents were after bigger fish. So too were British Prime Minister Winston Churchill—who looked to become the broker between Moscow and Washington; and Soviet leader Joseph Stalin—whose belief that the conference would concentrate on politics was illustrated by his bringing only a single military adviser, Marshal K. E. Voroshilov, a general whose politics were more important than his generalship.[21] After all, Roosevelt was not the only wartime leader who looked to pick a political pocket or two.[22]

Even something as crucial as the military implications of the Second Front did not require the presence of the Big Three, as reporters took to calling them. The sensitive and decisive question of final Soviet approval of the Second Front—OVERLORD, the invasion of northern France—could have been solved by correspondence, even if Stalin had unintentionally reopened the issue by proposing that the Turks be forced to enter the war.[23] If what turned out at Teheran to be a nondebate over the cross-Channel attack is any indication, the exchange of messages would have gone something like this:

ROOSEVELT TO STALIN: If we conduct extensive operations in the Aegean/ Balkans, they will most likely delay OVERLORD. Moreover, where do we go from there? However, if you prefer that course of action, we will act accordingly.[24]

STALIN TO ROOSEVELT: We appreciate your offer to assist in the Balkans/ Aegean. Certainly the Turks should be told to join us or suffer the consequences. However, any delay of the Second Front in northern France is unacceptable. The Soviet people would not understand any postponement of that long-promised campaign.

CHURCHILL TO ROOSEVELT: Of course I support OVERLORD as I have from the outset. Had you asked for my comments, your direct message to Uncle Joe on this subject would have had my full and enthusiastic second, for I am as ever your loyal lieutenant in this and all our joint endeavors. My military chiefs do assure me that our proposed Aegean operations would have a minimal effect on OVERLORD. The Chiefs of Staff paper on this matter follows.[25]

The records of the meetings at Teheran illustrate that once Stalin gently but firmly told Churchill and Roosevelt early in their first plenary meeting that he considered an invasion of northern France the best way to defeat Germany and that he wanted a firm commitment from the Anglo-Americans, everything else was a matter of details. With Stalin's preference clear, Roosevelt steadfastly stuck to the American position—although his support for his military advisers was conditional on Stalin's decision. By the second plenary meeting, Soviet insistence on OVERLORD was no longer gentle. Churchill, who had made a career out of not knowing when he had lost, continued throughout the conference to throw up objections and suggest reasons that could delay the cross-Channel invasion, but the new Roosevelt-Stalin team would not back off.[26]

That Roosevelt essentially left the Second Front decision to Stalin only illustrates its overriding political significance. Although the President had embraced the American Joint Chiefs' strategy for defeating Germany, and while he was willing to stand up to Churchill and the British time and again when they tried to nibble at the edges of that strategy, he was also willing to listen to Stalin if the Soviet leader had misgivings about OVER-LORD. The goal was to defeat Germany, and if the Soviet Union, which had borne the brunt of the land war in Europe, had what it thought was a better way, then that should at least be considered.[27] Roosevelt still supported the cross-Channel invasion strategy, but by December 1943, how to work together to defeat Germany was less important than how to work together to create a stable postwar political situation. Creation of the "family circle" counted for more than did military strategy in what was a foregone conclusion.[28]

An unmistakable indication of Roosevelt's changing priorities came in June 1943, when he tried to arrange a one-on-one meeting with Stalin. The President had recognized the postwar potential of the Soviet Union by June 1941, when the Russians were forced to enter the war against Germany. A victorious USSR would be a postwar power of major geo-political strength, putting it in the same arena with the United States. What America had was economic and ideological superiority.[29] That as-sessment was behind Roosevelt's clumsy attempt to hide from Churchill a proposal for à deux talks with Stalin, a maneuver that finally ended with the President lying about who had proposed the meeting. Roosevelt should have been embarrassed, but was not. In a phrase used by two of his personal representatives, Joseph Davies and Averell Harriman, the purpose of a Roosevelt-Stalin meeting was to demonstrate how unneces-sary it was for Britain to be "the friendly broker" in transactions between the United States and the Soviet Union.[30] A second declaration of inde-pendence, as it were.

That image of independence was part of a conscious strategy on Roosevelt's part. The President had sought a meeting with Stalin well before getting Bullitt's gratuitous advice. In a 2 December 1942 message to Prime Minister Churchill, Roosevelt agreed that a Big Three meeting was necessary. But what is most interesting is that he crossed out draft wording suggested by his advisers that called for "us [Churchill and Roosevelt] going into that conference only after the fullest exchange of views and a complete understanding." Instead, the President questioned the advisability of giving "Stalin the impression that we are settling every-thing between ourselves before we meet him."[31] Not that Roosevelt was alone in that fear. Even the British had, at one time in 1942, scrapped plans for a visit by Eden to Washington in part out of fear that the Soviets would become suspicious of secret Anglo-American understandings.[32] Roosevelt and his closest adviser, Harry Hopkins, continued to express concern lest Stalin suspect Anglo-American conniving, and Harriman gave the same advice. Stalin may have assumed that the British and Americans were working closely together—he did express surprise at Roosevelt's desire for one-on-one discussions—but also sought to limit that cooperation, suggesting that the Soviet treaty with Britain should prevent Anglo-American agreements on postwar settlements.[33]

But it was the Americans who avoided prior agreements with London on postwar matters. And that pattern of holding Britain at arm's length became painfully clear to Churchill as the time for the Cairo/Teheran conferences approached. The Prime Minister found the President unwilling to meet for preconference talks. Roosevelt's excuses were legion and transparent. He could not leave Washington before Hull returned from Moscow. He rejected a proposal from Churchill (that Hopkins supported) for another meeting in Casablanca, claiming the harbor was too shallow for the warship on which he would travel. He wanted a Soviet representative present at any US/UK staff conversations. He proposed meeting after the Teheran talks. Even his flight out of Algeria to Cairo was delayed.[34] Whatever Churchill proposed, Roosevelt evaded it. Churchill's doctor, Lord Moran, captured the Prime Minister's distress: "What I find so shocking is that to the Americans the P.M. is the villain of the piece; they are far more skeptical of him than they are of Stalin. Anyway, whoever is to blame, it is clear that we are going to Teheran without a common plan."[35]

Even at the Teheran meeting, Roosevelt continued to evade Churchill's embrace. The President arranged an immediate one-on-one meeting with Stalin, much to Churchill's indignation (he muttered about obeying orders, then rhetorically threatened to give a dinner party on his birthday the next day, to get drunk, and then to leave the conference). Roosevelt turned down the Prime Minister's luncheon invitation for the next day. Then, during his third private meeting with Stalin, Roosevelt again stepped back from the British, commenting that "it was premature" to discuss with Churchill the American ideas for a postwar international organization, even though the President had already outlined those thoughts during his first meeting with Stalin.[36]

Part of the problem was Churchill himself. As one British official put it in August 1943: "Russian matters are pretty tricky at the moment. [Churchill] is the real snag. His statement the other day about consulting the Americans and informing the Russians was no slip of the tongue. It's his deliberate policy and it's going to land us in one hell of a mess."[37]

But what Roosevelt wanted was more complex than just convincing the Soviet leader that Britain and the United States were not "ganging up" on him. The purpose was to create a Soviet-American working relationship, a goal that necessitated disabusing the British and the Soviets of the notion that the United Kingdom was a suitable go-between in Soviet-American affairs. Perhaps Roosevelt was more the child of the age of flight—seeing a direct connection between Washington and Moscow—while Churchill, from a nation bound to the land and waters by a naval tradition and centuries of involvement with and in Europe, saw no way to Russia except through London.[38] In any event, Americans had long distrusted British policy as motivated by colonialism, greed, outmoded European-style power politics, and unwarranted arrogance. Early in the war, the President had remarked to Churchill that "Stalin hates the guts of all your top people. He thinks he likes me better, and I hope he will continue to do so." A year later, he told the Prime Minister that a private Roosevelt-Stalin meeting was a good idea because the Soviet leader would be "more frank" if Churchill were not there. During the trip to Teheran, discussions between Roosevelt and his advisers often depicted Britain as a stumbling block to Soviet-American cooperation.[39] Hopkins expressed annoyance and distrust about the effect the British would have on attempts to get along with the Russians. When he asked Joseph Davies, just prior to the Cairo/Teheran meetings, to assess Allied relations, Davies reported that Britain retained the strongest influence with the Soviets, although Hull had reported that, during the Moscow meetings, Molotov was more willing to discuss American ideas than those proposed by the British. Hopkins, fearing the British were playing the United States against the Soviet Union, took steps to insure that things like Lend-Lease could not be used by the British for that purpose. In fact, Hopkins' personal admiration for Churchill the man never erased his distrust for British politics and policies. Moran recorded angrily that when he encountered Hopkins in Cairo, the American was "full of sneers and jibes" about British attempts to delay OVERLORD.[40]

Postwar politics, not wartime planning, brought them together at Teheran—but what were Roosevelt's motives? Following the Moscow Foreign Minister's Conference, political analyst Walter Lippmann congratulated Roosevelt on what had been achieved during the talks. The President's response was wary, even cynical: "Sometimes . . . however, I feel that the world will be mighty lucky if it gets 50% of what it seeks out of the war as a permanent success. That might be a high average." Roosevelt's breezy charm deceived some into concluding he was all style and no substance. British diplomat Harold Macmillan sneered that the President "lived on charm. . . . Even thought he could charm Stalin." But as Lippmann observed a decade later, FDR was too cynical and distrusting of everybody to have tried naively to charm Stalin at Teheran. "What he thought he could do," said the columnist, "was to outwit Stalin, which is quite a different thing."[41]

Is that what FDR meant by the "family circle"? Were his stated goals regarding the Soviet Union merely a performance, at Teheran and throughout the war? Or was he serious about his hope and desire to bring the Soviet Union into some kind of broad, effective international system that would impose peace on smaller nations and preserve that peace by avoiding great power confrontations? The Teheran conference can only give us a snapshot of where Roosevelt stood as of late 1943, for perhaps more than either Churchill or Stalin, the President was willing to step backward, to back and fill, to compromise on tactical matters, in order to achieve progress toward what he considered truly important strategic issues. Teheran is only a part of that mosaic, but it is the crucial part. That meeting marked a clear reorientation in Roosevelt's priorities away from military concerns and toward shaping the postwar world. His proposals were vague and suggestive, as was so often the case, but the fundamentals he outlined there shifted later only in form, not substance.[42] But before Roosevelt played his part at Teheran, his secretary of state set the stage at Moscow.

The aura of power and excitement that surrounds the summit meetings of World War II has tended to obscure the important part played by lesser mortals at other conferences—in this case, the role of Cordell Hull at the Moscow Foreign Ministers discussions, held only a month before their chiefs met in Teheran.[43] Hull is frequently dismissed as a minor factor in American policy-making. After all, he was left at home while Roosevelt came to Teheran and used Harry Hopkins as his major adviser. But that is somewhat misleading. Hull was chronically ill—Admiral William Leahy, who acted as Roosevelt's chief of staff, reports that the secretary telegraphed from Moscow to say that poor health prevented his going to either Cairo or Teheran.[44] True, FDR wanted to be his own secretary of state, particularly at a "summit" conference. What he needed at such conferences was an alter ego with no ego—a role Hopkins was far better suited for than Hull. But that did not mean that the secretary of state could not speak for the President on certain broad issues.[45]

At Moscow, Hull represented not only his own views on the question of organizing the postwar world, he spoke for Franklin Roosevelt as well. Hull, an old Wilsonian, and Roosevelt, a young Wilsonian eager to avoid Wilson's mistakes, had differed and would differ even more as time went on, but in the autumn of 1943, Hull was the perfect missionary. He and Roosevelt met on 5 October 1943 and agreed about "what could be done toward arrangement of a more or less stable international agreement" following the war.[46] Hull had no interest in the debate over the cross-

Channel invasion or other military questions, so he would simply follow instructions on those issues. He saw a Soviet promise to enter the East Asian war as a political rather than just a military commitment to cooperate. He, like the President, saw Eastern Europe as an abyss that would swallow up any worldwide postwar organization. With Roosevelt, Hull saw China as a balance-weight against the United States being dragged into the same old cycle of petty European quarrels over ethnic and historic boundaries—whether in Eastern or Western Europe.[47] Roosevelt's famous disclaimer—"I am absolutely unwilling to police France and possibly Italy and the Balkans as well"—also summed up Hull's thinking. Both men looked with suspicion on British pretensions to play broker between East and West. And like Roosevelt, Hull believed that bringing their nation into a Wilsonian world required special care lest the United States Senate and electorate repeat their errors of 1919 and 1920. Strange as it may seem to generations of American globalists after World War II, in 1943 a retreat into unilateralism (invariably mislabeled isolationism) was a very real possibility.[48]

At Moscow, the dilemma of specifics versus grand designs came into sharp focus, with China and Eastern Europe providing the lens. Eastern Europe was the region where, in one form or another, both Britain and the Soviet Union proposed creating spheres of influence, something Hull opposed in principle. Perhaps as a tactic to avoid that outcome, he consistently treated Eastern Europe as a detail that the USSR and the United Kingdom should deal with—the same approach Roosevelt followed at Teheran. "Moscow Meeting: The Surrender of Eastern Europe" is how one British historian recently titled a discussion of the Moscow Foreign Ministers Conference. Churchill and Eden would have found that an apt phrase. From their viewpoint, the Americans were largely to blame. Eden proposed a "self-denying" ordinance designed to eliminate Great Power scrambling "to secure the allegiance of the smaller powers" in Europe, but Hull expressed opposition by saying that such matters were not the concern of the United States. When Eden, with dramatic disregard for nationalism, subsequently proposed the establishment of confederations in Eastern Europe—"to undo some of the political and economic damage . . . wrought by the break-up of the great empires . . . after the first World War"—Hull once again expressed disinterest. That despite the similarity of Eden's proposals to Roosevelt's scheme for the creation of Rhineland confederations called Walloonia and Flamingia.[49]

Eden's self-denying ordinance, of course, contradicted the creation of what would have been British-sponsored confederations, but either way, Molotov recognized that each proposal aimed at recreating the *cordon sanitaire* around the Soviet Union. Roosevelt and Hull found the scheme unworkable and transparent. The British goal was more than just to restrict Soviet political expansion. They hoped to extend their influence and, where that was not practical, create confused and chaotic buffer states. Eden's protests to the contrary notwithstanding, it was the old First World War–era solution all over again.[50] To blame the United States for the defeat of an unworkable and transparent scheme makes little sense, even if the British hardly had a copyright on the trumpeting of liberal ideas as camouflage for a sphere of influence. But the episode does illustrate Hull's insistence on avoiding what he saw as the Eastern European quagmire.

Averell Harriman expressed displeasure with both Hull and Roosevelt's preoccupation about bringing China into what they called the Four Powers. The ambassador later recalled that he thought Hull "would have been better advised also to apply his considerable leverage with the Russians in attempting to work out agreements to safeguard the independence of Poland and other nations in Eastern and Central Europe, whose liberation was foreseen in a matter of months." When Harriman pushed Hull to talk to Molotov about Poland, the secretary dismissed the suggestion, saying, "I don't want to deal with these piddling little things. We must deal with the main issues."[51]

And what were the main issues? Was Hull simply a fool, as Harriman later implied? "The main issue," wrote Harriman in his memoirs, "as Hull saw it, was his own four-power declaration, a document *breathing assurance that the Great Powers would behave with perfect decorum after the war was won.*"[52] All things considered, why was Poland more important than China? All things considered, what "considerable leverage" did Hull have with Molotov over Eastern Europe? This was, after all, in the wake of massive Soviet victories at Stalingrad and Kursk, even if the Kursk victory was not fully appreciated by the western allies or, it seems, by the Soviet high command.[53]

Hull's refusal to get bogged down in "piddling issues" reflected his commitment to a broader conception of postwar international relationships. His (and Roosevelt's) design, set out in the Four Power Declaration, called for the four powers—the United States, Great Britain, the Soviet Union, and China—to continue their wartime association "for the organization and maintenance of peace and security."[54] To achieve that goal meant obtaining the voluntary and constructive cooperation of the Soviet Union. Thus Hull agreed, at Molotov's request, to delete pledges of "joint" actions and consultations in occupied and liberated areas. The postwar world order would work only if the Soviets, and the other great powers, could be persuaded of their own volition to act decently (i.e., within liberal democratic/economic norms).

Hull's firm insistence that China be included reflected a belief that the postwar relationship between the United States and the Soviet Union should not be painted just in Eastern Europe, but on a far broader canvas. In that sense, he and the President overestimated even Stalin's designs and reach. Hull and Roosevelt insisted throughout the war that postwar planning must be on a worldwide basis, even if each of the Big Four ended up as, or would be groomed to be, the guardian for a region. In the spring of 1943, Eden had reported to Churchill that Roosevelt's executive committee of the United Nations Organization was simply the Big Four, yet the President followed that description with a warning: "It was essential . . . to organize all these United Nations organs on a world-wide basis and not on a regional basis.. . . [T]he only appeal which would be likely to carry weight with the United States public . . . would be one based upon a world-wide conception." Harry Hopkins likewise cautioned Eden against any attempt to create a European council, lest that prompt "isolationists" to do the same in the Western Hemisphere.[55]

But how are regional "policemen" to avoid the Orwellian temptation, even necessity, of creating a sphere of influence in their region?[56] How is such a region different from a Pax Britannica, a Russian Empire, or a Monroe Doctrine? That Roosevelt perceived a difference is clear. It was one of many apparent contradictions that Roosevelt never clarified.[b] When White House confidant, Forrest Davis, published "Roosevelt's World Blueprint" in a *Saturday Evening Post* article only a week after Eden's visit to Washington, the same ambiguities appeared. Roosevelt advocated creating "security commissions" in various regions—Europe and Asia, for example—while rejecting any notion of exclusive spheres of influence by proposing a "master commission" that would act as an international executive committee to deal with crisis situations. That Roosevelt recognized the difficulties is suggested by references to long-term evolution and a clear dismissal of universalist solutions—"universal rebirth" was the specific phrase.[57] What the President wanted to avoid was a series of regional groupings that excluded one or another of the major world powers. Not only would that encourage unilateralism (always called isolationism) at home, but it promised to set region against region in times of crisis.[58]

Later, in the autumn of 1944, when Roosevelt learned of plans for talks between Stalin and Churchill regarding a European settlement, the President's initial reaction was to tell the Prime Minister to go ahead—the United States did not care about the details of arrangements in Eastern Europe. Only after Hopkins and Charles Bohlen warned of dire consequences did the President tell Churchill that the United States was interested in everything, everywhere. What the Americans really feared was

[b] For Roosevelt's perception of, and problems with, the Good Neighbor Policy as an example of that difference, see " 'Baffled Virtue . . . Injured Innocence.': The Western Hemisphere as Regional Role Model."

disruptive Anglo-Soviet quarreling, although that concern pointed in the direction of globalism.[59] Roosevelt did not see Poland, then or in 1943, as the litmus test it later became for Cold Warriors in both the Soviet Union and the United States. As Stalin recognized, Roosevelt was not satisfied with merely a kopek or two. Winning Eastern Europe was too small a prize if it cost him the world.

And the world was what Roosevelt came to discuss at Teheran. The interlude at Cairo with Churchill and Chinese leader Chiang Kai-shek served largely to promote China as a legitimate postwar regional leader, even if the military campaigns promised to Chiang soon fell afoul of the realities of military logistics and strategy, as well as the politics of colonialism.[60] But at Teheran, the President came face-to-face with what could be a major challenge to his postwar design—Joseph Stalin and the Soviet Union. Roosevelt had entered the war thinking that, once Germany and Japan were defeated, European power politics and colonialism posed the greatest threat to a liberal, democratic, peaceful world—and those apprehensions had not left him. He had no confidence in the ability of Britain or other western democracies to lead Europe into an era of peace. After all, they had failed twice in the twentieth century. But such fears were soon joined by a realization that the Soviet Union had become a new player on the world scene, a development that greatly complicated things. For that reason, Roosevelt's private meetings at Teheran with Stalin—meetings whose very privacy angered Churchill—take on special meaning.

FDR put it clearly to the Soviet leader—we need to talk about "a great many other matters pertaining to the future of the world." When Stalin said they could discuss whatever they wished, Roosevelt launched into a description of the postwar international organization he envisaged. Stalin cut directly to the dilemma—would this body (an executive committee composed of the Big Four plus six other states) "make decisions binding on the world?" Roosevelt then spoke of the Four Policemen who would deal with emergency threats to the peace, but Stalin again asked the President to confront his dilemma, suggesting that the small nations might take exception to having the Big Four order them about. They would particularly resent China's acting in that capacity. When Stalin suggested instead that there be area committees with strictly regional membership, thus leaving China out of European affairs, Roosevelt obliquely commented that Churchill had made the same suggestion. The President then resorted to his favorite means of countering a proposal without taking a personal stand. He warned that the American Congress would not agree since that could require that American troops be sent to Europe. Stalin wondered how Europe could be policed without American military forces, and the discussion then slid off into the practical question of how to prevent a resurgence of German power. The Soviet leader found that much more pressing than Roosevelt's grand design, although the President managed to get in a mention of China's long-term potential. As one observer put it, Roosevelt was more interested in peace than war, while Stalin wanted to get down to business.[61]

Roosevelt showed deep concern about the threat posed by smaller nations to any concert of the Big Three. Memories of the First World War breaking out in the Balkans not only stimulated wariness about involvement in Eastern Europe, but also aroused fears that the same sort of indirect, war-by-proxy that had occurred in the Balkans could again pit the Great Powers against each other. Stalin understood that Roosevelt dismissed the smaller nations as players in the political system, but seems not to have discerned the President's fear that those nations might disrupt the grand scheme of international politics.[62] Speaking through Hull at the Moscow talks, Roosevelt had rejected Eden's scheme for a self-denying ordinance, returning instead to his long-held preference for disarming all but the major powers. The full range of the President's thinking is better displayed by an offhand comment he made just after the Teheran meeting. Responding to an inquiry about the military forces that postwar Greece and Yugoslavia would require, Roosevelt answered: "Will it be necessary for these states to defend themselves after this war?" Concluding that the President thought he had "arranged to banish war, from Europe anyway, for good," his questioner, in a written aside, skeptically asked, "but why should one quarrel with the faith of the worker in his work?"[63] Disarming *almost* everybody left unanswered the question of policing the policemen, and a later Roosevelt comment—"The maintenance of the moral prestige of the great powers is an essential element in any successful system of international cooperation"—reveals the difficulty of translating dreams into practicalities. Confronted by Sumner Welles with the conundrum, Roosevelt "dismissed as of little account the argument that no responsible government of a small country could be compelled to liquidate the military establishment upon which it believed the safety of the nation depended, unless the self-appointed policemen were prepared to occupy that country by force."[64] At Yalta, fourteen months later, the President agreed with Stalin's assertion that, while the small powers had rights that should be protected, those nations should not judge the actions of the great powers. Roosevelt added that the peace should be written by the Big Three. Churchill chimed in, remarking cynically: "The eagle should permit the small birds to sing and care not wherefor they sang."[65]

Domestic pressures and the regional nature of Roosevelt's design dovetailed in his conviction that American military forces could and should not be involved in any postwar settlement in Europe. Determining which came first is a chicken-and-the-egg question. The growing domestic consensus in the United States favoring participation in some sort of postwar international organization aimed at preserving peace gave Hull and Roosevelt a greater sense of freedom of action at Moscow and Teheran to push for postwar international cooperation. Even *Pravda* was pleased. But insular and unilateralist voices in America remained loud and frequent, and the Connally resolution, passed by the U.S. Senate on 5 November 1943, dodged the issue of using force for international peacekeeping.[66] Partly for that reason, but partly out of personal conviction, FDR repeatedly insisted that U.S. military forces would leave Europe as soon as possible. He told General Marshall that it would be necessary to keep a million men in Europe only for one or two years. Even the War Department premised its plans for the administration of postwar Germany on a short-term occupation.[67] Perhaps that reflected Roosevelt's understanding of the limits of American power. But whatever his reasons, that assumption was a major element in the definition of his postwar design.

But that did not solve one of the President's major dilemmas. European rivalries—sometimes in Europe, sometimes in their colonial empires—had plunged the rest of the world into a series of global conflicts, starting as far back as what Americans called the French and Indian War. Europe had given birth to two world wars in the twentieth century alone. What could be done to prevent that from happening again?

To start with, Germany had to be eliminated as a major European power. The intensity of that belief on Roosevelt's part is hard to overestimate. De-Nazification was agreed upon by all. So was postwar dismemberment, although the Big Three could not agree on the size and shape of the pieces. All agreed on the disarming of Germany, but again the means was not determined. Eden repeatedly insisted that disarmament required American occupying forces to remain in Germany; Roosevelt envisaged the virtual disarmament of all but the leading powers, which would let the Americans go home. It was one reason why Morgenthau's plan for the deindustrialization of Germany held such appeal for FDR. If Germany had no heavy, war production-capable industry, then Britain, the Soviet Union, and the rest of Europe could easily police the Germans.[68]

But that was only one of the potential problems for Europe. Decolonization of empires was another step, but that would not settle intra-European disputes dealing with Eastern and Central Europe, where the Soviet Union would meet the other of Europe's policemen, Great Britain. Roosevelt had long since dismissed the seductive mirage of an Anglo-American world that he and Churchill flirted with at Casablanca. Now the Americans also rejected Britain-as-broker between the Soviet Union and the United States, believing perfidious Albion too selfish and imperialistic to play such a role. But if Britain could not be trusted to get along with the Soviet Union, how was peace to be maintained? What Roosevelt did was to reverse the brokerage. He saw the United States, and more specifically himself, as the mediator between the Soviet Union and Britain, although that role would not include an American military presence in Europe. The Squire of Hyde Park would sit on the veranda of his Hudson Valley home, dispensing wisdom and justice to the world leaders who journeyed to his door.[69] Moreover, Roosevelt presumed that shared values—one of Churchill's constant themes—plus the leverage of American economic strength left the United Kingdom neither the leeway nor the desire to act independently.[70]

But the cooperation of the Soviet Union was another matter. Roosevelt repeatedly entertained the idea of using economic pressure to persuade Stalin to go along, but invariably he backed away when the time came to implement such a policy. His fleeting support for Harriman's recommendations at Teheran, and his sporadic interest in Morgenthau's proposals for postwar loans to the Soviet Union, are but two examples.[71] Ascribing that to a penchant for procrastination is too simple, even if postponement was a Roosevelt tactic. The President refused to choose confrontation with a touchy, suspicious, revolutionary nation of great and growing power. Blackmail had not worked in the late 1930s, and no one could be certain how Soviet leadership would respond. Playing Bullitt's "lady bountiful" to the Soviet "beggars" might bring the wrong answer. As the President once told Churchill: "Stalin must be handled with great care. We have always got to bear in mind the personality of our ally and the very difficult and dangerous situation that confronts him. No one can be expected to approach the war from a world point of view whose country has been invaded."[72]

Two issues threatened Roosevelt's plans for the development of postwar great power relationships: (1) the fate of Eastern Europe, seen by some as a litmus test for Soviet intentions, and (2) the broad issue of Soviet cooperation in an international system aimed at preserving peace. Roosevelt recognized that the Soviets would fail the first test, a failure that could jeopardize the transcendent goal of great power cooperation.[73] Therefore, in classic Roosevelt style, he (and Cordell Hull) evaded, avoided, and ignored specifics regarding Eastern Europe, hoping to insulate the more important objective—long-term collaboration.

Although one British participant at Teheran commented sourly that "Stalin has got the President in his pocket," the Soviet leader would hardly have agreed. Lippmann was right when he concluded that FDR hoped to outwit Stalin. Hopkins declared that Roosevelt was convinced "that even if he cannot convert Stalin into a good democrat, he will be able to come to a working agreement with him. After all, he had spent his life managing men, and Stalin at bottom could not be so very different from other people." Roosevelt was in Teheran to "come to terms with Stalin," and nothing was going to interfere with that goal.[74] The President did not come with his eyes shut. He arrived committed to getting Great Britain, the United States, and the Soviet Union all "mixed up together" in the postwar world, while avoiding the possessive embrace of Churchill who sought to limit the special relationship to the Anglo-Americans.[75] A Soviet translator at Teheran has FDR winking conspiratorially at Stalin; a British observer wrote of "How Stalin Found an Ally."[76] Neither was quite right; neither was quite wrong.

Historian/participant Herbert Feis speculated as to why Roosevelt did not leave Teheran with "gloomy forebodings" about a Europe dominated by Soviet military and political power. One reason, Feis speculated, could have been that FDR thought that Stalin would be content to live within his own, secure borders. A second could have been the perception that Stalin sought to advance Russian interests, not those of expansionist communism. Feis' third supposition seems closer to the mark:

> These issues of size, frontiers, relative power of the countries of continental Europe may have been deemed of only passing importance. If, it may have been thought, the three main members of the war coalition worked together in the new international political organization, such questions could be adjusted satisfactorily; while if they quarreled and failed to be true to their saving purpose, all of Europe would face a dark future howsoever they were settled at the moment.[77]

If we think of the "international political organization" as something far broader than just the United Nations Organization, and recognize the limitations of Feis' Eurocentrism, then this third supposition seems closest to the truth.

But it is an interpretation whose accuracy is demonstrated largely in the negative. Within a few months after the end of the war (some would say earlier), the Cold War set in. It was a war that remained "cold" only in Europe, where political walls, deterrence, self-interest, and ethnocentrism worked to preserve a stylized form of peace. It was a war that became "hot" outside of Europe—in China, Korea, and particularly in the former colonial world—long before the time predicted by Roosevelt. In fact, as the war went on and Big Three cooperation continued, the President had become more optimistic. In 1942 he told Molotov that "a peace could be established and guaranteed for at least twenty-five years, or as long as any of his and Stalin's and Churchill's generation could expect to live." Later, during the Yalta Conference, he said that "fifty years [of peace] were feasible and possible."[78] But that optimism was misplaced.

The collapse of Roosevelt's grand design for postwar cooperation may demonstrate that the lesser, excruciatingly detailed issues of borders, boundaries, and benefits cannot, in fact, be ignored; that grand conceptions are too vague and amorphous to be implemented. Or it may mean that FDR was, as some have argued, masking his own nation's ambitions in a facade of idealism. Or, more likely, it means that everyone—from Roosevelt to Churchill to Stalin—hedged their bets, as national leaders always do. Rivalries over economics, power, and ideology ("this is a struggle for the hearts and minds of the people") took over and, just as Roosevelt had feared, Eastern Europe became the birthplace for another storm. Roosevelt's successors did not share his calm assurance and sense of security about America's future, and their insecurities guaranteed that the Soviet Union's "muscular diplomacy in Eastern Europe" would eventually be met in kind.[79]

But as of the close of the Teheran Conference, and on into the Dumbarton Oaks and Yalta talks, Roosevelt's concept of international cooperation still had a chance. His concern for appearances, for cosmetic solutions to Eastern Europe's political quarrels, did not mean that he had abandoned his broad goal of creating a liberal, democratic world. It meant only that Wilsonianism had to be practical. His convictions were indirectly laid out in January 1944 in an offhand comment about King George II of Greece. At first glance, the remark appears naive and superficial. But the tying together of democratic experience and strength was no accident: "I like George very much—in fact I call him by his first name—but, of course, he is not a very strong or convincing person, as *he has not had the opportunity of conducting a Presidential campaign.*"[80]

An equally curious example of Roosevelt's conception of the "game of politics," was his proposal for what he called "Free Ports of Information." Taking advantage of modern communications, the establishment of such internationally controlled centers at key points around the globe would insure that dictators could not prevent uncensored news from reaching all the people of the world.[81] This from a man who regularly instructed the Federal Bureau of Investigation to uncover the source of "leaks," and who tried to manipulate the news.[82] But it was all a matter of degree. Roosevelt also depended upon the press to preserve his political support, and never gave any serious consideration to constitutional limitations on the First Amendment. To him, the free press was all part of the political game.[83] He would surely have preferred his "Free Ports of Information" to depend largely on government-managed news, but that too was part of the contest. What is significant is Roosevelt's casual acceptance, his assumption that information and democratic institutions were interdependent. The same assumption was the basis of his hopes for Eastern Europe—that "open spheres" would permit the flow of culture, trade, and information.[c] Whatever his youthful penchant for power politics while serving as Assistant Secretary of the Navy during World War I, he seems to have absorbed Woodrow Wilson's understanding of public di-

[c] See below, "Naked Reverse Right."

plomacy—the use of public statements and propaganda to influence the electorates of the liberal nations. It was either a commitment by Roosevelt to populist democracy, or a concession that ultimately people had power.[84]

Roosevelt also had a personal dilemma. His refusal to think systematically meant that he could not reconcile power politics (Bismarckian-European style, decadent and degenerate) with his plans for a regional power structure of the Big Four, because that attempt to make Wilsonianism practical ended up looking like just another form of exclusive spheres of influence. Thus, he squirmed awkwardly when faced with explaining how the Four-Power system was not just realpolitik, telling Eden that "the only appeal which would be likely to carry weight with the United States public . . . would be one based upon a world-wide conception."[85]

To conclude a Big Three dinner meeting at the British legation, Roosevelt likened the relationship between the three great powers to the coloration of a rainbow:

> We have proved here at Teheran that the varying ideals of our nations can come together in a harmonious whole, moving unitedly for the common good of ourselves and of the world.
>
> So as we leave this historic gathering, we can see in the sky, for the first time, that traditional symbol of hope, the rainbow.[86]

A lovely image, but, as so often with Roosevelt, amorphous. As the Teheran Conference closed, what was his vision of the postwar world? What was he pursuing? Were his goals sufficiently defined for Roosevelt himself, much less historians, to grasp? How did he intend ideas like the Four Policemen and regional responsibility to be translated into reality? He evidently wanted, and assumed, that the great powers would, eventually, operate from a set of common political principles; principles that are best described by the word liberalism or, perhaps, Americanism. The Holy Alliance which followed the Napoleonic Wars, was founded on a common ideology and may have worked better than Roosevelt's Four Policemen, which lacked that common basis. But Roosevelt seems to have instinctively understood that a balance of power (irrespective of what one called it) could not work unless it rested firmly on a political equilibrium, as in the case of the nineteenth century's Concert of Europe—at least until nationalism broke it apart. The Concert operated under a set of common if broad political principles, precisely the way in which the Four Policemen were to behave.[87]

Based upon the President's words and actions at Teheran, his vision of the international political structure that was both desireable and possible is defined largely in the negative. What he did not want is much clearer than what he wanted. He did not want war, and the sine qua non for that was avoiding any confrontation between the major powers. Everything else followed. He did not want the United States involved in Europe's quarrels, particularly those of Eastern Europe. Small nations, there and elsewhere, were not to be players in world politics lest they disturb great power cooperation. He rejected Britain as intermediary between the United States and the Soviet Union. He did not want old-fashioned, exclusive spheres-of-influence/power-politics relationships, by which he meant both Metternichian coalitions against change and geopolitical Bismarckian alliances. He did not want to repeat the errors made by Wilson after the First World War; errors that prevented the United States from playing an appropriate international role. He did not want his support at home threatened by arguments over either the Monroe Doctrine or the issue of using American troops overseas.

Two early statements of United States war aims—the Atlantic Charter and the Four Freedoms—were too vague and unformed to act as practical guidelines, although they provided a clearer picture of his political economy. The economic and ideological segments of Roosevelt's thinking would become more and more clear in the months that followed. But the political superstructure offered at Teheran was flimsy—too flimsy to support the edifice.

At the Yalta Conference, thirteen months later, Roosevelt tried to put into place the world order he had outlined at Teheran. Stalin and Churchill similarly tried to implement their own conceptions. The end result was what has come to be called the "Yalta system," conjuring up visions of the balance of power/spheres of influence structure that characterized the general peace created by the Concert of Europe in the nineteenth century. But that is a false image. The decades of the Cold War proved far from peaceful, even if the armed struggles pitted the Great (Super) Powers against each other only in wars-by-proxy. Roosevelt's fears came true as colonialism and nationalism created havoc, while the major powers tried to divide the world into two great spheres of influence. Part of the problem at Yalta was that, as one French diplomat wrote years later, the effort "fell afoul of conceptual and terminological differences, amounting to mutual incomprehension, over the nature of spheres of influence."[88] But that was only one of the details that Roosevelt slid past at the Teheran talks. More important was his failure, or inability, to explain to Stalin and Churchill, as well as most of his associates, how the Roosevelt system would work.[89] As British economist James Meade, in Washington in 1943 as part of John Maynard Keynes' team of negotiators on postwar monetary policy, put it: "The Americans have already decided against isolationism, but don't for the life of them know what sort of interventionism to practice. (And who indeed can blame them for that?)"[90]

Roosevelt's dilemma was to reconcile his vision with the need for practical solutions that faced up to political realities. His manner of dealing with this quandary was to postpone, avoid, evade, and dodge. He frequently took three steps back, two to the side, and then stood still before considering one giant step. The problem was that long-term visions take time to develop, and the immediate details always seemed to matter. Churchill once wrote to FDR that "when the war of the giants is over, the wars of the pygmies will begin."[91] His timing was off. The wars of the pygmies began even before the giants had concluded their efforts. Somehow it all had echoes of Greek mythology, with flawed Olympian giants finding their grand schemes frustrated by the mere mortals they sought to manipulate.

But what goes around, comes around. During the 1988 presidential campaign, a newspaper analysis summed up the policies of the Democratic candidate, Michael Dukakis:

There are two cornerstones to [his] approach to Soviet-American relations. One . . . was [the] repeated assertion that unrest in Eastern Europe is a "regional conflict," comparable to the situation in Central America, the Middle East or southern Africa. . . .

Although . . . [his] aides said this marked a departure from the Republican approach to Eastern Europe, neither . . . explained the specific implications this notion would have for American policy.

The second cornerstone is that the United States can hold out economic incentives for Soviet political and military concessions in Eastern Europe, such as . . . an easing of Soviet political control.

The Republican candidate, George Bush, could not disagree, and less than a year later, speaking as President, he speculated optimistically on the chances of "integrating" the Soviet Union into the community of nations.[92]

All that could pass for an analysis of Franklin Roosevelt's foreign policy at Teheran. The curious combination of regionalism and global involvement, the concern about domestic political criticism, and the notion that economic rewards would prompt more moderate Soviet behavior were all considerations in Roosevelt's thinking. Like Franklin Roosevelt, the candidates sought to find a way to reconcile liberal dreams with hard realities, and, after nearly fifty years, the solutions proposed were dramatically similar. But *plus ça change, plus c'est la même chose* is not quite accurate. American leaders in the late 1980s had the advantage of what Roosevelt always said he needed—the passage of time.

"The only true substitute for empire": Roosevelt in Mexico, 1943.

VI

"Baffled Virtue . . . Injured Innocence": The Western Hemisphere as Regional Role Model

In the Western Hemisphere for more than a
century there has been no such thing as a balance of power. That might, according to European experience, have meant the creation of an
American empire. It has, instead, led to a radical innovation in human affairs, and to the only
true substitute for empire, which we call the
Good Neighbour Policy.
  (*Walter Lippmann, 1944*[1])

FRANKLIN ROOSEVELT believed that his Good Neighbor Policy provided a paradigm for the postwar world. The verdict of Walter Lippmann, public philosopher and political observer, caught Roosevelt's beliefs, regardless of whatever personal and policy differences existed between the two.[2] But like the President, Lippmann refused to confront the very political and ideological tensions they both claimed to have solved. Like Roosevelt, Lippmann heaped scorn on the foolish notion of identifying "the rights of small nations with their right to have an 'independent' foreign policy, that is to say one which manipulates the balance of power among great states." Like Roosevelt, Lippmann believed that "the evil we have to find a remedy for is that of the shifting alliances of 'power politics.'" Lippmann went on to suggest a solution that resembled the regional approach proposed by Roosevelt: "The remedy for shifting alliances is to stabilize alliances. Regionalism seeks to do just that; each state would recognize that it belongs to one, and only one, larger strategic zone of security." Both men assumed that nationalism, which encompasses both

Some portions of this essay were presented at a conference on "Latin America between the United States and Great Britain in World War II," St. Antony's College, Oxford, England, 4–6 July 1986. Those remarks, which focused on Argentina, have been published in *Argentina between the Great Powers, 1939–46*, Guido di Tella and D. C. Watt, eds. (Basingstoke: Macmillan/St. Antony's College, Oxford, 1989).

revolutionary and elitist movements, could coexist peacefully with a Good Neighbor Policy that presumed the wisdom, rectitude, and hemispheric leadership of the United States.[3] Both assumed that international peace and order could not be maintained by a huge, vaguely democratic organization made up of every nation-state, and that smaller nations should not be permitted to exploit balance of power politics, pitting one great power against the other. Both assumed that the wartime alliance of the Big Four should continue, as the best hope of avoiding another world war. Both eschewed the use of the phrase "spheres of influence" to describe the role of the great powers, not merely out of deference to American dislike of power politics, but because they sought to construct a system that was different from those of Metternich and Bismarck.

But the ideas of President and pundit diverged in a number of ways. Both assumed the superiority of Western Civilization, but Lippmann's intense, almost myopic concentration on European geopolitics put him on a tighter, different path that led away from Roosevelt's broader horizons.[a] Perhaps both played on a global chessboard; but if so, Roosevelt either played a three-dimensional game or had more pieces. The President saw the United States deeply involved in what might be called bringing-up-China, and insisted on economic and cultural access to Eastern Europe, whereas Lippmann argued for clearer lines of demarcation. Using the word "orbit" instead of sphere, Lippmann described the Atlantic, Russian, Chinese, and Hindu/Muslim orbits as "the nucleus around which order can be organized." He went on to stress the natural unity of the Atlantic Community, arguing for limiting American power to that region (a later generation of geopoliticians would have had to label him a neo-isolationist). Roosevelt, leery of anything that smacked of the kind of exclusivity that characterized empires—exclusivity that later became typical of the Cold War—avoided any specific terms beyond the "Four Policemen" and "regions." Roosevelt insisted on disarming smaller nations; Lippmann rejected the idea that arms create tension. Nevertheless, the President surely included Lippmann when he claimed that "the intellectuals are nearly all with us" on the matter of United States participation in an organized postwar international structure.[4]

Whatever their differences, both Roosevelt and Lippmann premised their case for regionalism on the argument that the policies of the United States in the Western Hemisphere since 1933 demonstrated that the Good Neighbor approach worked. Roosevelt never publicly adopted Lippmann's habit of referring to the Good Neighbor Principle as the proper

---

[a] See the essays " 'The Family Circle' " and "Naked Reverse Right," for Roosevelt's broader conceptions about the postwar world order.

relationship between the major powers and the smaller states within their "orbit"—perhaps because the phrase was so identified with just Latin America—but the analogy lay in the President's mind, occasionally creeping into his statements. As he put it to Canadian Prime Minister Mackenzie King in April 1941, the Good Neighbor Policy had been "one of the greatest contributions we had made together to world affairs."[5]

However faulty the presumption that the Good Neighbor was a "radical innovation" and a "true substitute for empire," it was the model that both Roosevelt and Lippmann offered for the postwar world. In the Western Hemisphere, the United States had thought and acted differently from Europe. It was not a rejection of Woodrow Wilson, but rather their hero's ideas adapted to make them practical.

Roosevelt and Lippmann had good reason for their smug satisfaction with the Good Neighbor policy. Not only had it played a major role in establishing Latin American solidarity against Germany, but, in the pre-war years, fears over security in the hemisphere had proven to be the "side door" for Roosevelt's internationalism.[6] Even with the impact of global war, he remained concerned that the allegiance of Americans to internationalism was superficial. The President did not advocate global interventionism, preferring instead to advance his notion of regional leadership combined with international consultation at the great power level. But even that modest commitment seemed a dramatic change for Americans, forcing him to find ways to ease the nation into its new role. Now the Western Hemisphere could once again serve as the vehicle for smoothing the path of formal American involvement in a cooperative international structure.

Roosevelt had always seen the Good Neighbor Policy as one of active leadership and cooperation, not passive live-and-let-live. He defined its goals as: "First, to remove from their [Latin American] minds all fear of American aggression—territorial or financial—and, second, to take them into a kind of hemispheric partnership in which no Republic would obtain undue advantage."[7] The President had not only repudiated the right of the United States to intervene in the affairs of other states in the Western Hemisphere—but he had done so publicly, repeatedly, and with great fanfare. That public posturing was essential, and Roosevelt knew it. He encouraged and approved a calculated program of government propaganda to build the image of a Good Neighborhood. As Nelson Rockefeller, then head of the Office of Inter-American Affairs, put it to Harry Hopkins in April 1941, the United States should equate the Monroe Doctrine with "life, liberty and the pursuit of happiness," instead of domination from Washington. An "instructive, enlightened, educational" program that included motion pictures, radio broadcasts, magazines, and cultural exchanges reached its apogee during the war with an animated cartoon feature from Walt Disney that had José Carioca, a well-dressed Brazilian parrot, always one step ahead of Donald Duck.[8]

With blithe self-assurance, Roosevelt not only believed in the demonstrable superiority of his nation's institutions, but assumed that societies south of the border would one day choose to emulate the United States example. He told reporters in November 1942 that, during his trip to South America six years earlier, he had heard people in Rio de Janeiro, Buenos Aires, and Montevideo shouting, "Viva Roosevelt." But even more of them, he said, were shouting, "Viva la Democracia."

> What we sneer at, some of us, as a Good Neighbor Policy is becoming in-grained in all of the Americas. The people are beginning to believe that if we continue through another 10 years or 20 years to maintain it as a continental policy, that it will work. . . . They have got the idea, the Democratic form of government—Democracy—all through there.
>
> . . . In all the other [Latin American] Republics, whoever the president is next time, whoever is the government in different places, they will go along with the idea of "democracia," and the thought of the Good Neighbor.[9]

Moreover, the Good Neighbor Policy was exportable outside the hemisphere. According to an approved account by journalist Forrest Davis, while Roosevelt was at the Teheran Conference he conducted for Stalin's benefit a seminar on the Good Neighbor Policy, closing with the observations that the Soviet Union's job was easier since the Slavic nations that adjoined the USSR were "nearer in blood" to the Russians than were Latin Americans to the United States.[10] Nor was it an accident that Davis concluded his series on the Teheran Conference by noting that the President staked "much on his good-neighbor diplomacy with Moscow."

A year earlier, Roosevelt used the same confidant to lay out for the public how regionalism and internationalism should be reconciled. If, in mid-1943, wrote Davis, the President was given the job of drafting the outline

> of a United Nations organization, . . . his framework would markedly resemble the simple . . . and workable body of arrangements under which the American republics manage their collective affairs. This American association of nations has become a highly effective organization capable of expressing the hemi-sphere's united will. . . . Its bonds are loose. It . . . requires no large and indefi-nite grant of sovereignty from the member states. . . . The system functions as a continuing peace conference, which mediates before, not after, hostilities.[11]

It all sounded easy, but Roosevelt's conception of the Western Hemisphere as an example of a sphere of leadership and responsibility ran up against more mundane issues of economic and political rivalry with one of the designated Great Powers. Even more, that Great Power was Great Britain, America's closest ally. In fact, the subtitle of this essay perhaps should be "How to Run a Region," for it is the issue of control, of leverage over an area, that is illustrated by the story of Anglo-American relations in the Western Hemisphere during the Second World War.

Whatever the meaning of the so-called Monroe Doctrine and the hemispheric orientation of the *norteamericanos*, merely dismissing Washington's calls for hemispheric identity as little more than a desire to exploit the other nations of the Americas is an incomplete explanation of the foreign policy of the United States. In fact, a study of the Anglo-American "special relationship" brings an awareness that there are strong, persistent parallels between that phenomenon and the interaction of the United States and the rest of the hemisphere.

One such parallel is that of wartime relations with Canada. Canadians treasured their independence even while most cherished their special political relationship to Britain and the empire. Despite internal differences among Canadians, they had long looked to Europe with much more affection and admiration than did their neighbor immediately to the south. Canada had not joined in prewar efforts to organize the hemisphere along Pan-American lines, and had quickly supported Britain and France by declaring war on Germany in September 1939, posing problems for the official neutrality policy of the United States. Even so, Roosevelt looked on Canada as a natural, logical part of any regional system in the hemisphere. Defense considerations had prompted discussions between Canadian Prime Minister Mackenzie King and Roosevelt as early as March 1937, discussions that only reinforced the President's casual assumption that Canadians would look to the United States for regional leadership.[12] Early in the war, with the collapse of France and the prospect of a British defeat, the government in Ottawa lived up to Roosevelt's expectations, eagerly accepting suggestions to create various defense relationships. Canada rushed to Britain's aid with troops and supplies, partly out of a sense of common purpose, partly to insure that the threat stayed in Europe on the other side of the Atlantic. At the same time, Canadians recognized that the war was changing their relationship with the United States. The security of the hemisphere rested upon the United States, and Canada had either to cooperate on a regional level or face the possibility of the Roosevelt administration imposing its will in the event of a crisis.[13]

By mid-war, some Canadians openly speculated that joining the Pan-American Union not only made good sense, but was not incompatible with their relationship with Britain; but Roosevelt remained leery of offering inclusion in the Union to a member of the British Commonwealth. Prime Minister King concluded, after conversations with the President, that the Americans did not want to discuss economic and other matters in

front of a member of the British Empire—a concern about trade competition with Britain that was exhibited even more strongly elsewhere in the
hemisphere. By 1944, with victory over Germany certain, Canadian government and public opinion opposed joining an organization that so emphasized regional unity while Canada's economic and defense interests
remained worldwide, or at least empirewide.[14] But the lesson of Canada's
reliance on the United States rather than Britain was not forgotten.

Canadian-American wartime relations centered around immediate defense issues, making it difficult if not impossible to separate legitimate
American security concerns from a broader sense of the proper hemispheric relationship, and from what could also be interpreted as American expansionism. For example; disputes over command of various defense sectors along the east and west coasts of North America seemed to
center on the issue of placing each nation's soldiers under foreign com-
manders—something the military (and Parliament or Congress) firmly
opposed. Since United States forces would be used to defend places like
the Maritime Provinces and Newfoundland, American military leaders
insisted that those areas be in their sector.[15] Was that an understandable
military desire to maintain control of its own forces, or was it a reflection
of their convictions that Canada would naturally, by a sort of gravita-
tional pull, become part of the United States?[16]

More significant was the developing pattern of American bases in the
Western Hemisphere—particularly as Roosevelt's definition of that hemisphere expanded to include Greenland, Iceland, and a number of South
Atlantic and Eastern Pacific islands that hardly qualified as being in the
Americas. Security against Germany was invariably the given reason;
when Roosevelt spoke of "taking over the entire Atlantic sphere, including Greenland," it was all placed within the atmosphere of the Nazi
threat.[17]

In spring 1940, as Germany moved into Norway and Denmark,
Roosevelt equivocated at a reporter's query about whether Greenland, a
Danish possession, fell under the Monroe Doctrine. A week later, the
President told the press that "most of the American people today . . .
would O.K. it if this Government said tomorrow that Greenland is inside
the Monroe Doctrine."[18] It was creative, clever geography. With German
military aggressiveness fresh in their minds, Americans did not protest an
expanded concept of United States responsibilities.

Roosevelt had very little to say during the war about Canada and its
place in hemispheric affairs. With Churchill's Britain the major ally, Canada tended to be subsumed in Anglo-American negotiations over the conduct of the war—a pattern that alternatively pleased and annoyed Mackenzie King, who projected a world role for Canada while it remained the
most important member of the British Commonwealth. Latin America

posed problems for Roosevelt's plans for the hemisphere, whereas Canada's special relationship with Britain was being replaced by the special Canadian-American defense affiliation.

Still, one early window into Roosevelt's thinking about Canada's place may be through Adolf Berle, an assistant secretary of state, who was charged with handling the Greenland base issue in 1940–41, and who later became involved with Latin American affairs. Though it is dangerous to extrapolate Roosevelt's thinking or American policy based solely on one source, Berle provides a fascinating window into the mix of immediate practicality and long-term assumptions that characterized American actions and thinking about the hemisphere.[19]

In 1940–1941, following the German occupation of Denmark, Berle was deeply involved with deciding how to handle the Danish possessions of Iceland and Greenland. The immediate security threat was the possibility of a German occupation of the islands. The United States had longstanding objections to the transfer between European powers of any of their New World possessions, but the immediate concern was that Germany might build air bases from which they could bomb the United States.[20] The more fundamental question, however, was how to integrate the islands into the Western Hemisphere security system without bringing the war closer to home. The Iceland situation was resolved by a combination of that country's declaration of independence from Denmark and an invitation to the British to send troops. But when the Canadians proposed that their forces occupy Greenland, Berle—and Roosevelt—drew back. Berle was far more prickly about the Western Hemisphere than Roosevelt, but they both agreed that Iceland was so much "a part of the European system" that occupation by Britain was acceptable, even if the island fell within their expansive definition of the Western Hemisphere. But Greenland was a different kettle of fish.[21]

Canadian plans to construct a base on that island resulted in year-long discussions that gave Berle ample opportunity to express his concerns. The resolution of the debate—construction of an American base—is less interesting than the broad context of Berle's comments and his assessment of Roosevelt's attitudes, which offer a gloss on the evolution of the Good Neighbor Policy during World War II.

Even before the fall of France to the Germans, the threat of a transfer of New World colonies between European powers made Roosevelt unhappy. An Anglo-French occupation of Dutch islands in the Caribbean in May 1940, before the fall of France to the Germans, annoyed the President and prompted a State Department protest. When the British occupied Iceland, Roosevelt told Berle to tell British Ambassador Lord Lothian "that he [Roosevelt] had no particular objection to that; but if they tried the same trick with Greenland he would be very angry"—a

statement that echoed American protests against a possible British purchase of Greenland back in 1920.

By August, Berle was worried that a Canadian air base in Greenland
could bring the war to the United States. If the Germans tried to attack
the facility, that would bring "in the Monroe Doctrine with a vengeance.
. . . It is a step eastward which means a step into the furnace which is
raging there." His conclusion? Any Greenland base should be operated
by the United States.[22] Shortly after Roosevelt emphasized that it was
permanent changes in the ownership of places like Greenland and Iceland that he objected to, Berle wrote of using the "Greenland technique"
to extend American neutrality protection to places like West Africa.[23]
Whatever the President's intentions, for subordinates like Berle the fear of
war seemed to produce endless expansion of the Monroe Doctrine.

By February 1941, as Congress debated lend-lease and the first Ameri-
can-British-Canadian military strategy talks were taking place, Berle
complained to the Canadians that "they couldn't grab an air base" in
Greenland. Rather, "they should build an air field and have it open to the
other American nations for purposes of hemispheric defense. . . . This of
course is the first true 'strategic point' [European style]—a case where we
are forced into a move primarily lest a military enemy should grab it
first. . . . For the first time, the Monroe Doctrine has to be implemented
militarily on a frontier."[24] As out of step as Berle was with administration policy to aid Britain and even to involve the United States in the
war against Germany, his extraordinarily expansive conception of the
Monroe Doctrine reflected the atmosphere in the White House. It was not
long afterward that Roosevelt began to speak of Dakar, on the western
bulge of Africa, as crucial to the long-term security of the American
hemisphere.

As Roosevelt's talks with Prime Minister King at Hyde Park in April
1941 demonstrated, the President included Canada within the "neighborhood." His seemingly casual mention of Canada as a contributor to the
Good Neighbor Policy reflected his appreciation of the "unguarded border," the St. Lawrence River Seaway project, and similar examples of
friendly Canadian-American relations. But it also revealed the President's
assumptions about Canada's relationship with the hemisphere. Mackenzie King's response reinforced Roosevelt's assumption. "Canada as the
neighbor on this continent, the only one that really mattered," the Prime
Minister insisted, should get special treatment. Well briefed about King's
thinking, Roosevelt was ready to act as good neighbor and agreed to direct significant American spending to the purchase of Canadian defense
production.[25]

Because Canadians sought, within the clear limitations of their economic and military strength, to play a global role during and after the

war, hemispheric organizations and structures held no appeal. Nor did Roosevelt publicly associate Canada with the Good Neighbor Policy. But there was no need to do so. The war had demonstrated Canada's dependence on the United States for security against a great power threat, substituting a new special relationship for the one that had existed between Great Britain and its so-called Dominion. The intertwining of the Canadian and American economies and the continuance of institutions like the Permanent Joint Defense Board insured practical regional cooperation on the part of Ottawa. Shared political values and geography did the rest.

The development of United States policy toward its hemispheric neighbors is unique to each situation, but Roosevelt's broad scheme and the wide range of his dilemmas are illustrated by his wartime dealings with the two nations that represented both the geographic and political-cultural poles; Canada in the far north, and Argentina in the far south.

It was in Argentina that Roosevelt's attempt to offer the Good Neighbor Policy as a role model for the other major powers faced its most serious test.[26] Not only did the Argentines reject American leadership, but another great power, Great Britain, also threatened to challenge the United States.

Argentina was separated from the United States more than any other Western Hemisphere nation. Part of that distance was geographic, but, as with the Canadians, a strong Argentine identification with European political, cultural, and intellectual currents was even more important.[27] New Deal diplomats were frustrated from the outset by opposition from Buenos Aires to American leadership in the region. Roosevelt's Good Neighbor Policy and Hull's reciprocal trade proposals—two sides of the same coin—met with evasions and outright resistance. In 1933, the Argentines chose British markets over those in the United States by signing the Roca Agreement so as to escape the impact of the Imperial Preference (Ottawa) Agreements. A few months later, at the Montevideo Conference of Latin American nations, Argentina indirectly but firmly rejected American efforts to promote hemispheric unity.[28]

That pattern was repeated. In 1939–40, Roosevelt proposed trusteeships for Antarctica and for European possessions in the Western Hemisphere. The plan was in response to a perceived German threat to those territories, and was part of the administration's position that there would be no transfer between European nations of territory in the hemisphere as a result of Hitler's conquests. But the proposal for Pan-American trusteeships also illustrated the way in which FDR thought regional cooperation ought to work. Predictably, only Argentina opposed the scheme, suggesting instead that European colonies either become independent or, with the Malvinas/Falklands in mind, that they be incorporated into those Latin American nations which had claims to the territory.[29]

Thus, when Roosevelt spoke during the war of harmony in the hemisphere and the success of his new approach, he conveniently ignored Argentine decisions to opt out of the system the Americans sought to create. But he did not forget, for the Argentines continued to challenge American leadership, eventually letting a combination of anti-Americanism and a vague empathy for Germany and Italy put them in the position of seeming to side with the Axis powers.[30]

To comprehend the subtleties and nuances of the role played by Argentina—and all the Latin American nations—within the broader structure of international relations during World War II requires an examination of the Anglo-American relationship; for those two nations were the primary players in the Western Hemisphere. The Anglo-American relationship during the Second World War may fall into convenient phases, but it does not always fit into neat categories. There was, as there had always been, vigorous economic competition, yet there was a strong sense of common goals and a determination to subordinate conflict to cooperation. There was agreement that the Axis powers were dangerous military and ideological enemies, yet there was strong disagreement on how best to meet that threat, particularly as it pertained to Latin America. There were differences of perspective, created by geography, history, and nationalism—that most important "ism" of all.

An appreciation of nationalism is central to any study of Latin America within the broad framework of Anglo-American relations. The point is illustrated by a tale from Anglo-American history. In 1814, with both Britain and the United States searching for a way out of a war with each other that promised only stalemate, each side agreed to peace negotiations, despite strong emotional arguments to the contrary. But when those peace talks began, the Americans were chagrined and even insulted to find that they had been relegated to the small backwater of Ghent, in Belgium, and that Britain's first team, the top officials in the government, were all dancing, dining, and deciding the fate of the western world at the Congress of Vienna. Not only was Ghent far from the center of events, but so were the Anglo-American peace negotiations.[31]

Thus it was with Latin America in World War II. For Argentines, Brazilians, Chileans, and each and every Latin American nation, the war was seen from a national, even hemispheric perspective. But for Americans and Britons, the primary focus was Europe. Part of that was Eurocentrism, part was just common sense. After all, Hitler's Germany was a very real horror. But, for the most part, Latin America did not have to confront that horror, for it could and had to rely on Britain and the United States to deal with the problem. That left Latin America free to pursue its own agenda. At the same time, Latin America was, for Britain and the United States, a stage to be acted upon, rather than an actor in its own right.

The Anglo-American "special relationship," when taken in historical context, reached remarkable, even unique levels of cooperation and intensity during World War II. But the "special relationship" between Britain and the United States was subject to the same pressures as the rest of international relations. Common histories, common institutions and ideologies, a common language, and a common enemy can facilitate cooperation, but nations continue to pursue their interests even within a close partnership. When efforts to satisfy those interests are combined with rough equality of power, harmony and cooperation are easier. But when imbalance occurs, one nation sees opportunities while the other worries more and more about protecting its interests. Rough equality was the case for Anglo-American relations only in the early stages of World War II. While Britain's contribution was equal to or greater than that of the United States, and while both felt threatened by German and Japanese military successes, mutual cooperation could predominate—although a number of British officials warned in the late thirties that too close an embrace with the Americans could result in merely exchanging one master for another.[32]

But the reality of the Anglo-American equation during the Second World War was the predominance of the United States. In 1783, the Venetian ambassador in Paris, representing Europe's oldest diplomatic tradition, predicted that "with the favorable effects of time, . . . [America] will become the most formidable power in the world."[33] Time had done its work, and by the 1940s, the United States was in a position to demonstrate the truth of those words. The Great Depression of the thirties had temporarily masked American strength, but Hitler's destruction of order in Europe ended all that. Given the historic fears and jealousies of nations, it is reasonable to argue that Britain's relative weakness was an essential element in the extraordinary Anglo-American cooperation that others have attributed to a "special relationship."

In the broadest sense, then, the context of Latin America as affected by Anglo-American relations in the World War II era has two main elements: first, the growing predominance of the United States over Great Britain, and second, their mutual preoccupation with European and even Asian events over those taking place in Latin America. The former meant that Britain could not and would not dictate alliance policy in Latin America; the latter meant that Latin American concerns almost invariably were subordinated to other issues. Put another way, whenever the Americans insisted, their policies in Latin America would be followed, and those policies were shaped by changing American perceptions of the fortunes of war.

Take, for example, the American reaction to events in the Rio de la Plata in 1939–1940. Following a battle between German and British warships in waters off Uruguay, the State Department protested British violations of neutrality in language that assumed hemispheric solidarity against European interference. But Franklin Roosevelt's response to a summary of the engagement sent to him by Churchill took a different tone. The President thanked the then First Lord of the Admiralty for "that tremendously interesting account of the extraordinarily well fought action," and then switched to a brief discussion of British blockade regulations. His warning against alienating American public opinion could have applied to both issues, but Roosevelt's reaction to the naval battle was that of a cheerleader. "I am inclined to think that . . . it will turn out that the damage to the *Admiral Graf Spee* was greater than reported," he gleefully told Churchill.[34] The reaction was natural, for in 1939–1940, the possibility of a German victory in Europe followed by some sort of action in the Western Hemisphere seemed very real indeed.

In the same vein, in a Navy Day speech on 27 October 1941, the President insisted that he had documents proving that Germany planned to conquer Latin America; a map that scholars later proved bogus showed Nazi plans for the entire area. It carefully exploited raw political nerves in the region by picturing a greater Argentina that included Paraguay, Uruguay, and part of Bolivia, as well as a *Korridor* to the Pacific at Antofagasta, going on to incorporate Peru into Chile, and ending with a recreation of New Granada under the name *Neuspanien*. The map was accepted at face value in a Washington that was fast developing a seige mentality. In March 1942, the FBI distributed another map showing the areas in South America where Germany and Japan presumably controlled strategic war materials. Five swastikas, three Japanese rising suns, and two Italian flags, all drawn large, combined to create an impression of Axis domination on that continent.[35] Little wonder that, early in the war, Roosevelt contributed to the impression in Whitehall that State Department protests against British actions were pro forma and the product of Secretary of State Cordell Hull's personal idiosyncracies.

Contrast all that with the way the United States acted regarding Argentina in 1944, once winning the war had become only a matter of time, and when any German threat to the Western Hemisphere had long since dissipated. Britain again blamed Cordell Hull for being intransigent—British official historian Llwellyn Woodward wrote of "Mr. Hull's Policy in Argentina," and the wartime British ambassador in Washington, Lord Halifax, described the secretary's position as set in "a background of baffled virtue and somewhat injured innocence."[36] Yet time and again President Roosevelt backed his secretary of state. The issue was complicated, and invariably phrased in the rhetoric of antifascism, but it boiled down to American attempts to create broad hemispheric unity under the umbrella of an anti-Axis alliance. In United States terms, that unity required governments in Latin America that were compatible—Wilsonian liberalism was far from dead. Thus, Washington found unacceptable the new Argentine regime led by Edelmiro Farrell and Juan Perón, for it was a government that combined a sort of vague authoritarian rhetoric with a nationalism that often exhibited itself as anti-Americanism.

The Argentine-American quarrel had begun early in the war when Buenos Aires had refused to declare war on the Axis. That decision proceeded from a variety of complex causes—the memory of successful neutrality in World War I, a large population of German and Italian stock, anti-U.S. sentiments, and domestic uncertainty. Whatever the reasons, the result was that American leaders harbored a good deal of resentment against Argentina for not having rallied to the cause.

But by 1944, solidarity against Germany and Japan was hardly the real issue. Roosevelt signed off on one message to Churchill, drafted by Hull, demanding that Britain not sign a long-term meat contract with Argentina. Whatever the arcane details of the dispute over British imports of Argentine beef, the language of the President's message revealed the true goals of American policy, even while the war remained the ostensible motivation: "If we continue to stand firm, letting the Farrell regime understand, in a tone not necessarily unfriendly, that it cannot in violation of its pledge of hemispheric unity and solidarity support the Axis in opposition to its sister nations, there is a good chance that this entire matter can soon be cleared up."[37] Hemispheric unity and solidarity were the goals. The British recognized that and tried to work around U.S. demands, but to no avail.

In November 1944, the State Department drafted a message for Roosevelt that went so far as to couple an admonition to Churchill about the Argentine meat contract with a warning; "Our people tell me that the phase two lend lease discussions are going well": a blunt piece of blackmail that the President himself crossed out.[38] Even without the threat, Churchill recognized what was happening, but he could only try to stand the American position on its head by assuring Roosevelt that "owing to our financial relationship and the scale on which you are helping us to play our part . . . I would not allow money to count in the matter."[39] One of Churchill's close advisers, Lord Cherwell, put the matter in perspective when he told the Prime Minister that the Americans "are proving so friendly and forthcoming in so many much more important matters that it would seem entirely wrong to refuse to meet their view on a question relatively so trivial."[40] American concern about the meat contract was not a case of crass economic competition—the United States had little interest in buying Argentine meat that would compete with American production—but investments translate into influence, and officials in Washington had long suspected that Argentina was using Britain as a counterweight against the United States.[41] In the long run, Roosevelt may have had in mind the sort of proposal Henry Morgenthau, Jr., had made back in 1939 when he told the President: "I have worked out a financial Monroe Doctrine which I hope will be called the Roosevelt Doctrine, and is planned to make your 'Good Neighbor Policy' work."[42]

Cordell Hull had been preaching hemispheric unity ever since taking office in 1933. Whether or not his willingness to use coercion to achieve that goal was a violation of the Good Neighbor Policy, as some may argue, is not the point. Arguments went on within the State Department as to the best method to use, but the goal was the same, even among such bitter personal enemies as Hull and Under Secretary of State Sumner Welles—a Western Hemisphere with liberal institutions that looked to the United States for leadership.[43]

Welles has long been recognized as someone who reflected Roosevelt's thinking, but Hull must not be dismissed as an unimportant, uninfluential foreign policy figure, even if he had originally been appointed secretary of state primarily because of his influence on Capitol Hill. Long after that influence with Congress had waned, Roosevelt continued to rely upon Hull for leadership and advice in certain areas—one of which was Latin America. Perhaps the President did give Argentina to Hull as a plaything, as some have claimed, but from 1944 on, Roosevelt seemed to play by the same game rules.[44] The creation of a liberal, American-style hemisphere was essential to what both Roosevelt and Hull dreamed of, each in his own way. That is no contradiction of the primacy of self-interest, for it was in the self-interest of the United States to see such congenial economic and political institutions developed and preserved in Latin America. Woodrow Wilson had failed in his attempt to impose his Americanism on the world. Roosevelt and, perhaps, Hull had the same goal—to demonstrate that American liberal institutions were an exportable commodity. That necessitated effective leadership in Latin America, for how could the United States sway Europe and Asia if it could not lead South America? Authoritarian Brazil, like similar regimes that would later become America's allies, could be tolerated not only because it offered a counterweight to Argentine influence in South America, but because the Brazilians apparently accepted United States leadership and were thus susceptible to change instigated by Washington.[45] It was an eerie combination of an echo and a portent. Woodrow Wilson had found it necessary to preserve America's leadership role in the face of German violations of international law. Half a century later, his successors would find it necessary to preserve American credibility by trying to build a nation in Southeast Asia.

British officials fought tenaciously during World War II to retain economic and political influence in Latin America, but even Winston Churchill, that dogged defender of British interests, accepted such regionalism. His ramblings about the postwar world invariably assigned the Western Hemisphere to the United States. In March 1944, when asking for co-operation regarding Spain, he laid out the arrangement to the President: "I would venture to remind you that we have gone along with you in Argentina and that we feel entitled to ask you to take our views seriously into account in the Iberian Peninsula, where our strategic and economic interests are more directly affected than are those of the United States."[46] In other words, Spain and Portugal were in Britain's sphere of influence, just as Latin America was in that of the United States. Churchill would not permit Anglo-American differences in the Western Hemisphere to work against the creation of that postwar Anglo-American entente he so ardently desired.

In June 1944, when Churchill denied any desire to create a sphere of influence in the Balkans, he said so in a way that Cordell Hull interpreted, quite correctly, as an insinuation that the United States had a sphere of influence in Latin America. Hull's angry denial notwithstanding, the exchange illustrated the Prime Minister's thinking.[47] The secretary complained in September 1944 that the British were treating the Argentine affair "as a matter of minor and relatively unimportant policy."[48] He was correct, though not for the reasons he thought.

Churchill hoped to get Roosevelt to agree to British concepts of spheres of influence by acknowledging an American sphere in Latin America (not Canada). But Roosevelt's regionalism was quite different. In one sense, his vision of the postwar world was even more regional in orientation than Churchill's; the Prime Minister was, as it were, "singing to the choir." But the President rejected centralized control over a region. The British had proposed a London-based regional control commission for Western Europe, but the President was opposed. Not only would it facilitate British hegemony in the area, but it would set an even more dangerous precedent for Soviet conduct.[49] Instead, Roosevelt envisaged a looser framework within which the United States would convince the nations of the Americas to follow its lead, all the while prompting the other great powers to act responsibly within their regions. But translating those ideas into a noncoercive policy for the Western Hemisphere proved difficult.

Anglo-American policy—joint and national—during the Second World War toward Latin America was very much a function of Anglo-American relations. What is very clear is that Latin America did not play a significant role in shaping Anglo-American affairs. The United States tended to be rigorous in its demands for Latin American support; the British tended to defer to the domestic priorities of the Latin American nations. But that was as much a byproduct of their self-perceptions as anything else. Britain recognized that its influence in Latin America had far less impact than that of the United States, while the Americans were consumed with the need to prove that their leadership was effective.[50]

Even with that difference of approach, Britain and the United States were in general agreement regarding Latin America. Despite extensive British investments in Argentine railroads and industry, both Whitehall and Washington saw a declaration of war against Hitler's Germany as a litmus test for acceptance into the postwar community of nations.

Beyond Argentina, Latin America posed few difficulties for Anglo-American relations at the level of high policy. Vague, nonspecific fears were expressed by one or another diplomat or businessman that the United States was using the war to displace British interests, or that Britain was using lend-lease to preserve postwar markets, but these proved little more than slight bumps in the path.[51]

No one would claim that Latin America was unimportant or that Britain and the United States were disinterested in that area. But within the broad context of World War II, Latin America was not a significant factor in Anglo-American rivalry during World War II. Disagreements are not disputes, and Anglo-American disagreements over policy toward Argentina and Bolivia, the only areas where even strong differences existed, were more an irritant than a serious problem. Anglo-American competition for trade and influence existed, but within the context of agreement that Latin America was a region where United States leadership should predominate.

One British Foreign Office official complained bitterly in 1944 that American policies were, to say the least, a fraud:

> The "fascism" of Colonel Perón is only a pretext for the present policies of . . . the State Department; their real aim is to humiliate the one Latin American country that has dared to brave their lightning. If Argentina can effectively be cowed and brought to patent submission, State Department control over the Western Hemisphere . . . will be established. . . . This will contribute at one and the same time to mitigate the possible dangers of Russian and European influence in Latin America, and remove Argentina from what is considered to be our orbit.[52]

But as angry, and even accurate as those words were, they did not govern British policy. Foreign Secretary Anthony Eden summed up Britain's position in a worldwide circular of March 1945 titled "The Effect of Britain's External Position on Foreign Policy" in which he stated that in Latin America (as well as the Balkans), "we might have wished to assert ourselves *had it been possible.*" British diplomats all over South America disputed Eden's conclusions, but history suggests he was on the mark. There was commercial competition, but rivalry is too strong a word.[53]

In the immediate, practical sense, the Monroe Doctrine in the era of World War II was a sphere of influence conception that gave the United States self-assigned special "responsibilities" in the Western Hemisphere. Never mind that, at times, some American governments "invited" the United States to exercise that power. It was a sphere of influence irrespective of who asked. But Roosevelt wanted to avoid the use of military force, and wanted all the American nations to adopt liberal democracy as their political system.[54] That tension over leadership versus coercion (on grounds of national security) emerged during a White House interview with a friendly journalist. During a monologue that focused on Latin America, the President casually told journalist John Gunther that the Argentina problem could be solved if the United States were "to colonize it." Roosevelt went on to comment flippantly on everything from his first-name relationship with the president of Haiti to the notion that Iquitos, Peru, should be a free port. The tone was patronizing, but without threats of military coercion. Roosevelt was not at all serious about "colonizing" Argentina, but his use of what are now loaded words reflects his assumption that his nation should provide the example and strong leadership for the hemisphere. In other words, the United States had done it right—it was time for others to follow.

Roosevelt's Good Neighbor Policy superficially resembled the concept of "two-spheres," an idea as old as the European discovery of the Western Hemisphere. Two-spheres theorists had argued that conflicts in one sphere—be it Europe or the Americas—should not automatically spread to the other.[55] The concept treated the Western Hemisphere as a single unit, unlike the Monroe Doctrine which, at least in the public mind, assumed a guardianship role for the United States over the less powerful, less developed, and/or less capable nations of the Caribbean and Latin America.[56] Roosevelt assumed that the United States would be the regional leader in the Western Hemisphere, and in that sense moved in the direction of the Monroe Doctrine. His inclusion of Canada—an advanced, English-speaking (mostly), white society—may have been based on a sense of partnership, but the United States was, of course, the senior partner. That hierarchy grew out of the difference in strength rather than a belief that Canada had to be "led" in the direction of political and economic maturity.

Roosevelt's Good Neighborhood reformulation of the Monroe Doctrine was, by the end of the Second World War, part and parcel of his broad scheme for creating a peaceful world where the great powers worked separately, but together. Assistant Secretary of State Berle tried to make order out of ambiguity when he attempted to put Roosevelt's vague nostrums into less equivocal terms: "East of Germany, the task of American representatives . . . should be the continuous attempt to resolve differences between the major contending forces. . . . A Soviet 'sphere of influence' in these areas operated in somewhat the same fashion as we have operated the good neighbor policy in Mexico and the Caribbean area would be no threat to anyone." Berle went on to argue that the exercise of that sort of influence did not conflict with the interests of the peoples involved, nor did it threaten the British lifeline to the Middle East, although it would prevent "the attempt at economic exclusiveness sought by certain elements in the British Government."[57]

Yet, less than a decade after the war, one historian—speaking for many—rejected the distinction made by Roosevelt and Berle, derisively commenting that

> to most Americans the Good Neighbour Policy in Latin America and the Big Brother policy towards China seemed nothing less noble than the practical application of liberal, democratic principles to international relations.
>
> Yet American policy in Latin America bore a suspicious likeness to European practices which American statesmen so much deplored.[58]

Roosevelt had recognized that trap and tried to avoid it. The way he envisaged the regional concept would work was illustrated by his own actions in 1940 and 1941, before the United States entered the war against Germany. The Graf Spee episode, the extension of U.S. naval patrols into the waters around Iceland, the designation of Greenland as an American protectorate after Hitler's forces occupied Denmark—were all justified on grounds of Western Hemisphere defense against the Nazis. On a broader canvas, the President's attempts to establish "an intimate connection between the Good Neighbor and Allied aid" were successful.[59] Then, and subsequently during the war, the Latin American nations (except for Argentina—whose recalcitrance Roosevelt finally chose to ignore) rallied round Washington's leadership. It was the perfect model for Soviet relationships with Eastern Europe, for British relationships with Western Europe and the Mediterranean, and for Chinese relationships with East Asia—although it required the pressure of global war.

Roosevelt saw the Good Neighbor Policy as a paradigm for both great power relations with each other and for their relations with the nations in their sphere of responsibility. Anglo-American-Argentine relations during the war demonstrate the difficulty of translating that concept into practice. And another difficulty became quickly apparent in the postwar world. Roosevelt failed to confront the difference between the way the United States could dominate the Western Hemisphere, and the way that Britain and the Soviet Union could act within Europe. To dominate that region, those two policemen would have to exert overwhelming force. Britain neither could nor wanted to; but that is exactly what the Soviet Union did.

There was a final flaw in Roosevelt's scheme. Despite his perceptive recognition of frustrated nationalism in the colonial world as a menace to any postwar peace, his offhand, dismissive approach toward less powerful, less developed nations suggests that the Western Hemisphere's neighborhood "policeman" would have run up against serious obstacles.[60] Sometimes Latin American leaders assumed the United States would solve their problems. In late 1939, when a political crisis developed in Cuba, diplomat George Messersmith replaced the U.S. ambassador (who had died) and continued a hands-off policy. But Cuban politicians were "conditioned" to expect American intervention in a crisis. As Messersmith told the State Department, Cubans assumed that the United States spoke of nonintervention for "public consumption, but, in fact, [we] try to run the show from the inside."[61] That dilemma remained for Roosevelt: how to lead from a position of power and influence, without resorting to the use of power—however restrained. Even if the United States could have resisted the normal impulse to use economic and political pressure as part of its guidance and leadership, the insistence, even imposition, by a *patrón* of a broad political system was bound to stimulate resentment and opposition. Sometimes singers are more succinct:

Down to the banana republics,
Things aren't as warm as they seem;
None of the natives are buying
Any secondhand American dream.[62]

"It is something I think we should discuss with them at every opportunity":
Roosevelt, the Sultan of Morocco, and a "glum" Churchill.

VII

"In Search of Monsters to Destroy": Roosevelt and Colonialism

> "Well, Mr. President, you stated that you had
> not gotten very far with the British on this issue.
> Do you want us to bring it up again?" "Yes, by
> all means," the President said, "it is something
> I think we should discuss with them at every
> opportunity."[1]

THE "ISSUE" was decolonization of European empires, with Great Britain the primary target. And discussing that issue "with them at every opportunity" was precisely what Franklin Roosevelt did throughout the Second World War. Those discussions were an integral part of his unceasing public and private campaign aimed at eliminating European empires and setting the colonial world on the road toward independence.

Roosevelt's anticolonialism[2] has long fascinated historians, but their analyses have reached dramatically different conclusions. Was he an early Cold Warrior who found European allies against the Soviet Union far more important than eliminating the empires of those allies? Was his anticolonialism merely a stalking horse for America's own version of empire, informal or otherwise? Was he really a misguided "populist" whose ignorance and empty rhetoric actually impeded chances of rational decolonization by the Europeans? Was he just a politician, playing to the crowd with "sanctimonious" words about freedom and independence? Or was his anticolonialism both sincere and practical? To comprehend Roosevelt's wartime policy toward colonialism, that policy must be studied as a whole. Breaking it up into regional and national pieces clouds the picture and often misses the broad, consistent thrust of his words and actions.[3]

Fred E. Pollock, the primary author of this essay, is a Research Associate at Rutgers University in Newark, N.J. and was awarded the Bernath Article Prize by the Society for Historians of American Foreign Relations for his piece, "Roosevelt, The Ogdensburg Agreement, and the British Fleet: All Done with Mirrors," *Diplomatic History* 5 (Summer 1981), pp. 203–19. He has taught American history at Central High School in Newark, N.J. since 1971. Our thanks to Mark Stoler of the University of Vermont for his comments, and to Louise Sieminski for her assistance.

There was nothing unique about Roosevelt's general distaste for colonialism—it came with being an American. His specific critique owed much to Woodrow Wilson, for it built upon the self-determination concept set forth in the Fourteen Points. Along with most Americans, both men had concluded that European colonial competition had heightened, if not created, the tensions that contributed to global warfare. Not only had the race for empire set the European powers against each other in the early twentieth century, but it also worked against any reasonable settlement of differences during the First World War. Anglo-French war aims regarding territory and influence, from the Pacific to the Middle East, had helped guarantee that any mediation, whether by Woodrow Wilson or another third party, would fall on deaf ears. The negotiations at the Paris Peace Conference after the war only brought into the open the squalid scramble for empire, formal and informal, that had helped destroy Europe. It was a lesson that Franklin Roosevelt, and Americans of his generation, could not forget.[4]

Roosevelt's critique of colonial empire was consistent, at least while he was President, but not until the Second World War did he gain the opportunity to challenge that system. Whatever his personal distaste for colonialism on moral and humanitarian grounds, his fear that it would disrupt any peace settlement motivated his wartime actions. But the requirements of alliance politics restricted his freedom of action. It would do no good to decolonize Britain if, in the process, the wartime alliance collapsed, thus threatening either victory over the Axis or, equally important, postwar cooperation.[a] That balancing act sometimes required Roosevelt to back and fill, to make short-term adjustments and concessions.

Looked at in isolation, those moves seem important. What appeared trivial to him may have become crucial in a later era. What were intended as temporary fall-back positions became, in some cases, permanent fixtures with his death. But thin historical skeins break when stretched too far. Shall we blame Great Britain's decision to return the Philippine Islands to Spain in 1763 for America's involvement in the war with Japan in 1941? To ask that Roosevelt *achieve* either a forced or a negotiated decolonization of the British and French Empires posits a level of omnipotence that the United States never possessed.[5] He had already exceeded John Quincy Adams' advice to go "not abroad in search of monsters to destroy"—advice that the combination of Nazism and modern technology seemed to make irrelevant. In Roosevelt's mind, the monster of colonialism threatened to bite if not devour the world by plunging it into another huge war.[b]

---

[a] See " 'The Family Circle': Roosevelt's Vision of the Postwar World," elsewhere in this collection.

[b] For further discussion of Roosevelt's anticolonial views, see "Casablanca—The End of Imperial Romance," elsewhere in this collection.

But the British, the French, and the other European colonial nations saw things differently. Many British diplomats and bureaucrats understood that the era of formal colonial empires was ending, and they adjusted their thinking accordingly. Even Winston Churchill occasionally faced that reality, although he was much happier proclaiming "that never would we yield an inch of the territory that was under the British flag."[6] But British officials could all agree that Roosevelt and the United States should not set the terms for new imperial relationships. British leaders may have recognized their nation's decline relative to the United States and the Soviet Union, but they still hoped and planned to maintain a place of power in the postwar world. That required, thought many, some sort of special, if restructured, relationship with their colonial empire. Independence, interdependence, or something in between might have to come, but it would come through the Colonial Office and 10 Downing Street, not the State Department and Pennsylvania Avenue. The Churchill government's effective tactics throughout the war in countering Roosevelt's anticolonialism suggest that the British were less defeatist, or less realistic, about their postwar position than occasional bursts of pessimism might imply.[7]

On the issue of maintaining control over colonies, the French agreed with their allies across the Channel, whatever differences of style, policy, and personality existed between their leader, Charles de Gaulle, and Churchill. During World War II those two men allied to thwart Roosevelt's attempts to negotiate peaceful, planned decolonization. This "in-house" Anglo-French struggle against the United States over colonialism strained allied unity and forced Roosevelt, ever eager to avoid direct confrontation, to pursue postwar decolonization circumspectly.

Besides convincing the British and French that the end of empires was inevitable, Roosevelt also had to persuade nationalist leaders in the various colonies that the United States was genuinely committed to their future independence. As Japan's forces swept through East Asia, Tokyo's propagandists had effectively exploited the racial and political antagonism subject peoples held for "Europeans," including the United States.[8] To dispel the widely held assumption that the United States supported the return of the colonial powers, the administration conducted an extensive worldwide propaganda effort.[9]

While the Office of War Information emphasized American differences with the allies over colonialism, the President launched his own campaign. He traveled around the colonial world throughout the war, stopping in Gambia, French Morocco, Egypt, Malta, and Iran. In almost every case, he made a point of holding private talks with nationalist leaders. Yet he avoided visiting Great Britain despite repeated invitations from Churchill. He repeatedly sent his official and unofficial representatives around the globe to preach the gospel of independence. Everywhere he and his emissaries went, they discussed postwar self-government and freedom with nationalist leaders, emphasizing American differences with the Europeans. At presidential press conferences, the President's favorite forum for public diplomacy, he lashed out repeatedly at the British and French for obstructing progress toward independence. Simultaneously, Roosevelt publicly pushed plans for immediate postwar independence for the Philippines—a clearing of the decks, so to speak—before launching his attack on the colonial empires of others. His intention was that Philippine independence reverberate throughout the European empires, proving that colonial powers could (and should) prepare their "dependencies" for self-government.[10]

Roosevelt shared the prevailing Western view that much of the colonial world was not ready for self-rule and that immediate postwar independence for many colonies would only lead to widespread disorder and conflict. But Roosevelt's own ethnocentrism and distasteful racial notions are not the issue here. Without question, his anticolonialism came with the burdens of paternalism, belief in white and Western superiority, cultural bias, and ignorance; though that hardly warrants comparison with Nazi racial theories. But Roosevelt also believed that, like it or not, complete freedom was inevitable for almost all the European colonies. Some, like India, were nearly suited for independence.[11] Others, like Indochina, required a period of education and training as well as the creation of appropriate internal political structures. If that process were left to the tender mercies of the European colonial powers, little would happen, and their foot-dragging would only create resentment and threaten violence. What some nationalists (and some historians) labeled "gradualism" on Roosevelt's part seemed hasty and precipitous to Churchill.

Roosevelt's political solution for decolonization was an adaptation of a scheme he had proposed for the Western Hemisphere back in 1939. First concerned that Hitler might move into Antarctica, then worried about German expansion into the New World possessions of Nazi-occupied European countries, the President had proposed a Pan-American trusteeship over those territories.[12] He may not have had postwar decolonization in mind when he came up with his hemispheric trusteeship proposal, but when the time came to offer a scheme for the staged, worldwide elimination of the European empires, he proposed an international, institutional framework whereby colonies would be put into a kind of protective custody—what he again called trusteeships. Under this system, an emerging nation would prepare itself for independence with the guidance of one or more experienced nations, sometimes even including the European "parent" state. Being responsible for the "training and education" of colonies held no terror for the European empires. The mandate scheme after World War I had levied similar duties, but to little effect.

What frightened the British and other colonial powers was the President's unshakable insistence on international accountability as the enforcement mechanism for the trusteeship scheme. However vague the details, trusteeship would require the ruling state to follow international (United Nations) rules and to prepare a colony for independence.

The British, recognizing the threat to their freedom of action, sought to modify any trusteeship formula that included international accountability. An advisory role for other nations was the most interference they would accept. When Roosevelt proved insistent, they decided not to negotiate the issue, and evaded American attempts to take up the matter.

Another major obstacle for Roosevelt's anticolonial plans came from China. Although he often "credited" Kuomintang leader Generalissimo Chiang Kai-shek with the idea of placing Indochina and the other Asian colonies into trusteeship, in point of fact, Chiang never endorsed trusteeships on mainland Asia, even if he appeared willing to let the Pacific islands come under that system.[13] Despite evidence of growing internal corruption in Chiang's regime, as well as a reluctance to fight the Japanese, the President handled relations with China gingerly. Not only was that nation's potential enormous, but it was America's most important third world (nonwhite is the phrase that would have been used during World War II) ally, slated to be one of Roosevelt's four postwar "policemen."[c] Concerned that Japan's extensive antiwhite propaganda campaign threatened America's future interests in Asia and Africa, the President carefully promoted Chinese-American friendship as a bridge to the non-European world. He believed China would remain militarily weak for many years, but its inclusion as one of the Big Four publicly demonstrated interracial cooperation between East and West. For psychological reasons, if nothing else, Roosevelt wanted to keep China fighting—whatever that meant—in the war against Japan.

Roosevelt consistently used his vast presidential powers to push for a phaseout of colonial empires, although he sometimes sidetracked his anticolonial initiatives when such moves conflicted with immediate wartime or postwar military and geopolitical objectives. These calculated postponements, particularly those involving India and Indochina, were controversial and brought charges that Roosevelt had abandoned his commitment to colonial independence. But he never wavered in his determination to rid the world of colonial empires. He treated both India and Indochina as metaphors of an antiquated imperial era—two important symbols of a colonial system that would eventually dissolve. What emerges is a President who was not subject to mere whims and impulses, bantering about anticolonial rhetoric for self-satisfaction or to pacify

[c] See " 'The Family Circle,' " for a discussion of the Four Policemen concept.

public opinion and gain domestic support, but a serious world leader who believed that decolonization and independence were the directions in which the world was going. Better that the West lead than follow in the wake of revolution. Better to be part of the process than to lose all influence. It was the classic position of the moderate American reformer, seeking the middle ground between reaction and radical change.

Roosevelt began his anticolonial campaign even before the United States entered the war. A few months prior to the Pearl Harbor attack, the President began pushing for self-government for India, with speedy independence the goal. Given India's symbolic value as the "crown jewel" in the empire, wartime British-sponsored home rule there would signal a turning point in the colonial world. At the same time, Roosevelt argued, a self-governing India would become a more motivated Asian ally against Japan, helping to undermine Japanese propaganda that charged Europeans with keeping yellow and brown people in slavery.[14]

Despite deteriorating British military fortunes in 1940–41, they resisted American suggestions about India. In fact, the military situation in the subcontinent became a justification for British intransigence. Indian Muslims, the largest minority in the land, feared any Hindu-controlled state. The British claimed that, without agreement between the two groups, the bitter dispute would destroy any independent Indian nation and, more to the point, a premature promise of independence could cripple the Imperial Indian Army, which had a large proportion of Muslims. It was an argument they used throughout the war. Thus, in the spring of 1941, when Secretary of State Cordell Hull raised the issue of self-government for India with the British, he got a firm rejection. The British Government had, in 1940, made a vague promise of home-rule and eventual independence, but specifics would come only after the war. When the Americans pushed for a faster timetable, British officials defended the empire, testifying to pro-British Indian loyalty and an already existing wide degree of home-rule for the Indian provinces.[15]

Roosevelt hoped to get a firm British commitment to Indian self-government from Churchill when the two first met in August 1941 at the Atlantic Conference. Even before that meeting, the President had recognized Churchill's stubbornness on the issue, and chose to avoid a confrontation by proposing a purposely vague statement supporting self-determination. The Prime Minister, even more eager to avoid confrontation lest it interfere with his pleas for American aid, quickly tried to exclude the empire with the condition that the phrase applied only to previously self-governing nations conquered by Germany. But then, apparently thinking he had defanged the commitment, Churchill agreed to include it in their joint statement of broad war aims—the unsigned document that was released to the press as the Atlantic Charter.[16]

Roosevelt had, in a classic exercise of public diplomacy, outmaneuvered the Prime Minister. Pro-independence nationalists read the Charter as an unequivocal commitment to independence, as the President intended. Moreover, public attention had been focused on the issue, a form of pressure that Roosevelt used consistently for the rest of the war. Finally, the statement gave the United States the moral high ground in the eyes of the nationalists.[17]

When Roosevelt, in his "day that will live in infamy" speech on 8 December 1941, emphasized that the "*Empire* of Japan" had attacked the United States, Churchill should have been forewarned.[18] The shock and sense of crisis that followed the bombing of Pearl Harbor did not long distract Roosevelt from his anticolonial campaign. When the Prime Minister made a quick trip to Washington,[19] only two weeks after the Japanese attack, to discuss military strategy, the President surprised Churchill by suggesting that Britain commit itself publicly to Indian independence. According to the Prime Minister's own account, he exploded, saying he would resign before granting independence to India. Roosevelt retreated, Churchill said, because "I reacted so strongly and at such length that he never raised it [India] verbally again."[20]

But Churchill chose his words carefully when he wrote his memoirs, leaving a misleading impression. Time and again, Roosevelt raised the issue in correspondence or through intermediaries, although Churchill's personal intensity prompted the President to avoid wasting time with direct discussions on the future of India. Even before the ARCADIA Conference ended, Roosevelt made an indirect move by proposing that the allies issue a Declaration by the United Nations, to be signed by all those fighting the common enemies. Their war aims were to be guided by the vague principles of the Atlantic Charter. By proposing that India be one of the signatories, the President once again raised the flag of independence. Some British officials opposed Indian ratification of the declaration, recognizing that it would link the colony to the Atlantic Charter and further encourage the separatists. But Roosevelt insisted, and after much haggling got his way.[21] The British secretary of state for India, Leo Amery, a staunch defender of empire, bemoaned the fact that a native representative "has signed on behalf of India to yet another resounding declaration which bases itself upon the Atlantic Charter, so it can hardly be said now that India is excluded from its purview."[22] Roosevelt would not have disagreed.

In early 1942, factions in Britain and India—encouraged by the Atlantic Charter and the Declaration by the United Nations—publicly pressured the British war cabinet to fulfill its 1940 pledge of self-government and independence.[23] Roosevelt tried to take advantage of the controversy by arranging for a push from a different direction, using his connection with Chiang Kai-shek—a tactic the President resorted to frequently thereafter. The Generalissimo had visited India, with FDR's endorsement, in February 1942. Ostensibly, Chiang's purpose was to boost Indian morale in the face of a possible Japanese military threat, but privately he tried to get Congress party leaders Mohandas K. Gandhi and Pandit Nehru to support the war. They withheld any commitment, but before Chiang left India he openly challenged Britain to move quickly toward independence for the colony. India's participation in the war, he said, should be a turning point in its struggle for freedom. Chiang then told Roosevelt that internal disunity in India would enable the Japanese military to enter the colony virtually unopposed. But "if the political situation in India were to change for the better, this may prevent the enemy from having any ambitions to enter India."[24]

Roosevelt, armed with Chiang's views, instructed Averell Harriman, then in London as the President's "Special Representative," to bring up discreetly the India question with Churchill. The Prime Minister ignored the subterfuge and responded directly to the President, raising the traditional "white man's burden" defense of Britain's role in the subcontinent. India would be thrown into internal chaos and violence, on the eve of a Japanese invasion, if one or another of the competing separatist/nationalist groups were recognized. Britain had commitments to many minorities—untouchables, various princes, and Moslems (who made up much of the Indian Army) that could not be ignored.[25]

To deflect growing pressure for Indian independence, the British government announced, on 11 March 1942, that Sir Stafford Cripps, an outspoken Labourite supporter of negotiated independence for India, would go on a mission to the subcontinent to offer a proposal for an eventual postwar self-government settlement. To encourage and also be associated with any accommodation, the President sent Louis Johnson to India as his "personal representative," a designation that would give him a special status in the public mind. Johnson arrived in India eager to play an active role as mediator while gaining worldwide recognition for American efforts. But Roosevelt hedged, knowing the high risks involved in the mission, and gave Johnson only unofficial support lest the United States be blamed for a breakdown in talks. The President's fears were well founded, for the British War Cabinet, led by Churchill and the Viceroy in India, Lord Linlithgow, scuttled efforts to gain an understanding.[26] Learning about the breakdown in talks, an exuberant Churchill "danced around the cabinet room. No tea with treason, [he said], no truck with American or British Labour sentimentality, but back to the solemn—and exciting—business of war."[27]

In a cable to Roosevelt, the Prime Minister blamed the Congress party, but the President knew better. Briefed by Johnson, FDR knew that the British had blocked a settlement. Roosevelt immediately sent Churchill a blunt response recommending that Cripps continue his efforts. The President, always careful of his personal relationship with Churchill, warned that "American public opinion" and "the American people" thought Britain responsible for the failure of the mission, and he hinted darkly of the consequences should an unmotivated and passive India fall to the Japanese invaders. But Churchill would not back down and told visiting presidential adviser Harry Hopkins that he would resign rather than yield on India. Faced with Churchill's stonewalling and the threat of a possible Japanese invasion of India, Roosevelt backed off, only to try again when the fear of an invasion of the colony diminished.[28]

Even though the situation in India remained tense, Roosevelt initiated an effort to enlist Soviet support for his broad, ambitious plans to end the colonial order. When Soviet Foreign Minister V. Molotov visited Washington in May–June 1942 to discuss the Second Front and Soviet frontiers, Roosevelt seized the opportunity. He proposed ending the old League of Nations mandate system, replacing it with a temporary international trusteeship scheme that would pave the way for colonial independence. In addition to the mandates, colonies like Indochina, Siam (Thailand), the Malay States, and the Dutch East Indies would be included in the plan: "Each of these areas would require a different lapse of time before achieving readiness for self-government, but a palpable surge toward independence was there just the same, and the white nations thus could not hope to hold these areas as colonies in the long run." Molotov was more interested in postwar controls over Germany and Japan, but agreed that "the President's proposals could be effectively worked out."[29]

By the summer of 1942, Churchill and Roosevelt had developed the technique of discussing decolonization through intermediaries, often presidential adviser Harry Hopkins. As the allied military situation in the Far East improved that summer, Roosevelt continued to prod Churchill on self-government for India. Again, Chiang Kai-shek served as the channel of communications. Disingenuously, Roosevelt passed to Churchill, without comment, a Chiang-to-Roosevelt message which, as the Prime Minister knew, reflected the President's position on Indian independence. Again, Churchill resisted the pressure. Objecting to Chinese interference in what he called Britain's internal affairs, he repeated his argument that the colony's Hindus and Moslems were at fault for their failure to reach an accommodation. He ended by asking Roosevelt to restrain Chiang.[30]

Instead, in autumn 1942, FDR shifted the pressure. His tactic was to focus world opinion on Indian self-government and decolonization in general, by sponsoring Wendell Willkie's overseas tour. Willkie had run for president on the Republican ticket against Roosevelt in 1940, but whatever their political rivalry, they both foresaw that rising nationalism foredoomed colonialism. Each believed that the United States should cultivate relations with emerging nations, offering Americanism as a practical model. Speaking in China, Willkie challenged the imperial powers to give freedom to their colonial peoples. His proposals for immediate commitments, "firm timetables," and international control over the process, all mirrored Roosevelt's thinking.[31] Willkie's repeated condemnations of colonialism prompted Churchill's most famous endorsement of Britain's empire. The declaration came before the luncheon guests, but its real target was Roosevelt: "We mean to hold our own. I have not become the King's First Minister in order to preside over the liquidation of the British Empire."[32]

Rumors of a possible breakthrough in India prompted Roosevelt to again try to act as mediator late in 1942. British officials, misled by Roosevelt's purposefully vague statements, requested a replacement for Louis Johnson, believing that the administration would send someone who would report Britain's side with sympathy and understanding. When Roosevelt announced the appointment of career diplomat and Anglophile William Phillips, the British thought they had gotten their man. But they had only given Roosevelt another opportunity to apply pressure.[33]

Phillips arrived as the President's new "personal representative" in New Delhi on 8 January 1943. He initially kept his cards close to his vest, hoping to avoid an immediate confrontation with the British Viceroy, Lord Linlithgow. For two weeks, Phillips traveled throughout the subcontinent, listening to both pro-British and independence advocates. In the process, he came to support a proposal for self-government offered by Devedas Gandhi, son of the Mahatma. The scheme called for the Mahatma to support Mohammed Jinnah, the Muslim League leader, as India's first Prime Minister, as a way to gain League support for a united India. But young Gandhi pointed out that such an agreement was not possible so long as the British forbade discussions between his father and Jinnah.

Upon returning to New Delhi, Phillips told the Viceroy about Devedas Gandhi's proposal for self-rule and offered to mediate the dispute. But Linlithgow refused to discuss the matter, suggesting instead that the American resume touring the colony to learn more about its problems. Thereafter, Linlithgow thwarted any attempts by Phillips at mediation or involvement. When Mohandas Gandhi, in prison for his separatist activities, began a twenty-one day, life-threatening fast, Linlithgow directed Phillips not to say anything publicly about the matter and denied the American's request to visit Gandhi.

As Gandhi's health deteriorated, the Indian press began to criticize the United States for its silence, labeling the Americans as Britain's collaborator. Aware that Gandhi's death would not only tarnish America's reputation, but also bring chaotic violence that would threaten the war effort and U.S. military personnel in India, Secretary of State Hull pressed the British ambassador in Washington, Lord Halifax, not to let Gandhi die in prison and suggested reviving the Cripps formula as a basis for new discussions with the Congress party. Halifax rejected the proposal, insisting that the administration stay out of the situation. That convinced Roosevelt that Hull should instruct Phillips to approach Linlithgow directly with a blunt message: "President Roosevelt and I [Hull] suggest that you seek an informal interview with the Viceroy and convey to him an expression of our deep concern over the political crisis in India. Please express to His Excellency our hope that a means may be discovered to avoid the deterioration of the situation which would be almost certain to occur if Gandhi dies."[34]

Linlithgow, confident of Churchill's support, continued to reject what he considered improper American intervention in British internal affairs, but Phillips persisted, asking permission to publicize his visit with the Viceroy concerning Gandhi. Borrowing a page from Roosevelt's tactical manual, Phillips disingenuously blamed the American press, claiming that, while he had no desire to cause problems, the press was "ugly" about the matter and demanded to know what the United States was doing. Linlithgow suggested that Phillips merely tell reporters that his function was "to keep in touch with things, . . . but that he had nothing more to say." Phillips retorted that he was in an awkward position, "not so much because of the local press, to which he attached no importance, but because of the American press, by which he was being besieged."[35]

Feeling the heat, Linlithgow complained to Churchill about American interference in the crisis. Once again, the Prime Minister went directly to the source. His message warning the administration to back off went through Halifax to the State Department, but the true addressee was Roosevelt. Once again, the President had to face the fact that American pressure would not alter British policy.[36]

As the administration prepared to disassociate itself from Britain's India policy in the event of Gandhi's death, Phillips continued his extensive travels, privately assuring Indian citizens that American concerns for self-government were being discussed at higher levels, although he could issue no public statement about the situation. But despite the diplomatic constraints on Phillips, the Viceroy remained uneasy. Phillips should leave India, he told London, and then perhaps the Roosevelt administration would finally stop its meddling. But with public attention in India focused on Gandhi, Phillips could not leave without visiting the Indian leader. Since alliance politics prevented the British from demanding the recall of the President's "personal representative," Linlithgow, unable to rid himself of the American, finally allowed Phillips to publicize the re- quest—and the Viceroy's rejection—to visit Gandhi. With that announce- ment, the Indian press blamed the British for Phillips' failure to visit the Mahatma. Phillips hung on for nearly two months, hoping in vain to visit Gandhi. But finally, with the American image of anticolonialism safe for the time, and hopes for a negotiated settlement dashed, his presence served no purpose, and he finally left.[37]

Even while Phillips remained in India trying to mediate a settlement, Roosevelt opened another front in his campaign to phase out the colonial order. Speaking before the Pacific War Council, the President admitted that the defeat of Japan would require a "redistribution of sovereignty of Pacific Islands," but insisted that control of key strong points remain with the "United Nations," not specific nations. He continued that theme during British Foreign Secretary Anthony Eden's visit to Washington in mid-March 1943.[d] Roosevelt hoped to persuade the British to accept American proposals for a trusteeship system, outlined in a Declaration on National Independence that the State Department had worked on since the summer of 1942. The Americans wanted a joint declaration with the British, but all the two had done was exchange drafts for nearly a year. Fundamental British concerns were expressed by Eden when he mistak- enly told the Foreign Office that the proposal "does not favour intrusive interference by outsiders."[38] Disabused of that notion shortly before he left Washington, Eden countered with a joint postwar colonial declara- tion that avoided any commitment to binding international accountabil- ity for the colonial powers, instead leaving such matters in the hands of the "parent" nation. Once again, the Roosevelt administration faced ada- mant, unyielding British opposition to American colonial solutions for India, Hong Kong, or anywhere else.

During one meeting with the President, Eden tried to blunt the pro- posal for international accountability, offering a poison apple by suggest- ing that the Japanese island mandates should come under United States control. That would undermine the notion of international accountabil- ity, and perhaps encourage Roosevelt to abandon the international trus- teeship principle. The President waited a few days, then reaffirmed the American position. With deft casualness, he tossed out various sugges- tions on how to assign postwar responsibility for the colonial world. But the key words, repeated time and again, were "*international* trusteeship"

---

[d] The talks with Eden are also discussed in " 'The Family Circle,' " elsewhere in this collection.

and "*international* administration." Eden had refused to negotiate any colonial settlement that would dismantle the British Empire, but as Hull later told Soviet Ambassador Maxim Litvinov, the United States would press its decolonization objectives despite British stonewalling on India, though with caution so as to avoid any "serious breach."[39]

The revised Declaration on National Independence outlined Roosevelt's wartime agenda for moving colonies toward independence, under the auspices of the postwar international organization soon to be known as the United Nations. The statement reaffirmed the principles of the Atlantic Charter as well as the Declaration by the United Nations, tightly joining all three documents in a commitment to future independence for colonial peoples. It provided for international accountability as the enforcement mechanism. It required colonial powers to prepare their dependent peoples for independence through education and self-government, and to publish timetables for the process. The British were unequivocally opposed, and Roosevelt backed off—but not for long.[40]

With Eden's departure, Roosevelt again turned to his Chinese connection to keep up the pressure on Churchill and the British. Madame Chiang Kai-shek had been in the United States since November 1942, staying part of the time in the White House and talking at length with the President. British officials believed she had great influence on Roosevelt, but at a press conference in April 1943 she presented his proposals on trusteeship as if they were her own, even going so far as to praise the United States for its independence commitment to the Philippines. If the Big Four led the way, she argued, less powerful nations would follow and cooperate in promoting future independence for colonies. India's freedom was the immediate priority. To gain Indian Congress party support for the war, she insisted that the British should immediately release the nationalist, Pandit Nehru, from prison so he could support the war effort. The script could have been, and indirectly must have been, written by the President.[41]

By early 1943, Roosevelt's indirect campaign for decolonization was in high gear. He had already placed British India and all colonial empires "in the dock," to use Churchill's phrase,[42] by sending Phillips to India, and by pushing the Declaration on National Independence. Meanwhile, at the Casablanca Conference in January 1943, with an annoyed Churchill looking on, the President gave his views on decolonization to a receptive Sultan of Morocco, and again privately for Charles de Gaulle, who sided with Churchill on reimposing the prewar colonial order.[e]

There was nothing to be gained by bringing up India or the colonial

---

[e] Roosevelt's meetings with the Sultan and de Gaulle at the Casablanca Conference are discussed in more detail in "Casablanca—The End of Imperial Romance."

issue during his talks with Churchill in Washington in late May 1943. But Roosevelt kept up his backdoor approach by instructing William Phillips to talk with Churchill about the situation in India. Phillips' experience in India had made him sharply critical of British policy, but he still believed that Roosevelt could have done more to press for an independence solution. The President had been pleased by Phillips' tough position but wanted his emissary to experience Churchill's stubbornness.[43]

Phillips soon learned the lesson. When he told the Prime Minister of finding "distrust of British promises for ultimate Indian independence" throughout the subcontinent, Churchill bitterly retorted: "Take India if that is what you want! . . . But I warn you that if I open the door a crack there will be the greatest blood-bath in all history." As Roosevelt had expected, Phillips found it "hopeless to argue."[44]

By the summer of 1943, the British Government, faced with the Declaration on National Independence, began to question whether negotiations with the Americans could ever bring about an acceptable joint position on colonialism. In an aide memoire, the Government rejected the Declaration: for its timetables for independence, for its commitment to international trusteeship, and for not distinguishing between colonial dependencies and sovereign nations which had lost their independence during the war. But their gravest concern was reserved for the word "independence." Forced into a public decision, the Government told the House of Commons it was committed to a unilateral British resolution of the colonial question.[45] Thereafter, they evaded, avoided, and rejected any further negotiations with the Roosevelt administration on decolonization.

The President, however, had shifted his attack to his other favorite target, the French and Indochina. During a 21 July meeting of the Pacific War Council, the President declared that "Indochina should not be given back to the French Empire after the war." After complaining about French exploitation of the region, he held up the Philippines as a model for the way to train a people in democracy, and then concluded that Indochina should be held as a "trustee" while such training took place. A few weeks later, at the first Quebec Conference, Roosevelt handed Churchill a copy of the Declaration on National Independence, hoping the Prime Minister would discuss American proposals. But Churchill refused to comment on the document. When Cordell Hull pressed Eden, the British Foreign Secretary finally decided "to be perfectly frank. . . . It was the word 'independent' which troubled him."[46]

That prompted Roosevelt to shift his campaign to a broader stage, this time the Foreign Ministers Conference in Moscow in October. When the conference began, Hull sent a copy of the Declaration on National Independence to Soviet Foreign Minister Molotov, at the same time alerting Eden of American intentions to discuss the matter with the Soviets. But Eden refused to discuss the topic during a conference session, and prevented Hull from including the Declaration in the conference official record. When Molotov supported Eden's position, the issue was dropped, even though the Soviet Foreign Minister agreed that the subject was of great importance.[47]

Blocked again by British tactics, Roosevelt also faced opposition of a different sort to his decolonization program. This time Chiang Kai-shek challenged the President's trusteeship agenda for Asia. Despite Chiang's repeated genuflections toward the principles of the Atlantic Charter and his assurances that he did not want Indochina, Roosevelt had reason to doubt the Chinese leader's commitment to true independence for Asia. Americans feared that the Chinese hoped to establish relationships with the smaller nations of East and Southeast Asia based upon dependency on China.

Chiang's reaction to the creation of the Southeast Asia Command (SEAC) in August 1943 suggested a postwar political agenda. The Chungking government's considerable military problems and unimpressive performance against the Japanese did not deter Chiang from resisting Anglo-American plans to shift Thailand from his control to the SEAC, which was commanded by British Admiral Lord Louis Mountbatten. Even when Chiang finally compromised and agreed that SEAC operations could include both Thailand and Indochina, he insisted that his government first be consulted about any military or political activities in those areas.[48]

By late 1943, Roosevelt began to realize that Chiang opposed the thrust of American plans for Asia, including trusteeships and the international accountability they would bring. Instead, the Chinese leader insisted on immediate postwar independence for Indochina and other Asian colonies. The Pacific War had been caused, in large measure, by American opposition to the Pan-Asianism that accompanied Japanese expansion. Now Roosevelt faced a similar threat from a different quarter. He had to find a power to replace Japan in East Asia if his scheme for a great power condominium were to work. To give Britain the leading role would only restore colonialism. To let the Soviet Union expand its influence in Asia went way beyond the President's policy of cooperation and, moreover, again introduced European ("white" would have been the word used by Roosevelt) leadership. Direct and acknowledged American dominance went against the grain of American thinking, including that of the President, although a China under the tutelage of the United States was a comfortable concept. Having China act as one of the Four Policemen massaged Chiang's insistence that China be "one of the greatest and strongest nations," and helped keep it in the war against Japan. But Chiang's anti-colonialism, with its heavy emphasis on what the Americans saw as precipitous independence for all Asian colonies, threatened to create unstable governments in former colonies untrained for self-rule. That could necessitate and justify Chinese-sponsored Pan-Asianism, leading Asia in the direction of becoming an exclusive sphere of influence—an unacceptable outcome for Roosevelt.[49] Shortly after the Cairo talks in December 1943, the President commented to General Joseph Stilwell that he hoped Chiang would soon be overthrown, and that the United States was ready to cooperate with his successor.[50] But Chiang hung on, forcing Roosevelt to move to prevent exchanging British, French, and Dutch imperialism in East and Southeast Asia for that of the Chinese.

Roosevelt tried to limit Chinese expansionism by offering Chiang an indirect quid pro quo—an American commitment that China would regain Manchuria, Formosa, and the Pescadore Islands. The President claimed to have received China's support on trusteeship for Indochina at a dinner meeting with Generalissimo and Madame Chiang during the Cairo Conference in November 1943. In separate accounts of the meeting, both FDR and his son, Elliott, repeated that the President told Chiang that the French would never again control Indochina, though they could return as a trustee provided they worked within the United Nations to advance the colony toward independence. In contrast, the Chinese summary makes no mention of trusteeships on mainland Asia, instead emphasizing independence for Indochina, a hint of Sino-American differences that neither Roosevelt mentioned. Chiang also refused to discuss Hong Kong until the President first discussed the colony's future with the British. Chiang opposed Roosevelt's proposal to turn Hong Kong into a free port after Britain returned the colony to China, and the Chinese avoided further talks with the Americans on the colony's future.[51]

Still looking to restrain Chinese expansion, Roosevelt first convinced Chiang, then Churchill, and finally Soviet leader Joseph Stalin (who was not at the Cairo Conference), to issue a press release on Allied Pacific war aims. This "Cairo Declaration" promoted China as a wartime ally, and pledged to return its lost territories. But the President got his quid pro quo, for the document included a specific renunciation by the Chinese of any intentions to expand in Asia.[52]

From Cairo, Roosevelt traveled to Teheran for the first Big Three conference, and for his first meeting with Stalin. During their initial get-together, the Soviet leader brought up the subject of French reactions to nationalist demands in Lebanon,[53] which quickly led the President into a discussion of French colonial rule in Indochina. Stalin told FDR that he did not want the "Allies to shed blood to restore Indochina, for example, to the old French colonial rule," going on to support independence for all colonial subjects. Delighted with Stalin's views, Roosevelt commented "that after 100 years of French rule in Indochina, the inhabitants were worse off than they had been before." When the President brought up his scheme for international trusteeships, implying that Chiang Kai-shek agreed, Stalin gave his support. They then agreed that there was no sense in discussing the question of India with Churchill, and on that note the meeting ended.[54]

To insure the Prime Minister got the message that the Americans were casting about for Soviet support on the issue, Harry Hopkins leaked the substance of the Roosevelt-Stalin talk.[55] Once again, the President avoided a fruitless direct exchange with Churchill while keeping the independence issue in front of the Prime Minister. Nor did Churchill have long to wait before hearing Stalin's views on Indochina.

At dinner that same evening, Stalin again commented that he opposed France's regaining its empire. The President quickly chimed in with his idea for international accountability through trusteeships, limiting his examples to the French possessions of New Caledonia in the Pacific, and Dakar on the west coast of Africa, thus avoiding a clash with Churchill. New Caledonia, said Roosevelt, posed a threat to Australia and New Zealand, and as spokesman for twenty-one American nations, he was concerned that a hostile Dakar would pose a threat to the Western Hemisphere. Churchill interrupted, hoping to change the focus from trusteeships to unilateral control over the islands. He pledged that Britain did not want new territory from the war, but since the Big Four would have the responsibility for postwar peace, some strategic global points should be placed under their individual control. Stalin, ignoring the Prime Minister's remarks, reiterated that France must not have any postwar strategic possessions outside its own border. After Roosevelt became ill and retired early, Stalin continued to argue with Churchill that the French Empire should not be returned to France.

The next evening, the President led his colleagues into a discussion on international trusteeships that prompted a sharp reply from Churchill. Roosevelt stated that the occupation of bases and strongholds in the vicinity of Germany and Japan must be placed under trusteeship. After Stalin agreed, Churchill took the offensive. He denied any British intention to expand its empire, but adamantly insisted that "nothing would be taken away from England without a war." If independence came, it would be as Britain decided. Stalin, who had supported the President's suggestion, sarcastically remarked that Britain's admirable performance during the war warranted an increase in the British Empire, particularly around Gibraltar. Hoping for a quid pro quo, Churchill inquired as to

Soviet territorial interests. But Stalin, content with having planted the seed, deferred, promising to address the matter "when the time comes."[56]

Even before the Big Three had shaken the dust of Teheran from their shoes, Roosevelt returned to his anticolonial campaign. Back in Washington by mid-December, he told the ambassadors from Great Britain, the Soviet Union, Turkey, Egypt, and Iran about his trusteeship plans for Indochina. Because the Indochinese had not been properly prepared for immediate independence, he suggested that a trusteeship would enable the country to develop along the Philippines model. The discussion prompted Churchill again to procrastinate, telling Eden that "until we are officially apprised of these declarations we should . . . have no part in them and must reserve our opinion." The Prime Minister followed with a memorandum, passed to Secretary of State Hull, that outlined official British policy goals for Indochina. At the same time, Halifax was asked to learn more about Roosevelt's plans.[57]

The British ambassador could not get a straight answer from Hull, but, a few weeks later, Roosevelt laid out his position before his favorite soundingboard on colonialism, the Pacific War Council. Although he did not mention Indochina, his proposal of trusteeship for Korea as well as the islands south of the Equator had a familiar ring. Shortly afterward, the President breezily remarked to Halifax that Indochina would be included in the trusteeship plan, although neither the British nor the Dutch had to worry since they "had done a good job" with their colonies.[58]

Roosevelt's private assurances could hardly have convinced the British, since he returned to his public attacks on colonialism almost immediately. At a press conference on 1 February 1944, the President chose "to respond" to Indian nationals who charged that the United States supported British imperialism. Even while he insisted that the military defeat of Japan remained primary, he linked Allied policy to America's postwar liberation objectives in the Philippines. The British and Dutch were "brothers in arms," he insisted, determined to liberate Burma, Malaya, and the East Indies from Japan, just as America sought to liberate the Philippines.[59]

But such solidarity was short-lived. As the British feared, Roosevelt soon dropped the other shoe. Only four days later, during another press conference, he delivered his most ringing condemnation of the evils of colonialism. Speaking to a group of black American publishers, he used Gambia, a small British colony in West Africa, as his case in point:

It's the most horrible thing I have ever seen in my life. . . . The natives are five thousand years back of us. . . . The British have been there for two hundred years—for every dollar that the British have put into Gambia, they have taken out ten. It's just plain exploitation of those people. . . . Those people, of course, they are completely incapable of self-government. You have got to give them some education first. Then you have got to better their health and their economic position. . . . The United Nations ought to have an inspection committee of all these colonies that are way, way down the line, that are not ready to have anything to say yet because the owning country has given them no facilities.

And if we sent—sent a committee from the United Nations . . . to go down to Gambia, "If you Britishers don't come up to scratch—toe the mark—then we will let all the world know."

After that unusually detailed description of how decolonization should work, Roosevelt went on to mock what he said was Churchill's attempt to embarrass the United States by sending an international committee to investigate conditions in the American South. Gleefully, the President passed on his retort: "Winston, that's all right with me. Go ahead and do it. Tell the world. But—what you people were talking about—we call it freedom of the press, and you also call it 'pitiless publicity'—you can right a lot of wrongs with 'pitiless publicity.' "[60] It was a bravura performance.

As so often with Roosevelt, the public target was not the primary one. Granted, he genuinely castigated European colonialism in Africa, and his condemnation of Britain's failures in Gambia were sincere. But it is difficult to determine just where Africa fit in Roosevelt's decolonization scheme. He relegated sub-Saharan Africa to that group of societies that were not ready for even rudimentary forms of self-government, but his promises to the Sultan of Morocco suggests a more ambitious schedule for North Africa. In any event, the blame lay with the failure of the European nations to develop native economies or to prepare their colonies for home rule. The President's visits to and public support of the two independent black African states, Ethiopia and Liberia, was interpreted by Africans, Afro-Americans, and the European colonial powers as a gesture of support for decolonization. Although Roosevelt did not respond directly to a campaign by American Pan-African groups to get a public commitment to independence for African colonies, a separate division of African affairs was established in the State Department by January 1944.[61] But the decolonization of Africa would come once the principle was established firmly in India and Indochina.

Likewise for Korea. Roosevelt's comments regarding a trusteeship for that nation promised "ultimate independent sovereignty," although a training period of "perhaps forty years" would be needed. But, as Under Secretary of State Sumner Welles told Roosevelt in April 1942, following a Chinese government suggestion of a public commitment to Korean independence, it made no sense to make such a promise until the more important question of independence for India was resolved. The specifics of colonial independence always posed a whole new set of problems—as specifics so often did for Roosevelt. Thereafter, the question of Korean independence became tangled with the decision whether to recognize one or another specific nationalist group, although United States policy was, as in so many other cases, affected by gradualism and a failure to appreciate the intensity of Korean nationalism.[62] Roosevelt had picked his targets—India and Indochina. The people of societies like Gambia and Korea would have to be patient.

The British Foreign Office, recognizing that Indochina served as a precedent for all the colonial world, proposed countering Roosevelt's trusteeship plans with a scheme designed to enable the French to regain the colony. But Churchill wanted no part of any sort of Anglo-American discussions about decolonization, and counseled delay until after the fall 1944 presidential election. As he wrote to Eden: "I do not consider the chance remarks which the President made in conversation should be the basis for setting all this ponderous machinery in motion."[63]

But Roosevelt's proposal was far from being "chance remarks." To get around Churchill's stonewalling, the President instructed Undersecretary of State Edward R. Stettinius to prod the British on American proposals during an upcoming trip to London in April. During briefings for Stettinius and Dr. Isaiah Bowman, a State Department adviser on colonial affairs, both FDR and Hull voiced their opposition to European colonialism and stressed the need for Anglo-American negotiations. "Hull complained that the British and French were 'taking great amounts of wealth' out of the Middle East and leaving 'very little for the peoples themselves.' The policy of the United States, he concluded, should be to 'work for a more equitable economic system.' "

Bowman wanted direction on tactics: "Well, Mr. President, you stated that you had not gotten very far with the British on this issue. Do you want us to bring it up again?" "Yes, by all means," the President said, "it is something I think we should discuss with them at every opportunity." Roosevelt went on to criticize French rule in Indochina in the same vein as his "chance remarks" about Gambia, pointing out that the British feared that the solution proposed for Indochina would be applied to British colonies in places like Malaya and Burma. Wishfully, the President insisted that Chiang Kai-shek did not want Indochina because "its people and the country as a whole were completely different from their own. He thought a trusteeship would be an ideal arrangement."[64]

Following their longtime policy, the British Government refused to budge from its own colonial declaration during talks with Stettinius and Bowman. Indochina never came up for consideration. Bowman's eagerness to arrange a joint Anglo-American agreement on decolonization prompted him to drop the American Declaration on National Independence and to accept limitations on the responsibilities of the trustees. With these apparent concessions, some British officials falsely believed that progress was made in convincing the Americans to lessen their demands. But the British soon learned otherwise.[65]

Even while Anglo-American negotiations were again getting nowhere, the administration continued to send signals supporting freedom for the colonial world. During the spring of 1944, both Vice President Henry Wallace and Secretary Hull each voiced support for independence. British concern over the public campaign against them heightened during the summer when Wallace visited China in an attempt to rebuild the spirit of Willkie's visit there two years earlier.[66] Then, in July, British anxiety levels soared when columnist Drew Pearson printed most of the text of a confidential report William Phillips had earlier sent to FDR concerning India. This report (leaked, one somehow suspects, at the pleasure if not connivance of the President) was strikingly similar in tone to the messages from Chiang Kai-shek in 1942 that had criticized British rule in India. In addition, Pearson accurately described Churchill's outburst during Phillips' visit to London. Whatever Roosevelt's role in the matter, the episode highlighted his opposition to British policy in India.[67]

Roosevelt had long treated Indochina as a matter for Anglo-American negotiations, since he refused to recognize de Gaulle's leadership of France. Nevertheless, in the wake of Churchill's intransigence on decolonization, the administration decided not to pursue the contentious issue at the Dumbarton Oaks Conference in August 1944, where the allies negotiated over the creation of the future United Nations Organization.[68]

But the British did more than just balk at negotiations on the colonial issue. In the summer of 1944, they helped Gaullist agents to enter Indochina. Later that year, Churchill allowed French military personnel to participate in activities of the Southeast Asia Command. Such actions should have had Roosevelt's approval and, in fact, the British had obtained the go-ahead from the American military chiefs for the SEAC mission. The military had failed to pass this information immediately to the White House, but that made little difference. Ignorant or not of the arrangement, Roosevelt, to prevent the French from getting their foot in the door, rebuffed all proposals from within the administration and from British and Gaullist representatives to approve the French mission at SEAC. Anticipating a confrontation, British and American officials prepped their respective leaders for a discussion of Indochina during the second Quebec Conference scheduled for September, but the two avoided the subject during their face-to-face talks. Roosevelt tried to thwart Anglo-French designs in Indochina indirectly by continuing to withhold recognition of de Gaulle's Committee of National Liberation (FCNL) as the legitimate French authority. But the pressure of events forced the President finally to give in and accept de Gaulle in late October. Even so, Roosevelt continued to insist that France play no official military role in Indochina.[69]

The usual Churchill-Roosevelt indirect approach on the colonial issue was discarded at Quebec by the Prime Minister, and on the most sensitive issue of all—India. Angry over the President's failure to disavow the criticisms of British policy attributed to Phillips by the Drew Pearson column, the Prime Minister spoke bitterly of the difficulties of administering the colony, and bemoaned "the lack of understanding in the United States about the Indian problem." Death, ignorance, poverty, disease—all indicated the need for the British to stay in India. Knowing that he could not convert Roosevelt, Churchill offered a sarcastic proposal: "I will give the United States half of India to administer and we will take the other half and we will see who does better with each other's half." The bickering once again demonstrated the irreconcilable nature of the two leaders' postwar colonial goals.[70]

In the closing months of the war—and Roosevelt's life—the fate of Indochina came to dominate his efforts to implement the scheme for decolonization and trusteeships. He had consistently rejected suggestions to return France to its prewar imperial status. Instead he planned to include Indochina in the trusteeship system—a move that would limit French or Chinese control over the colony—and pave the way for independence. This, in conjunction with sovereignty for the Philippines and for India, would begin the unraveling of the entire colonial structure.

But avoiding the issue could not put the President's plan into operation. Churchill had already maneuvered past the White House to arrange for French representation at SEAC—a first step in his plan to have France regain sole control over Indochina. The President refused to legitimize that presence and, in mid-October, rejected a plan to provide materials to resistance groups inside Indochina. Despite his desire to disrupt Japanese military operations, he withheld approval because the French were to be consulted. He chose not to try to expel them from SEAC lest that damage allied unity while other options, particularly the upcoming Yalta Conference, were still available. At the same time, he instructed his subordinates not to recognize the French mission at SEAC or engage "the French or anyone else" in political issues in Asia. When Churchill tried to present the French presence in Indochina as a fait accompli—something Mountbatten had recommended six months earlier—Roosevelt, after some delay, rejected the proposal, telling Stettinius on 1 January 1945: "I still do not want to get mixed up in any Indochina decision. It is a matter for post war. By the same token, I do not want to get mixed up in any military effort toward the liberation of Indochina from the Japanese. You can tell Halifax that I made this very clear to Mr. Churchill. From both the military and civilian point of view, action at this time is premature."[71]

Churchill had already received a warning from Halifax that the State Department was again pushing Roosevelt's trusteeship scheme. The Department first wanted to discuss the matter informally with British officials, then hold talks with Colonial Secretary Oliver Stanley, who could visit Washington before returning home from a scheduled trip to the British West Indies. The news prompted Churchill to remind Eden about protecting British interests:

> There must be no question of our being hustled or seduced into declarations affecting British sovereignty in any of the Dominions or Colonies. . . . If the Americans want to take Japanese islands which they have conquered, let them do so with our blessing and any form of words that may be agreeable to them. But "Hands off the British Empire" is our maxim, and it must not be weakened or smirched to please sob-stuff merchants at home or foreigners of any hue.

Eden assured Churchill not to worry, but about two weeks later, the Prime Minister again cautioned the Foreign Secretary that British sovereignty over the colonies had to be protected by avoiding any commitment to binding international accountability.[72]

Although Roosevelt told Halifax he would not support the military campaign proposed by Britain for Indochina, the President seemed to compromise his position when, on 4 January 1945, without telling subordinates, he approved Mountbatten's request to use French commandos for an operation inside Indochina aimed at destroying Japanese communications.[73] The President may have believed the operation would hasten victory over Japan and ultimately save American lives, and that it was too small to serve as a means to restore Indochina to French control. But more likely, Roosevelt viewed this as a special, unofficial situation and, moreover, had begun to accept the necessity of France's being a "trustee" for Indochina, even while insisting that colonialism be eliminated.

When Oliver Stanley visited Washington in mid-January, the President avoided a confrontational policy debate on the future of the European empires; but, in a jaunty style that belied the intensity of his convictions, he reaffirmed his plans for the dissolution of the British, French, and Dutch empires. Indochina would not be returned to France, but would be "administered by a group of nations selected by the United Nations." Burma, Java, Sumatra, Dutch New Guinea, Hong Kong, Gambia, and Morocco all came up in a context that made clear to Stanley that Roosevelt believed the impulse toward independence was irreversible, and that the United States would play an important role in bringing it about.

The President did allow that the United States wanted to occupy "as guardian" a few of the North Pacific islands which had been a Japanese mandate since World War I. This reinforced the British belief that the Americans intended to act in old colonial style, expanding in the Pacific as a means of becoming that region's key Western player.[74]

Churchill hoped to use what he saw as American colonial aspirations to defuse Roosevelt's trusteeship design. The British were quite happy with "guardianship" so long as it came without international accountability. But they failed to grasp what the President had in mind. Although he believed that American security interests required base sites in the Pacific, the relationship was to be modeled on the Anglo-American agreements in the Western Hemisphere. The islands were to retain their sovereignty. Where islands were not yet ready for independence, international regional commissions would supervise progress toward that goal.[75] Once again, the key was international accountability.

Stanley's visit had only reaffirmed British stubbornness over decolonization, driving home to Roosevelt the need to increase the pressure. Thus, at Yalta, the President stepped up his campaign to enlist Stalin in the cause. The Soviets had already approved the trusteeship principle and wanted it included in the Charter of the United Nations Organization. When Roosevelt met privately with Stalin he got the Marshal's support for trusteeships over Korea and Indochina. The President repeated his earlier promise to support Soviet access to Darien as a warm-water port, but he coupled that with international control over the port city because of its similarity to Hong Kong. Echoing the past dreams of countless American traders, Roosevelt called for the British to return that city to the Chinese, who would turn it into "an internationalized free port." Stalin readily agreed.[76]

But Stalin's support, however useful and for whatever motives, did not spell victory for Roosevelt. He had to gain British approval, or at least acquiescence, for decolonization and the trusteeship scheme. After all, the President's overall postwar system depended upon great power cooperation—and Britain was to be one of the Four Policemen. A military confrontation with Great Britain over the issue of empire was unthinkable; but the President had no qualms about applying heavy pressure on Churchill. After all, one speaks to members of the family with a candor and bluntness that would alienate an outsider. Stalin had to be treated with care lest his suspicions become irreversible; Churchill spoke the same language, so there was less need to be so careful.

The next day, with Stalin's support, Roosevelt had Secretary of State Stettinius spring the trusteeship plan on an unsuspecting Churchill. The Prime Minister's initial reaction was predictable:

I absolutely disagree. I will not have one scrap of British territory flung into that area [trusteeships]. After we have done our best to fight in this war and have done no crime to anyone I will have no suggestion that the British Empire is to be put into the dock and examined by everybody to see whether it is up to their standard. No one will induce me as long as I am Prime Minister to let any representative of Great Britain go to a conference where we will be placed in the dock and asked to justify our right to live in a world we have tried to save.[77]

Churchill calmed down a bit after Stettinius deceptively told him that the British Empire was not included in the trusteeship scheme. As the secretary of state explained it, the trusteeship plan included three categories: existing League of Nations mandates, territory that would be taken from the enemy, and territory that might be placed in trusteeship voluntarily. This explanation apparently satisfied the Prime Minister, for he initialed a hastily written memo composed by the Americans that put the trusteeship protocol into the United Nations Charter.

It was a move reminiscent of Churchill's actions back in August 1941 when he agreed to a self-determination clause in the Atlantic Charter.[78] In both instances, he thought Britain was exempt, while the President planned otherwise. Perhaps the Prime Minister wishfully accepted Stettinius' explanation at face value; perhaps the American pressure persuaded Churchill that the colonial issue was jeopardizing his plans for an Anglo-American postwar entente; perhaps he failed to recognize that British-controlled mandates were automatically included in the trusteeship formula. But most likely, the word "voluntary" lulled him into thinking the entire agreement was harmless, since the decision to "volunteer" a colony for the scheme would be at Britain's time and pace.

But the "voluntary" formula did not render the trusteeship system harmless to Britain's empire. Roosevelt, satisfied with what he had won, agreed to postpone further discussions on the specific territories to be included in the trusteeship formula until after the United Nations conference, scheduled for May 1945 in San Francisco. But the President was confident that "pitiless publicity" would force the European imperial powers toward decolonization and his trusteeship plan, and to initiate that process, he renewed his public campaign, returning once again to the crucial question of the French Empire in Southeast Asia.[79]

Roosevelt had not raised the Indochina issue with Churchill during their Yalta talks, but enroute home aboard the USS *Quincy*, in an "off the record" exchange with reporters, the President vigorously attacked the French and British Empires, contrasting them unfavorably with the admirable Dutch commitment to colonial independence and the successful United States performance in the Philippines.[80] His condemnation of

French colonial rule in Southeast Asia again echoed, sometimes almost word for word, his tirade of a year earlier about British rule in Gambia. The mention of a French return to Indochina seemed a major shift, but their role was to be as one of a group of trustees, all subject to international accountability:

> They [the French] have been there over a hundred years and have done nothing about educating them [the Indochinese]. For every dollar they have put in, they have taken out ten. The situation there is a good deal like the Philippines were in 1898. The French have done nothing about it.
>
> With the Indo-Chinese, there is a feeling they ought to be independent but are not ready for it. I suggested at the time, to Chiang, that Indo-China be set up under a trusteeship—have a Frenchman, one or two Indo-Chinese, and a Chinese and a Russian because they are on the Coast, and maybe a Filipino and an American—to educate them for self-government. It took fifty years for us to do it in the Philippines.
>
> Stalin liked the idea. China liked the idea. The British don't like it. It might bust up their empire, because if the Indo-Chinese were to work together and eventually get their independence, the Burmese might do the same thing to the King of England.[81]

At this point, Roosevelt's two key postwar designs—great power collaboration, and decolonization of European empires—pulled against each other. Although the Soviet Union had expressed support for both, the British continued their adamant rejection of American prescriptions for the colonial world. That adamancy was only intensified by de Gaulle's insistence that restoration of the empire was a prerequisite for French cooperation after the war, since Churchill feared that an American withdrawal from Europe could leave Britain facing the Soviet Union alone. If the British refused to negotiate on the question of empire, then Roosevelt had to back off lest direct coercion jeopardize the establishment of his Four Policemen.

But how to avoid confrontation without losing the battle? Colonialism threatened the postwar settlement, but so would great power disputes. France and Britain refused to negotiate decolonization, so the trick was to commit them to that result in a politically palatable way. Hence international trusteeships, even ones that permitted the "parent" state to oversee the process. Roosevelt's decision to work with France and Britain was not a case of blind Eurocentrism—though there was much of that in the State Department and even among some White House advisers. Rather, his postwar scheme depended on harmonious great power cooperation.[82]

Indochina remained the test case for the President's trusteeship plan, but it was increasingly difficult to prevent some type of French reoccupation of that colony. French forces had already been admitted into SEAC, and there were new plans every day calling for more and more French involvement in that theater of operations, particularly after the Japanese formally displaced the remnants of the Vichy regime on 9 March. Chiang was no alternative since he was unable (or perhaps unwilling) to prosecute the war, and seemed to have imperial designs of his own, although General Albert Wedemeyer, Roosevelt's representative on Chiang's China-Burma-India Command, insisted that Indochina belonged to that theater of operations.[83] Ever optimistic, Roosevelt sought to make a silk purse out of a sow's ear. Let France be the sole trustee for Indochina, Roosevelt told adviser Charles Taussig during a discussion about empires and the postwar world, but under the formula agreed to at the Yalta talks.

> If we can get the proper pledge from France to assume for herself the obligations of a trustee, then I [Roosevelt] would agree to France retaining these colonies with the proviso that independence was the ultimate goal. I asked the President if he would settle for self-government. He said no. I asked him if he would settle for dominion status. He said no—it must be independence.[84]

As was so often the case with Roosevelt, what seemed a new idea was, in fact, something that had been in his mind for some time. Back in the autumn of 1942, during discussions about the future of European colonies in the Caribbean, he mused about a federation of those islands with the other concerned nations—that is, the United States and the colonial powers—acting as "a joint trust or international supervisory authority, or as a sort of holding company."[85]

Roosevelt's conditions for French reinvolvement in Indochina were a trap designed to get them to dissolve their entire empire, not just in Southeast Asia. By gaining sole trusteeship under terms of the agreement signed by Churchill at Yalta, the French would accept international accountability. By agreeing to independence as the goal, the French would tie progress toward that end to international supervision by the United Nations, an organization where the Great Powers, including the United States, would set the standards. Sole trusteeship and international trusteeship would achieve the same result, independence. Thus, Roosevelt tried to preserve his principles while allowing the French back into its Southeast Asian colonies. His trusteeship scheme—with the international accountability mechanism in place—was designed to prevent just the sort of struggles for national liberation that engulfed France and later the United States in Indochina.

In fact, some British officials suspected just what Roosevelt intended.[86] While Churchill and Eden refused to admit that trusteeship would radi-

cally affect British colonial policy and the future of the empire, Oliver
Stanley read the President correctly:

> Colonel Stanley thought that it would be very difficult to go ahead on the old
> basis in view of the Protocol. We could hardly argue that we did not know
> what territorial trusteeship meant, as if we did, it would be open to the Ameri-
> cans to inquire why in that case we had signed the Yalta Protocol. He was
> inclined to think that the Americans meant by territorial trusteeship something
> on the lines of the old mandate system, but modified to make supervision more
> strict.[87]

The British embassy in Washington soon confirmed Stanley's fears. On
23 March, Halifax reported a State Department proposal calling for the
United Nations to have wide-ranging monitoring powers over progress in
the colonies. Under this new proposal, an apparatus of experts—doctors,
sanitary engineers, social workers, economists, and the like—would report their findings to the world organization. Anxiety in the War Cabinet
increased as British officials waited for the next American proposal aimed
at dismantling the empire. Those fears only heightened as the San Francisco Conference drew nearer, particularly since Australia, New Zealand,
Canada, and India all indicated support for the substance of American
proposals on trusteeship. This forced Churchill to suggest that "as a
matter of tactics," the Dutch and the French should take the lead in objecting "to arrangements for placing their colonies under voluntary
trusteeship."[88]

While the British were busy devising a defensive strategy to protect the
empire, Roosevelt worked on offensive plans for escalating the pressure.
The State Department outlined the President's scheme for international
accountability in a memorandum that State hoped would gain acceptance
at the San Francisco Conference. Turning, as usual, to public diplomacy,
the administration sought to promote worldwide support for the formula
by releasing the "secret" Yalta trusteeship protocol.[89]

On 5 April, in Warm Springs, Georgia, at what turned out to be
Roosevelt's last press conference, he turned up with Philippine President
Sergio Osmena in tow. FDR suggested that reporters prepare stories they
could release in a week or so, once Roosevelt returned to Washington. He
and President Osmena had had "a nice talk," remarked FDR, and he had
pledged that when the islands were cleared of Japanese troops, the Philippines would gain immediate independence. The granting of "immediate"
independence, even before the war had ended, would send an unmistakable notice to the European powers that the prewar colonial order was
over, and the President wanted to be sure the reporters passed on the
message.

At that same meeting, Roosevelt publicly outlined American plans to exercise control over various Pacific islands. His, and the military's, explanation was that such control would prevent Japan from ever posing a threat to peace in the region. But some interesting concepts accompanied the plan. First, "the Filipinos and ourselves would . . . take care of that section of the Pacific." Second, there was no mention of China and its role in the Pacific—an omission reminiscent of Sherlock Holmes and the dog that did not bark in the night. Nor would Roosevelt brook any interference from the military over trusteeships for those Pacific islands. He sympathized with their concerns, and planned to install bases in a number of strategic Pacific locations, but he rejected American sovereignty over the islands and insisted instead that the territories be included in the United Nations trusteeship system.[90] Assistant Secretary of State Adolf Berle, the diplomat assigned the task of negotiating postwar airbase agreements, sensed the temptation, writing in his diary that such bases tend "to delimit what might be called the 'American Empire'—except that we do not propose to make it an empire."[91]

Roosevelt suspected that some of his own people did not either understand or accept his approach, and no wonder. That Harry Hopkins seemed to favor a return of France to Indochina, and Henry Stimson was lukewarm about the trusteeship conception, may have warned FDR that old State Department hands like James Dunn and a weathervane like Edward Stettinius might go so far as to deny that the President ever intended to keep France out of Indochina. Perhaps that is why he scheduled a meeting with military and State Department personnel for 19 April, only a week before the start of the San Francisco Conference, to ensure that they presented his proposals on trusteeships.[92] According to Roosevelt's instructions, State Department officials were to discuss trusteeship plans with British, Soviet, French, and Chinese officials prior to the conference. But British officials were reluctant to engage in these talks.[93] Churchill's approval, wittingly or not, of the trusteeship concept at Yalta posed serious problems. With much of the colonial world slated for trusteeship, how could the British prevent their colonies from petitioning and gaining that status? India already had limited self-government and a vague promise of independence. Full freedom would, no doubt, follow the war, irrespective of American efforts. Indian independence and aiming Indochina toward that status through trusteeship spelled the end of the colonial order—and not on a schedule to Britain's choosing.

At the time of his death on 12 April 1945, Roosevelt had taken steps to press his trusteeship scheme at the San Francisco meeting and beyond. Whatever short-term concessions he thought expedient, he never retreated from his insistence on the need to phase out the European colonial empires that threatened the peace of the world. Granted, trusteeships were far from a cure-all. His sensitivity to the desires of the native populations was superficial at best. All Koreans, for example, could agree that what was acceptable for "the uncivilized aborigines of the South Seas" was an insult to a nation with a history of forty centuries of independence.[94] But consensus was Roosevelt's style, and, given his commitment to independence for the colonial world, such complaints would likely have prompted a change in the trusteeship category or a firm schedule for independence.

Does this mean that Franklin Roosevelt, like other Americans before and after him, was "protected from having to come to terms with the contradictions in nation building by the conviction . . . that America had a special talent for liberating colonized people?"[95] There is no question that FDR considered that he, speaking for the American nation, possessed a special and enlightened perspective about colonialism. And, compared to his other partners in the Big Three, that was true. He was far more prescient about the fate of colonial empires than either Churchill or the supposed revolutionary, Stalin, although even the President failed to predict the speed and suddenness of the demise of the European empires. The problem for Roosevelt was not so much "protection" from the contradictions of power and principle, as it was the dilemma of trying to encourage, even force, negotiated decolonization without destroying the basis for trust and cooperation built up during the war. The postwar Soviet-American confrontation should not obscure the fact that both China and Britain (with France) were integral to the great power system that Roosevelt believed necessary to prevent, or at least postpone, another war. He saw colonialism as a dangerous anachronism, something his successors found out in Vietnam.

But what gain was there in eliminating colonialism at the cost of alienating Britain? It was the same dilemma he faced in relations with the USSR: how to strike a balance between the absolute need to include that nation as a cooperative partner in the postwar system, and the threat to that cooperation posed by certain Soviet political goals. In trying to gain the trust of Stalin and the Soviets, Roosevelt drew condemnation as an appeaser (although there are those who claim he did not go far enough). In trying to force the elimination of colonial empires, he drew the criticisms of those who claim that he not only compromised too much, but that he laid the seeds as well for an American Empire.[96] But narrow self-interest was not the explanation for Roosevelt's insightful analysis of colonialism and nationalism, even if his solution was compatible with what seemed best for the United States. The American "blind spot" regarding colonialism in the Philippines must be viewed in the context of the President's commitment to immediate Philippine independence—the indispensable first step. The inevitable special relationship between colonized and colonizer that followed had imperial overtones, both economic and political, but that is a different problem. This also applies to America's relationship with all regions previously dominated by the European empires. It was Roosevelt's successors, operating in the changed circumstances of the postwar world, either lacking or not sharing his vision, who set the United States on a different course.

"Two steps left close": Roosevelt meets with Polish-Americans.

VIII

Naked Reverse Right: Roosevelt, Churchill, and Eastern Europe, from TOLSTOY to Yalta—and a Little Beyond

On 28 September 1944, President Franklin D. Roosevelt cabled Prime Minister Winston S. Churchill a brief, but revealing, message: "I think we are all in agreement . . . as to the necessity of having the U.S.S.R. as a fully accepted and equal member of any association of the great powers formed for the purpose of preventing international war. It should be possible to accomplish this by adjusting our differences through compromise by all the parties concerned." Then, in a phrase added to the draft in his own scrawl, Roosevelt laid out the essence of his policy toward the Soviet Union: "and this ought to tide things over for a few years until the child learns to toddle."[1]

What follows is an examination of Roosevelt's and Churchill's Russian policies as they are reflected in the correspondence of the two wartime leaders. Such a view from the top is both out of style and far from the full story. Nevertheless, we can learn from the exchanges between those two national leaders, for each was, after all, the single most influential policymaker for his nation.

During the Quebec Conference in the fall of 1944, Roosevelt and Churchill apparently discussed plans for a tripartite conference with Joseph Stalin. Roosevelt reportedly claimed that he could not attend such a meeting until after the November presidential election. After disdainfully commenting that the Red Army would not stand and wait for results, Churchill decided to arrange his own meeting with Stalin. Convinced that Anglo-American military successes in France had changed the balance of power between the Soviet Union and the Western Allies, he vowed to press the advantage and work out an agreement with Stalin about Eastern Europe, particularly Poland. On 27 September, Churchill cabled Stalin to suggest a meeting between the two in Moscow, with a Big Three meetings to follow after the American presidential election. Churchill hoped to operate as the spokesman for both the British and the Americans during his

Originally published in *Diplomatic History* 9 (Winter 1985), pp. 1–24. Copyright 1985 by Scholarly Resources Inc. Reprinted by permission of Scholarly Resources Inc. Portions of this essay were adapted from the author's *Churchill & Roosevelt*. An earlier version was presented as the Georgetown University Department of History's Distinguished Alumni Lecture, 2 May 1984.

meeting with Stalin, and at first Roosevelt agreed. When the Prime Minister cabled that "the bulk of our business will be about the Poles, but you and I think so much alike about this that I do not need any special guidance about your views," FDR wished him "every success in your visit to U.J." and agreed that Ambassador Averell Harriman needed only to "be available for advice and consultation."[2] But Harry Hopkins, whom Churchill mistakenly believed to be Britain's best friend at the White House, convinced Roosevelt not to let the Prime Minister assume the role of broker between the United States and the USSR. Roosevelt finally cautioned Churchill:

> I can well understand the reasons why you feel that an immediate meeting between yourself and Uncle Joe is necessary before the three of us can get together. The questions which you will discuss there are ones which are, of course, of real interest to the United States, as I know you will agree. I have therefore instructed Harriman to stand by and to participate as my observer, if agreeable to you and Uncle Joe, and I have so informed Stalin. While naturally Averill [sic] will not be in a position to commit the United States—I could not permit anyone to commit me in advance—he will be able to keep me fully informed and I have told him to return and report to me as soon as the conference is over.[3]

While Churchill reserved the right to hold "private tête-à-têtes" with the Soviets, Roosevelt had put himself in his favorite position—uncommitted and free to swing his weight to one side or the other.

The 1944 Moscow Conference between Churchill and Stalin began on the evening of 9 October and concluded on the evening of 17 October, an unusually long meeting. Those talks, and the ones held between Foreign Ministers V. M. Molotov and Anthony Eden were unique. With the exception of the 1941 discussions between Eden and Molotov, which that early in the war were necessarily exploratory and inconclusive, the Moscow conversations were the only time undisguised power politics predominated at a wartime conference. With the United States represented only by Ambassador Harriman, who acted as an observer rather than a participant, Churchill and Stalin spoke as if matters in Eastern Europe were theirs and only theirs to decide. That was particularly true during their private, informal conversations when the American ambassador was not present. Although both Churchill and Stalin passed on the gist of their talks to Harriman and the President, the atmosphere of those talks—an atmosphere that can be recreated from the British minutes—was missing from those reports.[4]

A spheres-of-influence arrangement with the Soviets was nothing new for Churchill. On 1 October 1939, when he was First Lord of the Admiralty, he had justified in part the Nazi-Soviet nonaggression pact as a legitimate expression of Soviet interests. Speaking publicly, Churchill labeled Russia "a riddle wrapped in a mystery inside an enigma," but he went on to explain that the puzzle might be solved by looking at "Russian national interest." "That the Russian armies could stand on this line [the Soviet-German border in what had been central Poland] was clearly necessary for the safety of Russia against Nazi menace," although Churchill "wished that the Russian armies should be standing on their present line as the friends and Allies of Poland instead of as invaders." Even in the context of Britain's fears in 1939, this is little short of an endorsement of Soviet boundary claims.

In the same speech, Churchill spoke of "the Community of interests to prevent the Nazis' carrying the flames of war into the Balkans and Turkey." He also noted that any German designs on the Baltic states threatened "the historic life-interests of Russia." Despite Churchill's claim that he merely "put the best construction on their [the Russians'] conduct," he had sent a clear message to Stalin—the Baltic states were in the Soviet sphere of influence. Later in 1939, and again during the Eden-Molotov talks in December 1941, the British did refuse formal recognition of Soviet annexation of those states, but that refusal stemmed primarily from concern over American opposition to territorial agreements, not because Churchill had changed his mind. In fact, he never recanted his de facto acceptance of Soviet control over Lithuania, Latvia, and Estonia. Churchill further demonstrated his consistent pursuit of a spheres-of-influence settlement in Europe in late spring 1944, when he eagerly sanctioned Soviet predominance in Rumania in exchange for British control in Greece, a proposal opposed by the State Department but approved by Roosevelt.[5]

Despite the President's acceptance of a temporary Soviet sphere of influence in Rumania, he had later tried to limit Churchill's freedom of action during the 1944 Moscow Conference by asking Stalin to consider the talks "as preliminary to a meeting of the three of us." The request puzzled the Soviet premier, since he had assumed that Churchill spoke for the Anglo-American alliance. Nevertheless, once the TOLSTOY talks began, both Churchill and Stalin did not hesitate to make just the kind of agreements that the American professed to oppose. Roosevelt was not unaware of such moves. Although Harriman was not present at the most sensitive of the TOLSTOY conversations, he managed to find out what was going on. In an early report to the President, the ambassador accurately reported the spheres-of-influence arrangement that was developing for the Balkans: "Churchill and Eden will try to work out some sort of spheres of influence with the Russians, the British have a free hand in Greece and the Russians in Rumania and perhaps other countries. The British will attempt to retrieve a position of equal influence in Yugoslavia. They can probably succeed in the former but I am doubtful about the latter objective." Roosevelt's response illustrates the difference between his own concerns and those of his advisers at the White House and the

State Department. Hopkins and Secretary of State Cordell Hull had expressed grave concern over any spheres-of-influence arrangement in Eastern Europe, but the President told Harriman, "My interest at the present time in the Balkan area is that such steps as are practicable should be taken to insure against the Balkans getting us into a future international war," leaving open the question of spheres of influence.[6]

The key Churchill-Stalin meeting came on 9 October, the first day of the talks. Faced with rapidly expanding Soviet political and military influence in southeastern Europe, Churchill sought to protect Britain's position in Greece and Yugoslavia. The British Army had landed in Greece on 4 October and would arrive in Athens on 14 October, but Churchill remained concerned about Soviet support for the partisans. Moreover, he may have suspected that Stalin would permit the Bulgarians, who were about to sign an armistice with the Soviet Union, to realize age-old territorial ambitions by expanding into northern Greece (Thrace and Macedonia) and eastern Yugoslavia (Serbia).

Poland, which had been the major Eastern European problem in Anglo-American affairs, took a back seat to the more pressing issue of maintaining British dominance in the Mediterranean. Stalin and Churchill exchanged crude remarks about the Poles, agreed that Poles were quarrelsome (Stalin remarked that "where there was one Pole he would begin to quarrel with himself through sheer boredom"), and put off any further discussions until representatives of the Polish government at London could come to Moscow. The impression left by Churchill's comments was that of a statesman willing to give the Soviets their way in Poland in return for their cooperation elsewhere. The Prime Minister labeled the Polish leaders at London "unwise," callously noted that General Tadeusz Bor of the Warsaw Underground would no longer trouble the Soviets since "the Germans were looking for him," and accepted Stalin's position that the London Poles would have to negotiate with the Polish Committee of National Liberation—a group controlled by the Soviets.

With the Polish question out of the way for the time being, the two leaders concentrated on the Balkans. Ambassador Harriman was excluded from the meeting, so Churchill and Stalin could speak in words of blatant power politics, although the Prime Minister cautioned that "it was better to express these things in diplomatic terms and not to use the phrase 'dividing into spheres,' because the Americans might be shocked." According to a Foreign Office account, which was later amended before making it official, Churchill "produced what he called a 'naughty document' showing a list of Balkan countries and the proportion of interest in them of the Great Powers."[7] Some of the percentages were later modified during lengthy talks between Eden and Molotov, but the basic structure remained. The Soviet Union would have 90 percent influence in Rumania and 75 percent in Bulgaria, with Britain exercising 90 percent in Greece.

Yugoslavia and Hungary were to be split 50–50, although Eden later granted the Soviets 75 percent influence in Hungary. During the discussion that followed, Stalin agreed with Churchill's insistence that "Britain must be the leading Mediterranean power," an admission the Soviets followed with a request that they gain unrestricted access to the Mediterranean from the Black Sea, necessitating the cancellation of the Montreaux Convention, which permitted Turkey to close the straits leading to the Aegean Sea. Ignoring centuries of British policy aimed at denying Russia such access, Churchill quickly agreed, calling the convention "inadmissable" and "obsolete."

All in all, it was not Churchill's finest hour, although he had little room to maneuver. His arguments during this first meeting had an air of desperation. Aware and proud of Britain's prewar power and influence, the Prime Minister was frequently forced to use the Soviet Union against the United States, and vice versa, in order to maintain the form if not the substance of the British Empire. In spite of a request from Roosevelt not to discuss the results of the Dumbarton Oaks Conference, Churchill came out in favor of great-power unanimity (the veto) in any postwar international organization, because without it "supposing China asked Britain to give up Hong Kong, China and Britain would have to leave the room while Russia and the U.S.A. settled the question." Churchill's plea for Stalin to restrain the Italian Communists (Stalin said they were not always controllable, but he would try) likewise demonstrated Britain's dependence upon the goodwill of the other two great powers.[8] Harriman's reports captured a good deal of what went on between Churchill and Stalin, but the Prime Minister made no attempt to fill the gaps. What little he told Roosevelt about the famous percentage deal seemed to indicate that Churchill had cut his losses and concentrated on two areas of traditional interest to Britain:

> Arrangements made about the Balkans are, I am sure, the best that are possible. Coupled with our successful military action recently we should now be able to save Greece and, I have no doubt that agreement to pursue a fifty-fifty joint policy in Yugoslavia will be the best solution for our difficulties in view of Tito's behavior and changes in the local situation, resulting from the arrival of Russian and Bulgarian forces under Russian command to help Tito's eastern flank. The Russians are insistent on their ascendancy in Roumania and Bulgaria as the Black Sea countries.[9]

As for the now controversial issue of the makeup of the government of liberated Poland, Stalin seems to have been quite clear—well before the Yalta talks. On 22 October, Churchill told the President:

> After the Kremlin dinner we put it bluntly to Stalin that unless Mik [Polish Premier Stanislaw Mikolajczyk] had 50/50 plus himself the western world

would not be convinced that the transaction was bona fide and would not believe that an independent Polish government had been set up. Stalin at first replied he would be content with 50/50 but rapidly corrected himself to a worse figure. Meanwhile Eden took the same line with Molotov who seemed more comprehending. I do not think the composition of the government will prove an insuperable obstacle if all else is settled. Mik had previously explained to me that there might be one announcement to save the prestige of the Lublin government and a different arrangement among the Poles behind the scenes.[10]

Roosevelt's response to that news is enlightening, considering accusations that he was duped at YALTA: "I am delighted to learn of your success at Moscow in making progress toward a compromise solution of the Polish problem. When and if a solution is arrived at, I should like to be consulted as to the advisability from this point of view of delaying its publication about two weeks. You will understand."[11] The President recognized that Soviet insistence on a "friendly" government in Poland meant that Poles in the West would be most unhappy with the "compromise" that seemed to be developing, and a two-week delay would take him past the election.

As for Stalin, Roosevelt's message to him may have led the Soviet premier to believe that the United States agreed to the percentages division of Eastern Europe worked out at the TOLSTOY Conference.[12] As Roosevelt wrote Stalin:

> I am delighted to learn from your message and from reports by Ambassador Harriman of the success attained by you and Mr. Churchill in approaching an agreement on a number of questions that are of high interest to all of us in our common desire to secure and maintain a satisfactory and durable peace. I am sure that the progress made during your conversations in Moscow will facilitate and expedite our work in the next meeting when the three of us should come to a full agreement on our future activities and policies and mutual interests.[13]

Granted, FDR reserved the right to disagree, but there is not even a hint of concern in this message about the Churchill-Stalin agreement.

Since there were overtones of a Poland-for-Greece swap in the talks between Churchill and Stalin, a brief explanation of the confused and confusing situation in Greece is in order. Basically, the Americans and the British differed over the form of the postwar government in Greece. The subject had come up at various times during the war, but the German evacuation of Greece brought matters to a head. Guerilla resistance to the German occupation had been led primarily by a coalition of antimonarchical political groups, particularly the Greek Communist party. This coalition (EAM) and its National Popular Liberation Army (ELAS) gained the respect of much of the Greek populace while the royal government of George II, already tainted by its association with the prewar dictatorship that had governed Greece, had lost much of its support. Churchill and the British government, however, believed that ELAS would be anti-British and therefore opposed attempts by the antimonarchists to arrange a plebiscite before the royal government could return to Greece. The fratricidal nature of the struggle was intensified by German use of "Security Battalions" of armed Greeks against the supposedly Communist ELAS, who were accused of planning to hand Macedonia over to the Bulgarians. By the time the Germans left, the hatred between those two groups had reached the point that neither could trust the other.

Expecting EAM/ELAS to attempt to seize control, the British rushed forces into Athens to "restore order" and install the royal government. Then, in a move that almost guaranteed violence, the British brought in two elements of the Royal Greek Army, both purged of all but loyal monarchists, and the old German-organized security battalions to act as a sort of national guard. Little wonder that members of ELAS refused to turn in their arms. In such an atmosphere of mutual hatred and mistrust, the inevitable "incident" occurred, and between ten and twenty-one demonstrators were killed and over one hundred wounded. Churchill quickly took charge and, without consulting his cabinet, gave orders to maintain the Greek government in power, using British military force as necessary. For the next two months, Greece was torn apart by a brutal civil war.[14]

Churchill came under heavy attack in both the British and American press for what seemed to be unwarranted intervention in the internal affairs of an ally. A debate and vote of confidence in the House of Commons was far more bitter and serious than Churchill let on, and a public statement by the new secretary of state, Edward R. Stettinius, Jr., criticizing British policy in Italy, issued on 5 December, contained an indirect but obvious reference to Greece that angered the Prime Minister.[15] When Churchill telephoned Hopkins to protest an order forbidding the use of American shipping to supply British forces in Greece, Hopkins persuaded the Prime Minister not to send an angry cable to the President. Hopkins interceded to get the naval order withdrawn, but Churchill sent the draft to Hopkins anyway. The Prime Minister's defense of his actions was well taken, for Roosevelt had approved the transfer of British forces for the very purpose of preventing a coup by EAM/ELAS:

> The reference in the last sentence of Mr. Stettinius's Press release has of course been taken all over the world and in Greece as a suggestion that the United States is against the action we have taken in Greece, and this undoubtedly makes our task more difficult and costly in British and Greek life. If our forces had not been on the spot, the whole of Greece would now be in the hands of a Communist-run E.A.M. Government against the will of what I am assured is the vast majority of its people. Being upon the spot, our troops could hardly stand by as spectators of the massacre which would have ensued, followed by a ruth-

less terror in the name of a purge. I am sure you would not like us to abandon this thankless task now and withdraw our troops and let things crash.[16]

Misled by the rhetoric of American criticism of British colonialism, EAM leaders and many Greeks on the streets of Athens believed that the United States would prevent the British from imposing a government on Greece. In fact, Roosevelt sent Churchill a message which supported British policy within the limitations supposedly set by American public opinion. The President granted that Great Britain had full responsibility for Greece and asked only that Churchill understand why the U.S. government could not publicly support him.

The suggestions made in this cable were aimed at resolving the crisis, not at displacing British influence in Greece:

> I have been as deeply concerned as you have yourself in regard to the tragic difficulties you have encountered in Greece. I appreciate to the full the anxious and difficult alternatives with which you have been faced. I regard my role in this matter as that of a loyal friend and ally whose one desire is to be of any help possible in the circumstances. You may be sure that in putting my thoughts before you I am constantly guided by the fact that nothing can in any way shake the unit and association between our two countries in the great tasks to which we have set our hands.
>
> As anxious as I am to be of the greatest help to you in this trying situation, there are limitations imposed in part by the traditional policies of the United States and in part by the mounting adverse reaction of public opinion in this country. No one will understand better than yourself that I, both personally and as head of State, am necessarily responsive to the state of public feeling. It is for these reasons that it has not been [and I am afraid will not be] possible for this Government to take a stand with you in the present course of events in Greece. Even to attempt to do so would be of only temporary value to you and would in the long run do injury to our basic relationships. . . . I will be with you wholeheartedly in any situation which takes into consideration the factors I have mentioned above. With this in mind I am giving you at random some thoughts that have come to me in my anxious desire to be of help.

Roosevelt went on to recommend a regency in place of George II and "the disarmament and dissolution of all the armed groups now in the country, . . . leaving your troops to preserve law and order alone until Greek national forces can be reconstituted on a non-partisan basis and adequately equipped." He then closed on a note of uncertainty: "I shall be turning over in my mind this whole question and hope you will share your thoughts and worries with me."[17]

At this point, the crises in Poland and Greece once again came together. Pressed by members of the Polish government in London who adamantly opposed any territorial concession to the Soviet Union, Mikolajczyk had resigned as prime minister. Churchill believed that the new government of Tomasz Arciszewski would be short-lived and that Mikolajczyk would return with increased strength. When Churchill made that prediction in a cable to Stalin, however, the Soviet premier responded with a call for Britain to support the Polish National Committee (Lublin). Stalin doubted that Mikolajczyk could be of any help and accused the London Poles of supporting anti-Soviet terrorists in liberated Poland.[18]

Mikolajczyk's resignation spawned a debate in the House of Commons on British policy regarding Poland, and on 15 December, Churchill made an extensive statement in which he praised Mikolajczyk and condemned the inflexible attitude of the new Polish government. Churchill warned that a reconciliation between the Polish government at London and the Lublin Committee (National Liberation Committee) seemed unlikely unless Mikolajczyk returned as prime minister, and he defended the territorial compromises worked out by Mikolajczyk during a trip to Moscow.

Prompted by Churchill's complaint that "the attitude of the United States has not been defined with the precision which His Majesty's Government has thought it wise to use,"[19] and with the election behind him, Roosevelt accepted State Department advice to release a letter he had sent to Mikolajczyk on 17 November. In that letter, he had supported "a strong free and independent Poland," but he had also added a vague statement supporting whatever Anglo-Soviet-Polish agreements could be worked out on territorial questions, including the idea of compensating Poland with German territory. To Mikolajczyk's distress, that veiled endorsement of the Curzon line was not accompanied by an American guarantee of Poland's new boundaries. The letter was released to the public on 18 December, but without any mention of compensation to Poland in the west.[20] When Churchill made a statement to the House of Commons implying American support for Poland's giving territorial concessions to the Soviet Union, a storm of protests arose from the American press and in Congress. That, combined with the crisis in Greece, prompted Hopkins to warn Churchill that American public opinion was increasingly critical of the President's policy of cooperation and might force Roosevelt to state publicly "our determination to do all that we can to seek a free and secure world."[21]

As Churchill quickly pointed out, however, Roosevelt had generally encouraged the British, particularly regarding the Polish settlement. Similarly, in a message to Stalin, the President made clear his willingness to make major concessions in Poland. Roosevelt outlined a four-point statement he planned to make public:

1. The United States Government stands unequivocally for a strong, free, independent and democratic Poland.
2. In regard to the question of future frontiers of Poland, the United States,

although considering it desirable that territorial questions await the general postwar settlement, recognizes that a settlement before that time is in the interest of the common war effort and therefore would have no objection if the territorial questions involved in the Polish situation, including the proposed compensation from Germany, were settled by mutual agreement between the parties directly concerned.

3. Recognizing that the transfer of minorities in some cases is feasible and would contribute to the general security and tranquility in the areas concerned, the United States Government would have no objection if the Government and the people of Poland desire to transfer nationals and would join in assisting such transfers.

4. In conformity with its announced aim, this government is prepared to assist, subject to legislative authority, and in so far as may be predictable, in the economic reconstruction of countries devastated by Nazi aggression. This policy applies equally to Poland as to other such devastated countries of the United Nations.

The proposed statement, as you will note, will contain nothing, I am sure, that is not known to you as the general attitude of this Government and is I believe in so far as it goes in general accord with the results of your discussion with Prime Minister Churchill in Moscow in the autumn, and for this reason I am sure you will welcome it.[22]

Although Roosevelt went on to ask Stalin to delay any formal recognition of the Lublin Committee as the provisional government of Poland, that could not hide the fact that the two western leaders had agreed to boundary changes and a forced removal of population that no Polish leader could or would accept.

Thus, by December 1944, a deal had been struck between the Soviet Union and the Anglo-American allies over Poland. As Churchill had demonstrated with matchsticks earlier at Teheran, Poland and the Polish people would have to take two steps "left close." Stalin, pointing to the increasingly vocal anti-Soviet leaders of the London Poles, had quickly refused to delay recognition of the Lublin Committee, so that matter was ended. Thus, before the Yalta meeting ever started, the Polish question had been decided. Little wonder then that Stalin ignored later attempts to reopen the issue.

The President tried again to convince Stalin not to take the irrevocable step of recognizing the Lublin Committee as the provisional government of Poland. Roosevelt's precise goals in this instance are difficult to determine. It is tempting simply to agree with the weight of historical opinion by claiming that Roosevelt was just procrastinating again, hoping that in some inchoate way the problem would solve itself. But the bulk of the evidence in the Churchill-Roosevelt exchanges indicates that the President, although he did not always keep the State Department informed of his views, was far from the disorganized random thinker that historians have described. Roosevelt's statement to congressional leaders that the Soviet Union "had the power in Eastern Europe," as well as his earlier acquiescence in Anglo-Soviet bargains regarding power sharing in eastern and southeastern Europe, all suggest that he accepted the fact of Soviet control in the area. Why then would he challenge that power, even as gently as he did? It may be that he viewed such wartime arrangements as temporary, subject to revision at a postwar peace conference. But that argument would mean that he failed to recognize the thrust of Soviet policy, something which is unlikely after the argument over the makeup of the Polish government and the Soviet refusal to aid the Warsaw uprising. It is also possible that the President placed Poland outside what he considered the Soviet Union's legitimate sphere of interest and hoped to preserve a significant degree of independence for the Poles. But again, the events of 1943 and 1944 demonstrated Soviet insistence on what they called a "friendly" Poland, and Roosevelt had continually worked to avoid a confrontation with Stalin.

Perhaps the real purpose of the President's moves was merely to get the Soviets to make some sort of small concession, even an unimportant one, just to get them used to cooperating with Britain and the United States. In the short run, this would enhance postwar harmony among the great powers. In the long run, however, Roosevelt may have been thinking of what one historian has called " 'open' spheres of influence," wherein a major power would exercise only enough authority to protect its physical security, instead of traditional "spheres of influence," which also included domination of a nation's internal policies and economic affairs. This would fit the President's vague but persistent notion of having "four policemen" who would keep order in the world without resorting to the kind of spheres-of-influence approach that had failed in the past.[23]

Secretary of State Stettinius's memo to Roosevelt on 31 October illustrates the point: "Postwar Poland will be under strong Soviet influence. In this situation, the United States can hope to make its influence felt only if some degree of equal opportunity in trade, investment, and access to sources of information is preserved." He went on to note that the Soviet Union would "insist on a Polish Government sympathetic to itself," although how exclusive that relationship would be could not be determined. Stettinius pointed out that the USSR was incapable of providing the things Poland needed for postwar reconstruction, whereas the United States could supply such goods "on a substantial scale."[24] Whatever his thinking, Roosevelt's plea to Stalin, copied as usual to Churchill, bears quoting:

> I am disturbed and deeply disappointed over your message of December 27 in regard to Poland in which you tell me that you cannot see your way clear to

hold in abeyance the question of recognizing the Lublin Committee as the provisional government of Poland until we have had an opportunity at our meeting to discuss the whole question thoroughly. I would have thought no serious
inconvenience would have been caused your Government or your Armies if you
delayed for the short period of a month remaining before we met.

There was no suggestion in my request that you curtail your practical relations with the Lublin Committee nor any thought that you should deal with or
accept the London Government in its present composition. I had urged this
delay upon you because I felt you would realize how extremely unfortunate
and even serious it would be at this period in the war in its effect on world
opinion and enemy morale if your Government should formally recognize one
Government of Poland while the majority of the other United Nations including the United States and Great Britain continue to recognize and to maintain
diplomatic relations with the Polish Government in London.[25]

Roosevelt protested that neither the London nor the Lublin governments
could legitimately claim to represent the Polish people and went on to ask
that Stalin delay recognition for a month, until they met at Yalta. Stalin
immediately refused, and formal Soviet recognition took place before the
Crimea Conference.

At the same time that the Polish question was apparently resolved, at
least for Churchill, Roosevelt, and Stalin, the situation in Greece stabi-
lized. The Soviets refrained from aiding EAM/ELAS, while British arms and
Churchill's reluctant agreement to establish a regency instead of reinstall-
ing George II brought an end to the fighting, although the scars still show
today. The Prime Minister's comment to Roosevelt "that we seek nothing
from Greece in territory or advantage" stands in stark contrast to the
percentages agreement he and Stalin had reached in Moscow a few
months earlier.[26] No one ever put in writing "Poland for Greece." But if
it looks like a duck, quacks like a duck, and acts like a duck. . . .

Thus, as the Yalta Conference approached, the Big Three seemed to
have sketched out the political settlement in Eastern Europe and the eastern Mediterranean. Still the details needed ironing out.

During Anglo-American discussions at Malta, just before the Crimea
Conference, Stettinius, Eden, and their subordinates did briefly discuss
political issues, including Allied participation in the reorganization of Rumania, Hungary, and Bulgaria, as well as the Polish-German frontier. A
revealing comment came from Eden who had recommended a "fusion" of
the Polish governments at London and Lublin (then situated at Warsaw),
leading to free elections. He now supported a *new* interim government"
made up of representatives from various factions. At the same time, Eden
noted that "there are no good candidates from the Government in London," although the inclusion of men like Mikolajczyk would make it
easier for the Allies to recognize a new Polish government. That sort of

reasoning, which seemed to be a confused attempt to combine public promises to the London Poles with secret arrangements made during the TOLSTOY talks, characterized the discussions about Poland which took place during the Yalta Conference.[27]

If frequency of discussion is any gauge, the Polish question dominated the Yalta Conference. The issue was complicated, but it had taken shape long before the three leaders met in the Crimea. By that time, with Soviet military forces firmly in control in Poland, Churchill and Roosevelt were forced to scramble for a compromise acceptable to Stalin and at home. The Prime Minister, already muttering warnings to Eden about a general election in Britain once Germany surrendered, feared both Russian expansionism and his own electorate—or at least Parliament—yet he was unwilling to force a confrontation with Stalin over Poland, particularly without full support from the United States. Deeply worried that Americans would reject the activist role in world affairs he favored, Roosevelt did not want controversy over the Polish question to turn domestic and congressional opinion against a postwar international organization or continued great-power cooperation.

The relationship between Poland and the Soviet Union—for that was the basic issue—had been set by the events of World War II and sketched out at the Teheran Conference and the Churchill-Stalin talks in Moscow in October 1944. Given the opportunity to occupy areas that had been claimed by tsarist and Soviet leaders, Stalin had insisted from the outset of the war that portions of what had been eastern Poland be "returned" to the Soviet Union, with territorial compensation for Poland in eastern Germany. Throughout the war, whenever Soviet-Polish relations came up, Stalin made the territorial settlement a prerequisite to agreement on other questions. Churchill and Roosevelt had offered no overall objections to the Soviet demands, although they had both suggested minor modifications to the boundaries proposed by Stalin. The problem was that at no time during the war was the Polish government at London willing to accept such territorial changes. At the same time, the two Allied leaders agreed that Stalin had every right to insist that any postwar Polish government be friendly to the Soviet Union—a requirement that ruled out any restoration of the London Poles to power.

During the Yalta discussions neither Churchill nor Roosevelt challenged these Soviet demands. Rather, they sought to create the impression that any government in postwar Poland would meet the high standards of political freedom set forth in the Atlantic Charter. They hoped the inclusion of a few members of the London Polish regime would legitimize the entire government, whether it was a "new" provisional government or just a broadened version of the Soviet-sponsored Lublin (Warsaw) group. At eight of the nine plenary meetings during the Crimea conference, Churchill and/or Roosevelt tried to get the Soviets to grant at least cosmetic concessions, but Stalin and Molotov gave very little. All the British and Americans could achieve was a vague promise that "all democratic and anti-Nazi parties" would have a right to take part in "free and unfettered elections" in Poland.[28] A tripartite commission was to discuss the reorganization of the Polish government, but this commission's authority was even less than that of the Allied Control Commission in Italy, which had been used so effectively to deny the Soviets any functional role. Churchill and Roosevelt recognized that implementation of the compromises they had negotiated depended upon Soviet goodwill, and the Allied leaders seemed to have believed wishfully that Stalin would be lured by the possibility of long-term cooperation instead of immediate gains. They counted on Stalin to understand their requirement for appearances, but both commented to subordinates that the Soviets could implement the agreements as they saw fit, without formally violating them.

The essence of the Yalta agreement was not in the joint protocols signed by Churchill, Roosevelt, and Stalin, however. They approached the conference believing that it provided a unique opportunity to create a long-lasting peace, but each had a different perception of how that peace could best be achieved. The "Declaration on Liberated Europe," part of the final protocols, promised peace, political freedom, and relief to the liberated peoples of Europe, but the three leaders each interpreted those objectives differently. Churchill viewed Europe from the perspective of Soviet expansion and Britain's own economic weakness. Stalin seemed convinced that his nation's security required that Eastern Europe come under Soviet domination. Roosevelt consciously tried to play the role of broker—guarding American interests, placating the Soviets, reassuring the British, converting his own State Department, and maintaining the support of the American Congress and public.

The President's attempts to deal with almost all the negotiable problems of the postwar world, from colonialism to buttressing the Chinese government, and to postpone the intractable ones lest they wreck the conference, betray his suspicions that Yalta would be his last chance. Spurred on, perhaps, by his failing health, Roosevelt seemed intent upon creating great-power harmony then and there, a difficult task even without the suspicion that characterized Anglo-Soviet-American relations. Desperate to satisfy so many constituencies, Roosevelt ended up pleasing none. In Poland, for example, the British saw Soviet expansion as a threat, the Soviets thought they had Anglo-American agreement, the State Department believed that Stalin had lied, and Polish-Americans felt betrayed. Given Roosevelt's penchant for procrastination, there is great irony in suggesting that he could have accomplished more if he had tried to accomplish less.

Despite the Soviets' unpleasant, peremptory style and their refusal to make even cosmetic concessions in Poland, the Yalta settlement on East-

ern Europe was a logical extension of the earlier TOLSTOY agreements.
The President and Prime Minister left the Crimea thinking they had come
to an understanding even while recognizing that Stalin could "stretch"
the agreements almost as far as he cared to. As Churchill commented
shortly afterward, "Poor Nevile [sic] Chamberlain believed he could trust
Hitler. He was wrong. But I don't think I'm wrong about Stalin."[29] Yet a
month after the Prime Minister had returned home, British policy
changed sharply.

Even though he continued to advocate cooperation with the Soviets
and cautioned against any direct confrontation, Churchill now took the
position that he and Roosevelt had been "deceived" at Yalta. Despite an
awareness that the Declaration on Liberated Europe signed at Yalta was
vague and imprecise, Churchill castigated Soviet officials for interpreting
it to suit their own purposes. Moreover, the thrust of the Prime Minister's
argument was not that he intended to live up to the spirit of his own
agreements with Stalin reached during the TOLSTOY talks, but that Britain
and the United States need only to avoid openly violating those accords.
Churchill was well aware of the contradiction inherent in any condemnation of Soviet spheres of influence while Britain struggled to maintain
control over Greece, Yugoslavia, and the Middle East. What is unclear is
when and why the Prime Minister and his government moved away from
the spheres-of-influence settlement outlined in the TOLSTOY talks.

The results of the 1944 meeting, the spheres of influence, were not
challenged during the Yalta Conference, although the Declaration on Liberated Europe did seem contradictory in spirit. Without specific, firm
changes to the Churchill-Stalin arrangements, however, the Declaration
was more for public consumption than actual implementation, something
Churchill and Roosevelt apparently recognized. Why the change? There
is no question that Soviet moves in Rumania, Bulgaria, and Hungary were
blunt and brutal. In each of those countries Soviet military power was
translated in direct political influence, and regimes presumably faithful to
direction from Moscow were soon put into place. But this had not fundamentally changed British or American policy. Appeals from King Michael
of Rumania for aid brought only verbal protests from London and Washington that the Soviets had acted without first consulting their allies, and
anti-Soviet forces soon realized that they were on their own. Yet despite
the practical if not very pretty agreement with the Soviet Union of October 1944 regarding Eastern Europe, Churchill now tried to persuade the
President that the time had come to get tough, at least over Poland and,
to a lesser degree, Rumania.

But the Prime Minister was playing a tricky game. At the same time he
tried to push Roosevelt toward a firmer stand against the Soviets, Churchill chastised his own foreign secretary for allowing the Foreign Office
and diplomats in Rumania to criticize Soviet actions in that country. "We

really have no justification for intervening in this extraordinarily vigorous manner for our late Rumanian enemies," he wrote Eden on 5 March, "thus compromising our position in Poland and jarring Russian acquiescence in our long fight for Athens." A week later, on 13 March, Churchill again warned Eden to keep in mind "that we, for considerations well known to you, accepted in a special degree the predominance of Russia in this theatre [Rumania]."[30] British interests in Greece and the eastern Mediterranean were obviously too important to risk by confronting the Soviets over an area occupied by the Red Army, but if the Americans could be persuaded to make the challenge, Britain could still appear faithful to the TOLSTOY accords. Churchill had learned well the art of statecraft from his mentor, David Lloyd George.

Churchill had come to believe that Stalin was not as eager to cooperate with the West as he had previously hoped. That was particularly true in Poland, a nation that the Soviets had never viewed as a trusted wartime ally. Already predisposed to distrust the "Bolsheviks," Churchill settled on a tougher policy when Stalin moved to consolidate Soviet authority without any pretense of elections or other face-saving gestures for the West. The Prime Minister continued his tactic of subtly placing Great Britain in the position of "broker" by candidly admitting to Roosevelt that any British protest about Poland would "lead to comparisons between the aims of his actions and those of ours"—a reference to the Anglo-Soviet arrangement in Eastern Europe that left Britain a free hand in Greece. Perhaps Churchill was sincere in arguing that British troops in Athens had protected democracy whereas Soviet political and military power had repressed freedom in Poland, but there is no doubt that he understood that Stalin would not see the distinction. Thus, the Prime Minister hoped to get the United States to take the lead over Poland as well, not only because Britain alone would be ineffective, but because it left him free to maneuver, just as he had done at the TOLSTOY talks.

But British electoral politics also played a role in the decision to draw the line over Poland. Even though Churchill assumed that victory against Germany would bring a wave of gratitude from voters, with a general election in the offing, he was searching for a coalition that would return him to office. The political "peace of the castle" in Britain would end with Germany's surrender, and Labour party chances for a win at the polls appeared good. As Churchill had predicted, the Yalta agreements on Poland received vigorous criticism in Parliament. Some members of the Labour party had grown restive within the constraints of the wartime coalition government, and one of the party's leaders condemned the Yalta conferees for deciding the fate of Poland without Polish representatives taking part. On the other side of the aisle, the Conservatives would provide the bulk of Churchill's electoral support, and they were even more sensitive to the plight of the London Poles and to "Bolshevik" expansion. Those most concerned were often the same Tories who had favored the appeasement of Germany in the 1930s, then on the grounds that a strong Germany would limit the Soviets. Even Roosevelt and Hopkins detected Churchill's concern about domestic politics from some of the Prime Minister's remarks during the Yalta talks. With the Greek situation well in hand by early March, the Prime Minister may have decided it was an opportune time to make a gesture toward "saving" the Poles, though it is hard to determine what he thought such opposition could accomplish outside of mending some political fences at home.[31]

The State Department and Foreign Office reactions to Soviet moves in Eastern Europe leave no doubt that British and American officials were very angry and embarrassed that not even the pretense of great-power consultation or "democratic" processes had been preserved. It is likely, however, that many of those officials, not having been at Yalta, failed or refused to understand the cosmetic nature of the Declaration on Liberated Europe. But Churchill did understand and still chose to move toward confrontation with the Soviet Union over Eastern Europe—not over some perceived threat to Western Europe. A key to figuring out British policy may be found in instructions sent to Ambassador Lord Halifax in Washington. After the United States had rejected a Foreign Office proposal for a strong protest against Moscow's insistence on recognizing the Soviet-sponsored Lublin government while excluding representatives of the London Poles, Eden instructed Halifax "to point out the danger that, if we did not now intervene to get fair treatment for the anti-Lublin Poles, . . . we and the Americans would be accused—rightly—of having subscribed at the Crimea Conference to a formula which we knew to be unworkable."[32] Churchill's repetition of those fears suggests that his public image, not Soviet expansion, was the real problem. Whatever the reason, this following long message was a call for Anglo-American unity against the Soviet Union:

I feel sure you will be as distressed as I am by recent events in Roumania. The Russians have succeeded in establishing the rule of a Communist minority by force and misrepresentation. We have been hampered in our protests against these developments by the fact that, in order to have the freedom to save Greece, Eden and I at Moscow in October recognized that Russia would have a large preponderant voice in Roumania and Bulgaria while we took the lead in Greece. Stalin adhered very strictly to this understanding during the thirty days fighting against the Communists and ELAS in the city of Athens, in spite of the fact that all this was most disagreeable to him and those around him.

Since the October Anglo-Russian conversation in Moscow Stalin has subscribed on paper to the principles of Yalta which are certainly being trampled down in Roumania. Nevertheless I am most anxious not to press this view to such an extent that Stalin will say "I did not interfere with your action in Greece, why do you not give me the same latitude in Roumania?"

This again would lead to comparisons between the aims of his action and those of ours. On this neither side would convince the other. Having regard to my personal relations with Stalin, I am sure it would be a mistake for me at this stage to embark on the argument.

The news from Moscow about Poland is also most disappointing. I must let you know that the government majorities here bear no relation to the strong under current of opinion among all parties and classes in our own hearts against a Soviet domination of Poland.

Labour men are as keen as Conservatives, and Socialists as keen as Catholics. I have based myself in Parliament on the assumption that the words of the Yalta declaration will be carried out in the letter and spirit. Once it is seen that we have been deceived and that the well-known communist technique is being applied behind closed doors in Poland, either directly by the Russians or through their Lublin puppets, a very grave situation in British public opinion will be reached.

As to the upshot of all this, if we do not get things right now, it will soon be seen by the world that you and I by putting our signatures to the Crimea settlement have under-written a fraudulent prospectus. . . .

I think you will agree with me that far more than the case of Poland is involved. I feel that this is the test case between us and the Russians of the meaning which is to be attached to such terms as Democracy, Sovereignty, Independence, representative Government and free and unfettered elections.[33]

From there on, Churchill kept up a drumfire of cables designed to bring Roosevelt around to the British point of view, but, as the Prime Minister finally realized, the President was not listening. In fact, Churchill sent a message on 17 March apologizing for sending so many messages and remarking on the infrequency of Roosevelt's replies. The observation was well taken. FDR had gone on what proved to be his final journey to Warm Springs, Georgia—where it seems he always went when he felt ill as opposed to just tired. While there, he complained of sleeplessness, so the bulk of the Churchill-Roosevelt correspondence was handled by the White House staff. Still, he kept his usual busy schedule, and cable traffic was routed to him. The careful way in which messages drafted for FDR's approval dealt with Churchill's insistent pleas for action suggests that Roosevelt's policy of cooperation with the Soviet Union still governed U.S. policy—a commitment that stemmed from more than just concern that the USSR fulfill its promise to participate actively in the war against Japan. Unlike Churchill, the President was unwilling to go beyond the text of the Yalta agreements on Poland. Not only did the State Department and Admiral William Leahy look with some suspicion on the "alleged" abuses reported by the London Poles, but they also emphasized the need to be practical. Roosevelt and his advisers avoided making an appeal to Stalin lest the Soviet premier give the wrong answer and thus force a confrontation or retreat. As the President put it in a cable to Churchill:

> Your message points directly to an urgent necessity of our taking every practicable means of accomplishing the corrective measures in Poland that are envisioned in the agreements reached at Yalta.
>
> The Yalta agreements, if they are followed, should correct most of the abuses alleged in your message.
>
> In my opinion . . . we should leave the first steps to our Ambassadors from which we hope to obtain good results.
>
> When and if it should become necessary because of the failure of the Ambassadors we may have to appeal to Marshal Stalin for relief for the oppressed inhabitants of Poland.[34]

Churchill and the Foreign Office wanted to draw the line in Poland, making it a clear-cut "test case" on Soviet willingness to cooperate with the West. Roosevelt and the State Department preferred to avoid any kind of ultimatum in the hope that the Soviets could be persuaded to follow more liberal policies. Although Harriman and others had come to the conclusion that Soviet leaders understood only harsh language and tough actions, their superiors in the State Department were not yet ready to give up on cooperation, particularly with the San Francisco Conference to plan the international peacekeeping organization about to begin.

The Prime Minister answered the President the next day:

> At Yalta also we agreed to take the Russian view of the frontier line. Poland has lost her frontier. Is she now to lose her freedom? That is the question which will undoubtedly have to be fought out in Parliament and in public here.
>
> I do not wish to reveal a divergence between the British and the United States Governments, but it would certainly be necessary for me to make it clear that we are in the presence of a great failure and an utter breakdown of what was settled at Yalta, but that we Britons have not the military strength to carry the matter further and that the limits of our capacity to act have been reached.
>
> The moment that Molotov sees that he has beaten us away from the whole process of consultations among the Poles to form a new government, he will know that we will put up with anything. On the other hand, I believe that combined dogged pressure and persistence along the lines on which we have been working would very likely succeed.[35]

By mid-March, the appearance of unity which had characterized the Yalta discussions had completely disappeared. The Soviet Union now openly insisted that the Lublin Poles could accept or reject all persons proposed by other Polish groups for positions in the provisional government, meaning that all noncommunists could be excluded. The British had come to demand open and free elections which would be held under the supervision of representatives of the tripartite Moscow Commission. The United States, trying to find a middle ground acceptable to Churchill, Stalin, the American public, and Congress, pushed for a "new" Polish government rather than just the continuation of the Lublin Committee under a new name. Both Roosevelt and the State Department seemed intent upon preserving great-power cooperation, and they were convinced that the British approach would only bring outright rejection from the Soviet Union.

It is perhaps typical of Roosevelt's policy that he would—in the midst of such tension—suggest increased economic cooperation with the Soviets in Greece:

> What would you think of sending a special mission for developing the productive power of Greece rapidly by concerted, non-political action? Such a mission could consist of people like [Oliver] Lyttelton, [A. I.] Mikoyan, the People's Commissar for Foreign Trade of the U.S.S.R. and Donald Nelson, who is back after a very successful similar mission in China. It would not take them long and might have a highly constructive effect on world opinion at this time.
>
> I take it that they could meet in Greece in about a month's time. I am not taking it up with the Soviet Government until I get your slant.[36]

In spite of his admission that the Soviet Union had lived up to its promise not to interfere in Greece, Churchill had no intention of asking the Soviets to come in through the front door. But it was not just the Russian bear that worried the Prime Minister. Roosevelt's proposal indicated that American business was interested in the Greek market, and Churchill's suggestion for a joint Anglo-American committee to dispense financial and economic advice to the Greek government suggests that the British wanted to make sure that the United States did not operate alone. As Churchill wrote:

> I am attracted by the suggestion in your No. 723 that a high-powered economic mission should visit Greece, but I am rather doubtful whether this is an appropriate moment to bring the Russians in. We cannot expect any help from the Russians in the economic sphere, and to include them in the mission would be a purely political gesture. As such, it might be valuable if we could be sure that the Russian representative would behave correctly and make a public demonstration of his solidarity with our policy, but this assumption seems very doubtful. There is the further disadvantage that at a time when the Russians are firmly excluding both you and us from any say in the affairs of Roumania, it would be rather odd to invite them unsolicited to assume some degree of responsibility in the Greek affairs.[37]

At this point—with Churchill firmly insisting that a-deal-was-a-deal in Greece and Stalin assuming the same in Eastern Europe—we can leave the unhappy story of that part of the world, knowing what will happen.

Slowly but surely, the State Department moved toward the British position. Roosevelt was less able to direct policy actively, even though his subordinates still put his name at the end of messages to Churchill. On those occasions when the President spoke his own mind, he did not abandon his conciliatory approach for that of East-West confrontation, despite what has been said by historians trying to make FDR into a belated but convinced Cold Warrior. A message sent to Churchill over the President's name on 6 April seemed unusually belligerent:

> I am in general agreement with your opinion, and I am pleased with your very clear strong message to Stalin.
>
> We must not permit anybody to entertain a false impression that we were afraid.
>
> Our Armies will in a very few days be in a position that will permit us to become "tougher" than has heretofore appeared advantageous to the war effort.[38]

But so cryptic a message as this does not mean that the President had finally accepted the idea of a postwar Soviet threat and was advocating an early form of military containment. This message merely endorsed the strong British protests over Soviet accusations stemming from the German surrender talks in Bern; it did not refer to the broader issue of Eastern Europe and Soviet actions there. Moreover, it came right after Roosevelt had rejected Churchill's plea for a drive on Berlin and earlier proposals for Allied forces to move into Austria and Czechoslovakia. Nor was the language that of the President. The cable was drafted by Admiral Leahy, who supported pleas from Harriman in Moscow and others for a change in policy toward the Soviet Union. Harriman believed that the Soviets understood only power and that the United States should demand a quid pro quo for any aid. Sent to Warm Springs for Roosevelt's approval, the telegram was returned to Washington without comment in only one hour and twenty-eight minutes, hardly time enough for Roosevelt to have reconsidered and redirected the entire thrust of his wartime and postwar policy toward the Soviet Union. In fact, one wonders if the President gave this message any consideration at all, particularly in view of his poor health.

In one of the very few messages the President drafted personally during his stay at Warm Springs, moreover, he characteristically chose to emphasize the optimistic side of Anglo-American relations with the Soviet Union. The suggestion that they "minimize" the problems caused by the Soviets epitomizes Roosevelt's approach to a host of issues. Partly creative procrastination based on a belief that many crises solve themselves if left alone, and partly an attempt to direct the thinking of others in the belief that the way one approaches a problem can be the key to the solution, Roosevelt's style was an integral part of his substance:

> I would minimize the general Soviet problem as much as possible because these problems, in one form or another, seem to arise every day and most of them straighten out as in the case of the Bern meeting.
>
> We must be firm, however, and our course thus far is correct.[39]

There was a sharp reversal in presidential policy once Harry S Truman took over that office. In a memo sent the day after Roosevelt's death, Secretary of State Stettinius summarized international problems. The style and content differed clearly from those of the late President: "The present situation relating to Poland is highly unsatisfactory. . . . Direct appeals to Marshal Stalin have not yet produced any worthwhile results. The Soviet Government likewise seeks to complicate the problem. . . . We have invoked this declaration [on Liberated Europe] for Roumania [a minority government imposed by intimidation] and Bulgaria [in anticipation of unfair elections]."[40]

The striking difference in style and policy under Truman was translated into action by the new President within two weeks after Roosevelt's death. Soviet Foreign Minister Molotov, enroute to the San Francisco Conference, stopped in Washington for talks with Truman. In an oft-told exchange, when the President upbraided the Soviets for their actions, particularly in Eastern Europe, Molotov complained, "I have never been talked to like that in my life." "Carry out your agreements and you won't get talked to like that," Truman shot back. Less well known is the reaction of Harriman who was also in the room. Surprised by the President's remarks, Harriman recognized the shift in approach and attitude, and expressed displeasure "that Truman went at it so hard because his behavior gave Molotov an excuse to tell Stalin that the Roosevelt policy was being abandoned. I regretted that Truman gave him that opportunity."[41]

Why were arrangements sketched out at TOLSTOY and Yalta reversed in only six months? Certainly Soviet behavior is a factor, although it is equally clear that neither Churchill nor Roosevelt believed that getting tough would lift the political oppression settling in over Eastern Europe. Pretty or not, moral—amoral—or immoral, the TOLSTOY and Yalta agreements had sanctioned Soviet predominance in that area. What was there about that modified spheres-of-influence arrangement—nothing new for the British—that made it so short-lived?[42] It seems that Roosevelt's death provided an opportunity for what came to be called Cold War ideology to set the broad strategy for American diplomacy. At the same time, the Munich analogy came to govern American tactics, although no one used that precise phrase.

The reasons for the British reversal are even less certain, although domestic politics seem to have been a major factor. Nevertheless, if Soviet control in Eastern Europe was acceptable in October 1944, why was that not so in March 1945? If Churchill chose to compromise in the autumn, why did spring bring confrontation, especially when that confrontation would not change the political realities? If picking dates and events that signal the start of the Cold War is a valid exercise, then you have my nominations.

1990 Addendum to "Naked Reverse Right"

A historian, reviewing a book on the Cold War, commented that it was much easier to "develop the strongest possible moral indictment against an inherently evil Soviet state if one concentrates on Soviet political oppression rather than upon a Big Three diplomacy that tends to raise awkward questions and to blur the moral clarity of an issue."[43] This essay raises awkward questions and blurs moral clarity.

Since 1985, when the essay was originally written, a number of excellent studies touching on the same issues have appeared, but nothing in them has persuaded me to change my basic interpretation.[44] None explain, to my satisfaction, why Winston Churchill made such a striking reversal of policy toward the Soviet Union after the Crimea Conference. Somehow, he seemed to have forgotten his own cynical contention that "the right to guide the course of history is the noblest prize of victory."[45]

Granted, the Prime Minister had always been ambivalent toward his wartime partners in Moscow. Old images of Russian expansion into spheres of British influence, from Afghanistan to the eastern Mediterranean, merged easily with the revolutionary rhetoric of Bolshevism. At the same time, Churchill seemed genuinely convinced that he could establish a workable modus vivendi with Stalin, as his comments following the TOLSTOY and Yalta conferences demonstrate. That ambivalence disappeared with his March 1945 calls for confrontation. What had the Soviets done that was so surprising, so unexpected? What had they done that brought Churchill to demand dramatic changes in Anglo-American policy? Perhaps Stalin's political crudeness had finally convinced the Prime Minister that anything less than firm opposition to the Soviets would

Much to my surprise, a number of people are unfamiliar with the terminology of American football, and therefore do not comprehend the meaning of "Naked Reverse Right." When a runner on the offensive team hands the ball to a teammate running toward the opposite side of the field, that is called a reverse. When all the offensive blockers pretend to be blocking for the runner who handed-off the ball, leaving the player with the ball without any blocking, that is called a "naked reverse." The title refers to the unexplained (i.e., no blocking) reversal Churchill made after Yalta regarding the Soviets and Eastern Europe.

open him up to charges of being an "appeaser," a frightening label for a British politician in 1945. After all, Harry Hopkins recalled that, during the Yalta talks, whenever Churchill was stubborn about something, Roosevelt would remark that "we've got to remember that Winston has an election coming up."[46] The Poles were the ostensible reason and the moral justification for Britain's entry into the war. But it was Winston Churchill at the Teheran talks, who proposed executing the drill parade maneuver, "left close"—moving all of Poland's boundaries to the west (leftward); even if Stalin had, in 1942, proposed compensating Poland in the west (Germany) for territory taken by the Soviet Union in the east.[47] Later arguments with the Soviets over the precise demarcation—which Oder-Neisse line?; is the city of Lvov Polish or Soviet?—were mere details compared to the initial concession advanced by Churchill.

Although this essay was not written with the same focus on Roosevelt as the others in this collection, it illustrates how Roosevelt's decision to go along with the regional (spheres-of-influence) agreement made at the TOL-STOY meeting was always modified by his own peculiar conception of regionalism and his opposition to exclusivity within those regions. His suggestion that there be international "Free Ports of Information" that would help prevent the creation of closed spheres, further reveals his thinking.[48] Assistant Secretary of State Adolf Berle articulated the President's scheme in a September 1944 report to the State Department's Policy Committee. Berle supported a Soviet "sphere of influence" in Eastern Europe modeled on America's role in Mexico and the Caribbean. A few paragraphs later, he condemned all " 'closed' systems, whether of commercial intercourse, . . . or travel, et cetera." American citizens must have, he argued, the same privileges as those exercised by what Roosevelt would have called that region's Policeman. During the Moscow Foreign Ministers and Teheran Conferences late in 1943, Roosevelt and Hull treated the issue of a settlement in Eastern Europe as a quagmire, a bottomless pit that could destroy the worldwide system they hoped to create. That conclusion lay at the root of the President's policies toward Eastern Europe until the day he died. As Berle put it: In Eastern Europe, where American influence would be "nominal," the United States should be coy, with its "participation sought, and granted rather rarely."[49]

By autumn 1943, Roosevelt and his advisers were noting that Stalin had the power to do as he wished in Poland and the Baltic States. "Do you expect us and Britain to declare war on Joe Stalin if they cross your previous frontier?" he asked the Polish ambassador, going on to comment: "Even if we wanted to, Russia can still field an army twice our combined strength, and we would just have no say in the matter at all."[50] Roosevelt's opposition in 1941–42 to Stalin's demands for an agreement on Soviet boundaries, particularly regarding the Baltic states, sprang more from the President's desire to avoid premature discussions about such issues, than from a belief that opposing what Stalin proposed would achieve anything useful.[51] Time and again, Roosevelt emphasized appearances, almost invariably recommending plebiscites as the appropriate mechanism. "Russia should take the trouble to go through the motions of getting that [a plebiscite] done," he commented to Hopkins in March 1943. Roosevelt had often expressed faith in plebiscites, telling Churchill in July 1941 that "the plebiscite was on the whole one of the few successful outcomes of the Versailles Treaty."[52]

Roosevelt's apparent willingness to sacrifice the Baltic states in order to "appease" Stalin is, at first glance, hypocritical. But the President's thinking about the postwar international order suggests otherwise. Roosevelt believed in self-determination, but on a worldwide scale. To argue in the short-term for democracy in the Baltic states would jeopardize the longer-term hopes he had for bringing the Soviet Union into the community of responsible leadership—the "family circle." What would it profit the Baltic states if, by taking a principled stand, the United States convinced Stalin that brute force was required? Hence, in 1941 and thereafter, the President tried to accustom Stalin to the idea that nationalities ought to have some voice in their own affairs, even if that voice was carefully controlled in the interests of Soviet geopolitical security. Freedom and democracy are habit-forming, as glas'nost in the late 1980s illustrates, and Roosevelt's postwar plans assumed such evolutionary change. As President George Bush put it nearly fifty years later, what we seek is the "integration of the Soviet Union into the community of nations."[53]

Roosevelt's expectation that the Soviets would permit some degree of internal autonomy and political diversity in Eastern Europe failed to materialize in his lifetime, or for decades thereafter, but he was not as naive and foolish as some would have it. Stalin's actions during the war suggest that he had no desire to incorporate Poland into an informal Soviet empire, but at the same time insisted that any Polish regime pose no ideological or political threat. Similar requirements were levied on Finland, Rumania, and Austria where the Soviets permitted coalition governments to exist. Stalin's demands for Polish compliance were, of course, intensified by Poland's military and political potential. Nonetheless, that is a far cry from some sort of master plan for empire. Archibald Clark Kerr, the British ambassador in Moscow during the war, neatly caught the conundrum: "Soviet Russia genuinely favors the revival of an independent Poland, but at the same time expects so much from the Poles in the way of exemplary behavior that it would require a miracle for them to live up to the standard demanded of them without complete subservience." Stalin could not find politicians he could work with among the London Poles, and the Polish Communist Party (PPR) could not gain any semblance of noncommunist support. In the end, Stalin and the Polish Communists found it necessary to rule with crude and brutal force.[54]

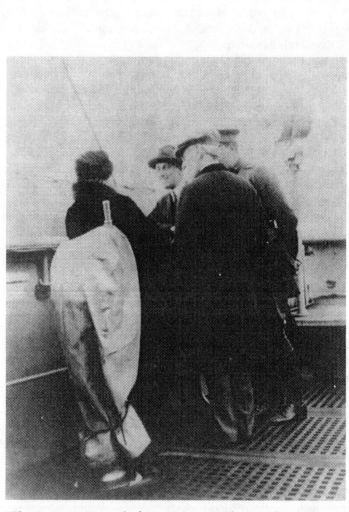

"This Persistent Evangel of Americanism": The Founding Fathers—
Woodrow Wilson and Franklin Roosevelt, 1919.

IX

"This Persistent Evangel of Americanism"

BY TRYING to systematize Roosevelt's thinking, we automatically distort, since he never articulated a cohesive philosophy. He avoided contradictions rather than trying to reconcile or confront them.[1] Nevertheless, his actions—successful or not—show a conceptual consistency that reveals his assumptions. It is trite but true to say simply that Roosevelt was a nationalist, an American whose ethnocentrism was part of his outlook. National leaders are always so, regardless of whatever facade of style and statement they construct. Franklin Roosevelt was no ideologue, but he had an ideology—"basic assumptions" is a less politicized phrase.

Roosevelt saw no sense in letting ideology stand in the way of common sense. But that is misleading. Idealism and realism are not mutually exclusive. Rather, they deal with different levels of thought and action. Realism, in the political sense, is a response to geopolitical necessities; to the tangible forces of power and wealth, arms and boundaries. Geopolitical issues invariably take precedence in the actions of politicians, for such matters are the "fires" that leaders must fight every day. Using strict geopolitical terms, Robin Edmonds, a thirty-year veteran of the British Foreign Service turned historian, perceptively contrasted differing United States and British international perspectives:

> This difference did not lie in a simple contrast between a naive American idealism and a mature British belief in what the Treaty of Utrecht had described, nearly two and a half centuries earlier, as "a just balance of power, the best and most solid foundation of mutual friendship and a lasting general concord." The real contrast lay rather between American perception of US national interests in Asia and their perception of US interests in Europe.

Edmonds quoted Hopkins telling Soviet leader Joseph Stalin in May 1945: "The interests of the United States were world-wide and not confined to North and South America and the Pacific Ocean. . . . President Roosevelt had believed that the Soviet Union had likewise world-wide interests and that the two countries could work out together any political or economic considerations at issue between them." Edmonds went on to label that a "Kissingerian concept of the superpower relationship."[2]

True as far as it goes, but it does not go far enough. Idealism relates to assumptions, to beliefs about the nature of humankind and society, to the political economy that underpins a nation's institutions. To treat those leaders as if they operated on only one or the other level is a false dichotomy. Roosevelt was never simply a "realist," any more than Woodrow Wilson was simply an "idealist." Harry Hopkins would have been the first to agree. When Roosevelt reversed Wilson's phrase to ask whether democracy could make the world safe from another war, instead of the war making the world safe for democracy, he illustrated the aptness of Eliot Janeway's characterization of FDR as a practitioner of "the politics of principle," aware of the ways that democracy compromises idealism. Later critics, blaming him for failing to solve everything from colonialism to war, claimed he elevated "evasion of reality into a principle." But for Roosevelt, good politics could achieve even the most lofty of goals.[3]

Franklin Roosevelt was a true twentieth-century American liberal—inspired by his cousin Theodore, tutored by Woodrow Wilson, and trained by Josephus Daniels. He possessed a calm, quiet conviction that Americanism (a better word than liberalism) was so very sensible, logical, and practical, that societies would adopt those values and systems if only given the chance. It was the city-on-a-hill/an-example-for-all-the-world-to-follow approach that FDR preferred, even if coercion and force were sometimes legitimate means to the end.[4] Put another way, his Four Policemen concept for the postwar world was a plan for peaceful coexistence, even if the peace officers had to be armed. The final goal was progression toward a homogeneous world—however unlikely full achievement might be. John Winthrop and the Puritans would have been proud.[5]

For Franklin Roosevelt, that Americanism was largely the product of the three great events of his lifetime: World War I, the Great Depression, and World War II. In the First World War, the United States came to rescue and reform Europe, but failed. Then, in the Depression, the New Deal saved the Old Order by reforming it. (It is worth mentioning that Roosevelt never rejected Hoover's assessment that the Depression was caused by international events; FDR just never accepted the argument that the solution lay outside the United States.)[6] Lastly, just as the Depression had offered a chance to reform America, so the Second World War offered an opportunity to reform the world, not so as to enrich America, but to preserve the nation and proselytize its values.

Let me suggest some of Roosevelt's assumptions:

1. European leadership had not only failed, but the locus of power had, by 1943, shifted eastward, toward the Soviet Union. Moreover, that failure was bound to spread and be compounded so long as the Europeans held on to their old empires, ignoring liberalism and nationalism.[7]

2. The efficacy of the American system was demonstrated in its successful response to the Great Depression. Historians may agree that the New Deal

failed to end the economic crisis, but there is near-unanimous agreement that government actions dampened the social crisis. For Roosevelt, that social stability was a precondition to solving economic problems and hence far more important—a conclusion he would extend to his foreign policy. For him the New Deal was a model. It had succeeded socially, and not failed economically, even if it had occasionally stumbled a bit.[8]

3. Woodrow Wilson had the right idea—stability and security (peace and prosperity?) for the United States can be achieved only on a worldwide scale. Peace is indivisible, or so the phrase goes. But Wilson erred in being too structured, too specific, too inflexible, too unwilling to be practical and accept the realities of great power relationships.[9]

Putting all those assumptions together, Roosevelt's policies and actions begin to fall into place. The retrograde, the reactionary, the unprogressive had to be brought into the present; the angry, the disenchanted, the revolutionary had to be convinced that their interests lay in the creation of a stable world where change took place without destruction. When he commented to Stalin that India could be reformed from below, Roosevelt revealed his belief that reform could be extensive without being violent.[10] The means was an extension of the New Deal or, to put it more accurately, an extension of American social, economic, and political liberalism—what is better called Americanism.[11] Tucked away at the end of his famous "Dr. Win-the-War" talk with reporters in December 1943, came the connection:

And when victory comes, the program of the past [the New Deal], of course, has got to be carried on, in my judgment, with what is going on in other countries—postwar programs—because it will pay. We can't go into an economic isolationism, any more than it would pay to go into a military isolationism.

That is not just a question of dollars and cents, although some people think it is. It is a question of the long range, which ties in human beings with dollars, to the benefit of the dollars and the benefit of the human beings as a part of this postwar program.[12]

This was not some kind of crude imperialism, but the normal, human impulse to convert the unenlightened in a practical, mutually beneficial way.

The economic side of that Americanism can be identified, although it is impossible to separate politics and economics for very long. Determining the role and nature of economic politics in Roosevelt's thinking, as with most things, depends largely on long-term patterns of action and inaction. For example, it may be true that the President appointed Cordell Hull as secretary of state largely because of Hull's influence on Capitol Hill. And it may be true that the President did not trust Hull to negotiate with the major powers during the war. But Hull was in office for eleven and a half years and, once the early, brief struggle with George Peek and the protectionists ended, the secretary of state's campaign for "the removal, in so far as possible, of all economic barriers and the establishment of an equality of trade conditions among all the nations" (to use the words of Woodrow Wilson's Fourteen Points), was the economic foreign policy of the United States. In Latin America, Hull was left largely in charge—suggesting that the economic side of Americanism was the next step for the continent.[13]

Nor is Hull the only window into Roosevelt's economic politics. International monetary policy rested with the turf-conscious, aggressively loyal Secretary of the Treasury, Henry Morgenthau, Jr. As early as 1936, Roosevelt's support for a cooperative international monetary system was displayed in the Tripartite Monetary Agreement. The immediate purpose of the pact was to shore up the liberal democracies of Western Europe against the external threat of Nazism and the internal threat of Bolshevism, particularly in France where early fears that the government of Leon Blum would be radical had given way to fears that its weakness would stimulate a communist or fascist coup. The monetary agreement was specifically aimed at combatting the economic nationalism of Germany and Italy. It would be, said Morgenthau, a warning "to Japan, Germany and Italy that we won't stand any monkey business. . . . This is a notice to the boys—achtung!" But the arrangement also foreshadowed American proposals for an international monetary system based on the United States-as-world-banker design finally agreed to at the Bretton Woods meeting in the summer of 1944.[14] In a message to that conference, Roosevelt tied together his economics and his Americanism, telling the delegates that "commerce is the lifeblood of a free society. We must see to it that the arteries which carry that blood stream are not clogged again."[15] That seems trite at first, for trade is essential to any modern society. But to make that commerce intrinsic to a *free* society illustrates the connection the two had in Roosevelt's thinking.

As the sense of crisis in Europe deepened during 1938 and thereafter, Roosevelt emphasized aid and deemphasized reform. Measures to help France and Britain prepare for and fight a war included requirements that those nations spend money in the United States on capital expansion of war industries, but that was a short-term demand that would increase employment while it enhanced American preparedness. Long-term reforms of the kind advocated by Hull were postponed, but not forgotten. The Lend-Lease Act of March 1941 left repayment to the President's discretion, but Hull's repeated suggestions that Britain should post collateral—in the form of various British empire assets or even a Caribbean island or two—augured the shift that took place once the crisis had subsided and postwar reforms could be considered.[16]

Even as the United States was formulating the precise "invoice," as it were, for Lend-Lease, the Roosevelt administration issued a clear signal of what was to come. At the Atlantic Conference in August 1941, the first of the Roosevelt-Churchill meetings, the Americans insisted on a broad postwar commitment from the British granting commercial access to their empire, irrespective of Britain's existing Imperial Preference Agreements. Regardless of any legalisms and niceties that seemed to give Britain room to maneuver, the thrust of the declaration was unmistakable: "[Great Britain and the United States] will endeavor, with due respect for their existing obligations, to further the enjoyment by all states, great or small, victor or vanquished, of access, on equal terms, to the trade and to the raw materials of the world which are needed for their economic prosperity."[17]

The negotiations on a master agreement to settle accounts on Lend-Lease, which began only a few months after the Lend-Lease Act became law, demonstrated Roosevelt's acceptance of Hull's vision—or, to be more precise, of a modified version of Wilson's vision, set forth in the third of his fourteen points. There was to be no adding of costs or shipping back of unused materials. British payment was to be in the form of policy concessions.[a]

Nor did it end there. As the United States came to dominate the Anglo-American war effort, economic Americanism came to the fore. Roosevelt, sometimes speaking for himself, sometimes speaking through his advisers, continually pushed for access on American terms to the markets and empires of the world. American concern over Imperial preference was subsumed in larger arguments against any and all restrictions on American commercial activity within Britain and the empire. The Bretton Woods monetary arrangements, and arguments over everything from civil aviation rights to British meat contracts with Argentina, all revolved around the concept of "access, on equal terms, to the trade and to the raw materials of the world." Combined with American visions of how the postwar world's political structure should look, it constituted a powerful organizing force in postwar planning.

The world, not just Britain, was the target. The Bretton Woods Conference went further toward establishing the American vision of a universal political economy than Roosevelt ever got with his international peacekeeping structure. The tie-in of politics and economics, of a "free" society to a structure of commercial and monetary openness, provided the appa-

---

[a] See above, "Lend-Lease and the Open Door."

ratus that facilitated United States economic dominance throughout the world. Even the Soviet attempt to operate independently posed no challenge to American monetary and, therefore, economic, supremacy. The Bretton Woods "system" set the political economy for the postwar world until, in the late sixties/early seventies, a combination of European/ German and Japanese growth, plus the economic demands of continuing the Vietnam War, combined to force the United States out of its role as the world's banker and investor.[18]

In Latin America the process was well underway.[b] The Good Neighbor policy was never designed to let those states develop (or fail to develop) completely on their own. It substituted American leadership and persuasion for military action. After all, open coercion had proven incapable of creating self-sustaining stability. Northern Africa would break away from European colonial control, encouraged and helped by American example and trade.[c] Sub-Saharan Africa remained in the background, a place where colonialism had been a dismal failure.[19] Societies there would need a great deal of help before they could cut their ties to Europe. "Those people, of course, are completely incapable of self-government," he told the Negro Newspaper Publishers Association in 1944. "You have got to give them some education first. Then you have got to better their health and their economic position." International pressure and even accountability would prevent further exploitation in the name of assistance. American bases in Dakar and Bathurst would insure that aggressors could not threaten the Western Hemisphere from West Africa, as well as providing American watchdog presence to guarantee progress toward independence.[20] In Asia, the spread of Americanism required hands-on contact, something that further justified what Japan's attack at Pearl Harbor had made an apparent national security necessity—the extension of American military and economic influence across the Pacific. With the complete defeat of Japan, the weakness of China, and the inevitable elimination of Great Britain and France as colonial powers in that part of the world, only the United States was left as guide and guardian for the Pacific, though always with international accountability.[21] In all these cases, the economic problems of the colonial world were part and parcel of the political problems. Roosevelt clearly believed that stable democracy required economic security—a conviction that had characterized his handling of the Great Depression—and the wealth of the United States could be crucial to the creation of that security.

[b] Roosevelt's thinking about Latin America and its relationship to the United States is discussed above in " 'Baffled Virtue . . . Injured Innocence.': The Western Hemisphere as Regional Role Model."

[c] See above, "Casablanca—The End of Imperial Romance."

In Europe the problem was more difficult. Not only did reaction and revolution meet there, but they met with vast force. It had been Europe that forced the collapse of Wilson's dream, at home and abroad, and FDR had no intention of letting that happen again. But how to involve the United States in Europe without unleashing the same forces that had destroyed Wilson after World War I? In some instances the answer was to use whatever political and economic leverage was available to force others to adopt American norms. In other cases, particularly where the Soviet Union was involved, the answer was to lead by example; to keep cultural, educational, social, and economic channels open; and thus tie Europe into the broad consensus structure—economic and political—that would follow.[d]

Looked at from this perspective, Roosevelt's "Four Policemen" notion, one he mentioned repeatedly during the war,[22] meets all his criteria.[e] The concept is comfortably vague, leaving ample room for maneuver and compromise, yet it recognizes the imperatives created by powerful nation-states. It had the appearance of international equality while, in fact, it assumes a weak China and an Anglo-Soviet standoff in Europe. It solves the dilemma of how to insert American influence into Europe without maintaining a military presence,[23] and assumes the success of Americanism in the Western Hemisphere. As the colonial empires recede, American economic and political leadership (not domination) fills the void. Just as the New Deal coalition, led by Franklin Roosevelt, managed to create consensus among disparate groups of Americans, so this new international coalition would find consensus within Americanism. The result would be nations connected by common economic and social systems, guided and led by statesmen (elected philosopher-kings?) who managed affairs through broad agreement. The United Nations Organization would be a device for creating that consensus, not a place for votes and confrontation. As Roosevelt regularly pointed out, what became the General Assembly should only be a talking shop. "They don't decide anything, do they?" asked one reporter. "No," the President answered.[24] The great powers would "keep" the peace.

In a world where human beings follow a philosophy even while refusing to analyze it, there is no foreign policy without ideology. In this modern world of nation-states, where the survival of the state and nation are synonymous (at least in the eyes of the state), there is no foreign policy without national self-interest. Any analysis that treats the two separately

---

[d] See above, "Lend-Lease and the Open Door" and "Naked Reverse Right."

[e] See above, " 'The Family Circle': Roosevelt's Vision of the Postwar World," for a fuller discussion of the Four Policemen and Roosevelt's thinking on the structure of the postwar world.

is, by definition, flawed. The challenge for historians, and policymakers, is to determine the relative significance of each. We are all eager, perhaps too eager, to assign tangible, material self-interest the primary role. There is little difference between the doctrinaire Marxist who finds economics loitering beneath every rock, and the doctrinaire realist who finds power politics lurking around every corner. An illustration. The French Revolution posed a very real political threat when it continued the search for hegemony that began with Louis XIV. But, there is little doubt that the European response to revolutionary France was also ideological. The final result was neither a revolutionary nor a conservative Europe, but something in between. Unhappily, that unplanned compromise came only at great loss of life and unnecessary cost.

That need to reconcile ideology and geopolitical reality is evident in Franklin Roosevelt's wartime policies toward his two great allies, Great Britain and the Soviet Union. The President often acted more like a fixer and manipulator than a statesman, as contemporaries and historians have pointed out repeatedly. Perhaps Richard Hofstadter's famous label for Roosevelt—"the Patrician as Democrat"—with its insinuation of sham and charlatan, captures the widely accepted image of FDR in foreign affairs as well as at home.[25] But one characteristic example is his "Second Front diplomacy." In 1942, during talks between Roosevelt and Soviet Foreign Minister V. Molotov, the Russian diplomat pushed hard for a promise of an early Anglo-American invasion of Europe. Despite warnings from the British and advice from his own military chiefs about the limits of Allied capabilities, Roosevelt agreed to an elliptical and misleading public statement, drafted by Molotov, indicating that "in the due course of the conversations full understanding was reached with regard to the urgent tasks of creating a second front in Europe in 1942." It was a short-term expedient intended by Roosevelt to boost Soviet morale and counter the ever-present danger of a negotiated settlement between Moscow and Berlin. "I am inclined to think that at present all the Russians are a bit down in the mouth," he cabled Churchill. "But the important thing is that we may be and probably are faced with real trouble on the Russian front." The public statement was cute and clever, never spelling out the nature of the "full understanding." But it backfired when the Soviets chose to treat it as a firm, unconditional commitment.[26]

But beneath the quick fixes, fire-fighting, and political balms and soothing oils lay Roosevelt's assumptions in action. There as elsewhere, ideology combined with interest. Determining how the three nations and their leaders, particularly Franklin Roosevelt, defined those forces during World War II may help cut through the exaggerated rhetoric and reactive policies that characterized the day-to-day events, as well as illuminating FDR's assumptions, strategy, and tactics—in the end, his Americanism.

Wartime high politics and strategy were invariably a tripartite affair, particularly as Britain and the United States interacted with the Soviet Union. After all, even while working together, they oftentimes also worked hard to foster their own goals by manipulating each other. Soviet leaders seemed to assume Anglo-American collusion, but they too seized opportunities to play one against the other, as events at the Teheran Conference and the Churchill-Stalin meeting in October 1944 demonstrate.[f] Soviet-American relations were always affected and deflected by British actions and policies. Americans may have had their own intellectual and cultural perceptions of the Soviet Union, but in the wartime period Roosevelt's foreign policy was almost always influenced by what the British had done and were doing.

That is not to say that American foreign policy was a prisoner of Winston Churchill at 10 Downing Street—far from it. Anglo-American relations during the war were characterized by an extraordinary degree of cooperation, made necessary by the crisis but made possible by the continuing bonds of a common language, an intersected history, and a great deal of intellectual and cultural common ground. But in the mind of Franklin Roosevelt and his closest advisers, this was a combative kinship with the British.[27] Tension and distrust had always been paired with the sense of a special relationship. The American Revolution developed out of very real political differences and commercial rivalry. Throughout the nineteenth century, Americans saw Britain as their major European adversary, less threatening than Amerindians and internal dissension, but the only European state capable of projecting its strength across the Atlantic. It was Britain that seemed to challenge United States interests in Texas, Oregon, California, Mexico, Central America, Brazil, and Cuba. Her Majesty's Government had even meddled in the Civil War. The American electoral game of "twisting the lion's tail" reflected very real anti-British sentiments, and not just among Irish-American voters. As for World War I, Americans included Britain as part of that reactionary Europe which had rejected United States prescriptions for a just world and a lasting peace.[28]

Anglo-American relations during the Second World War built on that mixed legacy. Roosevelt's actions demonstrate his conviction that Britain could not and should not be the broker for Soviet-American relations. If anything, it was the United States that should act as a "balance wheel" between the British Empire and the Soviet Union. The President believed that Britain was a barrier to the creation of an atmosphere of trust and cooperation between Stalin and the West. "Stalin had taken Britain's desire to have a *cordon sanitaire*," he observed in 1944, "as an excuse now

---

[f] See above, " 'The Family Circle' " and "Naked Reverse Right."

for Russia's intention to have Czechoslovakia, Poland, and other nations whom it could control around it." Simply put, Soviet expansion into Eastern Europe, in Soviet eyes, was justified by British policy. It was just the sort of muddy-the-waters influence that Roosevelt feared.[29] After all, this was the same Franklin Roosevelt who, back in 1935, had written that the British "show a national selfishness towards other nations which makes mutual helpfulness very difficult to accomplish."[30]

Relations between the Soviet Union and the United States during the Second World War fall into no neat phases or categories. For much of the time, their contacts were minimal—an occasional meeting, discussions about aid, ambassadors arguing about a range of petty problems. The two nations often interacted through third parties—Great Britain, China, even Nazi Germany in its role as common enemy. The United States and the USSR were not "mixed up together," as Churchill aptly described the Anglo-American connection.[31] But, near the end of the war, as the Soviet Union became more powerful and the United Kingdom less so, the United States more and more was drawn—or stepped—into European affairs.

History is no zero-sum game that begins and ends at convenient dates, and that is particularly true for so brief an era as the Second World War. There is no need to dwell on the obvious fact that national self-interest, not altruism, brought the Soviet Union into the war against Germany in 1941; and that, likewise, American aid and cooperation were motivated by the same kind of self-interest. Self-interest is a given in relations between nation-states, but there is also a good deal of intellectual baggage that comes along with geopolitical realities. What seems by common agreement to be the greatest legacy for Americans and Soviets of their coalition is the memory of Franklin Roosevelt's policies. Soviet diplomat Andrei Gromyko, hardly a sentimentalist, has written of Roosevelt "with respect and affection, describing him as someone 'who knew how to conduct conversation freely, without any tension.' " Gromyko "detected 'a kind of gaiety' in Roosevelt that was 'evidence of a kind of inner strength.' "[32] That good feeling was in large part generated by Roosevelt's early and consistent recognition of the Soviet Union as a legitimate and major world power. Roosevelt's intuitive response to the German attack on Soviet forces in June 1941 was to offer acceptance and aid (albeit at British expense). Since the actual aid could not arrive in time to affect the outcome of the armed struggle for Moscow, acceptance was what mattered.[g] Four years later, Roosevelt wrote to Churchill: "I think we are all in agreement . . . as to the necessity of having the USSR as a

---

[g] This is discussed above in " 'They Don't Come Out Where You Expect': Roosevelt Reacts to the German-Soviet War, 1941."

fully accepted and equal member of any association of the great powers.
. . . It should be possible to accomplish this by adjusting our differences
through compromise by all the parties concerned." The President then
added in his own scrawl—"and this ought to tide things over for a few
years until the child learns to toddle."[33] The "child" Roosevelt wrote
about may have been the United Nations, but it could just as well have
meant the new, more reasonable, more liberal Soviet Union that FDR
hoped would emerge from the war—a hope that arose again some forty
years later in the days of *perestroika* and *glas'nost*.

Roosevelt's style may have prompted Soviet leaders (as well as American historians) to underestimate his "Americanism."[34] Practicality may
have masked his deeper assumptions. His acceptance of the fundamental
importance of the Soviet Union was supported by his military planners.
As Admiral Ernest King, the President's personal selection to head up the
Navy, put it bluntly to reporters in November 1942: "In the last analysis,
Russia will do nine-tenths of the job of defeating Germany."[35]

But there was a longer-term practicality as well. The image of Roosevelt's efforts to build on the wartime alliance in order to create an atmosphere of cooperation and trust with the Soviet Union is essentially correct, although his reluctance to share atomic secrets (with the USSR or
any other nation) was a cooperative opportunity lost that may have sabotaged the entire effort.[36] Of course it was easier for an American president
to call for compromise and conciliation with the Soviets, since Roosevelt
assumed that in the postwar world U.S. influence and forces would concentrate on the Western Hemisphere and the Pacific—England and the
Soviet Union would have to work things out in Europe. That was why he
accepted the political spheres-of-influence arrangement put together by
Stalin and Churchill in the summer and fall of 1944. Roosevelt had no
objections to special political relationships within the areas of Great
Power responsibility—and responsibility was the word he used—so long
as old-style, neomercantilist, exclusive spheres of influence were a thing
of the past.[h]

The President saw no sense in fighting World War II in order to prepare
for World War III. His "Four Policemen" were to be like four Dutch
uncles (one of his favorite phrases), gently chastising, hectoring, and lec-
turing the world into acting sensibly. With the world divided into four
arenas of responsibility, Roosevelt thought, the great powers would be
reasonably satisfied and too busy to get into each other's hair. Perhaps his
true conception of the glue that would hold this system together was revealed when he mused that he saw himself in retirement working with a

[h] See "Naked Reverse Right," above.

United Nations Organization, conveniently located in New York City, holding forth at Hyde Park as an elder statesman giving advice to world leaders who would trek up the Hudson to his home.[37]

Superficially, the pieces of Roosevelt's regional system were almost caricatures, the ultimate geopolitical structure. The Western Hemisphere appeared as an American sphere of influence, Asia a cardboard cartographic entity, and Eastern and Western Europe a hard reality. Africa was left down below, still largely splashed in the British-Empire-pink that covered classroom wall maps all over the United States. It was a picture that reflected American images of the world.

But Roosevelt had more in mind than just a political science–style model for an international system. He rejected British hints that his proposals could be adapted to the Churchill-Eden scheme for well-defined, centralized regionalism, believing that would only establish exclusive spheres of influence. The British version of collective security for Europe included a powerful regional council in London. A suggestion to Churchill that the regional councils be placed within the United Nations organization "set off a firecracker. The Prime Minister stamped around and said he would not stand for it a moment," even if some of his advisers favored the idea. Churchill's concept of the Big Four emphasized the creation of strong, structured regional councils whose members were powers in that region—much too autonomous and restrictive to suit Roosevelt.[38] Responsibility should not be the same as control.

The same was true for the Soviet Union. Shortly before the Yalta Conference the President identified his dilemma when he told congressional leaders that military occupation of liberated areas had raised the possibility of a spheres-of-influence solution. No one wanted to "force things to an issue," he said, concluding that the only option left was the use of American influence "to ameliorate the situation."[39] On 12 April 1945, the same day that Roosevelt died in Warm Springs, Georgia, Clement Attlee, who would soon replace Churchill as Prime Minister, received from an aide a memorandum analyzing American policy. The paper caught the essence of FDR's opposition to any reestablishment of the old European system: "It is more than doubtful, as I have said, whether the U.S.A. will join any Organization of which Russia was not a member since such an Organization would, in the long run, become an anti-Russian alliance, and the Americans are still controlled by their irrelevant and unrealistic historical phobia against 'alliances.' "[40] The memo correctly assessed Roosevelt's fears, even while it failed to recognize that Americans were about to embark on a new "historical phobia." When Roosevelt went "in search of monsters to destroy" he was not advocating global interventionism. Rather, he sought to prevent global "monsters" from intervening and destroying the peaceful American system that existed in the hemisphere and that he hoped would spread throughout the globe.

Nor did Roosevelt advocate a "closed" system in the New World. He and his advisers consistently opposed Latin American proposals for a regional security system in the Western Hemisphere. Hull rejected a seemingly innocuous pro-Allied association of nonbelligerent Latin American nations lest it establish a precedent for "united bloc action." Subsequently, during discussions about the structure of the United Nations Organization, the Latin Americans proposed creating regional security agencies that could take action to preserve the peace. The United States followed the same line it took with Britain and the Soviet Union, insisting that any peacekeeping enforcement have the prior approval of the United Nations Organization. The strong American reaction to British economic competition in Latin America (and elsewhere) was always couched in terms of open access. That may have been a dominant economic power's "imperialism of free trade," but the alternative was the kind of restrictive preferential trade agreements America had inveighed against since 1776, when they emerged on the world stage in the midst of a world of empires.

Not until early 1945 did the State Department, then headed by Stettinius, relax its opposition to regional security blocs. At that time, pressure from the Latin American governments fearful of both communism and great power manipulation, combined with some support from the U.S. military and Monroe Doctrine advocates in the United States, to force the State Department to modify its position. Ironically, Colombia's foreign minister even accused the United States of abandoning the Monroe Doctrine.[41]

Six months after Roosevelt's death, State Department adviser Charles Bohlen tried to distinguish between the Good Neighbor Policy and the Soviet sphere of influence in Eastern Europe that so concerned the Truman administration. In Latin America, wrote Bohlen, the United States had a "guiding voice" that was limited to "the politico-strategic aspect of their foreign relations."[42] It was an analysis that caught some of Roosevelt's distinction between regional leadership and dominant spheres of influence. Regions were to remain open, yet the major powers had legitimate regional security concerns that would, if ignored, create tensions and threats to the peace.

But Bohlen's distinctions were nothing new. Roosevelt and Hull had drawn similar distinctions in the mid-thirties when the Japanese claimed the Amamu Doctrine was Japan's Monroe Doctrine for East Asia. Again, early in 1940, when Nazi Foreign Minister Joachim Ribbentrop told Under Secretary of State Sumner Welles that all they wanted in Europe was the same security the United States gained in Latin America from the Monroe Doctrine, Welles retorted that the policy protected Hemispheric security without justifying American coercion or hegemony in the region.[43]

The President's 1943 proposal for "Free Ports of Information," and his suggestion for international free ports of trade in northern Norway are but two examples of the kind of accessibility he envisioned. A 1944 memo from Secretary of State Edward Stettinius to Roosevelt provided another example: "Postwar Poland will be under strong Russian influence. In this situation the United States can hope to make its influence felt only if some degree of equal opportunity in trade, investment, and access to sources of information is preserved."[44]

Whatever the dynamics of Anglo-Soviet shared responsibility in Europe, Roosevelt's early and continued commitment to cooperation, to peaceful coexistence, seems to offer a kind of vision that Soviet historians grudgingly admire. Even while they point to his "imperialism"—the acquisition of islands in the Pacific, an insistence on hegemony in Latin America, the struggle with Britain for economic advantage—they still treat the President and his closest advisers as a breed apart. This suggests that, first of all, there must be some sort of common ideological ground that makes Roosevelt understandable and less threatening. Second, it suggests that the Japanese are correct in their belief that style is in itself substance. How a leader does something is often as important as what is done, especially in this world of the "new diplomacy," where public relations and public posturing are forces to reckon with.

As for the common ideology, perhaps Roosevelt's relaxed if unshakable Americanism, combined with his seeming willingness to assign a sphere of influence to the Soviet Union while retaining one for the United States, suggested to Soviet leaders that practicality (geopolitical realism?) was the overriding factor.[45] They misjudged Roosevelt. He was far from the early Cold Warrior as some have claimed, but neither was he a simple, geopolitical "realist" playing with nations as if they were chess pieces on a board. His legacy is a mixed one that, in retrospect, often depends on the perspective and current agenda of the observer, but it is clear that he assumed the superiority and steady acceptance of American-style institutions.

Historian-diplomat George Kennan once accused Roosevelt of believing that personal charm could "melt" Stalin's ideological preconceptions, but that was not the President's thinking.[46] Roosevelt once described the process he envisaged to Sumner Welles. Assuming a peaceful world, American democracy and Soviet communism would continue to move toward each other, just as they had been doing since 1917. Following the revolution, the Soviet system moved toward "a modified form of state socialism," while the United States had traveled down the road toward "true political and social justice." Even if the two would never reach the middle together, on a scale where 100 stood for the distance that existed between the two in 1917 (with the United States at 100 and the Soviet Union at 0), they could lessen that distance enormously, perhaps getting to a point of 60 for the Americans and 40 for the Soviets. A crude but clear conception. That does not evade the question of whether or not Roosevelt would work with revolutionaries. Rather, it suggests that he believed, as had many of the progressives in the twenties and thirties, that revolutionaries and reformers would, given time, move toward the Golden Mean.[47] Perhaps war had calmed the revolutionary intensity of 1917, he told a friendly journalist; wise international leadership could bring "social as well as international peace, with progress following evolutionary constitutional lines."[48]

Roosevelt's ideology—his Americanism—is highlighted by his thinking on Germany. In part, his cautious optimism about the political evolution of the USSR was wishful thinking that flowed from what he perceived as a lack of choices. Nevertheless, the prerequisite for peace was a liberalized Soviet system. The fundamental German character, on the other hand, had been warped—"Prussianized" was his word—and thus he insisted on the unconditional surrender of Germany so that its society could be thoroughly reshaped. "We intend to rid them [the German people] once and for all of Nazism and Prussian militarism and the fantastic and disastrous notion that they constitute the 'master race,' " he told reporters after the Teheran talks. Upon returning from Yalta, the President stuck to his guns, warning that the Germans "must realize that only with complete surrender can they begin to reestablish themselves as people whom the world might accept as decent neighbors." His flippant comments about having Abyssinian doctors sent to Germany to practice their "particular brand of surgery" (emasculation), or of "castrating" the Germans if they continued to breed aggressive people betrayed the intensity of his feeling, even while they contain a hint of his appalling belief in genetic engineering.[49]

It is fascinating but ahistorical to speculate about what might have happened had Roosevelt not acted as he did, and when he did. Would a spheres-of-influence (regional councils) settlement have prevented the Cold War? What would the effect have been of open Presidential support for foot-dragging on aid to Russia? Would a "get tough" American policy have prevented the Soviet Union from later establishing its special relationship with Eastern Europe? Could Hitler then have played both sides against the middle and negotiated a separate peace with either the Soviet Union or the Anglo-Americans? Would Soviet military forces have been able to achieve the same kind of successes? Would the Americans have deserted the European theater for the Pacific? Would an open and early embracing of the Anglo-American alliance so desired by Churchill have forced the Soviets to act differently? The list of possibilities is endless.

It is easy to mock and condemn Roosevelt for his attempts to create a cooperative relationship with the Soviet Union, particularly in the light of Stalin's crude brutality. Even if the Cold War was inevitable because of Stalin's actions, which is by no means certain, FDR's attempt to work with the Soviet Union makes more sense than the belligerent, confrontational approach that was the alternative. Such ahistorical criticisms assume that a get-tough attitude toward Stalin would have brought about better results. That is a dubious conjecture given the Soviet leader's response to the tender ministrations of Harry Truman and his persuasive advisers.

Whatever the might-have-beens, Roosevelt treated the Soviet Union as an ally worth supporting, not an enemy or weak house of cards about to fall. His quick commitment to aid is evidence of the President's very early conviction that, like it or not, the Soviet Union should be treated as a major power in any postwar world. That was something of enormous psychological significance to a new, revolutionary state that saw itself, as the United States had in 1776, as a *novus ordo seclorum*—a new concept in social order.[50] It was a self-perception that outlasted the revolutionary era, remaining a fundamental part of United States foreign policy, just as it did in Soviet society. Whether in his efforts to pressure Britain to adapt its imperial system to an American-designed model, or his attempts to cajole the Soviet Union into acting "sensibly," Roosevelt's goal was consistent even while his expectations were moderate. He was trying to turn the conflict into the "Good War."

"No plan is perfect," he told Congress after the Yalta Conference. "Whatever is adopted . . . will doubtless have to be amended time and again over the years, just as our own Constitution has been. No one can say exactly how long any plan will last. . . . It ought to spell the end of the system of unilateral action, the exclusive alliances, the spheres of influence, the balances of power, and all the other expedients that have been tried for centuries—and have always failed."[51]

Writing in 1943, political commentator/columnist Walter Lippmann outlined his prescription for the postwar world: "This persistent evangel of Americanism in the outer world must reflect something more than meddlesome self-righteousness. It does. It reflects the fact that no nation, and certainly not this nation, can endure in a politically alien and morally hostile environment; and the profound and abiding truth that a people which does not advance its faith has already begun to abandon it."[52]

It could have been Franklin Roosevelt speaking.

Notes

Introduction

1. The hypothesis is that of historian Thomas McCormick. See William E. Leuchtenburg, "The Pertinence of Political History: Reflections on the Significance of the State in America," *Journal of American History* 73 (Dec. 1986), p. 593. However, before "political" historians have a smugness attack, it is sobering to survey the context within which Leuchtenburg's piece, an expansion of his 1986 address as president of the Organization of American Historians, appeared. Of a total of seven articles and notes in that issue of the *Journal*, all except Leuchtenburg's essay and a short eleven-page note (about the strategic bombing campaign during World War II) were on social history. Of those, two depend heavily on statistics for a narrow case study (Lynn, Massachusetts—everyone's favorite; and Concord, Massachusetts—such is the burden of locales that keep extensive records). Two others about steelworkers in Birmingham, and rural churches and reformers, work on a somewhat broader but not national canvas. The remaining article, about "Women, Politics, and Social Activism in the 1850s," manages to discuss those fascinating questions without even passing reference to the federal government, and only occasional mention of state governments. All things considered, one wonders whether Leuchtenburg's article would have been published had he not been president of the Organization of American Historians.

For thoughtful commentaries on the nature of diplomatic history, see Christopher Thorne, *Border Crossings* (Oxford: Basil Blackwell, 1988), "Introduction" and "The Prompting of History," pp. 3–28; Alexander DeConde, "Essay and Reflection: On the Nature of International History" *International History Review* 10 (May 1988), pp. 282–301; and Akira Iriye, "The Internationalization of History" *American Historical Review* 94 (Feb. 1989), pp. 1–10. That ongoing debate, which in itself illustrates the vigor of the field, can be followed in the lively pages of *Diplomatic History*, particularly over the last five years or so.

2. Eliot Janeway, *The Struggle for Survival* (New Haven: Yale Univ. Press, 1951), p. 71. Janeway goes on to argue strenuously that such statements, made apparently in 1940, were nothing but political sleight of hand since Roosevelt and Hopkins had abandoned the New Deal by then. An extreme example of the internationalization of the New Deal was the assertion of Treasury Secretary Henry Morgenthau, Jr., that his plan for postwar Germany should incorporate programs like the Rural Resettlement and Farm Security Administrations—both New Deal schemes. Morgenthau, memo of a conference at Red Rice, Andover, England, 15 Aug. 1944, Harry Dexter White papers (Princeton University), box 7. Roosevelt's belief in liberal, New Deal reforms is evident in his proposals to the Pacific War Council (Washington) for national rather than individual control of the sale of some basics like food, and his attack on high interest rates for public and quasi-public works; see minutes of the 23d and 28th Pacific War Council

meetings, 28 Oct. 1942 and 17 Feb. 1943, Map Room (MR) papers, Franklin D. Roosevelt Library (FDRL), Hyde Park, N.Y.

The externalization of the New Deal is perceptively presented in various chapters in John Morton Blum, *From the Morgenthau Diaries* (3 vols.; Boston: Houghton Mifflin, 1959–67), in particular the chapter entitled "A New Deal in International Economics," vol. III, pp. 228–78. Charles S. Maier in "The Politics of Productivity: Foundations of American International Economic Foreign Policy after World War II," *International Organization* 31 (Autumn 1977), pp. 607–33, argues that the New Deal experience shaped wartime planning. In particular, Maier sees belief in productivity and dislike of monopoly as keys to American thinking. See also Lloyd C. Gardner, *Economic Aspects of New Deal Diplomacy* (Madison: Univ. of Wisconsin Press, 1964) and his perceptive essay "The Role of the Commerce and Treasury Departments," in *Pearl Harbor As History*, Dorothy Borg and S. Okamoto, eds. (New York: Columbia Univ. Press, 1973), pp. 261–85. See Jürg Martin Gabriel, *The American Conception of Neutrality after 1941* (London: Macmillan, 1988), pp. 42–65, for a discussion of American monetary planning as a globalization of the New Deal. Another case study in the New Deal as foreign policy is my *Swords or Ploughshares? The Morgenthau Plan for Defeated Nazi Germany* (Philadelphia: Lippincott, 1976), esp. chap. 3.

3. Frank Ninkovich, "Interests and Discourse in Diplomatic History," *Diplomatic History* 13 (Spring 1989), pp. 135–61, argues that diplomatic historians must seek to understand the ways in which leaders sort and resort facts in accordance with their own perceptions of reality, i.e., their assumptions.

4. The supposed sterility of traditional diplomatic history is further belied by what has happened since 1973, following the opening of World War II archives in Great Britain and the United States. Debate began anew over everything from corporatism to colonialism to communism—demonstrating that traditional diplomatic history, with its emphasis on documents and records, still has something to offer, even for a period where a never-ending deluge of publications threatens to engulf us.

5. This is not the place to argue with Steiner about his classification of the United States as a "museum culture" society, destined for "near-greatness, a strength just below the best." Certainly Franklin Roosevelt would not have accepted that categorization; *In Bluebeard's Castle* (London and Boston: Faber & Faber, 1971), p. 86.

6. *United States* v. *Curtiss-Wright Export Corp*, 299 U.S. 304. Sutherland's opinion was *obiter dictum*, but reflected the reality of presidential power, even if the constitutional limits of such power remain open to question.

7. For some reason, FDR has often been either ignored or downplayed as a contributor to the growth of presidential power in foreign affairs. Walter LaFeber, in a discussion of contemporary concern during World War II about that trend, fits Roosevelt neatly into the chain. See LaFeber, "American Empire, American Raj," in *America Unbound: World War II and the Making of a Superpower*, W. F. Kimball, ed. (New York: St. Martin's Press, 1992), pp. 55–72.

8. This is recently argued with praise and admiration by Eric Larrabee, *Commander in Chief: Franklin Delano Roosevelt, His Lieutenants and Their War* (New York: Harper & Row, 1987), esp. pp. 1–95.

9. See, for example, the complaint of George Elsey, "Some White House Recollections, 1942–53," *Diplomatic History* 12 (Summer 1988), pp. 359–60.

Chapter One
The "Juggler"

1. Roosevelt quoting himself speaking to a special study group on Latin America; memorandum of a conversation between Roosevelt and Morgenthau, 15 May 1942, Presidential Diary, p. 1093, Henry Morgenthau, Jr., papers (FDRL).

2. On this matter of keeping a historical record, Roosevelt vociferously opposed keeping written accounts of policy deliberations. Here are but two examples: in 1934 he refused to let Henry Morgenthau's personal secretary take notes at cabinet meetings; in 1943 he rejected Churchill's proposal to publish the minutes of the Council of Four meetings from 1919 with the comment that "no notes should have been kept." Roosevelt to Hull, 16 Sept. 1943, U.S. Dept. of State, *Foreign Relations of the United States (FRUS)* (Washington: USGPO, 1865–), *Conferences at Washington and Quebec, 1943*, p. 1338n; Warren F. Kimball, *"The Most Unsordid Act" Lend-Lease, 1939–1941* (Baltimore: Johns Hopkins Univ. Press, 1969), p. 4. Sumner Welles, under secretary of state and a personal friend of the Roosevelts, complained of the President's "almost invariable unwillingness to dictate any memoranda of his conversations with foreign statesmen." Clearly that was neither laziness nor accident; *Seven Major Decisions* (London: Hamish Hamilton, 1951), p. 205.

3. My thanks to the resident Cretan philosopher of the University of Sussex, Christopher Thorne, for reminding me that, as usual, the Greeks said it first, and usually better. The story is related by Paul in his letter to Titus, 1.12.

4. Kent Roberts Greenfield, *American Strategy in World War II: A Reconsideration* (Baltimore: Johns Hopkins Univ. Press, 1963), p. 62.

5. Janeway, *The Struggle for Survival*, is particularly critical of Roosevelt's administrative shortcomings, especially his failure to establish a rational, structured war production/requirements system. Many of his complaints have been echoed subsequently. However, William R. Emerson, "Franklin Roosevelt as Commander-in-Chief in World War II," *Military Affairs* 22 (Winter 1958–59), pp. 183–92, argues persuasively that, in fact, Roosevelt established firm control of procurement, even if there was confusion at the next bureaucratic level. An example is provided in Albert A. Blum, "Birth and Death of the M-Day Plan," in *American Civil-Military Decisions*, Harold Stein, ed. (Birmingham: Univ. of Alabama Press, 1963), pp. 61–94.

6. Perhaps the best taste of that atmosphere is provided in William D. Hassett, *Off the Record with F.D.R., 1942–1945* (New Brunswick: Rutgers Univ. Press, 1958).

7. Hopkins' role is discussed in all the standard studies of Roosevelt's foreign policy and diplomacy. The classic study is by Robert Sherwood, a playwright and speechwriter in Roosevelt's White House, *Roosevelt and Hopkins: An Intimate History* (rev. ed.; New York: Grosset & Dunlap, Universal Library, 1950). Despite Sherwood's obvious sympathy for both subjects, the book remains the best source. For a general biography, see George McJimsey, *Harry Hopkins* (Cam-

bridge, Mass.: Harvard Univ. Press, 1987). Fraser Harbutt, "Churchill, Hopkins, and the 'Other' Americans: An Alternative Perspective on Anglo-American Relations, 1941–1945," *International History Review* 8 (May 1986), pp. 236–62, has drawn a picture of Hopkins as Churchill's man in the White House, the linchpin in the Prime Minister's "system" for manipulating Roosevelt. But who manipulated whom? Roosevelt, fully aware of the Churchill-Hopkins channel, used it even more effectively to influence the Prime Minister, particularly on major issues. Moreover, Hopkins' admiration for Churchill was balanced by his distrust of British policies. Like "the Boss," Hopkins supported decolonization of European empires and a we-can-work-together approach toward the Soviet Union, as the essays which follow illustrate.

8. See the interesting set of essays by John Morton Blum, *The Progressive Presidents: Roosevelt, Wilson, Roosevelt, Johnson* (New York: Norton, 1980).

9. For such criticism see below, chap. 9, n. 39.

10. Historian Elliot A. Rosen recalls Raymond Moley saying that the Roosevelt entourage never discussed foreign policy in the 1932 presidential campaign because they had no reason to differ with Hoover; Rosen to the author, 22 April 1987.

11. The quotations are from William R. Rock, *Chamberlain and Roosevelt* (Columbus: Ohio State Univ. Press, 1988), pp. 35, 85–86.

12. The quotation is from Donald Cameron Watt's description of Lord Halifax's conclusions following the German invasion of Poland; *How War Came: The Immediate Origins of the Second World War, 1938–1939* (New York: Pantheon, 1989), p. 540. A few weeks after the German attack, the Soviet Union, on the grounds of security, "occupied" those portions of eastern Poland assigned to the USSR in a secret protocol.

13. Charles C. Tansill's *Back Door to War: The Roosevelt Foreign Policy, 1933–1941* (Chicago: Henry Regnery, 1952) is the prototype for accusations that FDR consciously used war with Japan as a means of entering the war in Europe. The claim that Roosevelt knew beforehand of the Japanese attack on Pearl Harbor is demonstrably false, but keeps rising, phoenixlike, from the ashes of each and every refutation. A recent summary of the controversy is Larrabee, *Commander in Chief*, pp. 82–86.

David Reynolds, *The Creation of the Anglo-American Alliance, 1937–1941: A Study in Competitive Co-operation* (London: Europa, 1982) stresses Roosevelt's reluctance to actively enter the war even while he firmly believed Britain's survival indispensable to American security. Waldo Heinrichs, *Threshold of War: Franklin D. Roosevelt and American Entry Into World War II* (New York: Oxford Univ. Press, 1988) paints a picture of a President whose concern over the lack of American preparedness made him reluctant to take the final step to war. By implication, both suggest that public opinion was as much an excuse as a reason for Roosevelt's hesitation. I agree.

Hitler's decision was not as "gratuitous" as it appeared. Lend-Lease, convoying, and Roosevelt's extension of the "neutral" Western Hemisphere far out into the Atlantic were more than enough grounds for declaring that a state of war already existed between Germany and the United States—the phraseology used by the President regarding Japan the day after the Pearl Harbor attack. On

12 December, Hitler made an offhand remark that illustrates his assumption that the United States, in retaliation for the Japanese attack, would concentrate its military efforts in the Pacific—an assumption that proved false; conference between Hitler and Admiral E. Raeder, *Führer Conferences on Matters Dealing with the German Navy*, trans. and mimeographed by the Office of Naval Intelligence (Washington: Dept. of the Navy, ONI, 1947), II, p. 79. Hitler apparently missed a piece in the *Chicago Tribune* of 4 December that summarized an Anglo-American-Canadian agreement of Jan.–Feb. 1941 to concentrate on defeating Germany even in the event of a war with Japan.

14. To start with, see David Wyman, *Paper Walls* (Amherst, Mass.: Univ. of Massachusetts Press, 1968), and Richard Breitman and Alan M. Kraut, *American Refugee Policy and European Jewry, 1933–1945* (Bloomington: Indiana Univ. Press, 1987).

15. Paul Fussell has recently overdone this point in *Wartime* (New York: Oxford Univ. Press, 1989).

16. As of this writing (September 1990), promises from Soviet officials of access to their diplomatic archives have proven to be just that—promises.

17. William L. Langer and S. Everett Gleason, *The Challenge to Isolation* (New York: Harper & Bros., 1952) and *The Undeclared War, 1940–1941* (New York: Harper & Bros., 1953); A. Whitney Griswold, *The Far Eastern Policy of the United States* (New York: Harcourt, Brace & Co., 1938), chap. 11.

18. Henry L. Stimson Diary (Sterling Memorial Library, Yale Univ., New Haven, Conn.), 18 Dec. 1940.

19. As quoted in the Earl of Birkenhead, *Halifax: The Life of Lord Halifax* (London: Hamish Hamilton, 1965), p. 477.

20. John Harvey, ed., *The War Diaries of Oliver Harvey* (London: Collins, 1978), pp. 229, 31.

21. Barry Karl, *The Uneasy State* (Chicago: Univ. of Chicago Press, 1983), p. 207. Two major studies that emphasize Roosevelt the politician, hemmed in by his perception of public opinion, are Robert Dallek, *Franklin D. Roosevelt and American Foreign Policy* (New York: Oxford Univ. Press, 1979), and John L. Gaddis, *The United States and the Origins of the Cold War* (New York: Columbia Univ. Press, 1972). J. Garry Clifford, "Both Ends of the Telescope: New Perspectives on FDR and American Entry into World War II," *Diplomatic History* 13 (Spring 1989), pp. 213–30, emphasizes the need to continue to study Roosevelt through both the "narrow lens" of the domestic debate over foreign policy as well as with the "broadened focus" of international events—through "both ends of the telescope," as it were.

22. For "pitiless publicity," see " 'In Search of Monsters to Destroy,' " elsewhere in this collection; "Free Ports of Information" is discussed in Sherwood, *Roosevelt and Hopkins*, p. 708; and in " 'The Family Circle,' " elsewhere in this collection.

23. John Martin in *Action This Day*, J. Wheeler-Bennett, ed. (London: Macmillan, 1968), pp. 145–46. Martin's comment is echoed by Lord Normanbrook, ibid., p. 32.

24. Bert E. Park, M.D., provides a comprehensive survey of the various claims that Roosevelt's health gravely affected his foreign policy, in *The Impact of Illness*

on World Leaders (Philadelphia: Univ. of Pennsylvania Press, 1986), "Roosevelt: Structuring the Aftermath," pp. 221–94. Park notes that between April and September 1944, Roosevelt's blood pressure was so high as to constitute "a bona fide medical emergency," a condition that could cause damage to vital organs, including the brain. Park's examination of the historical and medical record illustrates that FDR experienced frequent incidents of stupor and forgetfulness, although these were usually measured in minutes not hours. Ibid., p. 235–36. Park concludes that Roosevelt's health left him enervated and prone to tire, but not mentally impaired. See also Kenneth R. Crispell and Carlos F. Gomez, *Hidden Illness in the White House* (Durham and London: Duke Univ. Press, 1988), pp. 75–159, and the comments in Hassett, *Off the Record*, pp. 307, 319, 327.

My own far less scientific research into the photographic record lends support to Park's conclusion that Roosevelt's episodes were transient. One symptom of encephalopathy is the same slack-jawed, vacuous look captured in the famous and oft-printed photograph of Roosevelt making a point to Churchill during the Yalta Conference. (See Crispell and Gomez, *Hidden Illness*, p. 139, and Park, *Impact of Illness*, p. 265.) But subsequent frames of the same 35mm film (taken by the U.S. Army Signal Corps and on deposit at the Defense Department Audio Visual Office in the Pentagon, Washington, D.C.) show little sign of that unhealthy, open-mouthed look. Perhaps Kathleen Harriman was right when she remarked three times in letters sent from Yalta about how relaxed and genial Roosevelt appeared; W. Averell Harriman and Elie Abel, *Special Envoy to Churchill and Stalin, 1941–1946* (New York: Random House, 1975). p. 392. Even the irrepressible Harry Truman, in his informal memoir, recalled that Roosevelt was healthy and chipper after returning from Yalta, although he tired quickly; *Where the Buck Stops: The Personal and Private Writings of Harry S. Truman*, Margaret Truman, ed. (New York: Warner Books, 1989), p. 67.

25. Larrabee, *Commander in Chief*, p. 11. Marshall was Chief of Staff of the U.S. Army.

26. The statement of Stephen E. Ambrose, *Rise to Globalism* (5th rev. ed.; New York: Penguin, 1988), pp. 27–28.

27. Two scholars have laid to rest the notion that Roosevelt meekly followed the advice of his military leaders; Kent Roberts Greenfield in *American Strategy in World War II*, and William Emerson in his article in *Military Affairs,* "Franklin Roosevelt as Commander-in-Chief." Greenfield argues that political matters did not seriously affect the decisions to overrule, except for the North African campaign, but Emerson claims that "the political motive was uppermost in Roosevelt's mind" (p. 206). Greenfield lists twenty overrules and twelve significant initiatives by FDR on military matters. Perhaps the key move was the creation of the Executive Office of the President in July 1939, an indication of just how much FDR wanted to hold the reins. Greenfield's speculation that Roosevelt may have believed, throughout the war, that the role of America was from first to last to serve as "the arsenal of Democracy" is worth considering. As he points out, the President repeatedly cut back on his Chiefs of Staff recommendations for a massive American commitment to the invasion of northern France (p. 74).

28. Warren F. Kimball, ed., *Churchill & Roosevelt: The Complete Correspondence* (3 vols.; Princeton: Princeton Univ. Press, 1984), II, C-414/6, C-567; III, C-617, C-750, and pp. 318, 523–24.

29. This is the argument of Mark A. Stoler, *The Politics of the Second Front* (Westport, Conn.: Greenwood Press, 1977).

30. As Stephen Ambrose pointed out, the decision not to race for Berlin had both political and military reasons, although the atmosphere of the decision was that General Eisenhower's summary of the options gave FDR the military justification to take the political decision he favored; *Eisenhower and Berlin, 1945: The Decision to Halt at the Elbe* (New York: Norton, 1967).

31. William A. Williams, *The Tragedy of American Diplomacy* (New York: World Publishing Co., 1959); Arthur Schlesinger, Jr., "The Origins of the Cold War," in *The Origins of the Cold War* (Boston: Ginn & Co., 1970), orig. pub. in *Foreign Affairs* 46 (Oct. 1967); Walter LaFeber, *America, Russia, and the Cold War* (New York: John Wiley, 1967), and "Roosevelt, Churchill, and Indochina: 1942–45," *American Historical Review* 80 (Dec. 1985), pp. 1277–95; Norman Podhoretz in the pages of *Commentary*.

32. "Ominous word" was the label of Oliver Harvey, a British Foreign Office official, when describing Eden's reliance on intuition; *War Diaries*, p. 365. Berlin is quoted in Robin Edmonds, *Setting the Mould: The United States and Britain, 1945–1950* (New York: Norton, 1986), pp. 14–15.

33. Comment delivered by George F. Kennan on 17 April 1974, meeting of the Organization of American Historians in Denver, Colorado. His personal impressions of Roosevelt are drawn largely from an episode when he was chargé d'affaires in Lisbon, Portugal. Kennan opposed policies for the Azores advocated by the military chiefs. He received no support from the State Department and flew to Washington to discuss the issue. He managed to meet with the President who, without consulting anyone, not only reversed the policy, but told Kennan he should not "worry about all those *people* over there," apparently a reference to both the military and the State Department. Kennan, *Memoirs, 1925–1950* (Boston: Little, Brown & Co., 1967), pp. 142–63.

34. The classic examples are Charles C. Tansill, who attacked from what might be called the Irish-right; *Back Door to War*, and Charles A. Beard, who proceeded from the progressive left; *American Foreign Policy in the Making, 1932–1940* and *President Roosevelt and the Coming of the War, 1941* (New Haven: Yale Univ. Press, 1946–48).

More recently, some historians, relying heavily upon a series of casual remarks attributed to Roosevelt, have concluded that the President consciously sought an "incident" in the Atlantic that would bring the United States into war against Germany. See, for example, Frederick W. Marks, *Wind Over Sand* (Athens: Univ. of Georgia Press, 1988), pp. 164–65, esp. n. 107. But for a different interpretation that stresses Roosevelt's distinction between a limited naval war and the kind of all-out participation hoped for by Britain (and the Soviets), see the persuasive arguments of David Reynolds, *Creation of the Anglo-American Alliance*, pp. 202, 213–20, esp. n. 116. See also Kimball, *Churchill & Roosevelt*, I, pp. 229–30. Heinrichs, *Threshold of War*, states that Roosevelt did not seek war (p. 151), but the overall thrust of his argument is that the President only sought to delay war while the United States built its military preparedness.

A useful look at the phenomenon of "revisionism," using World War II and Cold War historiography as examples, is Lawrence S. Kaplan, "The Cold War and European Revisionism," *Diplomatic History* 11 (Spring 1987), pp. 143–56.

35. One recent study gives Churchill the credit, or blame, for maneuvering the United States into the Cold War; see Fraser J. Harbutt, *The Iron Curtain: Churchill, America, and the Origins of the Cold War* (New York: Oxford Univ. Press, 1986).

36. Donald C. Watt, "Britain and the Historiography of the Yalta Conference and the Cold War," *Diplomatic History* 13 (Winter 1989), pp. 67–98, suggests a complex typology and provides an excellent, wide-ranging, occasionally argumentative historiographical survey of the World War II origins of the Cold War. The notes provide a comprehensive bibliography of Anglo-American-Soviet relations during the war.

37. As quoted by James T. Patterson, "Robert A. Taft and American Foreign Policy, 1939–1945," in Leonard P. Liggio and James J. Martin, eds., *Watershed of Empire: Essays on New Deal Foreign Policy* (Colorado Springs: Ralph Myles, 1976), p. 207, n. 76.

The research of the early critics has been superseded by the opening of the archives, but their emotional arguments are still with us, and their accusatory tone still makes occasional appearances. Two who condemn Roosevelt's actions at Yalta are George N. Crocker, *Roosevelt's Road to Russia* (Chicago: Henry Regnery, 1959), and Hanson Baldwin, *Great Mistakes of the War* (New York: Harper, 1950). A more recent example is Steven M. Miner, *Between Churchill and Stalin: The Soviet Union, Great Britain, and the Origins of the Grand Alliance* (Chapel Hill: Univ. of North Carolina Press, 1988), p. 7 and passim, who contemptuously dismisses the belief of Roosevelt (as well as of a number of others, including Churchill) that "he alone understood Stalin and knew the secret of winning his trust; each, in turn, failed." A much less scholarly and even more strident, bitter attack, couched in the rhetoric of the early Cold War, is Robert Nisbet, *Roosevelt and Stalin: The Failed Courtship* (Washington: Regnery Gateway, 1988). Nisbet takes all the evidence of Roosevelt's efforts to work with Stalin and, with the careful exclusion of anything that does not fit his thesis, creates Churchill the hero and Roosevelt the fool, albeit a calculating one. "Puerility, . . . political romanticism and misguided moralism," were all compounded by Roosevelt's personal diplomacy; see p. 107. Theodore Draper has engaged in a running battle with Nisbet and others in the pages of *The New York Review of Books* during the 1980s. One of those essays is reprinted in his *A Present of Things Past: Selected Essays* (New York: Hill & Wang, 1990).

38. Roosevelt also considered deindustrialization. See Kimball, *Swords or Ploughshares?*

39. The analogy is that of Robert Dallek in *Roosevelt and American Foreign Policy*, p. vii. I hasten to add that Dallek does not stop there.

Chapter Two
"They Don't Come Out Where You Expect"

1. Halifax to Sir John Simon, 21 March 1941, papers of Lord Halifax (microfilm, Winston S. Churchill Library, Churchill College, Cambridge).

2. There has been speculation, particularly among German historians, that Stalin was planning an offensive against Germany. Evidence for that thesis re-

mains dubious. See Gabriel Gorodetsky, "Stalin und Hitlers Angriff auf die Sowjet Union." *Vierteljahrsheft für Zeitgeschichte* 4 (1989): 645-72. More subtle is the thesis of H. W. Koch, "Hitler's 'Programme' and the Genesis of Operation 'BARBAROSSA,' " *The Historical Journal* 26 (1983), pp. 891–920, who presents Hitler's policies in rigidly geopolitical terms. Koch argues that Hitler had good reason to worry about Soviet moves, particularly in Finland, hence the German attack was both preventative and aggressive. He denies that Hitler had a detailed "programme" for conquering the Soviet Union.

Likewise, the Roosevelt administration has been accused both of provoking a war with Japan in order to enter the war in Europe on Britain's side, and of trying to goad Germany into a war over shipping in the Atlantic. See " 'The Family Circle,' " n. 83, and Kimball, *Churchill & Roosevelt*, I, pp. 229–30. A twist on that theme has Churchill manipulating intelligence, as was done with the Zimmermann Note during World War I, to hide from the Americans the knowledge that the Japanese were about to attack Pearl Harbor. In the absence of documentary evidence (though certain British records on relations with Japan during September through December 1941 remain closed), and despite the implausibility of either Roosevelt or Churchill permitting the bulk of the U.S. Pacific Fleet to be sunk, the belief persists. See John Costello, *The Pacific War* (New York: Wm. Morrow, 1981). The still-restricted materials are Premier (PREM) 3, files 252/5, 252/6, and 252/6B, located in the British Public Record Office (PRO), Kew, England.

3. See below, nn. 46–48.

4. A Soviet interpretation presented in *Soviet Foreign Policy, 1917–1945*, A. A. Gromyko and B. N. Ponomarev, eds. (Moscow: Progress Publishers, 1981), p. 418. David Reynolds has placed Roosevelt's reaction to the Soviet-German war in the context of "a President who preferred to contain Hitler by proxy rather than hurriedly to commit his country to formal war." See Reynolds, *Anglo-American Alliance*, pp. 204–7; and Reynolds, "Churchill and the British 'Decision' to Fight on in 1940: Right Policy, Wrong Reasons," in *Diplomacy and Intelligence during the Second World War*, ed. Richard Langhorne (Cambridge: Cambridge Univ. Press, 1985), pp. 147–67.

5. Gabriel Gorodetsky, *Stafford Cripps' Mission to Moscow, 1940–1942* (Cambridge: Cambridge Univ. Press, 1984), pp. 112–25. Gorodetsky is much concerned with exonerating Cripps for initially refusing to carry out Churchill's instruction to pass on such warnings to Stalin. Steven Miner, *Between Churchill and Stalin*, pp. 119–22, who is much more critical of Cripps, points out that Churchill's insistence on delivering a warning was based on ULTRA intelligence which was not available to Cripps. Whatever the verdict, the account illustrates Britain's uncertainty about the matter. An extensive summary of British intelligence indications of the German attack, operation BARBAROSSA, is in F. H. Hinsley, *British Intelligence in the Second World War*, 3 vols. (London: HMSO, 1979–88), I, pp. 429–83. Soviet histories generally make no reference to such warnings. German diplomats in Moscow quickly learned of the warning given by Cripps; see *Documents on German Foreign Policy*, series D, 12 (Washington: USGPO, 1962), pp. 604–5.

The British assumption that they were Hitler's primary military target is set forth in Hinsley, *British Intelligence*, I, pp. 481–83, and modified a bit in ibid., II, pp. 78–80. Reynolds, "Churchill and the British 'Decision' to Fight on in 1940," in *Diplomacy and Intelligence*, pp. 147–67, summarizes this evidence.

6. Hull to Steinhardt, 4 March 1941, *FRUS*, 1941, I, p. 714. See also Sherwood, *Roosevelt and Hopkins*, p. 259; Heinrichs, *Threshold of War*, pp. 60–61. Barton Whaley, *Codeword BARBAROSSA* (Cambridge: MIT Press, 1973), is a fascinating study of the intelligence warnings that preceded the German attack on the Soviet Union, although the book is marred by extensive speculation and use of undocumented claims. Whaley concludes that through disinformation and deception, Hitler convinced Stalin that war would come *only* if the Soviet Union rejected a German ultimatum. That ultimatum never came; pp. 222–45.

7. A convenient and readable summary of the warnings and Stalin's reaction is in Anthony Read and David Fisher, *The Deadly Embrace: Hitler, Stalin, and the Nazi-Soviet Pact, 1939–1941* (New York: Norton, 1988), particularly chaps. 53–54. A recent survey of Stalin's thinking and decisions is Louis Rotundo, "Stalin and the Outbreak of War in 1941," *Journal of Contemporary History* 24 (April 1989), pp. 277–99. See also Whaley, *Codeword BARBAROSSA*, passim and esp. pp. 36–37, 41–42, 66–73; Valentin Berezhkov, *History in the Making: Memoirs of World War II Diplomacy* (Moscow: Progress Publishers, 1983), p. 72; and Edward M. Bennett, *Franklin D. Roosevelt and the Search for Victory: American-Soviet Relations, 1939–1945* (Wilmington, Del.: SR Books, 1990), chap. 2. Khrushchev is quoted by Milton Leitenberg, "The Soviet Union and the Lessons of World War II," *SHAFR Newsletter* 19, no. 2 (June 1988), p. 11. See also Russel H. S. Stolfi, "BARBAROSSA: German Grand Deception and the Achievement of Strategic and Tactical Surprise Against the Soviet Union, 1940–1941," in *Strategic Military Deception*, D. C. Daniel and K. L. Herbig, eds. (New York: Pergamon, 1982), pp. 195–223. Soviet intelligence directed against Germany is surveyed with grudging admiration in Paul L. Kesaris, ed., *The Rote Kapelle: The CIA's History of Soviet Intelligence and Espionage Networks in Western Europe, 1936–1945* (Washington: University Publications of America, 1979).

A Soviet assessment of the intelligence that reached Moscow about German intentions is Janghir Najafov, "German Invasion of the U.S.S.R. and the U.S. Position," in *Soviet-U.S. Relations, 1933–1942* (Moscow: Progress Publishers, 1989), pp. 231–37. According to Soviet historian Oleg Rzheshevsky, the letters dismissing warnings of a German attack as Western "disinformation" were sent to Stalin by his secret police chief, Lavrenti Beria.

On 8 May 1989, *Pravda* published a detailed account of Soviet intelligence reports on German preparations for BARBAROSSA; reports were sent to Moscow as early as November 1940 (*International Herald Tribune*, 9 May 1989). On 25 June 1989, The *Sunday Times* (London) summarized an article by a Soviet army general published in *Ogonyok* that accused Stalin of "a cowardly awe of Adolf Hitler" and of ignoring a direct warning about Hitler's plans from the German ambassador, Friedrich von Schulenberg. In the era of *glas'nost*, when this is being written, it is difficult to keep up with the steady stream of "disclosures" appearing in Soviet newspapers and journals. Most are attacks on Stalin and, more recently, against Beria. Few come as surprises to western historians, and even fewer are accompanied by documentary evidence.

8. See Kimball, *"The Most Unsordid Act,"* pp. 189, 200–201, 216. The various amendments are examined from the point of view of the Roosevelt administration in an undated memorandum, "Objection to Amendment . . . ," Treasury Dept. files, "The Lend-Lease Bill" (Washington, D.C.). [Those files have presumably been transferred to the National Archives since they were sighted by the author in 1965.] See also Raymond Dawson, *The Decision to Aid Russia* (Chapel Hill: Univ. of North Carolina Press, 1959), pp. 23–25. Sherwood claims that Roosevelt firmly opposed anything that would prevent giving aid to the Soviets since it was "possible if not probable" that they would soon be at war with Germany and/or Japan; *Roosevelt and Hopkins*, p. 264.

9. Joint Army-Navy Board minutes, 3 Nov. 1941, as quoted in Edwin T. Layton, Roger Pineau, and John Costello, *"And I Was There"* (New York: William Morrow, 1985), pp. 176–77.

10. *Soviet Foreign Policy, 1917–1944*, p. 411.

11. Halifax reported to Churchill that the United States believed the B-17s in the Philippines would deter Japan from further expansion. Halifax to Churchill, 11 Oct. 1941, Halifax papers (Churchill Library). For a discussion of the American belief in B-17s as deterrents to Japanese expansion, see Heinrichs, *Threshold of War*, esp. pp. 175–76, 195–96.

12. Halifax to Eden, 7 July 1941, Avon papers-FO 954/29, US/41/116 (PRO). A summary of the details of the American response to the German attack can be found in Heinrichs, *Threshold of War*, pp. 92–117.

13. Hopkins as quoted in Jan Ciechanowski, *Defeat in Victory* (Garden City, N.Y.: Doubleday, 1947), p. 26. Dwight W. Tuttle, *Harry L. Hopkins and Anglo-American-Soviet Relations, 1941–1945* (New York: Garland, 1983), p. 86, uses this comment and a few similar statements by Hopkins to argue that he "disagreed with FDR's Russian policy." That interpretation flies in the face of all the other evidence, nor did Roosevelt cease to support the aid-to-Britain program. The turn-to-the-left pun, accidental or not, is from Sherwood, *Roosevelt and Hopkins*, p. 303.

14. Reynolds, *Anglo-American Alliance*, p. 206; Sherwood, *Roosevelt and Hopkins*, pp. 303–4.

15. Steinhardt to the secretary of state, 17 June 1941, *FRUS*, 1941, I, p. 765.

16. Bullitt to Roosevelt, 1 July 1941, in Orville H. Bullitt, ed., *For the President, Personal and Secret* (Boston: Houghton Mifflin, 1972), p. 522. Bullitt's penchant for gossip and flamboyance later made him a liability, and by 1942 his influence had waned. There are literally hundreds of similar warnings of the danger of Communists at home and abroad. Some of the more colorful public responses are in Wayne S. Cole, *Roosevelt and the Isolationists, 1932–45* (Lincoln: Univ. of Nebraska Press, 1983), pp. 434–35. See also Dawson, *The Decision to Aid Russia*, and Fred L. Israel, *The War Diary of Breckenridge Long* (Lincoln: Univ. of Nebraska Press, 1966), pp. 206–14.

17. Kennan, *Memoirs*, pp. 133–34.

18. See memorandum of a conversation between Henderson and Umansky, 2 July 1941, *FRUS*, 1941, I, pp. 784–85. Henderson's intensity may have been heightened by his marriage to a Latvian whose nationalism was quite fervent. In

addition, Washington officials held Umansky in contempt as a sycophantic bureaucrat. See Loy W. Henderson, *A Question of Trust: The Origins of U.S.-Soviet Diplomatic Relations: The Memoirs of Loy W. Henderson*, George W. Baer, ed. (Stanford, Calif.: Hoover Institution Press, 1986), pp. 195–98; Edward M. Bennett, *Franklin D. Roosevelt and the Search for Security: American-Soviet Relations, 1933–1939* (Wilmington, Del.: SR Books, 1985), pp. 174–75.

19. Roosevelt's statement is in a message to Churchill of 14 July 1941; Kimball, *Churchill & Roosevelt*, I, R-50x. Even though the message mentioned only rumors of British commitments to various Balkan groups, the stimulus for Roosevelt's comments was a memo from Assistant Secretary of State Adolf Berle that warned of British pledges regarding the Baltic states as well.

Stalin publicly assumed that the Baltic area was a legitimate part of the Soviet Union. Churchill later told the House of Commons that the Atlantic Charter applied, primarily, to nations "under the Nazi yoke . . . quite a separate problem from the progressive evolution of self-governing institutions in the regions, and people which owe allegiance to the British Crown." Sherwood, *Roosevelt and Hopkins*, p. 363. Miner, *Between Churchill and Stalin*, deals with the period from 1940 to mid-1942, focusing on Stalin's early demands for the Baltic states.

20. Memo of Conversation between Atherton (Acting Chief of the Division of European Affairs) and the Soviet ambassador (Umansky), 30 June 1941, *FRUS*, 1941, I, pp. 778–79.

21. The exchange of mid-June is in Kimball, *Churchill & Roosevelt*, I, C-100x. Roosevelt's response was sent indirectly through the American ambassador in London; Winston S. Churchill, *The Second World War* (6 vols.; Boston: Houghton Mifflin, 1948–53), *The Grand Alliance*, p. 369.

One example of American caution in promising aid is in a wordy memorandum of a conversation between Welles and Halifax (British ambassador in Washington), 10 July 1941, *FRUS*, 1941, I, p. 789. In that memo, Welles told Halifax that "whatever it was decided by this Government to send to Russia would be the subject of consultation between this Government and the British Government since it was a matter of common concern to all three Governments that the supplies which this country might have available be utilized in those particular places where, from the military standpoint, they might prove to be most useful."

22. A. A. Berle, Jr., to J. Edgar Hoover, 10 July 1941, *FRUS*, 1941, I, p. 790.

23. PREM 3/469/145–48 (PRO); Kimball, *Churchill & Roosevelt*, I, C-114x; Heinrichs, *Threshold of War*, p. 171.

24. See, for example, Marshall to Welles, memo of 10 July 1941, Larry Bland et al., eds., *The Papers of George Catlett Marshall* (vol. II; Baltimore: Johns Hopkins Univ. Press, 1986), pp. 564–65. Such assumptions have incensed Soviet historians. See, for example, Oleg Rzheshevsky, *World War II: Myths and the Realities* (Moscow: Progress Publishers, 1984), pp. 108–18.

25. There are literally hundreds of examples of such complaints in both the British and American files.

26. See Lloyd C. Gardner, "A Tale of Three Cities: Tripartite Diplomacy and the Second Front, 1941–1942," in *Soviet-U.S. Relations, 1933–1942*, pp. 104–20.

27. John Colville, *The Fringes of Power: 10 Downing Street Diaries, 1939–1955* (New York: Norton, 1985), p. 404. Bowing in the House of Rimmon is a biblical reference meaning someone who conforms to an immoral requirement or custom (II Kings 5, 18).

Colville's remark encourages a false image of Churchill as militantly opposed to working with the Soviet Union. To the contrary, he had argued that the Nazi-Soviet Pact was not in "the historic life-interests of Russia." See below, "Naked Reverse Right," n. 5. As Lloyd C. Gardner points out, Churchill treated "Russian actions as if they created an 'Eastern Front' against Germany" in 1939; *A Covenant With Power* (New York: Oxford Univ. Press, 1984), pp. 54–55. Miner, *Between Churchill and Stalin*, illustrates how Stalin hoped Germany would become entangled in wars against Britain, France, and Yugoslavia.

28. Cooper to Citrine, 7 July 1941, and Citrine to Cooper, 7 July 1941, Walter Citrine papers (British Library of Political and Economic Science/London School of Economics), file 4/7.

29. Stalin's quick seizure of even more territory than agreed upon with Hitler suggests that the Soviet leader had gambled for the big prize. This is also the argument of Miner, *Between Churchill and Stalin*, pp. 100–137. See also Anthony Read and David Fisher, *The Deadly Embrace*, which is a useful study despite inadequate citations. Chapters 41 and 42 discuss Soviet expansion beyond that called for in the treaty and its protocols. Even though the authors refer frequently to the "bribes" that the Germans offered Stalin, they generally reflect the long-held Soviet argument that Stalin agreed to the pact with Germany primarily because the Soviet Union was not prepared for war with Germany in 1939—a position Miner vigorously opposes; *Between Churchill and Stalin*, pp. 134-7/. By 1988, the "defensive" argument was being challenged even by a few Soviet historians, although they remained reluctant to ascribe territorial gain as Stalin's motive. Beginning in 1988, Soviet newspapers reported their historians suggesting that the Nazi-Soviet Pact may have been a great blunder that sowed seeds of intense distrust between the Anglo-Americans and the Soviet Union. For example, see the *New York Times*, 21 June 1988, p. A12. The most cursory glance at Soviet histories of the World War II era demonstrates that such suggestions were previously unthinkable—or at least unpublishable. However, the admission by the Soviet Foreign Ministry on 27 Feb. 1990 that they had found copies of the portion of the Nazi-Soviet Pact that assigned parts of Eastern Europe to the USSR may herald both access to those archives and a reassessment by Soviet historians.

30. Kimball, *Churchill & Roosevelt*, I, R-46x, and pp. 212–35.

31. Ibid., R-50x.

32. Gorodetsky, *Cripps' Mission*, pp. 196–98. In September, the British Foreign Secretary reported that Soviet Ambassador Ivan Maisky had "admitted the difficulties of an opposed landing on the coast," although there were times "when the political chiefs must be prepared to accept an over-riding responsibility." Maisky went on to inquire if, since a second front seemed to have been ruled out, renewed efforts could not be made to provide munitions and supplies. Eden to Cripps, 4 Sept. 1941, FO 371/29490 [100670] (PRO). Stalin, by his willingness to stick to discussions of supply matters during the Beaverbrook-Harriman talks,

made a similar admission, notwithstanding his taunting question to Beaverbrook: "What is the good of having an army if it doesn't fight?" Harriman and Abel, *Special Envoy*, p. 101.

33. Military Report by H. L. Ismay, 6 Oct. 1941, CAB 120/36, enclosure II to the report of the Moscow Conference, 29 Sept.–1 Oct. 1941 (PRO).

34. In fairness to the British, if the Soviets were defeated, logic as well as German military plans (plan ORIENT) called for an attack through the Caucasus and Turkey against British oil holdings in the Middle East. Hinsley, *British Intelligence in the Second World War*, II, pp. 67, 97.

35. Gorodetsky, *Cripps' Mission*, pp. 184, 194. The unfavorable British assessment of Soviet military capabilities had its roots in the 1930s. See James S. Herndon, "British Perceptions of Soviet Military Capability, 1935–39," in *The Fascist Challenge and the Policy of Appeasement*, Wolfgang J. Mommsen and Lothar Kettenacker, eds. (London: George Allen & Unwin, 1983), pp. 297–319.

36. Sheila Lawlor demonstrates in "Britain and the Russian Entry into the War," *Diplomacy and Intelligence*, pp. 168–83, that Churchill, the Foreign Office, and the various military services—each for their own reasons—were all inclined to resist Soviet requests for help.

37. *War Diaries of Oliver Harvey*, pp. 24, 33, 49. This same line of argument is suggested by Gorodetsky, *Cripps' Mission*, p. 198. A promise in July 1941 of two squadrons of "Hurricane" aircraft became impossible by August, and there are many examples of the same pattern. See also Joan Beaumont, *Comrades In Arms: British Aid to Russia 1941–45* (London: Davis Poynter, 1980) and John D. Langer, "The Harriman-Beaverbrook Mission and the Debate Over Unconditional Aid for the Soviet Union, 1941," in Walter Laquer, ed., *The Second World War: Essays in Military and Political History* (London and Beverly Hills: Sage, 1982), pp. 300–319. Evidence of British preoccupation with the Middle East is in all the official histories and memoirs of the era, and is well summarized in Reynolds, *Anglo-American Alliance*, pp. 208–10.

38. See *FRUS*, I, pp. 766–802, passim. Also memorandum from A. A. Berle, Jr., to Hopkins, 30 July 1941, Harry L. Hopkins papers, Sherwood collection, book 4 (Franklin D. Roosevelt Library [FDRL], Hyde Park, N.Y.); Marshall to Gen. Arnold, memo of 16 July 1941, *Marshall Papers*, II, pp. 567–68; Theodore Wilson, "In Aid of America's Interests: The Provision of Lend-Lease to the Soviet Union, 1941–1942," in *Soviet-U.S. Relations, 1933–1942* (Moscow: Progress Publishers, 1989), pp. 125–26.

39. Press Conference statement by Welles quoted in Welles to Steinhardt, 23 June 1941, *FRUS*, 1941, I, pp. 767–68. Soviet historians have correctly pointed out that American scholars long ago dismissed altruism as the motive for the decision to aid the Soviet Union. Even Joseph Davies, who had staunchly defended Soviet foreign policy during the 1930s, argued for aid to the Soviet Union in a 1941 letter to Harry Hopkins, on the grounds that anything else would aid Hitler in his attempts to get "an armistice or peace on the Russian front." Davies to Hopkins, 8 July 1941, Hopkins papers, Sherwood collection, book 4 (FDRL).

40. Roosevelt's belief that Stalin's foreign policy was fundamentally nationalist is illustrated by Bennett, *Roosevelt and the Search for Security*; Thomas R.

Maddux, "Watching Stalin Maneuver between Hitler and the West: American Diplomats and Soviet Diplomacy, 1934–1939," *Diplomatic History*, I (Spring 1977), pp. 140–54; Eduard Mark, "October or Thermidor? Interpretations of Stalinism and the Perception of Soviet Foreign Policy in the United States, 1927–1947," *American Historical Review* 94 (October 1989), pp. 937–62. Whatever Davies' penchant for finding excuses for Stalin's conduct, he did consistently portray the Soviet leader as a practical nationalist. See, for example, Elizabeth Kimball MacLean, "Joseph Davies and Soviet-American Relations, 1941–1943," *Diplomatic History* 4 (Winter 1980), pp. 73–93.

41. Heinrichs, *Threshold of War*, p. 104. By this time, the Neutrality legislation had become a farce, with the President applying it or not as suited his policies.

42. The first poll is cited in Mark, "October or Thermidor?" *American Historical Review*, p. 945. The second is from Bennett, *FDR and the Search for Victory*, chap. 2, n. 52.

43. Roosevelt had sent Harriman to Britain in February 1941 as the President's personal representative and lend-lease "expediter." In September that year, he and Lord Beaverbrook, British Minister for Aircraft Production and one of Churchill's close advisers, went to Moscow to work out a supply protocol with the Soviets. That mission is discussed briefly below.

44. Sherwood, *Roosevelt and Hopkins*, pp. 308, 315. The Anglo-American dispute over strategy in the Middle East is well summarized in Reynolds, *Anglo-American Alliance*, pp. 208–20.

45. Prime Minister's Operational Files (PREM) 3/224/2 (PRO), p. 66. British records are disappointingly devoid of memoranda or minutes regarding the Hopkins trip, particularly his conversations with Churchill.

46. Sherwood, *Roosevelt and Hopkins*, p. 321.

47. Hugh Dalton Diary, 21 July 1941 (London School of Economics Library); Alexander Cadogan Diaries, 17 July 1941 (Churchill Library); *The Diaries of Sir Alexander Cadogan*, ed. David Dilks (New York: G. P. Putnam's Sons, 1972), 21 July 1941, p. 393. Churchill makes no mention of Hopkins' attendance at cabinet in his memoirs. Neither does Martin Gilbert in *Finest Hour* (Boston: Houghton Mifflin, 1983). Gilbert mentions Hopkins' presence in England, but does not discuss the mission.

48. Chancellor of the Duchy of Lancaster (Duff Cooper) to Churchill, 22 July 1941, PREM 3/224/2 (PRO), pp. 69–70.

49. Ambassadors Maisky and Winant (U.S. ambassador in London) both take credit for the suggestion, but it was clearly Hopkins' idea. See Tuttle, *Harry Hopkins*, pp. 92–93. Others have suggested the proposal was Churchill's, although Sherwood specifically denies that. See McJimsey, *Harry Hopkins*, pp. 181–82.

50. Sherwood, *Roosevelt and Hopkins*, p. 318 (emphasis mine).

51. Ibid., pp. 321–22.

52. Ibid., pp. 308, 315; Cripps diary, 30 July 1941, as quoted in Gorodetsky, *Cripps' Mission*, p. 200.

53. Presidential diary, 4 Aug. 1941, Henry Morgenthau, Jr., papers (FDRL). Heinrichs, *Threshold of War*, pp. 146–79 summarizes the supply allocation struggle within the United States. Roosevelt's orders on aid given to Stimson are

216 NOTES TO CHAPTER TWO

quoted on p. 172; to Wayne Coy, on p. 140 and in *F.D.R. His Personal Letters, 1928–1945*, Elliott Roosevelt, ed. (3 vols.; New York: Duell, Sloan and Pearce, 1950), II, pp. 1195–96.

The story of FDR's administrative actions, before and after the Hopkins mission, aimed at making the aid to Russia program effective are well summarized in Marvin D. Bernstein and Francis L. Loewenheim, "Aid to Russia: The First Year," in *American Civil-Military Decisions* (Birmingham: Univ. of Alabama Press, 1963), pp. 97–149.

54. Averell Harriman believed that to be one of Roosevelt's motives in keeping the Russians in the war; Harriman oral history, Eleanor Roosevelt papers, acc. # 78–15 (FDRL). The best presentation of this thesis is in Reynolds, *Anglo-American Alliance*, passim, but especially pp. 206–7, 213–20.

55. A formal statement of that assessment, extensively discussed by U.S. Army planners, came in September 1941 in a Joint Army-Navy Board estimate:

> *The maintenance of an active front in Russia* offers by far the best opportunity for a successful land offensive against Germany. . . . Predictions as to the result of the present conflict in Russia are premature. However, were the Soviet forces to be driven even beyond the Ural Mountains, and were they there to continue an organized resistance, there would always remain the hope of a final and complete defeat of Germany by land operations. The effective arming of Russian forces, both . . . from the outside and by providing industrial capacity in the Volga Basin, or to the east of the Ural Mountains, would be one of the most important moves that could be made by the Associated Powers.

Sherwood, *Roosevelt and Hopkins*, p. 417.

56. See, for example, Churchill to Hopkins, 28 Aug. 1941, PREM 3/224/2, p. 37, where he warned that a "there has been a wave of depression . . . here about the President's many assurances about no commitments and no closer to war etc. . . . If 1942 opens with Russia knocked out and Britain left again alone, all kinds of dangers may arise."

57. The impact on Hopkins of requests for heavy production materials is mentioned in Leon Martel, *Lend-Lease, Loans, and the Coming of the Cold War* (Boulder, Colorado: Westview Press, 1979), p. 28; and Sherwood, *Roosevelt and Hopkins*, p. 344. The story of the trip is told in ibid., pp. 323–48, and McJimsey, *Harry Hopkins*, pp. 182–88.

58. Steinhardt to Hull, 1 Aug. 1941, *FRUS*, I, p. 815; Sherwood, *Roosevelt and Hopkins*, p. 330; Tuttle, *Harry Hopkins*, pp. 104–5. Cripps immediately noted a change in Steinhardt's attitude toward aiding the Soviets, and concluded he "suspected that he might be in danger of being removed unless he changed his tune." Gorodetsky, *Cripps' Mission*, p. 203. It was to no avail. Steinhardt was replaced in the fall, after Stalin complained to Harriman that the ambassador was a defeatist and concerned primarily with his own safety. Harriman and Abel, *Special Envoy*, p. 93.

59. Sherwood, *Roosevelt and Hopkins*, pp. 330, 344–45; memorandum of a conference at the Kremlin on 31 July 1941, Hopkins papers, Sherwood collection, book 4. Roosevelt had expressed similar criticisms, calling Stalin's rule "a dictatorship as absolute as any other dictatorship in the world." Quoted in David

Mayers, *George Kennan and the Dilemmas of US Foreign Policy* (New York: Oxford Univ. Press, 1986), p. 102.

60. Hopkins to Roosevelt, Hull, and Welles, 1 Aug. 1941, *FRUS*, I, p. 814.

61. Miner, *Between Churchill and Stalin*, p. 152.

62. One item in the Hopkins papers indicates that some, if not all of those reports were written after the Atlantic Conference. Hopkins' reports are in his papers at the Roosevelt Library. Extensive portions of them are printed in Sherwood, *Roosevelt and Hopkins*, and *FRUS*, 1941, I.

63. Elliott Roosevelt, *As He Saw It* (New York: Duell, Sloan and Pearce, 1946), p. 22. Elliott Roosevelt's recreation of dialogue is hardly credible. There is no evidence that he kept notes, journal, or diary. But his recollection of his father's attitudes and sentiments consistently fits with other evidence, and the conversations he creates may well have taken place, though at different times and places.

64. Sherwood, *Roosevelt and Hopkins*, pp. 353, 356, 359.

65. As quoted in Larrabee, *Commander in Chief*, p. 240. It was their only meeting.

66. Gorodetsky, *Cripps' Mission*, pp. 200–205, argues that Cripps manipulated and helped convert a reluctant Hopkins. From my reading of the documents, it is not clear who manipulated whom. McJimsey argues that Hopkins had a more cautious view of aid to Russia, and that he wanted the autumn conference to be an exchange of information on needs and production capabilities that concentrated on broad planning. It was Beaverbrook, writes McJimsey, who convinced Harriman to accept Soviet supply requests "at face value." My own reading is that Hopkins supported no-questions-asked aid, even while he quite sensibly proposed that long-term planning issues be discussed. McJimsey, *Harry Hopkins*, pp. 189–90.

67. Harriman to Roosevelt, 29 Oct. 1941, *FRUS*, 1941, I, p. 851 (emphasis mine). See also Harriman, *Special Envoy*, pp. 86–108.

68. Heinrichs, *Threshold of War*, p. 193.

69. Marshall to Stimson, memo of 14 Oct. 1941, *Marshall Papers*, II, p. 645; Roosevelt to Stalin, 30 Oct. 1941, *FRUS*, 1941, I, p. 851; Roosevelt to Stettinius, 7 Nov. 1941, ibid., p. 857. For detail on Roosevelt's strategies in dealing with Congress on this issue, see Sherwood, *Roosevelt and Hopkins*, p. 264; Dawson, *The Decision to Aid Russia*; and Kimball, *"The Most Unsordid Act,"* pp. 189, 200.

70. George C. Herring, Jr., *Aid to Russia, 1941–1946* (New York: Columbia Univ. Press, 1973), p. 286. Soviet estimates of four percent are based on lend-lease goods that actually reached the Soviet Union, whereas Herring's statistics were for goods shipped before they ran the gauntlet of German submarines, air, and surface ship attacks in the Norwegian Sea. Halving the difference, a figure of seven percent seems a reasonable estimate.

71. Stalin's attitude regarding future aid was clear. At a dinner that concluded the Beaverbrook-Harriman mission, he toasted "American industry and said that the war would be won by industrial production. . . . He said that the United States is giving more assistance as a non-belligerent than some countries in history had

given as allies." The sarcasm was unmistakably directed at the British. Steinhardt to Hull, 3 Oct. 1941, *FRUS*, 1941, I, p. 840.

Two and one-half years later, in another toast, Stalin acknowledged publicly the crucial role of Lend-Lease: "The most important things in this war are machines. . . . Without the use of those machines, through Lend-Lease, we would lose this war." *FRUS, Tehran*, pp. 469, 584–85.

72. See Richard Leopold, *The Growth of American Foreign Policy: A History* (New York: Knopf, 1962), pp. 558, 561–62; Bennett, *Roosevelt and the Search for Security*, pp. 181–86; Dallek, *Roosevelt and American Foreign Policy*, pp. 209–12. Roosevelt held off any application of the Neutrality legislation to the conflict—ostensibly so as to permit arms sales to the Finns.

73. Roosevelt's later opposition to Britain-as-Broker is discussed in this collection in the essays "Naked Reverse Right" and " 'The Family Circle.' "

74. See, for example, Llewellyn Woodward, *British Foreign Policy in the Second World War*, II (London: HMSO, 1971), pp. 28–35; Gorodetsky, *Cripps' Mission*, pp. 251–52; Miner, *Between Churchill and Stalin*, p. 167; and reports from Ambassador Steinhardt in *FRUS*, I, 907–11. Reports of Stalin's offer of a deal to Hitler cropped up a Bulgarian newspaper and in Soviet magazines and newspapers (e.g., the *Moscow News*) in the spring of 1989. See *The Sunday Times* (London), 28 May 1989, p. A18. The evacuation of Moscow in mid-November 1941 was done in an atmosphere of general panic. But by then Roosevelt had already decided to provide large-scale aid. It is important to keep in mind that, as of mid-1989, none of these "revelations" in the Soviet or East European press have been accompanied by archival, documentary evidence subject to verification.

75. My argument for Roosevelt's careful hedging is set forth elsewhere in this collection, particularly in "Naked Reverse Right."

76. This has been the major and recurring theme of the Soviet papers given at the meetings, which began in 1986, of the IREX-sponsored Soviet-American project on the History of the Second World War.

Chapter Three
Lend-Lease and the Open Door

1. Historians have only begun to grapple with the intriguing questions posed by William Appleman Williams in *The Tragedy of American Diplomacy* (rev. ed.; Dell—Delta Books, 1962). His treatment of the late 1930s is quite brief, but he asserts that America entered World War II firmly believing that only continued expansion of its own economic system would guarantee prosperity and democracy; see p. 200. That broad theme, with variations, has been taken up by Lloyd Gardner in *Economic Aspects of New Deal Diplomacy*; Robert F. Smith, "American Foreign Relations, 1920–1942," in Barton J. Bernstein, ed., *Towards a New Past: Dissenting Essays in American History* (New York: Pantheon, 1968), pp. 232–62; and Gabriel Kolko, "American Business and Germany, 1930–1941," *Western Political Quarterly* 15 (1962), pp. 713–28. Kolko has vigorously put forward the same thesis for the later war years in *The Politics of War: The War and United States Foreign Policy, 1943–1945* (Vintage ed.; New York: Random House, 1970). The more commonly accepted viewpoint which emphasizes power

politics and Wilsonian idealism is the one presented in the two volumes by Langer and Gleason, *The Challenge to Isolation* and *The Undeclared War*. Their position is seconded by Robert A. Divine, *The Reluctant Belligerent* (New York: Wiley, 1965), as well as by most of the current textbooks in American foreign policy and diplomatic history. None of these more traditional treatments really deal with the question of America's overall economic goals and their effect on foreign policy.

2. *The Great Evasion* (Chicago: Quadrangle, 1964), p. 47.

3. See Kimball, *"The Most Unsordid Act."*

4. Hull's economic notions over the years have received considerable attention from historians. For example, see Richard N. Kottman, *Reciprocity and the North Atlantic Triangle, 1932–1938* (Ithaca, N.Y.: Cornell Univ. Press, 1968); Arthur W. Schatz, "The Anglo-American Trade Agreement and Cordell Hull's Search for Peace, 1936–1938," *Journal of American History* 57 (1970), pp. 85–103; William R. Allen, "The International Trade Philosophy of Cordell Hull, 1907–1933," *American Economic Review* 43 (1953), pp. 101–16; Allen, "Cordell Hull and the Defense of the Trade Agreements Program, 1934–1940," in Alexander DeConde, ed., *Isolation and Security* (Durham, N.C.: Duke Univ. Press, 1957). Most of the more general treatments of American diplomacy in the prewar period discuss Hull's obsession with what he called free trade.

5. Cordell Hull, "The Outlook for the Trade Agreements Program," speech delivered before the 25th National Foreign Trade Convention, New York City, 1 Nov. 1938, printed in U.S. Dept. of State, Commercial Policy Series 54, Pub. 1261 (Washington: USGPO, 1938).

6. This concept of the "imperialism of equality" is challenged by those who argue along lines of neoclassical trade theory. They assume that the flow of foreign exchange to the United States which would follow American domination of foreign markets would force other nations to turn to the short-term solution of currency devaluation or the longer-range policy of trade and currency controls. Thus, the United States could dominate British markets only so long as Britain accepted capital transfers. In other words, balance of payment factors can offset absolute trade advantages. Radical historians would argue that America was creating an informal, neomercantilist empire which essentially integrated the British economy under American domination, thus eliminating the equalizing forces operating within the classic free marketplace. Such mechanisms as the International Monetary Fund and the International Bank for Redevelopment implicitly and explicitly regulate the fiscal and monetary policies of member countries, more often than not in ways beneficial to American economic expansion.

7. Perhaps the most ludicrous example of Hull's obsession with economic solutions to problems occurred shortly before the Japanese attack at Pearl Harbor. While American intelligence was warning of some sort of military action by Japan, Hull outlined the American peace program largely in terms of long-range economic concepts. Out of a total of nine general principles which would provide a basis for peace, six dealt with trade, particularly the elimination of discriminatory practices. U.S. Dept. of State, *The China White Paper* (Stanford, Calif.: Stanford Univ. Press, 1967), I, pp. 464–65.

8. Richard N. Gardner, *Sterling-Dollar Diplomacy* (exp. ed.; New York: Oxford Univ. Press, 1969), p. 19.

9. *FRUS*, 1937, II, p. 14.

10. Ibid., 12 Feb. 1937. Hull also gives an account of his talks with Runciman in *The Memoirs of Cordell Hull* (2 vols.; New York: Macmillan, 1948), I, pp. 524–26.

11. *FRUS*, 1937, II, pp. 2–3.

12. U.S. Dept. of Commerce, Bureau of Foreign and Domestic Commerce, "Economic Review of Foreign Countries, 1937," economic series, no. 2 (1938), pp. 1–17.

13. The Morgenthau Diary (FDRL) is replete with examples. One such is the meeting of 4 June 1937, vol. 71, pp. 245–46, 251.

14. Kottman, *Reciprocity*, pp. 183–85. See Robert A. Divine, *The Illusion of Neutrality* (Chicago: Univ. of Chicago Press, 1962), for a treatment of the motives behind the "cash and carry" concept.

15. Harold L. Ickes, *The Secret Diary of Harold L. Ickes* (2 vols.; New York: Simon & Schuster, 1953–54), II, pp. 470, 474; U.S. Dept. of Commerce, Bureau of Foreign and Domestic Commerce, "Foreign Long-Term Investments in the United States, 1937–1939," economic series, no. 11 (1940), p. 10, table 3; U.S. Congress, House Committee on Foreign Affairs, *Hearings on H.R. 1776: A Bill Further to Promote the Defense of the United States and for Other Purposes*, 77th Cong., 1st Sess., 1941, p. 81.

16. Kimball, *"The Most Unsordid Act,"* p. 74.

17. Ibid., pp. 64, 74, 116, 159–60, 222–26, and Kimball, " 'Beggar My Neighbor': America and the British Interim Finance Crisis, 1940–1941," *Journal of Economic History* 29 (1969), pp. 758–72.

18. Hopkins to Churchill, 17 Feb. 1941, Franklin D. Roosevelt papers, Franklin D. Roosevelt Library (FDRL), Hyde Park, N.Y., President's Personal File (PPF), 4096.

19. Memo from Joel Pinsent (British financial counselor) to Acheson, 27 Mar. 1941, U.S. Dept. of State, decimal file 841.24/48-1/2 (hereafter State Dept. plus the file number), National Archives, Washington, D.C. The problem of the "old commitments" is treated in Kimball, " 'Beggar My Neighbor,' " *Journal of Economic History*. Lloyd C. Gardner briefly discusses the negotiation of the Master Lend-Lease Agreement with Britain in *Architects of Illusion: Men and Ideas in American Foreign Policy, 1941–1949* (Chicago: Quadrangle, 1970), pp. 113–19; his view of American goals during those negotiations corresponds with mine.

20. Kimball, *"The Most Unsordid Act,"* passim, esp. pp. 105–9, 143, 157–58, 159–60, 222–26, 231–32, 237–38. See also Blum, *From the Morgenthau Diaries*, II.

21. Roosevelt to Hull, 11 Jan. 1941, in *F.D.R. His Personal Letters*, II, pp. 1103–5; Kimball, *"The Most Unsordid Act,"* pp. 143–44.

22. Culbertson, "Introduction" to Hugh O. Davis, *America's Trade Equality Policy* (Washington: 1942), p. x.

23. Memorandum from Roosevelt to Morgenthau, 13 Mar. 1941, Roosevelt papers (FDRL), President's Secretary's File (PSF): Dept. Correspondence-Treasury Dept., Henry Morgenthau, 1941–42.

24. The suggestion is that of Gaddis Smith, who commented on this paper at the OAH meeting in April 1970.

25. Blum, *From the Morgenthau Diaries*, II, pp. 242–43.

26. Memo from Oscar Cox to Hopkins, 6 June 1941, State Dept. 841.24/593-1/2; memo from Morgenthau to Hull, 25 Apr. 1941, ibid., 841,24/531-1/2; memo from Hull to Morgenthau, 14 May 1941, ibid., 841.24/601-1/2. The Treasury approach is fully illustrated in the Cox papers (FDRL), particularly in materials in "Lend-Lease Files (aid to Britain, vol. 6), box 62, file V, esp. the memo from Cox to Edward Foley, "Financial Terms of Disposition to Britain Under H.R. 1776," 27 Feb. 1941, and memo from H. D. White to Morgenthau, "Possible Sources of Payment for Materials sent to England under the Lend-Lease Act," 14 Mar. 1941, both in that file.

27. Moffat, *The Moffat Papers: Selections from the Diplomatic Journals of J. Pierrepont Moffat, 1919–1943*, Nancy Hooker, ed. (Cambridge: Harvard Univ. Press, 1956), pp. 352–53.

28. Roy F. Harrod, *The Life of John Maynard Keynes* (New York: Harcourt, Brace, 1951), p. 504.

29. Draft of Lend-Lease Agreement, 8 Apr. 1941, State Dept. 841.24/587.

30. "Notes on the conversation of May 3rd," 31 May 1941 (author unknown), FDRL, PPF 1820; Gardner, *Economic Aspects*, p. 276, and Theodore Wilson, *The First Summit* (Boston: Houghton Mifflin, 1969), p. 180 state, without details, that using the lend-lease agreement as a means of breaking the Imperial Preference system had been discussed well before Keynes arrived in the United States on 10 May 1941. Langer and Gleason, *The Undeclared War*, pp. 678–79, claim that Keynes galvanized the State Department into action, and R. N. Gardner, *Sterling-Dollar Diplomacy*, pp. 41–42, accepts that interpretation.

31. Only the day before, a State Department draft had still retained the vague and ambiguous language of the early drafts when it merely called for discussions designed to revise existing trade agreements. See Draft of Lend-Lease Agreement, 21 May 1941, State Dept., FW 841.24/603-1/5 and Draft of Lend-Lease Agreement, 22 May 1941, ibid. The Leo Pasvolsky file in the Dept. of State Archives contains a number of earlier drafts in box 2, all of which lack any specific demand for an end to discriminatory agreements, even though officials agreed that such was their goal.

32. Morgenthau Diary, 9 June 1941, vol. 406, p. 160; Roosevelt to Hull, 16 May 1941, *FRUS*, 1941, III, pp. 5–6; Morgenthau to Roosevelt, 20 May 1941, PSF: dept. Correspondence-Treasury Dept., Henry Morgenthau, 1941–42. Morgenthau Diary, 4 June 1941, vol. 404, pp. 269–339, contains a transcript of a long discussion between Morgenthau, his staff, and Dean Acheson, in which the overall views of Treasury and State are fully argued.

33. This overview of Keynes' position generally follows that presented in all the sources and secondary works which deal with this subject. Among the more informative are Blum, *From the Morgenthau Diaries*, II, pp. 244–48; Langer and Gleason, *The Undeclared War*, pp. 679–81; Harrod, *Keynes*, pp. 505–16. Dean Acheson, *Present at the Creation: My Years in the State Department* (New York: Norton, 1969), pp. 29–32, refers to Keynes as "delightful," "engaging," and "brilliant," and claims that the Englishman did not put him off as Keynes did so many others in the American government. Acheson's description of the talks with Keynes, however, leaves the distinct impression that the assistant secretary was

also annoyed by Keynes' lack of deference. For those who like their information straight from the sources, Morgenthau's diary is best; see in particular, Morgenthau Diary, 13 May 1941, vol. 397, pp. 221–24, memo of a talk between Morgenthau, Keynes, and Merle Cochran, and similar conversations in vol. 411, pp. 89–90, and vol. 414, pp. 132–38. There is also a substantial amount of material in the State Department archives, some of which is printed in *FRUS*, 1941, III, esp. pp. 6–7, 9–15, 19–22. As usual, Hull's memoirs are useless if not downright misleading and do not even mention Keynes at any point. Hull claims that the Master Lend-Lease Agreement was held up "largely because a few Tory members of the British Cabinet objected" to any interference with the empire preference system, which is just not so; Hull, *Memoirs*, II, pp. 1151–53. See also R. S. Sayers, *British Financial Policy, 1939–1945* (London: HMSO, 1956), pp. 405–13.

34. Morgenthau Diary, 6 May 1941, vol. 395, pp. 148–51; 13 May 1941, vol. 397, p. 225; 15 May 1941, vol. 399, p. 143. Defense information was defined in the Lend-Lease Act as "any plan, specification, design, prototype, or information pertaining to any defense article"; Kimball, *"The Most Unsordid Act,"* p. 243.

35. Draft of Lend-Lease Agreement, 23 May 1941, State Dept. 841.24/636-1/2; memo for the President, 29 May 1941, ibid.; memo, "Possible Types of Payment by the British of their Lend-Lease Obligations," ibid.

36. Morgenthau Diary, 4 June 1941, vol. 404, pp. 240, 246. The "millennial blueprint" comment is from ibid., p. 276. Feis' objections are in a memorandum he wrote to Acheson, 28 July 1941, State Dept. 841.24/643-1/2. A similar objection came from James C. Dunn in a memorandum to Acheson, 19 May 1941, ibid., FW 841.24/601-1/2. A comparative analysis of the State and Treasury Department drafts is in Morgenthau Diary, vol. 404, pp. 264–66.

37. Sayers, *Financial Policy*, pp. 406–7. The details of the redrafting process can be found in the various sources used in this study. The following documents are of particular interest: memo from Cox to Hopkins, 6 June 1941, Cox papers, FDRL, box 74, file "V. Lend-Lease Files: Lend-Lease, May-June, 1941"; memo from Welles to Roosevelt, 9 June 1941, PSF: State Dept., 1941; Keynes to Acheson, 17 June 1941, State Dept. 841.24/603-3/5; memo of conversation between Acheson and Keynes, 15 July 1941, PSF: Welles, 1941–43; memo from Roosevelt to Welles and Acheson, 18 July 1941, ibid.

38. Memo of a conversation between Keynes and Acheson, 20 June 1941, Roosevelt papers, PSF: Lend-Lease, box 55; Harrod, *Keynes*, p. 512.

39. Blum, *From the Morgenthau Diaries*, II, pp. 245–48; Sayers, *Financial Policy*, pp. 390–94.

40. "Draft Proposal," 28 July 1941, *FRUS*, 1941, III, p. 15.

41. Memo of a conversation by Acheson, 28 July 1941, ibid., pp. 10–13; Keynes to Acheson, 29 July 1941, ibid., pp. 16–17. For his reaction in hindsight, see Acheson, *Present at the Creation*, pp. 29–30. See also Sayers, *Financial Policy*, p. 411.

42. Wilson, *The First Summit*, esp. pp. 188, 190–202, 205, 208–9, 247–49, provides an excellent treatment of the Atlantic Conference. See also Langer and Gleason, *The Undeclared War*, pp. 688–89.

43. The American view of the White Paper negotiations is sketched in *FRUS*, 1941, III, pp. 22–26. The British version—which leaves an entirely different im-

pression—is well presented in Sayers, *Financial Policy*, pp. 398–405. There is additional data in State Dept. 841.24 and 740.0011 Eur. War 1939.

44. Hull to Winant, 27 Sept. 1941, *FRUS*, pp. 36–37.

45. Hull to Winant, 26 Sept. 1941 (not sent), State Dept. 740.0011 Eur. War 1939/14570; memo from Feis to Hull, 27 Sept. 1941, ibid.

46. Stettinius to Hull, 1 Oct. 1941, State Dept. 841.24/956; Acheson to Stettinius, 30 Oct. 1941, ibid.; minutes of the meeting of the Committee on Foreign Trade Problems, 26 Sept. 1941, State Dept., Pasvolsky file, box 2.

47. Winant to Hull, *FRUS*, 1941, III, pp. 37–38.

48. Memo of conversation by Acheson, 3 Oct. 1941, ibid. One example of congressional pressure is found in a letter from Roosevelt to Sen. Arthur Vandenberg, 4 Oct. 1941, State Dept. 841.24/893B.

49. Memo of a conversation between Halifax and Welles, 9 Oct. 1941, *FRUS*, III, p. 40.

50. Hawkins to Acheson, 10 Oct. 1941, State Dept. 841.24/902-1/2.

51. Memorandum of conversation by Acheson, 17 Oct. 1941, *FRUS*, III, pp. 40–43; Acheson, *Present at the Creation*, p. 31.

52. Memo, Hawkins to Acheson, 20 Oct. 1941, State Dept. 841.24/921-1/2; memo, Feis to Acheson, 23 Oct. 1941, ibid., 841.24/922-1/2; memo, Acheson to Hull and Welles, 28 Oct. 1941, ibid., 841.24/942-1/2.

53. Memo from Hickerson to Acheson, 4 Nov. 1941, ibid., FW 841.24/942-1/2. Ray Atherton and James Dunn indicated their agreement with Hickerson's point of view.

54. Memo, Hull to Roosevelt, 19 Nov. 1941, ibid., 841.24/1073B; Hull to Winant, 3 Dec. 1941, *FRUS*, III, pp. 45–46; Hull to Winant, 9 Dec. 1941, ibid., pp. 46–47; memo, Pasvolsky to Hull, 12 Dec. 1941, "Possibilities of Conflict of British and American Officials Views on Postwar Economic Policy," State Dept., Pasvolsky file, box 2. For Acheson's comment about Hull and Pasvolsky, see Acheson, *Present at the Creation*, p. 55.

55. The invitation and Elliott's paper are in State Dept. 841.24/1125-1/12. The various calls and conferences concerning the Elliott talk are in ibid., 841.24-2/12,-3/12,-4/12.

56. Memo of conversation by Hull, 29 Dec. 1941, *FRUS*, III, p. 53; memo from Hull to Roosevelt, 30 Dec. 1941, PSF: Safe file, box 1, "Great Britain"; memo by Acheson of conversation with Roosevelt, 29 Jan. 1942, State Dept. 841.24/ 1224. Winant to Hull for Roosevelt, 4 Jan. 1942, ibid., 740.0011 Eur. War 1939/ 18151, outlines the British problems, as does a memo by Acheson of a conversation with Halifax, 30 Jan. 1942, ibid., 841.24/1238. The British delaying tactics and the American response are in Hull to Winant, 30 Jan. 1942, *FRUS*, I, pp. 525–27; Winant to Hull, 3 Feb. 1942, ibid., pp. 527–29; Roosevelt to Churchill, 4 Feb. 1942 [drafted by Dean Acheson], ibid., p. 529.

57. Winant to Hull, 6 Feb. 1942, ibid., pp. 529–32. This document includes the proposed explanatory notes as well as Eden's remarks. For additional information on the British position, see memo of conversation between Welles, Acheson, and Halifax, 7 Feb. 1942, ibid., pp. 532–33. A harsh response from within the State Department is Hawkins to Acheson, 4 Feb. 1942, State Dept. 841.24/ 1125-8/12.

58. Memo of a conversation by Acheson, 7 Feb. 1942, *FRUS*, 1942, I, pp. 533–34; Winant to Hull, 9 Feb. 1942, ibid., pp. 534–35; Roosevelt to Churchill (# 105), 11 Feb. 1942, ibid., pp. 535–37. The background to Roosevelt's cable to Churchill is in State Dept. 841.24/1125-9/12b,-10/12. The cable was drafted by Hopkins, Acheson, and Welles. See ibid., 841.24/1208A and /1209 for data on the submission of the draft to the dominions. The text of the statement issued by the United States on the announcement of the signing is in ibid., 841.24/1240A. See Acheson, *Present at the Creation*, for additional details. The final text of the interim Master Lend-Lease Agreement, which was finally signed on 23 Feb. 1942, is in Dept. of State, *Bulletin*, 28 Feb. 1942, p. 190.

59. David Reynolds has made full use of the British documentation in his work and, although we differ on some minor interpretive points, we ended up in much the same place. He does suggest that Roosevelt was not fully aware of the implications of the State Department's draft of a master lend-lease agreement, and that the hard line adopted by the White House was in reaction to Keynes' abrasive attempts to "teach Washington some rudimentary economics. . . . One might even call it [the American insistence on multilateralism] 'The Diplomatic Consequences of Mr. Keynes.' " I remain more impressed by the consistency of the American campaign against imperial preference and other "discriminatory" trade systems. Roosevelt may not have read the draft agreement carefully, but he had long supported the economic reforms advocated by Hull, Welles, and Acheson; *The Anglo-American Alliance*, pp. 274–80. Alan Dobson has made good use of the British documents in "Economic Diplomacy at the Atlantic Conference," *Review of International Studies* 10 (1984), pp. 143–63.

60. James Meade diary, British Library of Political and Economic Science (London School of Economics, England) file 1/1, p. 67.

61. Thorne, *Allies of a Kind* (New York: Oxford Univ. Press, 1978); Louis, *Imperialism at Bay* (New York: Oxford Univ. Press, 1977); Dobson, *US Wartime Aid to Britain, 1940–1946* (London: Croom Helm, 1986).

62. Nor did the Anglo-American coalition in World War II end such suspicions. Roosevelt remained convinced that British and other European colonialism posed a serious threat to postwar peace. At the same time, the image of British commercial shrewdness dominated American thinking. See " 'In Search of Monsters to Destroy' " and " 'Baffled Virtue . . . Injured Innocence,' " elsewhere in this collection. George Herring, "The United States and British Bankruptcy, 1944–1945: Responsibilities Deferred," *Political Science Quarterly* 86 (June 1971), pp. 260–80, remains the definitive description of the wartime persistence of American jealousies and fears of British commercial abilities.

Chapter Four
Casablanca

1. Elliott Roosevelt, *As He Saw It*, p. xiii.

2. The Casablanca Conference between Roosevelt, Churchill, and their advisers, primarily their military chiefs, took place in Casablanca, Morocco (with a side trip to Marrakech), 14–25 January 1943. The codename for the meeting was SYMBOL.

3. This is also the argument of A. E. Campbell, "Franklin D. Roosevelt and Unconditional Surrender," *Diplomacy and Intelligence during the Second World War,* ed. Richard Langhorne (Cambridge: Cambridge Univ. Press, 1985), pp. 219–41. In the aftermath of the Japanese attack on Pearl Harbor, Roosevelt told reporters on 9 December that "the United States could accept no result but victory, final and complete"; quoted in James MacGregor Burns, *Roosevelt: The Soldier of Freedom* (New York: Harcourt Brace Jovanovich, Harvest ed., 1970), p. 172.

4. Harriman and Abel, *Special Envoy,* p. 191 (emphasis added).

5. Dilks, ed., *Cadogan Diaries,* p. 312.

6. Sherwood, *Roosevelt and Hopkins,* pp. 241–42. Ellipses have been omitted to enhance readability.

There are many references by Harry Hopkins to Churchill's prowess as a drinker. Here are but two; a Churchill to Hopkins memo dated 21 Jan. 1943 read: "*Dinner.* At the White House (Dry, alas!); with the Sultan. After dinner, recovery from the effects of the above." [The White House referred to Roosevelt's villa at Anfa, the suburb of Casablanca where the Casablanca Conference was held.] The following day, Hopkins described finding Churchill "in bed in his customary pink robe, and having, of all things, a bottle of wine for breakfast." Sherwood, *Roosevelt and Hopkins,* pp. 685, 688. Hopkins' admiration for Churchill's prowess as a drinker may have been tinged by wishfulness; Hopkins was forbidden by his doctors to drink, although he regularly ignored their advice. Even as he lay dying, in part from cirrhosis of the liver, Hopkins ruefully complained to Churchill that the disease was "not due, I regret to say, from taking too much alcohol." Hopkins to Churchill, 22 Jan. 1946, quoted in McJimsey, *Harry Hopkins,* p. 397. Another wine-for-breakfast story about Churchill is recounted by General Alan Brooke, though in that case it was preceded by two whiskeys and soda during the flight from Marrakech to Cairo. See Arthur Bryant, *The Turn of the Tide* (Garden City, N.Y.: Doubleday, 1957), p. 464. Whiskey for breakfast was apparently not the exception, for Anthony Eden, in his diary, mentions Churchill taking a "stiff whiskey and soda, at 8:45 a.m." Eden, *The Reckoning* (Boston: Houghton Mifflin, 1965), p. 494. A foreign office official described dining with Churchill in May 1953: "A varied and noble procession of wines with which I could not keep pace—champagne, port, brandy, cointreau: W. drank a good deal of all, and ended with two glasses of whiskey and soda." David Carlton, *Anthony Eden* (London: Allen Lane, 1981), p. 328. Secretary of State Edward Stettinius noted in his diary that Churchill drank "an extraordinary number of brandies and ports" after they ate lunch together at the Prime Minister's country residence in Chequers; Thomas Campbell and George Herring, eds., *The Diaries of Edward R. Stettinius, Jr.* (New York: New Viewpoints, 1975), p. 44. C. P. Snow quipped that Churchill was no alcoholic, for no alcoholic could drink that much. (Raymond O'Connor to W. Kimball, 21 Dec. 1987) Some of Churchill's aides have seriously claimed his image as a drinker has been exaggerated, that he watered and nursed his drinks. Those arguments are not persuasive, but such is the fate of iconoclasm. When Roosevelt and Canadian Prime Minister Mackenzie King met in April 1940, they spent much of the time gossiping about Churchill's drinking; J. L. Granatstein, *Canada's War* (Toronto: Oxford Univ.

Press, 1975), p. 117. Wendell Willkie, asked by Roosevelt in 1941 if Churchill was a drunk, replied that he had as much to drink as Churchill did when they met, "and no one has ever called me a drunk." The darker side of Churchill's alcoholism—for that is clearly what it was, irrespective of his obvious ability to function—is argued in caustic and accusatory fashion by David Irving, *Churchill's War: The Struggle for Power* (Australia: Veritas Publishing Co. Pty., 1987), pp. 225–28. The Willkie quotation is from p. 506.

Of course that does not confront Churchill's other vice—cigar smoking. In my hours of going over snapshots of Churchill taken during the war, I have never found any photograph of him without that omnipresent cigar. In fact, what I at first thought to be a curious signet ring, turned out to be a cigar band slipped over his ring finger. Averell Harriman once commented that Churchill did not smoke very much at meetings because he talked all the time (a third vice, perhaps), but the cigar was always there as pointer and punctuator. O'Connor to Kimball, 21 Dec. 1987; see also Ian Jacob in *Action This Day*, Wheeler-Bennett, ed., p. 182.

7. *FRUS, Yalta Conf.*, p. 729; Sherwood, *Roosevelt and Hopkins*, p. 864. Even Stalin seems to have detected Churchill's concern about the election; see ibid., p. 852. Churchill himself expressed apprehension to those around him. See, for example, Lord Moran [Charles Wilson], *Churchill: Taken from the Diaries of Lord Moran* (Boston: Houghton Mifflin, 1966), p. 240.

8. Sherwood, *Roosevelt and Hopkins*, p. 232.

9. Ibid., p. 238.

10. Minute by Alexander Cadogan, 25 Jan. 1941, quoted in Joseph P. Lash, *Roosevelt and Churchill, 1939–1941* (New York: W. W. Norton & Co., 1976), p. 282.

11. Sherwood, *Roosevelt and Hopkins*, p. 364. Randolph Churchill held up the Churchill-Roosevelt caravan enroute to Marrakech after the Casablanca conference in order to read a passage from Machiavelli to the President; see Moran, *Diaries*, p. 89.

12. Campbell and Herring, eds., *Stettinius Diaries*, entry for 17 Mar. 1944, pp. 39–40. W. Averell Harriman wrote that the President held "a fundamental belief that the old order could not last." Harriman, *Special Envoy*, p. 191.

13. See, for example, Thorne, *Allies of a Kind*, pp. 666–67. Actually, Roosevelt became quite concerned about Chinese intentions in Southeast Asia, and searched for ways to keep Indochina from China's embrace while escaping that of European colonialism. See " 'In Search of Monsters to Destroy,' " elsewhere in this collection.

14. Harriman, *Special Envoy*, p. 191. Churchill is quoted in Moran, *Diaries*, entry for 5 Feb. 1945, p. 240. In February 1945, Roosevelt labeled Churchill a mid-Victorian regarding colonial empires; Ted Morgan, *FDR: A Biography* (London: Grafton Books, 1986), p. 759. For the British complaint, see J. Harvey, ed., *War Diaries of Oliver Harvey*, p. 171 (23 Oct. 1942).

Churchill's criticisms of the New Deal had already raised the hackles of some members of the Roosevelt administration. Memoirs, diaries, and histories by and about New Dealers, from Adolf Berle to Henry Morgenthau, Jr., refer regularly to Churchill as unsympathetic to the reforms they advocated. Since Roosevelt and many of his advisers often saw New Deal–style reform as the solution for international problems, this image of British conservatism spilled over into foreign relations. The New Deal solution is further discussed in "The 'Juggler,' " elsewhere in this collection. The same issue is discussed in Harbutt, *The Iron Curtain*, esp. pp. 15–19.

15. The Eisenhower comment is in Alfred Chandler et al., eds., *The Papers of Dwight David Eisenhower: The War Years* (vol. II; Baltimore: Johns Hopkins Univ. Press, 1970), p. 928. FDR expressed similar suspicions commenting that de Gaulle would show up whenever Churchill and the Foreign Office chose; see Elliott Roosevelt, *As He Saw It*, p. 71.

16. An example of American suspicions came after the Casablanca meeting when General Marshall's advisers concluded that the adoption at Casablanca of a strategy of "periphery-picking" was due "to the superior skill and cunning of British conference tactics." Michael Howard has disputed that conclusion arguing that the realities of logistics and military feasibility persuaded the Americans to go along. That may be true, but within a few months the Americans felt they had been duped; Howard, *Grand Strategy, August 1942–September 1943*, pp. 278. Thorne in *Allies of a Kind*, p. 273, quotes one American diplomat: "To our allies the conduct of the war is a function of overall political and economic policy." See also Kimball, *Churchill & Roosevelt*, II, p. 121 and, for example, R-270; and Maurice Matloff, *Strategic Planning for Coalition Warfare, 1943–1944* (Washington: Office of the Chief of Military History, 1959), chaps. 1 & 2.

17. Wilson, *The First Summit*, 1969, pp. 121–24.

18. Sherwood, *Roosevelt and Hopkins*, p. 680. De Gaulle himself does not use those words in his memoirs, but they clearly capture his feelings; de Gaulle, *The Complete War Memoirs of Charles de Gaulle* (New York: Clarion Book, Simon & Schuster, 1972), pp. 382–88.

19. The Roosevelt-Giraud talk of 17 Jan. 1943 is in *FRUS, Casablanca*, pp. 609–11. The Roosevelt-de Gaulle talk is in ibid., pp. 695–96 (emphasis added). It is worth noting that de Gaulle mentions the "strange" atmosphere created by Harry Hopkins lurking in the darkness of a balcony during the initial Roosevelt-de Gaulle meeting. Hopkins' presence is not indicated in the official notes, but Hopkins himself stated: "I attended all the meetings of the President and De Gaulle." Navy Captain John McCrea, an aide of the President who took notes during the conversation, admits that de Gaulle spoke too softly to be heard, particularly since McCrea was supposedly hidden behind a door only "slightly ajar"; ibid., p. 694; Sherwood, *Roosevelt and Hopkins*, p. 686; de Gaulle, *War Memoirs*, p. 391. Roosevelt's commitments to Giraud are outlined in Arthur L. Funk, "The 'Anfa Memorandum': An Incident of the Casablanca Conference," *Journal of Modern History* 26 (Sept. 1954), pp. 246–54. For additional background, see Funk, *Charles de Gaulle: The Crucial Years, 1943–1944* (Norman: Oklahoma Univ. Press, 1959), chaps. 1–2.

20. Elliott Roosevelt, *As He Saw It*, p. 72. Throughout much of the war the British conducted a debate over the future of the empire, but that had little effect on American thinking. See Thorne, *Allies of a Kind*, pp. 209–24. LaFeber, "Roosevelt, Churchill and Indochina, 1942–1945," *American Historical Review*, pp. 1277–95, is a fundamental reinterpretation of Roosevelt and colonial empires, even if I find that it underestimates the consistency of FDR's active opposi-

tion to colonialism. American pressure for a promise of independence for India had prompted Churchill to state publicly in November 1942, before any proposals were made for what became the Casablanca Conference, that he had "not become the King's First Minister in order to preside over the liquidation of the British Empire." Sherwood, *Roosevelt and Hopkins*, p. 656. See also M. Gilbert, *Road to Victory*, (Boston: Houghton Mifflin Co., 1986), p. 254, esp. n. 2.

21. Churchill's position on preferential trade is discussed more fully in "Lend-Lease and the Open Door: The Temptation of British Opulence, 1937–1942," in this collection. An example of his willingness to acknowledge that the Baltic states were part of the Soviet Union is his message to Roosevelt of 7 March 1942 in Kimball, *Churchill & Roosevelt*, I, C-140. The broad question of the American critique of inter-war European diplomacy is discussed briefly with references in ibid., I, p. 14.

Harry Hopkins told the British that Roosevelt thought Churchill (like Hull, Halifax, and Norman Davis) was too old, unteachable, and "too steeped in the past" to make the peace. He "loves Winston as a man for the war, but is horrified at his reactionary attitude for after the war." *War Diaries of Oliver Harvey*, 11, 29 Mar. 1943, pp. 228, 239–40.

22. Poet Arthur Hugh Clough as quoted by Churchill in a speech of 27 Apr. 1941; see Kimball, *Churchill & Roosevelt*, I, p. 178. Just one example among many of the "cherubic" descriptions is in William Manchester, *The Last Lion, Winston Spencer Churchill: Visions of Glory, 1874–1932* (Boston: Little, Brown & Co., 1983), p. 36. Roosevelt's initial impression of Churchill was rather less favorable, and until Hopkins' visit to London in January 1941, the President harbored vague suspicions about Churchill's attitude toward the United States and even FDR himself. See Reynolds, *The Anglo-American Alliance*, pp. 114, 179–80. Reynolds is also one excellent source of information on Churchill's commitment to a "special" Anglo-American relationship. In particular, see ibid., pp. 263–64, 283–84, 371–72n.

23. Raymond G. O'Connor pointed out to me that the "romance" between Roosevelt and Churchill as well as that of Anglo-American cooperation meet "Napoleon's definition of history, i.e., 'a lie agreed upon' created in the euphoria of war." I would add that the myth was perpetuated, particularly by Churchill, in the spirit of a Cold War alliance. In any event, even if the picture of complete harmony is illusory, Casablanca should still be seen by historians as the point at which that illusion became, or should have become, evident.

24. Kenneth Pendar, *Adventure In Diplomacy* (New York: Dodd, Mead, 1945), p. 149. Pendar rented Flower Villa from an American; Churchill and Roosevelt rechristened it Pansy Palace; see Kimball, *Churchill & Roosevelt*, II, pp. 618–19.

Roosevelt had flown in a Ford trimotor from Albany, New York, to Chicago to receive the Democratic Party nomination for president in 1932.

25. On 19 November 1942, Roosevelt telegraphed Stalin that "both Churchill and I want to consult with you and your staff" concerning future Anglo-American operations in the Mediterranean. USSR, Ministry of Foreign Affairs, *Stalin's Correspondence with Roosevelt and Truman, 1941–1945* (New York: Capricorn Books, 1965), pp. 39–40, 42–44. On 14 November, the President suggested send-

ing a very small Anglo-American staff group to Moscow to discuss "operations springing from the Eastern Mediterranean," but it was not until 25 November that he cabled Churchill to propose a major conference with the Russians. Even then the President wrote in terms of a staff conference rather than the Big Three meeting he had proposed to Stalin. Churchill, who had met with Stalin in Moscow in August 1942, responded by stating that Stalin had expressed willingness to meet them in Iceland. The Churchill-Roosevelt exchanges are in Kimball, *Churchill & Roosevelt*, I, R-211, p. 674; II, R-222, p. 42; C-214, p. 43. The unsuccessful joint Churchill-Roosevelt attempts to persuade Stalin to meet with them can be followed in the two sources cited in this note. Soviet documents and histories give no indication of what, if any, alternatives Stalin considered.

26. While that encouragement included limited military and economic aid, the promise of future aid and a Second Front made up the essence of Anglo-American policy toward the USSR prior to the Casablanca Conference. See the essay " 'They Don't Come Out Where You Expect': Roosevelt Reacts to the German-Soviet War, 1941," elsewhere in this collection for additional detail on this point.

27. *FRUS, Casablanca*, p. 506; William D. Leahy, *I Was There* (New York: Whittlesey House, 1950), p. 147. Vojtech Mastny, *Russia's Road to the Cold War* (New York: Columbia Univ. Press, 1979), pp. 73–74, finds hints of such thinking by Stalin a few months before the Casablanca Conference.

The notion that Stalin might pursue a separate peace was not new. See, for example, a memorandum of 5 Feb. 1942 by Orme Sargent (deputy under secretary in the British Foreign Office), and the accompanying minutes, printed in Graham Ross, ed., *The Foreign Office and the Kremlin: Documents on Anglo-Soviet Relations, 1941–45* (Cambridge: Cambridge Univ. Press, 1984), pp. 127–30; and minutes, 7th Pacific War Council meeting, 13 May 1942, MR-FDRL.

28. Stalin to Churchill, 16 Jan. 1943, USSR, Ministry of Foreign Affairs, *Stalin's Correspondence with Churchill and Attlee, 1941–1945* (New York: Capricorn Books, 1965), p. 85. Hinsley, *British Intelligence in the Second World War*, II, pp. 68, 108–11. Churchill did receive some ULTRA material in the form of the 'Sunset' series of telegrams prepared by British Naval Intelligence; Gilbert, *Road to Victory*, pp. 295–96. On 14 Jan., at the opening of the Casablanca talks, Gen. Sir Alan Brooke mentioned the military situation at Stalingrad, but without any hint of awareness of the overall importance of the battle. See *FRUS, Casablanca*, p. 537. See also Howard, *Grand Strategy*, p. 329 and Matloff, *Strategic Planning*, p. 20. Elliott Roosevelt states that "every one of us was excited over the great news that was coming in from the eastern front," but that sense of excitement is not borne out in the conference minutes or other memoirs; *As He Saw It*, p. 67. Secondary studies frequently assume Churchill and Roosevelt took the Stalingrad victory into consideration during the Casablanca talks, but offer no evidence.

29. As Mastny points out, Soviet historians have asserted that Stalingrad established only "a balance of forces" between Germany and the USSR; *Russia's Road to the Cold War*, p. 73. Even if that was true, hindsight demonstrates that "balance" spelled defeat for a Germany that had planned and relied upon speedy victory. Churchill did speculate earlier that, if the Red Army should reach Rostov-on-the-Don, "a first class disaster may overtake the German Southern Armies."

But that is a far cry from foreseeing the kind of Soviet offensive that would develop. Churchill to Roosevelt, 24 Nov. 1942, Kimball, *Churchill & Roosevelt*, C-211, II, p. 39.

30. Elliott Roosevelt, *As He Saw It*, pp. 61, 89, and Arthur Bryant, *The Turn of the Tide*, p. 455, both describe the scene. Churchill states that the vessel was "gutted by fire and beached"; *The Hinge of Fate*, p. 620. LTJG (now Professor) Arthur Funk recalls that by July 1943, when his destroyer escort pulled into Casablanca harbor, "the ship was tied to a dock. . . . That one of her four great turret guns was broken off was the only thing noticeable. Otherwise she looked as if she were ready to take off at any time"; letter from Funk to Kimball, 12 July 1987. That the warship was refloated by July and later that year sailed to the United States for full repairs, only reinforces my point, as does the location of the Casablanca Conference in Morocco, ostensibly still part of the French Empire. For details on the refitting of the *Jean Bart*, see Marcel Vigneras, *Rearming the French* (Washington: OCMH, 1957), pp. 220–21.

31. Above, pp. 4–8. For the exchanges about India, see Kimball, *Churchill & Roosevelt*, I, C-34 draft A, C-34, C-35, C-41, R-116 draft A, R-116, C-67, R-132, and C-68 draft A. The issue of independence for India is taken up in " 'In Search of Monsters to Destroy.' "

32. A classic example is the demand by de Gaulle for the expulsion from Morocco of then U.S. Army 2d Lieutenant Archibald Roosevelt (grandson of Theodore Roosevelt). Young Roosevelt had established contacts with various nationalist elements in what were then the French colonies of Tunisia and Morocco, and had written reports critical of American government support for French policy in the area. Perhaps Lt. Roosevelt was completely on his own; then again. . . . See Archibald Roosevelt, *For Lust of Knowing* (Boston: Little, Brown & Co., 1988), pp. 108–13. See also the essay " 'In Search of Monsters to Destroy,' " elsewhere in this collection.

33. Roosevelt-Churchill discussions at Quebec about India are mentioned in *FRUS, Quebec Conf., 1944*, p. 298. For further discussion on this, see " 'In Search of Monsters to Destroy' " in this collection.

34. Roosevelt's reaction to the radicalization of William Phillips in India is in Roosevelt to Hopkins, 19 Mar. 1943, *F.D.R. His Personal Letters, 1928–1945*, II, p. 1414. As usual, the President continued to keep the pressure on the British by instructing Harry Hopkins to show the Phillips memorandum to British foreign Secretary Anthony Eden. The "radical" portion of the statement is quoted in a number of sources; e.g., Thorne, *Allies of a Kind*, p. 359. This episode is put into fuller context in the chapter " 'In Search of Monsters to Destroy,' " elsewhere in this volume.

35. Harold Macmillan, *The Blast of War, 1939–1945* (New York: Harper & Row, 1968), p. 201. Macmillan was British Minister Resident at Allied Military Headquarters in Algiers; i.e., Churchill's political representative in North Africa. Other descriptions of the dinner are in E. Roosevelt, *As He Saw It*, chap. 4, esp. pp. 108–16; Sherwood, *Roosevelt and Hopkins*, p. 690; *FRUS, Casablanca*, pp. 701–4 and the sources cited on p. 693. Gilbert in *Road to Victory* makes no mention of the talks with the Moroccans.

36. De Gaulle, *War Memoirs*, p. 923.

37. *FRUS, Casablanca*, pp. 632–33. The British minutes of that same meeting (18 January) present Marshall's position in far gentler and more politic words: "It was a question of weighing up the necessity of placating the Russians, against the very real help which we should receive elsewhere by the discontinuance of these convoys." CAB 120/75 XC 100848 (PRO), p. 7.

38. Kimball, *Churchill & Roosevelt*, I, R-210, C-189. The American debate over priorities between the Pacific and European theaters is discussed in Mark A. Stoler, "The 'Pacific-First' Alternative in American World War II Strategy," *The International History Review* 2 (July 1980), pp. 432–52.

39. For discussions of the strategic decisions taken at Casablanca, see Stoler, *Politics of the Second Front*; Howard, *Grand Strategy*; Matloff, *Strategic Planning*; *FRUS, Casablanca*; and Kimball, *Churchill & Roosevelt*, II, pp. 117–21. Emerson, "Franklin Roosevelt as Commander-in-Chief," *Military Affairs*, pp. 195–99, emphasizes the confusion of American military planning at the talks, which may be true, although I do not share his evaluation that the conference was a "complete victory for British strategic conceptions." Even the American Army agreed that an invasion of Sicily made sense, and FDR refused to move into the eastern Mediterranean despite Churchill's arguments. In any event, that very confusion provides an opportunity to judge Roosevelt's own thinking.

It was Secretary of War Henry Stimson who, a few months after the Casablanca Conference, expressed the fear that Aegean campaigns would rekindle Anglo-Russian bickering over that area. But such thoughts were likely present in January as well; see Stoler, *Second Front*, p. 80.

40. Stalin to Roosevelt, 13 Jan. 1943, *Stalin's Correspondence with Roosevelt*, p. 50. See also Dallek, *Roosevelt and American Foreign Policy*, pp. 368–71.

41. *FRUS, Casablanca*, p. 506. The entire issue of the Second Front (capitalized as a proper noun because it was a political issue far broader than just the idea of an invasion in force of Western Europe) is discussed neatly and intelligently in Stoler, *Second Front*. Stalin's response to Roosevelt's suggestion of a visit from Marshall was strikingly similar to his rejection of Roosevelt's proposal for a Big Three meeting: "I am not quite clear about his [Marshall's] mission. Kindly advise me." The very next paragraph contained strong criticism of the slowness of the Anglo-American advance in North Africa. In turning down the Big Three meeting, Stalin wrote: "I do not know as yet what were the specific matters that you . . . wanted discussed." The next paragraph raised the issue of the Second Front; *Stalin's Correspondence with Roosevelt*, pp. 44, 50.

42. Kimball, *Churchill & Roosevelt*, I, p. 312, and R-135/1. As late as January 1945, Roosevelt remained uncertain about Burma, telling aides, "I don't know yet just how we will handle that situation." As quoted in Thorne, *Allies of a Kind*, p. 595.

43. Elliott Roosevelt, *As He Saw It*, p. 72.

44. As quoted in Dallek, *Roosevelt and American Foreign Policy*, pp. 377–78.

45. De Gaulle's fears of British intentions are discussed in Keith Sainsbury, *The North African Landings, 1942* (Newark: Univ. of Delaware Press, 1976), pp. 47, 184n. See also Funk, *Charles de Gaulle*.

46. Churchill to Eden, 18 Jan. 1943, (STRATAGEM 78) CAB 120/76–02100848 (PRO), p. 2. Churchill's comments and the cabinet's reactions regarding the Casa-

blanca talks can be followed step-by-step in this file of messages given the code-name STRATAGEM. Additional information is in the British conference minutes found in CAB 120/75.

47. Howard, *Grand Strategy*, p. 279.

48. This strange tale is told by Terence Robertson, *The Ship With Two Captains* (New York: E. P. Dutton, 1950).

49. Kimball, *Churchill & Roosevelt*, II, R-256, 5 Feb. 1943 (emphasis added). Churchill used similar phrases, for example, ibid., C-263.

50. Henri Michel, *The Second World War* (New York: Praeger, 1975), p. 496.

51. Roosevelt's suspicion of French abilities to govern themselves predated and remained more important than his personal dislike of de Gaulle. See, for example, Kimball, *Churchill & Roosevelt*, II, R-457 and R-483/1, February 1944 messages to Churchill in which the President labeled France as Britain's "baby," and warned not to expect the United States "to keep in France my military force or management for any length of time." That is not to dismiss the personality conflict between Roosevelt and the French leader, but only to put it in perspective. The President's famous remark after Casablanca that, when de Gaulle arrived, "he thought he was Joan of Arc and the following day he insisted he was Georges Clemenceau," was prompted by substance as well as style. The quip was popular in Whitehall as well; Hassett, *Off the Record with F.D.R.*, 7 Feb. 1943, p. 153; *F.D.R. His Personal Letters, 1928–1945*, FDR to John Roosevelt, 13 Feb. 1943, p. 1400; *War Diaries of Oliver Harvey*, p. 225.

This is not the place to discuss the actual, as opposed to intended, effect of American programs for rearming the French; programs that clearly did involve the United States in the affairs of postwar France. Those questions are treated in Vigneras, *Rearming the French*, esp. pp. 78–82, 97–98; and James J. Dougherty, *The Politics of Wartime Aid* (Westport, Conn.: Greenwood Press, 1978).

52. Churchill, *The Hinge of Fate*, pp. 687–88. The falseness of Churchill's claim is neatly demonstrated by Forrest C. Pogue, *George C. Marshall: Organizer of Victory* (New York: Viking Press, 1973), pp. 32–35, and Raymond G. O'Connor, *Diplomacy For Victory: FDR and Unconditional Surrender* (New York: Norton, 1971), pp. 50–53. O'Connor throughout treats the long-term effect of unconditional surrender. Churchill's message to the War Cabinet of 19 January, sent before unconditional surrender was proclaimed, asking their advice about such a declaration is in the Prime Minister's Confidential Files (PREM 4) 72/1, STRATAGEM 98, as well as in CAB 120/76–02100848, both in the PRO.

53. See my *Swords or Ploughshares?*

54. The phrase of Michael Howard, *Grand Strategy*, p. 284.

55. A. E. Campbell scoffs at the idea that unconditional surrender was a conscious gesture directed at the Soviets, suggesting that Roosevelt could not have believed that Stalin would "be reassured by a phrase." Campbell, "Roosevelt and Unconditional Surrender," *Diplomacy and Intelligence*, p. 226. On the other hand, Vojtech Mastny and Lloyd Gardner, whose interpretations often differ dramatically, both conclude that the President and Prime Minister hoped to pacify Stalin, particularly since the conferees had agreed that the major invasion of Western Europe would not take place until 1944; Gardner, *A Covenant With Power*, pp. 60–61; Mastny, *Russia's Road to the Cold War*, p. 145. The most convincing piece of direct evidence to surface is a comment made by Roosevelt to General

Marshall just prior to the Casablanca meeting. As the minutes record: "The President said he was going to speak to Mr. Churchill about the advisability of informing Mr. Stalin that the United Nations were to continue on until they reach Berlin, and that their only terms were to be unconditional surrender." *FRUS, Casablanca*, p. 506. The persuasiveness of that evidence is substantially increased by its citation in the memoirs of Averell Harriman, one of Roosevelt's closer wartime advisers; *Special Envoy*, p. 190.

The long Anglo-American debate over whether or not to impose unconditional surrender on Italy is not relevant here, but it is neatly summarized in O'Connor, *Diplomacy for Victory*, pp. 57–61.

56. The deal with French Admiral Jean Darlan had been designed by American negotiators to insure that French forces in Africa that still accepted the authority of their government in Vichy would not fight against the Anglo-American invasion. Darlan had continued as head of the French Navy under the Vichy regime, and had been openly sympathetic to the Germans. But by the fall of 1942, he seemed willing to cooperate and order French forces not to fight back against the Americans. The full details of this complex and confusing story are related in Arthur L. Funk, *The Politics of TORCH* (Lawrence: Univ. of Kansas Press, 1974).

57. Sherwood, *Roosevelt and Hopkins*, p. 658. The Soviet Union's reaction to the North African invasion is, perhaps, reflected well in Soviet scholarship. Of three recent studies of wartime diplomacy published in English by Soviet historians, only one does more than merely mention the North African landings, and the phrasing is, at best, contemptuous: "On November 8, 1942, American and British forces began a landing in French North Africa. There were neither Germans nor Italians there. . . . Allied forces advanced eastwards, without any fighting. . . . They were stopped by German and Italian forces . . . and undertook no further offensive action right up to mid-March 1943." None of the books mentioned the Casablanca Conference or the unconditional surrender proclamation. The quotation is from Vilnis Sipols, *The Road to Great Victory: Soviet Diplomacy, 1941–1945* (Moscow: Progress Publishers, 1985). pp. 110–11. The other two books that did not discuss the North African invasion or the Casablanca talks are Rzheshevsky, *World War II: Myths and the Realities*, and Berezhkov, *History in the Making*. A general survey, *Soviet Foreign Policy, 1917–1945*, pp. 430–31, dismisses the Casablanca Conference in two sentences, mentioning only its failure to decide upon "the promised broad invasion of France in the spring." However, public statements by Soviet historians beginning in 1987 indicate a greater readiness to acknowledge the importance of the North African campaign. See the notes of the 3d Symposium of the US/USSR Project on the History of World War II (Moscow, Oct. 1988), in possession of the author.

58. There was some fuzzy thinking here. While the Anglo-Americans assumed the postwar devastation of the Soviet Union, they simultaneously believed that only the Soviet Army could defeat Germany in a way that could make unconditional surrender possible—whatever the claims for strategic bombing offered by the U.S. Army Air Force.

59. Howard, *Grand Strategy*, p. 285. Howard could have been echoing Woodrow Wilson's call for peace without victory, but the context suggests a more geopolitical interpretation. Even before the war was over, Churchill began to

think that German military strength would be a useful bulwark against the Soviet Union. See Arthur Smith, *Churchill's German Army* (Beverly Hills and London: Sage, 1977).

60. For American military assumptions about the indispensability of the Soviet Army in order to defeat Germany, see Mark A. Stoler, "From Continentalism to Globalism: General Stanley D. Embick, the Joint Strategic Survey Committee, and the Military View of American National Policy during the Second World War," *Diplomatic History* 6 (Summer 1982), pp. 312–13. The strategic bombing argument is summarized in R. J. Overy, *The Air War, 1939–1945* (London: Macmillan-Papermac, 1987), pp. 102–26, 204–6; Larrabee, *Commander in Chief*, pp. 579–622.

61. Stalin accepted unconditional surrender indirectly in November 1943 when Molotov signed the Four Power Declaration which began with a commitment to make that demand. *FRUS, 1943*, I, p. 755. Stalin's doubts are summarized in Albert Resis, "Allied Policy Toward the Future Germany, 1942–43," unpublished paper presented to the 3d Symposium of the US/USSR Project on the History of World War II (Moscow, Oct. 1988), pp. 27–32. However, Stalin objected to unconditional surrender only as a wartime tactic. The terms he wanted to impose on the Germans assumed the total defeat of Germany, not a negotiated peace. See, for example, his speech of 6 Nov. 1942, excerpted in Ross, *The Foreign Office and the Kremlin*, p. 123, and *FRUS, Tehran*, p. 513.

62. Eisenhower Diary, 5 Jan. 1953, as quoted in David Carlton, *Britain and the Suez Crisis* (Oxford, Basil Blackwell, 1988), pp. 5–6. Eisenhower believed that Churchill, again Prime Minister, was trying to recreate that "special place of partnership" that Britain had enjoyed during the Second World War. Eisenhower expressed gentle skepticism that such an Anglo-American condominium had really existed, and bluntly dismissed such hopes in 1953 as "completely fatuous."

63. See, for example, Averell Harriman's comments in *Special Envoy*, pp. 170, 191. The negotiations over the Master Agreement are discussed in "Lend-Lease and the Open Door" in this collection.

64. The "Lieutenant" comment is made in a number of places. See Kimball, *Churchill & Roosevelt*, I, C-148, C-180/1; II, C-205; and Harriman, *Special Envoy*, p. 172. Independence for India is one example of Roosevelt staying away from direct arguments with Churchill.

65. Moran, *Diaries*, p. 90; Sherwood, *Roosevelt and Hopkins*, p. 695. According to one source, the painting was at Hyde Park until Elliott Roosevelt sold it; Larrabee, *Commander in Chief*, p. 39. Whatever its history after that, it is currently (1989) owned by M. S. Forbes, editor of *Forbes* magazine. The "easy intimacy" remark was immediately followed by the warning that "neither of them ever forgot for one instant what he was and represented or what the other was and represented." Sherwood, *Roosevelt and Hopkins*, p. 363.

66. Kimball, *Churchill & Roosevelt*, II, C-259-A/1, p. 130.

67. Harold Macmillan, *War Diaries: Politics and War in the Mediterranean, January 1943-May 1945* (New York: St. Martin's Press, 1984), pp. 7, 8, 9, 10.

68. Churchill sent this German cartoon to Hopkins on 22 June 1943; PREM 4/72/1 XC/100818 (PRO), pp. 279, 285.

69. British worries were expressed in Chiefs of Staff Committee (London),

draft reply to J.S.M. 879, undated, Premier (PREM) 3/420/7/6–9 (PRO). Churchill wrote, "I fully concur" on the message and dated it 18 Apr. 1943. For the American suspicions, see Matloff, *Strategic Planning*; and Kimball, *Churchill & Roosevelt*, II, pp. 121ff., esp. R-270.

The attempt by Roosevelt to arrange private talks with Stalin, and the significance of that move, is discussed in ibid., II, R-280, C-309, C-328, and R-287. See also MacLean, "Joseph Davies," *Diplomatic History*, pp. 73–93.

70. Sherwood, *Roosevelt and Hopkins*, p. 665.

Chapter Five
"The Family Circle"

1. Franklin D. Roosevelt opening the First Plenary Meeting of the Teheran Conference, *FRUS, Tehran*, Bohlen minutes, p. 487. Not surprisingly, General Sir Alan Brooke, Chief of the British Imperial General Staff, thought Roosevelt's speech a feeble effort; Arthur Bryant, *Triumph in the West* (Garden City, N.Y.: Doubleday, 1959), p. 61. The Teheran Conference began on 27 November and concluded on 1 December 1943.

2. PSF, Bullitt folder, Roosevelt papers.

William C. Bullitt had visited Russia in 1919 at the request of the secretary of state, resigning when his recommendations for cooperating with the Bolsheviks were ignored. Roosevelt appointed him the first U.S. ambassador to the Soviet Union, an experience that convinced Bullitt of the need to confront Soviet and international communism. He subsequently acted as a personal trouble-shooter for Roosevelt, but by January 1943, had lost favor and held a minor assignment in the Navy Department. Additional detail on the Bullitt-Roosevelt relationship plus an edited version of this long letter is in Bullitt, ed., *For the President*, pp. 575–90. The letter foreshadows William Bullitt's postwar attack on Roosevelt in "How We Won the War and Lost the Peace," *Life* 25 (30 Aug. 1948), pp. 82–97. Gardner, *Architects of Illusion*, chaps. 1–2, analyzes American liberal foreign policy using Bullitt and Roosevelt as case studies.

3. *FRUS, 1943*, III, p. 22. Anthony Eden was British Foreign Secretary.

4. Averell Harriman, a staunch Democratic Party contributor, typifies the attitude of members of the President's stable of personal emissaries. He became ambassador to the Soviet Union in early October 1943. His cautious optimism is discussed below in this essay. Warnings from such State Department professionals as Loy Henderson and George Kennan are found throughout the various volumes of *FRUS, 1943*.

5. Sherwood, *Roosevelt and Hopkins*, p. 709.

6. These various references by Roosevelt to a postwar "police" function are found in Wilson, *The First Summit*, pp. 198–99; *War Diaries of Oliver Harvey*, p. 32; Martin J. Sherwin, *A World Destroyed: The Atomic Bomb and the Grand Alliance* (New York: Alfred A. Knopf, 1975), p. 88. The Molotov-Roosevelt conversation of 29 May 1942 is in *FRUS, 1942*, III, pp. 573–74. A convenient summary, sympathetic to jaundiced British reactions to Roosevelt's postwar conceptions as they developed during the war, is in Woodward, *British Foreign Policy*, V, chaps. 61–62.

The Moscow Foreign Ministers' Conference was held 19–30 Oct. 1943.

7. Molotov-Roosevelt conversation of 1 June 1942, *FRUS, 1942*, III, pp. 580–81. Hopkins' whisper must have referred to the Treasury Department plan for a monetary stabilization fund among the United Nations, and an international bank for reconstruction and development. That plan proposed loans at a mere three percent interest, but it was the principle that counted. Roosevelt approved the concept in May 1942. See Eckes, *A Search for Solvency*, pp. 42–57. See also Richard N. Gardner, *Sterling-Dollar Diplomacy in Current Perspective* (New York: Columbia Univ. Press, 1980), chap. 5. The President made a similar proposal on 24 Nov. 1942 for the Caribbean, suggesting that American investment in that area was needed but that the only profit would be a return of the government's investment. What he wanted to create was a "social and economic team." *Complete Presidential Press Conferences of Franklin D. Roosevelt* (25 vols.; New York: DaCapo Press, 1972), vol. 20 (July 1942–Dec. 1942), pp. 264–65.

In December 1941, with the World War I war debts controversy in mind, Roosevelt had labeled his idea "something brand new" when he suggested avoiding dollar debts in return for Lend-Lease; Kimball, *"The Most Unsordid Act,"* p. 121.

8. Molotov-Roosevelt conversation of 1 June 1942, *FRUS, 1942*, III, pp. 580–81. The quote about rifles is from Woodward, *British Foreign Policy*, V, p. 32. The talks with King are in J. W. Pickersgill and D. F. Forster, *The Mackenzie King Record* (3 vols.; Toronto: Univ. of Toronto Press, 1960), I, p. 431; the instruction to the military chiefs is in McCrea to Leahy, 28 Dec. 1942, as quoted in Wm. Roger Louis and Ronald Robinson, "The United States and the Liquidation of the British Empire in Tropical Africa, 1941–1951," in *The Transfer of Power in Africa*, Prosser Gifford and Wm. Roger Louis, eds. (New Haven: Yale Univ. Press, 1982), p. 33. See "The Juggler" in this collection for a discussion of Roosevelt's difficulties with the Second Front issue.

9. Eden's report to Churchill of the 27 March conference, sent by Ambassador Halifax on 29 March 1943, is in FO 371/35366, U1430/320/70, Public Record Office (PRO), Kew, England. The report is summarized in Eden, *The Reckoning*, pp. 436–37. Harry Hopkins' record of Eden's talk with Roosevelt and various other officials on 27 March is essentially the same; *FRUS, 1943*, III, p. 39. The three-tiered plan had been suggested by the State Department, and clearly took into account FDR's insistence that the great powers be in control. See Welles, *Seven Major Decisions*, pp. 178–79.

10. *War Diaries of Oliver Harvey*, 21 March 1943, p. 235.

11. *FRUS, Tehran*, p. 532. Chiang Kai-shek was the leader of the Kuomintang political movement, and the head of the Chinese Nationalist government and armies. Chiang's refusal to accept the role Roosevelt had in mind for China is discussed in " 'In Search of Monsters to Destroy' " in this collection.

12. Eden, *The Reckoning*, p. 432.

13. Sherwin, *A World Destroyed*, pp. 82–89.

14. Harry S. Truman, *Year of Decisions*, vol. I of *Memoirs* (Garden City, N.Y.: Doubleday, 1955), p. 11. For Leahy's earlier doubts about the bomb, see Sherwin, *A World Destroyed*, p. 125n.

15. There is an indication that, at Yalta, Roosevelt considered telling Stalin about the A-bomb, but that was only because of talk of telling the French, and the

President believed that the secret would quickly leak out from Paris. See Gilbert, *Road to Victory*, p. 1265. Neither Stalin nor the French were told. The speed with which the Soviet Union developed its own atomic bomb may have been due to the work of captured German scientists rather than either espionage in the U.S. and Britain or Soviet scientific capabilities.

As Christopher Andrew explains, the sharing of information between the Soviet Union and the Anglo-Americans was, in reality, extensive by the standards of past wars, but pales in comparison to the unique degree of information exchange during World War II between Great Britain and the United States. See Andrew, "Intelligence Collaboration between Britain and the United States during the Second World War," unpublished paper (1st draft).

Edmonds, *Setting the Mould*, pp. 52–53; Sherwin, *A World Destroyed*, pp. 63, 85–86, 96, 100–102, 104. As Lloyd Gardner points out, the decision not to share atomic secrets with the Soviets was paralleled by a refusal to provide them with four-engine bombers under lend-lease; see "The Atomic Temptation, 1945–1954" in *Redefining the Past*, L. C. Gardner, ed. (Corvallis: Oregon State Univ. Press, 1986), p. 179. Burns, *The Soldier of Freedom*, pp. 456–57. David Holloway, *The Soviet Union and the Arms Race* (2d ed.; New Haven: Yale Univ. Press, 1984), pp. 17–19, concludes that Stalin's 1943 decision to launch a Soviet bomb project was a "hedge against uncertainty," which suggests that Stalin did not comprehend the bomb's potential. We can deduce how much the Soviets knew about the bomb, but only currently closed Soviet archives or still unpublished memoirs can provide insights into Stalin's understanding of the weapon. Recent additions to the literature are Timothy J. Botti, *The Long Wait: The Forging of the Anglo-American Nuclear Alliance, 1945–1958* (Westport, Conn.: Greenwood Press, 1987), and Richard Rhodes, *The Making of the Atomic Bomb* (New York: Simon & Schuster, 1986), and J. Samuel Walker, "The Decision to Use the Bomb," *Diplomatic History* 14 (Winter 1990), pp. 97–114.

Churchill and Roosevelt determined early in the war not to include the Soviets in their joint military planning; see Kimball, *Churchill & Roosevelt*, I, p. 293. Bradley Smith argues that there are some strong indications of a limited sharing by the British of intelligence with the USSR, in "Sharing ULTRA in World War II," *International Journal of Intelligence and Counterintelligence* 2 (Spring 1988), pp. 59–72. But Christopher Andrew, in his forthcoming *KGB: Foreign Operations*, shows that there was no sharing of SIGINT (signals intelligence, i.e., MAGIC and ULTRA) techniques or knowledge between the Soviets and the Anglo-Americans, as does Geoff Jukes, "The Soviets and ULTRA," *Intelligence and National Security* (April 1988), pp. 233–47, and "More on the Soviets and ULTRA," ibid. (forthcoming). The Soviets and the Anglo-Americans did occasionally tell each other of certain strategic and even tactical intelligence gleaned from SIGINT (e.g., bombing targets in Germany), but the source was always carefully protected. That may have fed Stalin's suspicions, since he probably knew by 1940 (certainly not long afterward, given the talent of Soviet spies) that the British had broken the Enigma codes.

16. For Roosevelt's question to Eden, see the opening quotations. In a 16 March 1943 conversation with Hull, Eden said he did not agree with what was called "the Bullitt thesis," although the United States and Britain should do every-

thing possible to avoid "the determined hostility and antagonism of Russia," and "to pave the way for international cooperation with the Soviet Union." *FRUS, 1943,* III, p. 22. Roosevelt's interview with Forrest Davis, published as "What Really Happened at Teheran," *Saturday Evening Post* 116 (13 and 20 May 1944), served as a public refutation of Bullitt's thesis.

17. O. Bullitt, *For the President,* pp. 554–55. W. Bullitt, "How We Won the War," *Life,* 30 Aug. 1948.

18. Bullitt to Roosevelt, 12 May and 10 Aug. 1943, PSF-Bullitt (FDRL); O. Bullitt, *For the President,* pp. 591–94, 595–99.

19. Meade Diary (BLPS), file 1/1, 3 Oct. 1943.

20. Roosevelt's inability to stand and walk made him very prone to various respiratory problems—discomforting and even dangerous when flying, especially in an era when aircraft cabins were often not pressurized or lost pressurization. He traveled across the Atlantic on the USS *Iowa,* but then spent some forty hours flying to Cairo, Teheran, and back again. The log of the President's trip, including mileage, is in *FRUS, Tehran,* pp. 270–300, 459–74, 655–61. Following the Teheran Conference, he suffered a serious attack of what he called the "grippe" and what doctors diagnosed as hypertension and congestive heart failure. The best summary of evidence on Roosevelt's health, particularly as it affected his actions during World War II, is in Park, *The Impact of Illness,* pp. 221–94. Park concludes that Roosevelt's intermittent bouts of brief forgetfulness (encephalopathy) did not trouble him during the Teheran meetings; ibid., pp. 231–33, and above, pp. 14–15. Other assessments are in Burns, *Soldier of Freedom,* pp. 448–50; Howard G. Bruenn, "Clinical Notes on the Illness and Death of President Franklin D. Roosevelt," *Annals of Internal Medicine* 72 (1970), pp. 579–91; Kimball, *Churchill & Roosevelt,* II, R-430; III, R-506; Jim Bishop, *FDR's Last Year* (New York: William Morrow, 1974).

21. As Stalin put it, he did not bring his military staff, but "Voroshilov would do his best." *FRUS, Tehran,* p. 496. Harriman later surmised that Stalin kept his generals away so as to "control the discussion." Harriman and Abel, *Special Envoy,* p. 266. See Thorne, *Allies of a Kind,* pp. 141, 381, 384, for evidence of Britain-as-broker thinking in the Foreign Office.

22. Milovan Djilas quotes Stalin's characterization of Churchill as "the kind who, if you don't watch him, will slip a kopek out of your pocket. . . . By God, a kopek out of your pocket! And Roosevelt? Roosevelt is not like that. He dips his hand only for bigger coins." Djilas, *Conversations with Stalin,* as quoted in Stoler, *The Politics of the Second Front,* p. 158.

23. We still do not know why Soviet leaders at the Moscow Conference proposed bringing Turkey into the war and then getting Anglo-American assistance in the Balkans—a scheme that prompted Churchill to hope and Roosevelt to wonder if Stalin no longer thought a massive invasion of northern France the best Anglo-American contribution to the defeat of Germany. Keith Sainsbury, *The Turning Point: Roosevelt, Stalin, Churchill, and Chiang Kai-shek, 1943; The Moscow, Cairo, and Teheran Conferences* (New York: Oxford Univ. Press, 1985), pp. 97–99, offers logical speculations, but only Soviet archives can provide final answers.

24. On 8 October 1943, Roosevelt actually did cable Churchill: "Strategically,

if we get the Aegean Islands, I ask myself where do we go from there and vice-versa where would the Germans go if for some time they retain possession of the Islands." Kimball, *Churchill & Roosevelt*, II, R-381.

25. This is, of course, a fictitious dialogue. Still, the imagined response uses a technique Churchill often adopted in disputes with Roosevelt—the Prime Minister's own arguments came in the form of a paper from his military chiefs.

26. USSR [Ministry of Foreign Affairs], *The Tehran, Yalta and Potsdam Conferences: Documents* (Moscow: Progress Publishers, 1969), pp. 7–16; *FRUS, Tehran*, pp. 487–508, 535–39; Berezhkov, *History in the Making*, pp. 265–82.

Mark Stoler, in his excellent *The Politics of the Second Front*, demonstrates the unbreakable connection of military and political strategy during World War II. My argument does not contradict that conclusion. Rather, in this case, Roosevelt was willing to put international politics above the military strategy so strongly recommended by his chiefs of staff. Once Stalin made his choice, the President could go on to other things. As Stoler wrote on p. 146: "This meeting had, in effect, determined future Allied strategy in Europe." After the first plenary session at Teheran, discussions by Roosevelt and Stalin on military matters related exclusively to the possible effect on OVERLORD of other military plans such as the invasion of southern France or Aegean operations.

Roosevelt's loyalty to the military arguments behind the OVERLORD concept was due in good measure to the persuasiveness of his Army Chief of Staff, General George Marshall. Those efforts are neatly summarized by Stoler in *George C. Marshall: Soldier-Statesman of the American Century* (Boston: Twayne, 1989), pp. 89–108.

27. That raises the question of determining why Stalin pushed so hard for the cross-Channel invasion, particularly with the Stalingrad and Kursk victories behind him. Did he and his advisers realize that the Normandy invasion was probably not needed to defeat Germany? Was Stalin tempted to take off the pressure for the Second Front, thus delaying an Anglo-American return to the continent and perhaps permitting even further Soviet penetration into Western Europe? Stalin's decision is clear and unequivocal. But what were the circumstances of that decision? Were Soviet leaders as yet unaware of the extent of their military superiority? Did they believe that Anglo-American assistance in the west was necessary to Soviet victory in the east? Did they consider eastern Mediterranean operations by Britain as politically motivated? Harriman thought that Soviet leaders desired only to relieve the enormous strain of war and end it as quickly as possible—though to claim that Soviet leaders ignored political issues and thought only of winning the war is patently false (memo by John McCloy of a talk with Harriman, 21 Nov. 1943, *Frus, Tehran*, pp. 265–66. This cable specifically challenged the suggestions of General Deane that the Soviets had slackened off in their demands for OVERLORD). The Soviet position suggests that, even as late as December 1943, Stalin had limited goals in Europe and was not tempted by the opportunity to "liberate" more of Europe while the Anglo-Americans stayed offshore. Soviet histories offer a simple Manichean dichotomy between Roosevelt and Stalin—the American was worried about the postwar Anglo-American position in Europe, whereas the Russian simply wished to win the war, nothing more; e.g., Sipols, *The Road to Great Victory*, pp. 159–60. Taking just one example among many—the

matter of Soviet-Polish relationships in the postwar world—it is crystal clear Stalin had the postwar Soviet position in Europe in mind. Again, Soviet archives offer the only hope for an answer.

28. Even an astute career diplomat like Charles Bohlen missed the forest for the trees, later claiming that, in preparing for the Moscow and Teheran meetings, "Roosevelt and his chief assistant, Harry Hopkins, were concerned mostly with the present. That meant that they focused on military decisions, because the immediate problem was turning back the Nazis." Charles E. Bohlen, *Witness to History* (New York: Norton, 1973), p. 121.

29. See " 'They Don't Come Out Where You Expect,' " in this collection.

30. Harriman told Churchill that Americans would react unfavorably to a "three cornered meeting on British soil in which it would appear that he, Churchill, had been the broker in the transaction." Harriman to Roosevelt, 5 July 1943, PSF-Harriman (FDRL). Roosevelt's maneuvering over private talks with Stalin can be traced in Kimball, *Churchill & Roosevelt*, II, R-280, C-309, R-289 drafts A and B, R-289, C-328, R-297, C-334, C-336. The story is recounted in MacLean, "Joseph E. Davies, *Diplomatic History*, pp. 73–93. Davies had been a sympathetic ambassador to the Soviet Union in the late 1930s. Harriman, a staunch Anglophile (perhaps Churchill-phile would be more accurate), apparently did not recognize the significance of such talks for Soviet-American bilateralism. See Harriman and Abel, *Special Envoy*, pp. 216–19.

31. Kimball, *Churchill & Roosevelt*, II, R-224.

32. Memo by Welles, 30 Nov. 1942, *FRUS, 1943*, III, p. 2. In addition, the visit was delayed because the British War Cabinet feared that Eden would concede too much to the Americans.

33. The Soviet ambassador in London, Ivan Maisky, asked Eden not to enter into any detailed, definite postwar commitments during his forthcoming talks in Washington; Eden to Clark Kerr (Amb. in Moscow), 10 March 1943, Lord Avon (Eden) papers, FO 954 (PRO). Stalin's reaction, which may well have been feigned, is in MacLean, "Joseph Davies," *Diplomatic History*, pp. 88–89. In March 1942 Roosevelt had proposed a similar one-on-one meeting with Stalin; Albert Resis, "Allied Policy Toward the Future of Germany, 1942–43," unpublished paper prepared for the 3d Symposium of the US/USSR Project on the History of World War II (Moscow, Oct. 1988). Harriman's comment is in a memo to the President, 4 Nov. 1943, *FRUS, Tehran*, p. 65.

34. Kimball, *Churchill & Roosevelt*, II, C-467, R-394 draft A, R-394, C-471, R-396, C-475, R-397, C-476 & 477, R-400 draft A, R-400, C-479, R-404, C-481, C-484, C-487, R-406, C-488, R-416, C-501, R-418, C-502, R-418/3. The same charade took place prior to the Yalta Conference in 1945.

35. Moran, *Diaries*, 25 Nov. 1943, p. 142. For similar comments by Hopkins, see Dilks, *Cadogan Diaries*, p. 581.

36. Harriman, *Special Envoy*, p. 265; Moran, *Diaries*, p. 136; *FRUS, Tehran*, p. 595.

37. G. Wilson (Northern Dept.) to Clark Kerr (Amb. in Moscow), 8 Aug. 1943, printed in Ross, *The Foreign Office and the Kremlin*, p. 134.

38. One of Roosevelt's "pet" journalists, Forrest Davis, made a remarkable claim for the President in an article that had White House approval (see n. 84

below): "A geographer and a power theorist, he was thinking globally when some recent advocates of global planning were confining their map reading to road maps." Davis, "Roosevelt's World Blueprint," *Saturday Evening Post* 115 (10 April 1943). Roosevelt's sensitivity to the potential of flight reached its apogee with his exaggerated assessment of the capability of German bombers to strike the United States from West Africa; Dallek, *Roosevelt and American Foreign Policy*, p. 175. The President paid great attention to postwar civil aviation questions, as Eden noted following his talks with Roosevelt in March 1943; Eden to Churchill (Halifax to Foreign Office), 29 March 1943, FO 371/35366, U1430/320/70.

39. Kimball, *Churchill & Roosevelt*, I, R-123/1; II, R-418, R-297; *FRUS, Tehran*, pp. 194ff.

40. McJimsey, *Harry Hopkins*, pp. 299–301, 305–6; Campbell and Herring, *Stettinius Diaries*, 11 Nov. 1943, p. 14. A reading of Sherwood, *Roosevelt and Hopkins*, illustrates that Churchill was badly mistaken when he thought Hopkins was his best ally in the White House. Moran, *Diaries*, p. 140.

41. Alistair Horne, *Harold Macmillan, vol. 1: 1894–1956* (New York: Viking, 1988), p. 165. Macmillan added that Churchill failed to realize "how devious FDR could be." Lippmann to Roosevelt, 2 Nov. 1943, Roosevelt to Lippmann, 8 Nov. 1943, PPF-2037 (FDRL). The later Lippmann quote is from Robert A. Divine, *Second Chance: The Triumph of Internationalism in America During World War II* (New York: Atheneum, 1967), p. 157.

42. This essay is not intended as a full description of either the Moscow, Cairo, or Teheran conferences, although I have offered a summary in *Churchill & Roosevelt*, pp. 605–13. British and American archives are open, and all three governments have published official histories or documentary collections of the conferences. Soviet archives might yield some surprises about their policy debates, but it seems safe to conclude that the facts are in. There have been Soviet assertions that publication of the records by the British and Americans broke promises of secrecy "with the aim of falsifying the Soviet policy and distorting the Soviet Union's stand on the vital issues of the World War II period." Berezhkov, *History in the Making*, p. 261. However, those documents the Soviets have published do not support that argument. The Soviet versions add some context and detail, although they omit material. See Stephen M. Miner, " 'The Other Side of the Hill': Soviet Sources on the Teheran Conference," unpublished paper presented at the 3d Symposium of the US/USSR Project on the History of World War II (Moscow, Oct. 1988).

43. That Stalin occasionally participated illustrates the importance of the meeting. Of the three books on the Teheran Conference published by Anglo-American scholars since 1985, only the one by British historian Keith Sainsbury, *The Turning Point*, treats the Moscow talks as important, devoting over one-third of his text to that meeting. It is the two Americans who downplay the conference. Keith Eubank, *Summit at Teheran* (New York: William Morrow, 1985) devotes only a handful of pages to the Moscow conference, and Paul D. Mayle, *Eureka Summit: Agreement in Principle and the Big Three at Tehran, 1943* (Newark: Univ. of Delaware Press, 1987), virtually ignores it. Dallek, *Roosevelt and American Foreign Policy*, p. 418, dismisses the conference as an opportunity for Roosevelt "to resolve domestic rather than diplomatic problems," although

the discussion that follows belies that statement. Herbert Feis, writing in the 1950s, gives the conference its due. He is critical of Hull's failure to pin the Soviets down on specifics, but treats the talks as an important part of wartime diplomacy. See his *Churchill, Roosevelt, Stalin* (Princeton: Princeton Univ. Press, 1957), esp. pp. 191–234. Berezhkov apparently reflects Soviet awareness of the significance of the conference; see *History in the Making*, pp. 204–39.

44. That may have referred to Hull's travel plans on the way home from Moscow. Leahy, *I Was There*, p. 207. See also the work of Irving Gellman regarding Hull's serious and chronic health problems.

45. Granted, Hull was not the President's first choice. Sumner Welles, whose personal life had given enemies like Hull the leverage needed to force the under secretary's resignation, was asked to go to Moscow as a final mission, but refused. But on the issue of organizing the postwar world, Welles and Hull were in fundamental agreement. Their differences had all along been more tactical and personal than ideological. Welles and Hull had been at odds since the thirties, largely because Welles, as an old personal friend of the Roosevelts, had direct and frequent access to the President. Welles frequently assumed the role of adviser and emissary that was normally reserved for the secretary of state. Hull was angered, but did not confront Roosevelt on the issue until the summer of 1943. The petty villain in the piece was William Bullitt, previously a member of Roosevelt's stable of personal envoys. With unseemly pride in his actions, Bullitt pushed the issue of reports of occasional homosexual advances by Welles. In a face-to-face meeting on 5 May 1943, the President angrily attacked Bullitt for having spread rumors— but that was only the proximate cause of Welles' departure. See Burns, *Soldier of Freedom*, p. 350; O. Bullitt, *For the President*, pp. 512–17.

Some anecdotes need retelling lest they be lost. William Leahy, hardly famous for his stand-up comedy, presented an unintentionally humorous defense of summitry: "At subsequent Big Three conferences, a Committee of Foreign Ministers was established. When some question arose about which an agreement could not be reached by the Big Three, it was frequently referred to these same foreign ministers who, in turn, were usually *unable* to reach an agreement." The unexpected negative in the final clause may not have been intended to provoke a smile, but one can hear Roosevelt chuckling softly in the background. Leahy, *I Was There*, p. 208 (emphasis added).

46. *FRUS, 1943*, I, pp. 541–43. For a discussion of the evidence of Roosevelt's eagerness to avoid Wilson's mistakes, see below, " 'This Persistent Evangel of Americanism,' " n. 8.

47. Roosevelt to Churchill 7 Feb. 1944, Kimball, *Churchill & Roosevelt*, II, R-457. The implications of that sense of disengagement from Europe are discussed in Kimball, *Swords or Ploughshares?*

48. Hull's angers and aspirations are laid out with more clarity than his diplomacy in his *Memoirs*.

49. Sainsbury, *Turning Point*, pp. 80–85. The quote is from ibid., p. 83, although it expresses Eden's thinking quite accurately. Eden's proposal for confederation had been made back in May 1943 to Roosevelt by Churchill; see Kimball, *Churchill & Roosevelt*, II, C-297/1. The official British version is in Woodward, *British Foreign Policy*, II, pp. 595–99. One British Foreign Office official (Owen

O'Malley) criticized the confederation idea arguing that smaller nations would refuse to be treated as merely "subsidiary features of the terrain on which the forces of the Great Powers are deployed." That recognition of nationalism was reinterpreted in a series of minutes as a dire warning of Soviet intentions in Eastern Europe, ending with a curt dismissal from Alexander Cadogan, the permanent under secretary: "I do not regard it as a helpful contribution." Ross, *The Foreign Office and the Kremlin*, pp. 127–30.

Roosevelt's notion of confederation in Western Europe, which seems less impractical in the light of various postwar Benelux cooperative schemes and the creation of the European Community, was brought up in November 1942 during his talks with a British official, Oliver Lyttelton, and again in March 1943 when the President spoke with Eden. Lord Chandos (Oliver Lyttelton), *Memoirs* (London: Bodley Head, 1962), pp. 309–10; Marks, *Wind Over Sand*, p. 397 n.40; Woodward, *British Foreign Policy*, V, p. 32.

50. For a contrary view, see Sainsbury, *Turning Point*, p. 122, where he reasons that after the Moscow Conference, the USSR had every reason to conclude "that there was a basis for the division of Europe into *de-facto* spheres of influence." Eden repeatedly insisted that he thought treaties between large and small nations were undesirable, and that collective security was his goal. But Churchill and Eden wanted a strong, centralized European regional council in London— something Hull, Roosevelt, and other administration officials thought smacked of power politics and exclusive spheres of influence. See Sherwood, *Roosevelt and Hopkins*, p. 717; *FRUS, 1943*, I, pp. 554–55, 626; Sainsbury, *Turning Point*, chap. 4; D. C. Watt, "Every War Must End," *Transactions of the Royal Historical Society*, 5th ser., 28 (1978), p. 168; Woodward, *British Foreign Policy*, V. Eden's assistant under secretary, Oliver Harvey, pointed out that the foreign secretary had "only superficial ideas" of Britain's future plans regarding European frontiers and postwar controls; *War Diaries of Oliver Harvey*, pp. 286–87.

51. Harriman and Abel, *Special Envoy*, pp. 236, 244. Hull also referred to the Soviet-Polish boundary question as "a Pandora's box of infinite trouble"; ibid., p. 244.

52. Ibid., p. 236 (emphasis added). Moreover, that is Cold War hindsight. In the midst of the Moscow talks, Harriman expressed cautious optimism that the Russians appeared to "want to do business with us." Harriman to Roosevelt, 21 Oct. 1943, *FRUS, 1943*, I, p. 590.

53. Stalin did not mention the Kursk victory during the Teheran talks. Marshal G. Zhukov is gently critical of Soviet failures to take full advantage of the Kursk victory. Reading between the lines in his memoirs, it appears that Soviet planners failed to realize the extent of German losses, particularly in tanks and tank crews. See G. Zhukov, *Reminiscences and Reflections* (English trans.; Moscow: Progress Publishers, 1985) pp. 207–9. In fairness, General S. M. Shtemenko, who was Chief of the Soviet General Staff's Operations Department for most of the war, asserts that the General Staff "realized the great import" of the Kursk victory, but he refers only to the need to prevent the Germans from withdrawing and establishing a strong defense line, not to the battle's broad strategic significance. Shtemenko, *The Soviet General Staff at War, 1941–1945* (Robert Daglish, trans.; Moscow: Progress Publishers, 1985), book 1, pp. 251–55. Mar-

shal I. Kh. Bagramyan, in his introduction to *World War II: Decisive Battles of the Soviet Army*, V. Larianov et al., eds. (Moscow: Progress Publishers, 1984), pp. 10–11, asserts that Kursk "ruined all the last hopes that Hitler's military and political leaders had entertained to regain the strategic initiative in the war." John Erickson, *The Road to Berlin* (London: Weidenfeld and Nicolson, 1983), pp. 123, 135, suggests that Stalin may actually have "overestimated the effect" of Kursk, although his demands for an immediate follow-up offensive to take advantage of the Kursk victory could be explained by the Soviet leader's penchant for overaggressiveness that Erickson portrays throughout the study. Erickson also suggests that Stalin pushed for a series of military victories in order to gain political advantage at the Moscow and Teheran conferences. Roosevelt had been trying throughout the summer of 1943 to arrange either a Roosevelt-Stalin or a Big Three meeting, but agreement on a Churchill-Roosevelt-Stalin meeting was not reached until after the Moscow Conference ended early in November, after the post-Kursk offensives. Nor did the Soviets brag at Moscow and Teheran about their military exploits. Eden complained to Molotov during the Moscow Conference that there was "less information on Soviet [military] action than before." At the first Roosevelt-Stalin talk the Soviet leader emphasized the difficulties of his military situation, probably with the Second Front in mind. *FRUS, 1943*, I, p. 659; *FRUS, Tehran*, pp. 529–33.

Whether or not Soviet wartime leaders appreciated the significance of the victory, Soviet historians (e.g., Bagramyan, *Decisive Battles*, pp. 10–11) criticize "bourgeois" historians for failing to treat the Kursk battle as one of the war's most important, particularly in memoirs like Dwight Eisenhower's *Crusade in Europe* (New York: Doubleday, 1948). That suggests ignorance not conspiracy, for as David Eisenhower has demonstrated, "Ike" was intensely aware of the crucial and overwhelming importance of Soviet military achievements. See David Eisenhower, *Eisenhower At War, 1943–1945* (New York: Random House, 1986). A finding of ignorance is further suggested by the apparent failure of British intelligence to comment by the time of the Teheran Conference about the scale and significance of the Kursk battle. Hinsley, *British Intelligence in the Second World War*, III, part I, mentions Kursk three times, but only in passing. None of those references suggest that British intelligence appreciated the military significance of the battle. Eubank, *Summit at Teheran*, pp. 105–6, 373, claims that the Kursk victory put Churchill and Roosevelt at a disadvantage and stimulated a change in Stalin's policies. If so, why was the battle never mentioned at Teheran? To the contrary, Lord Moran states that Churchill and Eden thought the Red Army was having problems since, during the Moscow meeting of foreign ministers, the Soviets had pushed so vehemently for the Second Front; Moran, *Diaries*, p. 143.

54. *FRUS, 1943*, I, pp. 600, 756.

55. Eden, *The Reckoning*, pp. 436–37; Eden to Churchill (Halifax to Foreign Office), 29 March 1943, FO 371/35366, U1430/320/70 (PRO). See also n. 38 to " 'This Persistent Evangel of Americanism,' " below. Churchill proposed three Regional Councils during talks with Roosevelt and Mackenzie King in May 1943; Pickersgill, *The Mackenzie King Record*, I, p. 513.

56. George Orwell in *1984* (published in 1949), depicted a world divided into three totalitarian empires (he too apparently dismissed China as a major player).

In his letters he stated that this reflected his concern about the post–World War II dividing of the world into spheres of power. William Pietz, "The 'Post-Colonialism' of Cold War Discourse," *Social Text*, 19/20 (Fall 1988), p. 61.

57. Davis, "Roosevelt's World Blueprint," *Saturday Evening Post*. Davis' piece was carefully vetted by the White House (see n. 84 below).

58. The same applied to Latin America, where the United States also opposed regional security arrangements outside the purview of the postwar international peacekeeping organization; see " 'Baffled Virtue . . . Injured Innocence,' " and " 'This Persistent Evangel of Americanism,' " elsewhere in this collection.

59. See "Naked Reverse Right" elsewhere in this collection. For Roosevelt's initial reaction and the final message to Churchill, see Kimball, *Churchill & Roosevelt*, III, R-625, R-626 draft A, R-626. The official record of State Department planning, [Harley Notter], *Postwar Foreign Policy Preparation, 1939–1945* (Washington: USGPO, 1950) demonstrates a consistent worldwide planning approach by department officials.

60. Hull and Roosevelt had agreed earlier that China was critical "both because of herself and because of her influence over British India." *FRUS, 1943*, I, pp. 541–42.

61. This paragraph is taken from *FRUS, Tehran*, pp. 529–33. Stalin later told Roosevelt that he agreed with the President's plan for a worldwide rather than a regional world organization; ibid., p. 596. The characterization of the two men's approach is that of Major General John Deane, head of the American military mission in Moscow. He was less perceptive about Churchill, claiming that the Prime Minister was just concerned about how to win the war; Mayle, *Eureka Summit*, p. 70. Stalin's own design for the postwar world is still a matter for debate. Some claim he merely responded to events, while others assert that expansion, either communist or Russian, was part and parcel of his policies. Albert Resis suggests a straightforward geopolitical set of goals centered around a pacified and dismembered Germany; see "Allied Policy Toward the Future Germany," pp. 7–9.

62. What neither Roosevelt nor Stalin, nor Churchill, for that matter, could predict was the way in which the atomic bomb would make war-by-proxy the only practical way for the Great Powers to fight each other.

63. John Iatrides, ed., *Ambassador MacVeagh Reports: Greece, 1933–1947* (Princeton: Princeton Univ. Press, 1980), p. 397. Roosevelt had similarly assumed a disarmed Poland, and wondered why France would need a large military once Germany was disarmed. *FRUS, 1943*, III, memo of a conversation between Roosevelt, Eden, and Hopkins, 15 March 1943, p. 17.

64. Roosevelt's comment about moral prestige was written in the context of discussions over voting procedures in the United Nations Security Council, but it reflects a consistent pattern of thinking. Kimball, *Churchill & Roosevelt*, III, R-666. Welles, *Seven Major Decisions*, pp. 171–72. Welles expressed regret that the President put such strong emphasis on Big Four authority; ibid., p. 182.

65. *FRUS, Yalta Conf.*, pp. 589, 590.

66. Divine, *Second Chance*, pp. 136–55.

67. For but three examples of Roosevelt's conviction that the U.S. would soon withdraw military forces from Europe, see *FRUS, Tehran*, p. 256; Kimball, *Churchill & Roosevelt*, II, R-483/1; memo Roosevelt to Stettinius, 21 Feb. 1944,

U.S. Dept. of State Archives, decimal file 740.00119 Control (Germany /-2-2144), National Archives (Washington, D.C.). War Department plans for occupying Germany are discussed in Kimball, *Swords or Ploughshares?* Shortly after the Yalta Conference, one of Deputy Prime Minister Clement Attlee's aides complained that they still had no idea how long the American would keep forces in Germany—yet the stability of Central Europe depended on that question; William Piercy papers, British Library of Political and Economic Science (BLPS), London School of Economics, London, England, file 8/11, 16 Feb. 1945.

68. See the strong feelings expressed below in " 'This Persistent Evangel of Americanism,' " where Roosevelt spoke of "castrating" the Germans; see also Kimball, *Swords or Ploughshares?*

Both British and American documents record that, at the Teheran Conference, Stalin accepted the principle of the dismemberment of Germany; *FRUS, Tehran*, pp. 602–4 (1 Dec. 1943). The published Soviet records of that meeting are couched in language that suggests Stalin opposed partition but was trying to be cooperative with his allies; USSR, *The Tehran, Yalta, and Potsdam Conferences*, pp. 48–50.

69. Presidential Diary, 25 Aug. 1944, p. 1391, Henry Morgenthau, Jr., papers, FDRL.

70. This Rooseveltian view of the postwar Anglo-American relationship is presented in a number of places, but a good place to start would be Sherwood, *Roosevelt and Hopkins*. The assumption is particularly clear during the Bretton Woods Conference regarding postwar economic/financial structures, and during negotiations over lend-lease. A number of historians have elaborated on this theme; Lloyd C. Gardner, Thomas Paterson, George Herring, Robert Hathaway, Alfred Eckes, and Donald C. Watt, to mention only a few. Three examples of the tough stand taken by Roosevelt are Kimball, *Churchill & Roosevelt*, II, R-474/1; III, R-509 and R-661. Henry B. Ryan, *The Vision of Anglo-America* (Cambridge: Cambridge Univ. Press, 1987), offers a persuasive case for Churchill's commitment to Anglo-American hegemony in the postwar world, as well as Roosevelt's insistence on a tripartite power-sharing.

However ruefully, Churchill and most Foreign Office officials shared that view. Llewellyn Woodward cites a long memorandum written in the early autumn of 1942 which assumed that Britain had to have a strong ally or allies in order to be a world power; *British Foreign Policy*, V, p. 5.

71. Harriman's recommendations, which became stronger as the war went on, that reconstruction aid and political issues be linked (to use a later term) are fully laid out in Lloyd C. Gardner, "The Riddle of the Sphinx: Russia and Reconstruction," an unpublished paper presented to the 3d Symposium of the US/USSR Project on the History of World War II (Moscow, Oct. 1988). The postwar loan issue is treated in Thomas G. Paterson, *Soviet-American Confrontation* (Baltimore: Johns Hopkins Univ. Press, 1973), pp. 33–41.

72. Kimball, *Churchill & Roosevelt*, I, R-171. The context of this 29 July 1942 message was military, but Roosevelt's uncertainty about Stalin's attitude continued throughout the war. The President repeatedly toned down Churchill's proposals for joint messages to the Soviet leader, commenting frequently that Stalin's latest cable seemed friendlier. For one example among many, see ibid., II, R-347.

73. For an example of Roosevelt's awareness of Soviet intentions and power in Eastern Europe, see *FRUS, 1943*, I, p. 542. After Roosevelt's death, Hopkins told Stalin that Americans considered the Polish settlement "a symbol of our ability to work out problems with the Soviet Union." As quoted in Edmonds, *Setting the Mould*, pp. 47–48. That Hopkins supported that view is unlikely; that Truman did is unmistakable.

74. Moran, *Diaries*, p. 143. The sour comment is that of General Alan Brooke, the Chief of the Imperial General Staff.

75. The quotation is of Churchill speaking to the House of Commons, 20 Aug. 1940, as quoted in Reynolds, *The Anglo-American Alliance*, p. 169.

76. Berezhkov, *History in the Making*, p. 267; Moran, *Diaries*, p. 143.

77. Feis, *Churchill, Roosevelt, Stalin*, pp. 275–76.

78. Sherwood, *Roosevelt and Hopkins*, p. 560 (25 years); *Stettinius Diaries*, 6 Feb. 1945, p. 242 (50 years). One cannot help wondering if there was any connection in FDR's mind between the prediction of twenty-five years of peace, and a subsequent prediction that France would not regain major-power status "for at least 25 years"; *FRUS, Tehran*, p. 195.

79. "Muscular diplomacy" is the happy phrase of Thomas G. Paterson. See his "Toward Spheres of Influence: United States Postwar Planning and Soviet-American Relations," a revised version of a paper written for the US/USSR Symposium on Soviet-American Relations in the Cold War (Moscow 1987), p. 17.

80. Roosevelt to MacVeagh, 15 Jan. 1944, *MacVeagh Reports*, p. 444 (emphasis added).

81. It was a notion he threw out to Anthony Eden when the British Foreign Secretary visited Washington in March 1943; Sherwood, *Roosevelt and Hopkins*, p. 708. Despite Sherwood's comment that "Roosevelt talked a great deal on the subject of a United Nations news service," the idea is not mentioned in the published American records of the Eden visit; *FRUS, 1943*, III, pp. 1–48. Nor did Eden include the proposal in his reports to London (FO 371, CAB 66, FO 954 all at the PRO) or in his memoirs. In fact, the idea seems not to have surfaced again. But that does not take away from its value as an insight into Roosevelt's thinking.

82. See, for example, Roosevelt's message to Churchill asking that the British reject a proposal from the Chicago *Tribune* (owned by one of Roosevelt's bitterest political opponents, Col. Robert McCormick) to publish a newspaper for American military personnel stationed in Britain; Kimball, *Churchill & Roosevelt*, I, R-190, C-161.

83. See Arthur Schlesinger, Jr., "War and the Constitution: Abraham Lincoln and Franklin D. Roosevelt," Fortenbaugh Memorial Lecture (Gettysburg: Gettysburg College, 1988), pp. 22–24. Roosevelt's contemporaries did not always agree. Col. Robert McCormick, owner of the Chicago *Tribune*, broke in 1933 with Roosevelt in part because the National Recovery Administration code for newspapers apparently threatened freedom of the press; James C. Schneider, *Should America Go to War?* (Chapel Hill: Univ. of North Carolina Press, 1989), p. 9.

Roosevelt's dedication to the Constitution is less convincing on the issue of making war. According to Churchill, during the Argentia Conference "he [Roosevelt] went on to say to me, 'I shall never declare war; I shall make war. If

I were to ask Congress to declare war they might argue about it for three months' "; Churchill to Smuts, 9 Nov. 1941, FO 954/4A/100670 (Dom/41/24), p. 340 (PRO). If the President said just that and meant it, then he *intended* to subvert the Constitutional provision that only Congress can declare war. On the other hand, Churchill most likely heard what he wanted to hear, while Roosevelt spoke of how he would act but only *if* he decided to do so.

Roosevelt and the manipulation of news is treated by Richard W. Steele in a number of articles and his book, *Propaganda in an Open Society* (Westport, Conn.: Greenwood Press, 1985); and by Allan M. Winkler, *The Politics of Propaganda: The Office of War Information, 1942–1945* (New Haven, Conn.: Yale Univ. Press, 1978). See also the interesting piece by Lorraine M. Lees, "National Security and Ethnicity: Contrasting Views During World War II," *Diplomatic History* 11 (Spring 1987), pp. 113–25, and Betty Houchins Winfield, *FDR and the News Media* (Urbana and Chicago: Univ. of Illinois Press, 1990).

84. The President applied public diplomacy at home when he gave sympathetic journalist Forrest Davis a series of special interviews that resulted in three *Saturday Evening Post* articles; "Roosevelt's World Blueprint," and the two-part piece, "What Really Happened at Teheran." All three pieces were submitted to the White House for prior approval; see Official File (OF) 4287 (FDRL), especially F. Davis to S. Early, 23 March 1944. Ernest R. May called Roosevelt's "fireside chat" following the Teheran Conference "a state paper," because it was so carefully prepared, going through eight drafts; *"Lessons" of the Past* (New York: Oxford Univ. Press, 1973), p. 4.

85. Eden, *The Reckoning*, p. 437. Despite Eden's presence at Teheran, his memoirs are disappointing. There are only three pages on the talks, and only the issue of Eastern Europe's frontiers is discussed; ibid., pp. 494–97.

See Ian Clark, *Reform and Resistance in the International Order* (Cambridge: Cambridge Univ. Press, 1980), pp. 180–83. An entire number of the *Review of International Studies* 15 (1989) is devoted to an interesting and useful discussion of the concept and history of balance-of-power politics in the modern era. Jürg Martin Gabriel has pointed out in *The American Conception of Neutrality*, pp. 66–70, that one of the ways Roosevelt sought to make Wilsonianism work was to make the United Nations Organization a much more hierarchical and centralized than the League of Nations.

86. *FRUS, Tehran*, p. 585.

87. This line of argument is suggested by a reading of Paul Schroeder, "The Nineteenth Century System: Balance of Power or Political Equilibrium?" *Review of International Studies* 15 (April 1989), pp. 135–53. My thanks to Steven Miner and other participants in the 3d Soviet-American Symposium on World War II for reminding me of the parallels between the Holy Alliance and the Four Policemen. See also Ian Clark's very useful *Reform and Resistance*, esp. pp. 133–68. See also Michael Howard, *War and the Liberal Conscience* (Oxford: Oxford Univ. Press, 1978), p. 118, where he argues that Britain aimed at the reestablishment of the Concert of Europe. Gordon A. Craig and Alexander L. George, *Force and State-craft* (New York: Oxford Univ. Press, 1983), pp. 101–12, speculate briefly but usefully on Roosevelt's postwar plans.

88. Watt, "Historiography of Yalta," *Diplomatic History*, p. 98, paraphrasing Jean Laloy.

89. Some of the President's advisers had a sense of where he was trying to go. Assistant Secretary of State Adolf Berle, even while blinded by his Anglophobia, often caught Roosevelt's thinking. Faced with Soviet advice to the President that the United States should "get tough" in the Western Hemisphere, Berle commented that such interference "would mean that the world is a straight, holy alliance, Metternich style"; Beatrice B. Berle and Travis B. Jacobs, *Navigating the Rapids, 1918–1971: From the Papers of Adolf A. Berle* (New York: Harcourt Brace Jovanovich, 1973), p. 473.

90. Meade Diary, file 1/1, 1943 (BLPS).

91. Kimball, *Churchill & Roosevelt*, III, C-914.

92. *The New York Times*, 21 Sept. 1988; Speech by President Bush at the U.S. Coast Guard Academy, 25 May 1989.

Chapter Six
"Baffled Virtue"

1. Walter Lippmann, *U.S. War Aims* (London: Hamish Hamilton, 1944), pp. 50–51.

2. Roosevelt often arranged for his views to be presented to the public indirectly by journalists and writers, but despite very occasional meetings between the President and Lippmann, including ones on 16 February and 8 April 1943, plus a few brief written exchanges (for example, see above, "'The Family Circle,'" n. 40), there is no indication that the President had any input into the columnist's two books on the postwar world, *U.S. War Aims* and *U.S. Foreign Policy* (London: Hamish Hamilton, 1943). Nor was Lippmann ever a social guest at the White House. According to the staff at the FDR Library, it appears that Roosevelt did not own a copy of *U.S. Foreign Policy*, although *U.S. War Aims* was in his library; FDRL to author, 3 March 1989. See also Ronald Steel, *Walter Lippmann and the American Century* (London: The Bodley Head, 1980); and the introductory essay by John M. Blum, *Public Philosopher: The Letters of Walter Lippmann* (New York: Ticknor & Fields, 1985). Sherwood does mention that Lippmann and Harry Hopkins became friends, but infers that was in 1944, after the publication of the two books; Sherwood, *Roosevelt and Hopkins*, p. 835. Lippmann and Secretary of State Edward Stettinius were also on good terms; Campbell and Herring, *Stettinius Diaries*, pp. 98–102.

3. Latin American challenges to the United States are not invariably "revolutionary," even if that is often the case. United States policy was often designed to co-opt the ruling elites, but the history of U.S.-Latin American relations is replete with examples of established elites that challenged the United States because of nationalistic pressures. Even a cursory look at what is called the Mexican Revolution raises serious doubts about the "revolutionary" nature of its domestic policies, but no doubts about the intensity of its nationalism.

4. These two paragraphs are taken from Lippmann, *U.S. War Aims*, with the quotations from pp. 37, 50–51, 119. Regarding the role of small nations in the postwar order, Lippmann wrote: "The problem of *world order* is, I believe, insoluble if we seek to constitute the order out of the sixty or more individual nations. It is soluble . . . if the world order is composed of the great regional constellations of states" (ibid., p. 52). For interpretations of Lippmann's thought, see Steel,

Walter Lippmann, and Blum, *Public Philosopher*. Roosevelt's remark about the intellectuals is quoted in Burns, *Soldier of Freedom*, p. 515. See also Divine, *Second Chance*, p. 167.

5. The Mackenzie King diaries as quoted in Granatstein, *Canada's War*, p. 141.

6. The "side door" phrase is that of Cole, *Roosevelt and the Isolationists*, pp. 357–62.

7. Roosevelt memo of 17 May 1942, quoted in Bryce Wood, *The Making of the Good Neighbor Policy* (New York: Columbia Univ. Press, 1961; Norton ed., 1967), p. 131.

The Good Neighbor Policy has been the subject of a number of excellent studies. For starters, see the study by Bryce Wood cited above, and his *Dismantling the Good Neighbor Policy* (Austin: Univ. of Texas Press, 1985); Dick Steward, *Trade and Hemisphere: The Good Neighbor Policy and Reciprocal Trade* (Columbia: Univ. of Missouri Press, 1975); Irwin F. Gellman, *Good Neighbor Diplomacy: United States Policies in Latin America, 1933–1945* (Baltimore and London: Johns Hopkins Univ. Press, 1979); David Green, *The Containment of Latin America: A History of the Myths and Realities of the Good Neighbor Policy* (Chicago: Quadrangle, 1971).

8. Gerald K. Haines, "Under the Eagle's Wing: The Franklin Roosevelt Administration Forges an American Hemisphere," *Diplomatic History* 1 (Fall 1977), pp. 380–87; Gellman, *Good Neighbor Diplomacy*, chap. 11.

The Office of the Coordinator of Inter-American Affairs (later the Office of Inter-American Affairs) was created by the White House with the dual mission of preventing German subversion in Latin America while promoting hemispheric unity. Much to Hull's distress, the agency did not come under the supervision of the State Department.

9. Press conference of 24 Nov. 1942, *Press Conferences of FDR* 20 (July 1942–Dec. 1942), pp. 264–65. See also Frances Perkins, *The Roosevelt I Knew* (New York: Harper Colophon, 1964), p. 351.

10. Davis, "What Really Happened At Teheran," *Saturday Evening Post*, p. 13, and "What Really Happened At Teheran," [part 2] *Saturday Evening Post*, p. 48.

Roosevelt's careless and ignorant use of phrases like "nearer in blood" should not be interpreted as plain, unadorned racism. Rather, call it what it was, an example of American cultural and political ethnocentrism, in which assumptions of biological superiority played a part.

11. Davis, "Roosevelt's World Blueprint," *Saturday Evening Post*, p. 110. Davis' articles were carefully vetted by the White House before publication. See " 'The Family Circle,' " n. 82.

12. Mackenzie King's "obsequious relationship" with the President (the phrase of one Canadian historian) may have encouraged Roosevelt to assume Canada's acceptance of American leadership, but the uncooperativeness of Argentine leaders did not dissuade FDR from making the same assumption; Denis Smith, *Diplomacy of Fear: Canada and the Cold War, 1941–1948* (Toronto, Buffalo, London: Univ. of Toronto Press, 1988), p. 13.

13. For some general studies of Canadian-American relations during the Second World War, see C. P. Stacey, "Twenty-one Years of Canadian-American

Military Co-operation, 1940–1961," in *Canada-United States Treaty Relations*, David R. Deener, ed. (Durham: Duke Univ. Press, 1963), pp. 102–22; Kenneth McNaught, *The History of Canada* (New York: Praeger, 1970); William R. Willoughby, *The Joint Organizations of Canada and the United States* (Toronto, Buffalo, London: Univ. of Toronto Press, 1979); R. D. Cuff and J. L. Granatstein, *Canadian-American Relations in Wartime: From the Great War to the Cold War* (Toronto: Hakkert, 1975); J. L. Granatstein, *Canada's War: The Politics of the Mackenzie King Government, 1939–1945* (Toronto: Oxford Univ. Press, 1975).

14. Stetson Conn and Bryan Fairchild, *The Framework of Hemisphere Defense* (Washington: OCMH, 1960), pp. 364–89; Smith, *Diplomacy of Fear*, pp. 11–14; Fred E. Pollock, "Roosevelt, the Ogdensburg Agreement, and the British Fleet: All Done with Mirrors," *Diplomatic History* 5 (Summer 1981), pp. 203–19. Canadian thinking about the Pan-American Union is from Hooker, *The Moffat Papers*, p. 373; C. Cecil Lingard and Reginald C. Trotter, *Canada in World Affairs, September 1941–May 1944* (Toronto: Oxford Univ. Press, 1950), pp. 138–43.

15. The Canadian Maritime Provinces are New Brunswick, Nova Scotia, and Prince Edward Island. At the time of World War II, Newfoundland was still a British colony and not part of the Dominion of Canada, but its defense became an American responsibility when the destroyer-bases arrangement gave the United States permission to have a military base on the island.

Canadian military leaders were likewise opposed to having their troops under the command of non-Canadian (i.e., American) officers; Conn and Fairchild, *Framework of Hemisphere Defense*, p. 381.

16. The gravity metaphor is that of Alfred Weinberg in his classic, *Manifest Destiny* (1935).

17. Roosevelt as paraphrased in John Gunther, *Roosevelt in Retrospect: A Profile in History* (New York: Harper & Bros., 1950), pp. 24–26.

18. Lash, *Roosevelt and Churchill, 1939–1941*, p. 122; press conferences of 12 and 18 April 1940. Roosevelt's cartographic legerdemain, which was not necessarily wrong, is discussed in Alan K. Henrikson, "The Map as an 'Idea': The Role of Cartographic Imagery During the Second World War," *The American Cartographer* 2 (1975), pp. 19–53. Roosevelt's casual cartography is displayed in a map, later shown to Churchill, that designated the eastern boundary of the Western Hemisphere. Not only was Greenland safely included, but so were the Portuguese Azores and, by virtue of a sharp curve to the east, Iceland; Sherwood, *Roosevelt and Hopkins*, p. 310. But that was not a new idea. General Billy Mitchell had told Congress in 1920 that Greenland could provide air bases between Europe and Asia in time of war, and in 1933, the State Department sent Roosevelt a paper reviewing the new importance of Greenland created by the development of air power. In 1939, Admiral Richard Byrd recommended that the U.S. acquire air base rights on the island, and the Senate followed by passing a resolution recommending the purchase of the island from Denmark; see Nancy Fogelson, "Greenland: Strategic Base on a Northern Defense Line," *Journal of Military History* 53 (January 1989), pp. 53, 57, 60–61.

19. Berle is, in some ways, a special case. His strong sense of continentalism led him to advocate neutralism toward the European war, and to view the Western Hemisphere in more exclusive terms than did the President. See the introduc-

tory essay by Max Ascoli in Berle and Jacobs, *Navigating the Rapids*, pp. xv–xxxvi.

20. Ibid., 6 Feb. 1941, p. 356.

21. Ibid., 20 Apr. 40, pp. 305–6; 24 June 40, p. 325. Berle's Anglophobia colored, or discolored, everything he said and did. "Low-grade English piracy" was his characterization of Whitehall's statement that they would treat Danish ships as enemy vessels after Germany took over Denmark; ibid., 23 Apr. 1940, p. 306.

22. Fogelson, "Greenland," *Military History*, p. 54; ibid., 27 Aug. 1940, p. 331.

23. Ibid., 7 Sept. 1940, p. 334; 9 Nov. 1940, p. 351.

24. Ibid., 13 Feb. 1941, pp. 356–57.

25. The quotations about Canada and the good neighbor are from the King diaries as quoted in Granatstein, *Canada's War*, pp. 141, 143. The agreement between Roosevelt and King is discussed in ibid., p. 143; R. D. Cuff and J. L. Granatstein, *Canadian-American Relations in Wartime: From the Great War to the Cold War* (Toronto: Hakkert, 1975), chap. 4, "The Hyde Park Declaration, 1941," pp. 69–92.

26. Mexican-United States relations during World War II were relatively smooth following Roosevelt's decision in 1940 to compromise over the issue of American claims to much of Mexico's oil rights.

27. See Samuel L. Baily, *Labor, Nationalism, and Politics in Argentina* (New Brunswick: Rutgers Univ. Press, 1967), esp. chap. 3; David Rock, *Argentina, 1516–1987* (Berkeley: Univ. of California Press, 1987).

28. Early New Deal economic policies toward Argentina are treated in Steward, *Trade and Hemisphere*, pp. 176–97. He goes on to argue that American trade policies, specifically Hull's reciprocal trade program, unintentionally sabotaged the sense of political unity that was the goal of the Good Neighbor Policy; see pp. 280–81.

The Imperial Preference System gave preferential monetary and trade privileges to members of the British Empire. To New Deal leaders, it symbolized everything that was outdated, selfish, and unethical about British economic policy. For additional detail, see "Lend-Lease and the Open Door," elsewhere in this collection.

29. Gellman, *Good Neighbor Diplomacy*, pp. 96–104. At a Pan-American meeting in Havana in July 1940, called largely in response to Hitler's conquest of France, the Low Counties, Norway, and Denmark, all the Latin American nations finally agreed to a series of steps that would permit them to establish joint trusteeships in order to prevent Germany (not mentioned by name) from taking over Western Hemisphere territories of the conquered nations.

30. The history of Argentine-United States relations during the war is recounted in Randall Bennett Woods, *The Roosevelt Foreign-Policy Establishment and the "Good Neighbor": The United States and Argentina, 1941–1945* (Lawrence: The Regents Press of Kansas, 1979).

31. Bradford Perkins, *Castlereaugh and Adams: England and the United States, 1812–1823* (Berkeley: Univ. of California Press, 1964), is the best study of the American actions and reactions at the peace talks at Ghent.

32. See Reynolds, *The Anglo-American Alliance*, esp. chap. 1.

33. As quoted in R. R. Palmer, *The Age of Democratic Revolution*, vol. I, *The Challenge* (Princeton: Princeton University Press, 1959), p. 239.

34. Kimball, *Churchill & Roosevelt*, I, R-2x. See also C-4x and C-8x, and Churchill, *The Gathering Storm*, pp. 529–30.

35. The German map can be found in the PSF, Safe: Germany (FDRL). The FBI map is from a report of March 1942, Hopkins papers, box 144 (FDRL). American concern about a German move into Latin America may have been exaggerated, as illustrated in Donald C. Watt, *Succeeding John Bull* (New York: Cambridge Univ. Press, 1984), pp. 78–79, 91; but it was not feigned, as shown by Patrick J. Hearden, *Roosevelt Confronts Hitler: America's Entry Into World War II* (DeKalb: Northern Illinois Univ. Press, 1987), pp. 110–12, 158–69. The origins of the German map are discussed in Stanley E. Hilton, *Hitler's Secret War in South America* (Baton Rouge: Louisiana State Univ. Press, 1981), p. 204. There are conflicting claims by British secret agents and historians as to the number of maps and their origins; see James F. Bratzel and Leslie B. Rout, "FDR and the 'Secret Map,' " *The Wilson Quarterly* 9 (1 Jan. 1985), pp. 167–73.

36. Woodward, *British Foreign Policy*, IV, chap. 49. Halifax, who became ambassador after Lothian's death in December 1940, is quoted in Wood, *Dismantling the Good Neighbor Policy*, p. 72. This is also the testimony of Sir Evelyn Schomburk, who was in the British embassy in Buenos Aires during much of World War II; remarks by Sir Evelyn Schomburk at the "Argentina between the Great Powers, 1939–1946," conference, St. Antony's College, Oxford, 3–5 July 1986.

37. Kimball, *Churchill & Roosevelt*, III, R-579 (emphasis added). Much of the detail of the controversy over British contracts for Argentine beef can be found in Woodward, *British Foreign Policy*, IV. See also Kimball, *Churchill & Roosevelt*, III, C-730, C-731, and ff.; *FRUS*, 1944, VII, pp. 327ff.

38. Kimball, *Churchill & Roosevelt*, R-651, p. 397.

39. Ibid., C-832 (emphasis added).

40. Cherwell to Churchill (in Halifax to the Foreign Office), 29 Oct. 1944, FO 954 (Eden papers)/14B, LA/44/37, p. 525 (PRO).

41. See, for example, Damonte Tabardo to Sumner Welles, 6 Feb. 1942, PSF-Welles 1942, box 96 (FDRL).

42. Morgenthau, Presidential Diary, 14 Oct. 1939, p. 352.

43. Those arguments are summarized in Bryce Wood, *Dismantling the Good Neighbor Policy*, and with some intensity in R. B. Woods, *The United States and Argentina, 1941–1945*. See also Gellman, *Good Neighbor Diplomacy*.

44. The U.S. economic counselor in Buenos Aires, 1942–1944, Merwyn K. Bohan, said in 1974 that he felt "Mr. Roosevelt more or less gave Argentina to Mr. Hull to play with, to keep him out of his hair." Oral interview, Harry S Truman Library, as quoted by Ronald C. Newton, "Great Britain, the United States, and the 'Nazi Menace' in Argentina, 1938–1947," in *Argentina between the Great Powers*, p. 111.

45. This liberal credo for Latin America is seen quite clearly in the statement made by U.S. representatives at the Buenos Aires conference in 1936. Hull's thinking is discussed in Schatz, "The Anglo-American Trade Agreement," *Journal of American History*, pp. 85–103, as well as in the books cited above in n. 43. A

good example of the limits of Roosevelt's liberalism is in his relations with the government of Panama; see John Major, "F.D.R. and Panama," *The Historical Journal* 28, no. 2 (1985), pp. 357–77. The role of Brazil is fully and persuasively discussed by Stanley E. Hilton, "The United States and Argentina in Brazil's Wartime Diplomacy, 1939–1945," in *Argentina between the Great Powers*, pp. 158–80. All this must be read in the light of the reports that flowed in constantly, particularly from the FBI, indicating that Argentina looked to Japan, Germany, and anywhere but Washington for friends and advice. See for example, J. Edgar Hoover to Harry Hopkins, 11 Feb. 1944, Hopkins papers, box 140-Special Assistant to the President, "FBI Reports: Argentina" (FDRL).

46. Kimball, *Churchill & Roosevelt*, II, C-297/1, pp. 222ff., and III, C-631.

47. Hull to Roosevelt, 17 June 1944, *FRUS, 1944*, V, pp. 124–25.

48. Hull to Roosevelt, 13 Sept. 1944, *FRUS, Conf. at Quebec, 1944*, p. 395. Churchill was not the only one to try to co-opt Roosevelt on this issue. Stalin also expressed willingness to relegate the Caribbean to the United States as a sphere of influence; see Anders Stephanson, *Kennan and the Art of Foreign Policy* (Cambridge: Harvard Univ. Press, 1989), p. 37.

49. See the discussion of the Moscow Foreign Ministers Conference in " 'The Family Circle,' " elsewhere in this collection.

50. A quick glance at either Cordell Hull's memoirs or the various books by Sumner Welles demonstrates American preoccupation with its leadership role in the Western Hemisphere. Hull, *Memoirs*; Welles, *Seven Decisions*, and *Where Are We Heading?* (New York: Harper's, 1946).

51. Such complaints were expressed frequently and with some fervor, but seem to have had no appreciable effect on Anglo-American relations at the time. In addition to citations in B. Wood, *Dismantling of the Good Neighbor Policy*, and Gardner, *Economic Aspects of New Deal Diplomacy*, pp. 212–13, Noel Fursman of St. Antony's College, Oxford, has been kind enough to provide a number of additional examples from British Public Record Office files. In each of the following documents, the drafter believed that the Americans were deliberately using the war to gain economic advantage: Reading (Min. of Economic Warfare) to Lyal (Dept. of Overseas Trade), 31/5/43, A55098/PRO 33901; Bonham Carter (Min. of Information) to Gallop (Foreign Office), 22/2/43, AS 1960/PRO 33903; Kelly (Amb. in Buenos Aires) to Foreign Office, 19/2/43, AS 2855/33907.

52. B.J.V. Perowne as quoted in B. Wood, *Dismantling of the Good Neighbor Policy*, pp. 96–97.

53. UE 813/PRO 45694 (emphasis added). I am once again indebted to Noel Fursman for this citation.

Perhaps the word rivalry is applicable at the local level, but a reading of Churchill-Roosevelt exchanges on Latin America indicates that it was not so at the level of high policy. See index entries under Latin America and Argentina in Kimball, *Churchill & Roosevelt*. A study of the broad issue of Anglo-American rivalry in World War II, D. C. Watt's *Succeeding John Bull* has no separate chapter or section devoted to Latin America, and properly so. The same is true for other recent studies like Alan Dobson, *The Politics of the Anglo-American Economic Special Relationship 1940–1987* (New York: St. Martin's, 1988); Dobson,

US Wartime Aid to Britain; and David Dimbleby and David Reynolds, *An Ocean Apart: The Relationship between Britain and America in the Twentieth Century* (New York: Random House, 1988).

54. To quote Roosevelt's youthful sentiments in 1914—"I do not want war, but I don't see how we can avoid it. Sooner or later it seems the United States must go down there and clean up the Mexican political mess. I believe that the best time is right now"—hardly demonstrates that his disavowal of the use of force was either insincere or hypocritical; Roosevelt as quoted in William Neumann, "Roosevelt's Options and Evasions in Foreign Policy Decisions, 1940–1945," *Watershed of Empire,* L. Liggio and J. Martin, eds. (Colorado Springs: Ralph Myles, 1976), p. 166.

55. This is one of the themes of Max Savelle's magisterial study, *The Origins of American Diplomacy* (New York: Macmillan, 1967), esp. pp. 210–15.

56. Fitzroy André Baptiste, *War, Cooperation, and Conflict: The European Possessions in the Caribbean, 1939–1945* (Westport, Conn.: Greenwood Press, 1988), emphasizes differences in the way the United States treated Latin America versus the Caribbean.

57. Berle report to the State Department Policy Committee, 26 Sept. 1944, Berle and Jacobs, *Navigating the Rapids,* pp. 464–65.

58. William H. McNeill, *America, Britain, & Russia* (New York and London: Johnson Reprint Corp., 1970; orig. pub. 1953), p. 317.

59. Gellman, *Good Neighbor Diplomacy,* pp. 74–92.

60. See " 'The Family Circle' " for other examples of Roosevelt's attitude toward the smaller nations.

61. Jesse H. Stiller, *George S. Messersmith: Diplomat of Democracy* (Chapel Hill and London: Univ. of North Carolina Press, 1987), pp. 149.

62. Jimmy Buffett, "Banana Republics," MCA Records, 1977.

Chapter Seven
"In Search of Monsters to Destroy"

1. Campbell and Herring, *Stettinius Diaries,* 17 March 1944, p. 39 (conversation between Isaiah Bowman and FDR).

2. This is not the place to try to reconcile or define how Americans use the words "colonialism" and "imperialism." Suffice it to say that when Roosevelt and his aides spoke of colonialism, they referred to formal colonial empire. Rule by "the white nations" was the President's frequent phrase. That excluded the Soviet Empire, but did encompass what he and his advisers called "inequitable exploitation," particularly in China. See Davis, "Roosevelt's World Blueprint," *Saturday Evening Post,* p. 110.

3. The nature of Roosevelt's anticolonialism has been the subject of extensive study. To start with, see LaFeber, "Roosevelt, Churchill, and Indochina," 1942–45," *American Historical Review,* pp. 1277–95; Louis, *Imperialism at Bay;* Thorne, *Allies of a Kind,* and "Indochina and Anglo-American Relations, 1942–1945," *Pacific Historical Review* 45 (1976), pp. 73–96; Lloyd C. Gardner, *Approaching Vietnam: From World War II through Dienbienphu, 1941–1954* (New York: W. W. Norton & Co., 1988); Gary Hess, *The United States' Emer-*

gence as a Southeast Asia Power (New York: Columbia Univ. Press, 1986), and *America Encounters India 1941–1947* (Baltimore: Johns Hopkins Univ. Press, 1971), and "Franklin Roosevelt and Indochina," *Journal of American History* 59 (1972), pp. 353–68; Watt, *Succeeding John Bull*, and "American Anti-colonialist Policies at the End of the European Colonial Empires, 1941–1962," in *Contagious Conflict: The Impact of American Dissent on European Life,* A.N.J. Hollander, ed. (Leiden: E. J. Brill, 1973), pp. 93–125; Robert J. McMahon, *Colonialism and Cold War: The United States and the Struggle for Indonesian Independence 1945–1949* (Ithaca: Cornell Univ. Press, 1981); George C. Herring, "The Truman Administration and the Restoration of French Sovereignty in Indochina," *Diplomatic History,* I (Spring 1977), pp. 97–117; John J. Sbrega, *Anglo-American Relations and Colonialism in East Asia, 1941–1945* (New York: Garland Publishing Inc., 1983); Raymond A. Callahan, *Churchill: Retreat from Empire* (Wilmington, Del.: SR Books, 1984). The popular, but exaggerated image of unyielding American anticolonialism seems to be giving way to an equally distorted belief that "the United States as a nation, expressing itself through its government, did not attempt to dismantle the European colonial empires in Asia at the end of World War II." See Neil Sheehan, *A Bright Shining Lie* (New York: Random House-Vintage, 1989), p. 150.

4. Warren I. Cohen's perceptive *The American Revisionists* (Chicago: Univ. of Chicago Press, 1967) recreates the atmosphere of cynicism and disillusionment America felt toward Europe.

5. This touches on the issue of what Lloyd Gardner has called the "Contradictions of Liberal Empire" and "A Covenant With Power." Certainly Wilson at Versailles and Roosevelt during World War II found themselves scrambling for a middle ground between popular revolutionary change (whether Bolshevism or nationalism in the colonial empires) and the elitist status quo (whether what Wilson called "reaction" or the colonial empires Roosevelt condemned); *Approaching Vietnam,* chap. 11; *A Covenant With Power.*

6. Quoted in Louis, *Imperialism at Bay,* p. 548.

7. British perceptions and concern about the changing colonial world are presented throughout Louis, *Imperialism at Bay,* and Thorne, *Allies of a Kind.* State Department adviser John Patton Davies was one of many who warned that the British would try to expand their empire in order to remain a first-class postwar power. Memo by Davies, "Anglo-American Cooperation in East Asia," 15 November 1943, American Committee for the History of the Second World War *Newsletter* (Spring 1989), no. 41, p. 33.

8. See Christopher Thorne, *The Issue of War: States, Societies, and the Far Eastern Conflict of 1941–1945* (New York: Oxford Univ. Press, 1985), chap. 5; John W. Dower, *War Without Mercy: Race and Power in the Pacific War* (New York: Pantheon, 1986), pp. 207–8. Dower goes on to demonstrate that such appeals to racial solidarity and anti-Western feelings were merely a precursor to Japanese domination of those Asian peoples; ibid., chap. 10.

9. Thorne, *The Issue of War,* see esp. pp. 146–52, 226–27, 590–91; Hess, *America Encounters India,* p. 81.

10. Hess, *The United States' Emergence as a Southeast Asian Power,* chap. 7.

11. The "almost all" qualification is necessitated by some exceptions Roosevelt made, usually on the grounds of U.S. national security (e.g., certain Pacific

islands), or extreme backwardness (e.g., New Guinea). See Lester J. Foltos, "The New Pacific Barrier: America's Search for Security in the Pacific, 1945–47," *Diplomatic History* 13 (Summer 1989), pp. 317–42. Even in those cases where Roosevelt insisted on maintaining military base rights, he believed "the sovereignty and civil administration of those areas are not a matter of profound concern." It apparently did not occur to him that the bases might become matters of "profound concern" to those peoples; minutes, 36th Pacific War Council meeting, 12 Jan. 1944, MR-FDRL.

For an example of Roosevelt's apparent acceptance of pseudo-scientific racial theories see Campbell to Cadogan, 6 Aug. 1942, reprinted in Sbrega, *Anglo-American Relations and Colonialism*, p. 285. The President's oft-quoted nasty comments about certain Burmese leaders were prompted by anger over their collaboration with the Japanese, although the tone hints at Roosevelt's prejudices; see Kimball, *Churchill & Roosevelt*, I, p. 312, and R-135/1. That does not, however, diminish the vigor or consistency of the President's anticolonialism.

In mid-1942, Roosevelt did tell the Pacific War Council that "India is not yet ready for home government. That takes time. The training of thousands of persons over a number of years is necessary for good government." He then pointed out that the United States learned by trial and error during the Confederation period—an analogy he had made to Churchill and one the Prime Minister had angrily mocked. Minutes, 17th Pacific War Council Meeting, 12 August 1942, MR-FDRL; Kimball, *Churchill & Roosevelt*, I, R-116.

12. See Gellman, *Good Neighbor Diplomacy*, pp. 96–104. The proposal is further discussed in " 'Baffled Virtue . . . Injured Innocence,' " elsewhere in this collection. Roosevelt also claimed that his 1936 arrangement with the British to postpone the issue of sovereignty over Canton Island was an early example of his trusteeship idea; *Stettinius Diaries*, 17 March 1944, pp. 38–39.

13. The Kuomintang, or Nationalists, was the politico-military organization behind Chiang's leadership of China. During most of the war, his government was located in Chungking.

14. Roosevelt and his advisers were very consistent on this point. After the Japanese invaded the Philippine Islands, the United States made a renewed and specific commitment to Philippine independence. That promise significantly limited the success of Japanese appeals to nationalism in the islands; Hess, *The United States' Emergence as a Southeast Asian Power*, pp. 219–28.

15. *FRUS, 1941*, III, p. 178.

16. On 1 August, the U.S. ambassador in London, John G. Winant, asked if he should raise the issue of dominion status for India with the British. Under Secretary of State Sumner Welles replied that Roosevelt "would wish to discuss it in a very personal and confidential way directly with Mr. Churchill." *FRUS, 1941*, III, pp. 178–79, 181.

For the details of the Atlantic Conference, see Wilson, *The First Summit*.

17. For example, Burmese nationalists immediately insisted that the British comply with the Charter's commitment to self-government. Amery pointedly remarked: "We shall no doubt pay dearly in the end for all this fluffy flapdoodle." John Barnes and David Nicholson, eds., *The Empire at Bay: The Leo Amery Diaries, 1929–1945* (London: Hutchinson and Co., 1988), p. 710; Reynolds, *The Anglo-American Alliance*, pp. 258–59.

18. The emphasis on the word "empire" is evident in recordings of the speech.

19. For the First Washington (ARCADIA) Conference, 20 Dec. 1941–14 Jan. 1942.

20. Churchill, *The Hinge of Fate*, p. 209.

21. *FRUS, Casablanca Conf.*, pp. 366–76. The Declaration by the United Nations is printed in *FRUS*, 1942, I, pp. 25–26.

22. Amery to Linlithgow, 5 Jan. 1942, *The Transfer of Power, 1942–1947*, Nicholas Mansergh, ed. (12 vols; London: HMSO, 1970–1983), I, document 5. Amery's sentiments and strategies on the empire are recorded in John Barnes and David Nicholson, *The Empire at Bay: The Leo Amery Diaries, 1929–1945* (London: Hutchinson and Co., 1988).

23. Immediately following the release of the Declaration by the United Nations, India again pressed for Dominion status. American public pressure supported their goals. See Mansergh, *Transfer of Power*, I, docs. 2, 10, 11, 12. See also, R. J. Moore, *Churchill, Cripps and India, 1939–1945* (Oxford: Oxford Univ. Press, 1979), p. 50; and Woodward, *British Foreign Policy*, IV, p. 492.

24. The Indian Congress Party, dominated by Hindus and led by Mohandas K. Gandhi and Pandit Nehru, had a long-standing demand for independence under a single, unified Indian state. The leading Moslem nationalist organization was the Muslim League, led by Muhammed Ali Jinnah. It advocated creation of a separate state, Pakistan. See Betty Miller Unterberger, "American Views of Mohammad Ali Jinnah and the Pakistan Liberation Movement," *Diplomatic History* 5 (Fall 1981), pp. 313–36.

Chiang Kai-shek's visit to India is discussed in Woodward, *British Foreign Policy*, IV, pp. 489–92; and Mansergh, *Transfer of Power*, I, starting with doc. 36. Also see Hess, *America Encounters India*, pp. 35–37; and Thorne, *Allies of a Kind*, pp. 237–38. Chiang is quoted in *FRUS, 1942*, I, pp. 604–6.

25. Kimball, *Churchill & Roosevelt*, I, C-35; Harriman and Abel, *Special Envoy*, pp. 129–31; Woodward, *British Foreign Policy*, IV, p. 492. British references to irreconcilable Moslem-Hindu antagonism were part of the traditional divide-and-rule tactics used by the British in India. Whether those references were accurate, or a self-fulfilling British prophecy, remains open to debate.

26. The British proposal called for the election of a constitutional assembly which would set out the framework of self-government. But this was to come only after the war, and included provisions that allowed any Indian state to opt out of the arrangement. In essence, that guaranteed the establishment of a Moslem state—Pakistan—and was unacceptable to leaders of Congress.

Hess, *America Encounters India*, remains the best overall survey of that subject. Moore, *Churchill, Cripps and India*, is harshly critical of Churchill's role in preventing Cripps from succeeding; see pp. 77–132. The Cripps mission is nicely summarized in Callahan, *Churchill: Retreat from Empire*, pp. 185–88. The Johnson mission to India is well analyzed in Kenton J. Clymer, "Franklin D. Roosevelt, Louis Johnson, India and Anticolonialism: Another Look," *Pacific Historical Review* 57 (1988), pp. 261–84. See also, *FRUS, 1942*, I, pp. 628–54; Sherwood, *Roosevelt and Hopkins*, p. 524; Thorne, *Allies of a Kind*, pp. 234–48; Mansergh, *Transfer of Power*, I, chaps. 3–5.

27. Quoted from Michael Edwardes, *The Last Years of British India* (London:

Cassell, 1963), in William L. Neumann, "Roosevelt's Foreign Policy Decisions, 1940–1945," *Modern Age* (Summer 1975), p. 284, n. 30.

28. Kimball, *Churchill & Roosevelt*, I, C-67, C-68 draft A, and R-132. Roosevelt's message was drafted by Sumner Welles and formally sent to Hopkins for delivery rather than directly to Churchill. Hopkins may have misled the Prime Minister by claiming that Cripps was using Johnson as a means of bringing the President into the controversy. Hopkins, usually suspicious of the British, believed they had made an honest effort in India; ibid., p. 448.

29. *FRUS, 1942*, III, pp. 578–83. The decolonization aspects of the talks with Molotov are summarized in Louis, *Imperialism at Bay*, pp. 155–58; and Akira Iriye in *Power and Culture: The Japanese-American War, 1941–1945* (Cambridge: Harvard Univ. Press, 1981), pp. 53–54, 77.

Roosevelt's incorrect inclusion of Siam as a colony is often cited as an example of his ignorance, since that nation had been independent for centuries. The implication is that Roosevelt's anticolonialism was equally ignorant, but history is the best judge of who was ignorant on that issue. Whatever the degree of independence possessed by Thailand (its British baptismal name was dropped, at least by Thais, in 1938), the country was sandwiched between the British colonies of Burma and Malaya, and French Indochina. The situation was complicated by official Thai cooperation with Japan and, in 1942, a declaration of war on the United States and Britain. The Americans ignored the declaration on the grounds it did not represent the will of the Thai people. The British argued that Thailand had "betrayed" British "friendship," and that they had to suffer the consequences. Moreover, the Americans were suspicious of the British failure to pledge the restoration of Thai independence after the war. Later in the war, the State Department reported rumors of British support for a federation of Malaya, Thailand, and Indochina under British sponsorship; Hull to Roosevelt, 8 Sept. 1944, *FRUS, Quebec, 1944*, pp. 262–63. Anglo-American arguments over Thailand are treated as "an extension of the clash over colonialism," by Hess, *U.S. Emergence as a Southeast Asian Power*, pp. 111–18. See also Thorne, *Allies of a Kind*, pp. 614–21.

30. Kimball, *Churchill & Roosevelt*, I, R-172, C-125; Woodward, *British Foreign Policy*, IV, pp. 494–96.

31. Roosevelt cabled Soviet Premier Joseph Stalin that Willkie was "heart and soul with my administration," and requested that Willkie be permitted to visit the Soviet Union during his world tour; USSR, *Stalin's Correspondence with Roosevelt*, no. 36, 9 Aug. 1942. See also Wendell Willkie, *One World* (New York: Simon & Schuster 1943), pp. 182–83. The British took Willkie's mission very seriously. See Thorne, *Allies of a Kind*, pp. 221–22. Willkie may have thought public opinion in Britain was even more anti-imperialist than it was in the U.S., but that was a far cry from what Churchill and Parliament were saying; ibid., p. 210. See also Gardner, *Approaching Vietnam*, p. 33.

32. Gilbert, *Road to Victory*, p. 254.

33. *FRUS, 1942*, I, p. 736; Mansergh, *Transfer of Power*, vol. II, doc. 749; ibid., vol. III, doc. 20.

34. While in London, Phillips claimed to have gained support for such mediation from Leo Amery and other British officials. This claim was quickly denied in

London by Amery, who instructed the Viceroy to stonewall Phillips. Mansergh, *Transfer of Power*, III, docs. 364, 366, 370, 374, 455. Hull message taken from Mansergh, *Transfer of Power*, III, doc. 485; *FRUS, 1943*, IV, p. 195.

35. This summary is taken from Mansergh, *Transfer of Power*, III, doc. 489. Phillips refused to issue a public statement fearing that the Americans would be associated with the British Government's policy concerning Gandhi. See also nos. 455, 486, 493, 495, 510; *FRUS, 1943*, IV, pp. 185–220; Hull, *Memoirs*, II, p. 1493; Thorne, *Allies of a Kind*, pp. 358–62. For a recent summary of the Phillips' mission, see Kenton J. Clymer, "The Education of William Phillips: Self Determination and American Policy toward India, 1942–1945," *Diplomatic History* 8 (Winter 1984), pp. 13–25; also Hess, *America Encounters India*, chap. 4.

36. Hull, *Memoirs*, II, p. 1493.

37. Clymer, "The Education of William Phillips," pp. 28–31. Also Mansergh, *Transfer of Power*, III, docs. 581, 590, 596, 635, 647, 667. In the event of Gandhi's death, the administration planned to disassociate the United States publicly from British policy in India; see *FRUS, 1943*, IV, pp. 203–4. Phillips was later declared persona non grata by the British Government when it appeared that he might be sent back to India; Thorne, *Allies of a Kind*, p. 476.

38. Minutes of the 28th Pacific War Council meeting, 17 Feb. 1943, MR-FDRL. Because he had not seen a redraft, Eden incorrectly "gathered" that the proposed declaration "does not favour intrusive interference by outsiders." Eden to Foreign Office, 29 March 1943, FO 371, U/1430/320/70.

39. Eden's own report to Churchill of his talks on colonial issues is in Halifax to the Foreign Office, 28 March 1943, FO 371/35366, U1430/320/70. See also Moscow embassy to Foreign Office, 28 April 1943, FO 954 [Avon papers] /30. For Roosevelt's response to Eden, see *FRUS, 1943*, III, pp. 28–39, 44–46 [emphasis added]; Hull, *Memoirs*, II, pp. 1234–36. Eden's visit to Washington is summarized in Louis, *Imperialism at Bay*, pp. 227–32, 177–79, and chap. 15. The meeting with Litvinov is in *FRUS, 1943*, III, pp. 44–46.

40. The Declaration on National Independence is printed in *FRUS, Washington and Quebec, 1943*, pp. 717–20. For a perceptive analysis of this issue, see Louis, *Imperialism at Bay*, pp. 231–32.

41. *The New York Times*, 15 April 1943; Mansergh, *Transfer of Power*, III, docs. 650, 661, 662, 675; Thorne, *Allies of a Kind*, p. 310. Madame Chiang Kai-shek was the wife of Kuomintang leader Generalissimo Chiang Kai-shek. British officials grossly exaggerated her influence, tending to see her as a Svengali, able to manipulate Roosevelt and official Washington at will. Amery concluded that one message from Hull to Phillips had been dictated by the President "but that the real source of it was Madame Chiang Kai-shek who is staying at the White House and over whom all America has gone crazy." "*Cherchez la femme*" is in Mansergh, *Transfer of Power*, III, doc. 494. Madame Chiang asserted that Nehru was a person with world vision. Like Roosevelt, she believed that Gandhi's perspective was clouded by his obsession with independence, despite the immediate requirements of war. One also suspects that her dislike of Gandhi stemmed from his stubborn refusal to accept any outside leadership, including that of the Chinese.

42. *FRUS, Yalta*, p. 856.

43. Roosevelt to Hopkins, 19 Mar. 1943, *F.D.R. His Personal Letters*, II, p. 1414.

44. William Phillips, *Ventures in Diplomacy* (North Beverly, Mass.: distributed by author, 1952), pp. 389–90.

45. These objections were raised in an aide memoire given to Ambassador Winant on 26 May 1943, the day after the TRIDENT Conference ended and Churchill left Washington; aide memoire, 26 May 1943, FO 371, U2381/130/G. For some reason, Winant never forwarded the memo to Washington. See Louis, *Imperialism at Bay*, p. 277 and chap. 15, esp. pp. 250–51; Hess, *The United States' Emergence as a Southeast Asian Power*, pp. 78–79. The statement in the House of Commons came on 13 July 1943.

46. Minutes, 33d Pacific War Council meeting, 21 July 1943, MR-FDRL. The Quebec discussions are covered in Louis, *Imperialism at Bay*, pp. 276–77; Woodward, *British Foreign Policy*, V, p. 73, n. 3; Thorne, *Allies of a Kind*, p. 348; Hull, *Memoirs*, II, pp. 1237–38; *FRUS, 1943, Washington and Quebec*, pp. 923–28. Eden is quoted in ibid., p. 926. The 1st Quebec Conference (QUADRANT) was held 14–29 August 1943.

47. *FRUS, 1943*, I, pp. 666–67. See also Louis, *Imperialism at Bay*, pp. 276–77.

48. Hess, *The United States' Emergence as a Southeast Asian Power*, pp. 84–85. When one leading Vietnamese nationalist, Nguyen Ai Quoc (Nguyen the Patriot), went to China in 1942 to work among various Vietnamese independence groups, the Kuomintang government threw him in prison, apparently because he was a communist. When he was released in September 1943, he changed his name to Ho Chi Minh ("He Who Enlightens"). Despite the treatment Ho had received, he concluded the Chinese sponsorship of Vietnamese independence was a sine qua non for success. For awhile, he managed to convince certain Kuomintang military leaders that he could be trusted to accept Chinese leadership, but eventually they lost interest, and Ho turned to American intelligence operatives (OSS) in Vietnam hoping to gain United States support; see Anthony Short, *The Origins of the Vietnam War* (London and New York: Longman, 1989), pp. 36–41; Gardner, *Approaching Vietnam*, p. 44.

49. This thesis is suggested by Hess, *The United States' Emergence as a Southeast Asian Power*, pp. 85–86. It also builds on the arguments of Iriye in *Power and Culture*, esp. pp. 49–95. The quotation from Chiang is on p. 54. As Wm. Roger Louis implies, Roosevelt's repeated claims that Chiang had come up with the trusteeship idea should be read as an attempt to co-opt the Chinese leader; Louis, *Imperialism at Bay*, p. 157. One excellent summary of American policy toward China during the war is Michael Schaller, *The U.S. Crusade in China, 1938–1945* (New York: Columbia Univ. Press, 1979).

50. Stilwell's Chief of Staff, General Frank Dorn, claimed that, after the Cairo Conference, Stilwell gave him a verbal order to assassinate Chiang Kai-shek. According to Dorn, Stilwell claimed that President Roosevelt was "fed up with Chiang," and wanted him replaced with "someone you can manage." Dorn came up with plans to give both Chiang and Madame Chiang faulty parachutes during an aborted flight to India. Dorn claims he did not execute the plan because Roosevelt never gave the final order to do so. See Schaller, *The U.S. Crusade in*

China, pp. 152–53. Given the communications problems between Roosevelt and Stilwell—the general viewed FDR with vulgar contempt—one can imagine the President saying, "We've got to get rid of Chiang," and that being translated by Stilwell or Dorn as assassination rather than the kind of political maneuvering that FDR himself was so adept at. Some of Roosevelt's talks with Stilwell are reported in Theodore H. White, *The Stilwell Papers* (New York: Schocken Books Edition, 1972), pp. 250–52.

Roosevelt's policies toward China's internal struggles are beyond the scope of this essay. Suffice it to say that the President disliked either of the two obvious options—Chiang and the nationalists, or Mao Tse Tung and the communists— and assumed for much of the war that the fighting would end with American military forces in China and in a position to influence, even determine the postwar political settlement in that nation. Whether or not the United States could ever have controlled the situation in China, an American invasion of Japan from Chinese bases never happened, and the leverage Roosevelt counted on never became available.

51. The Cairo (SEXTANT) Conference of 22–26 Nov. 1943, brought Roosevelt, Churchill, and Chiang together. The British and American leaders went on from there to the Teheran (EUREKA) meeting with Stalin (27 Nov.–2 Dec.), returning to Cairo for more Anglo-American discussions (2–7 Dec.). Roosevelt's discussions with Chiang are summarized in *FRUS, Tehran*, pp. 322–25. See also Louis, *Imperialism at Bay*, pp. 279–83; Thorne, *Allies of a Kind*, pp. 319–27; Hess, *The United States' Emergence as a Southeast Asian Power*, pp. 79–81; Roosevelt, *As He Saw It*, p. 165; *Stettinius Diaries*, pp. 39–40; Gardner, *Approaching Vietnam*, p. 41; Iriye, *Power and Culture*, pp. 154–61.

52. The Cairo Declaration is printed in *FRUS, Tehran*, pp. 448–49.

53. Lebanon, within the sphere of French imperial control since World War I, had been the scene of proindependence activities that were publicly supported by the United States. When the French suspended the local government, riots ensued. See *FRUS, Tehran*, p. 84, n. 2.

54. It was at this point that Roosevelt flippantly suggested that reform in India should come from the bottom up, "somewhat on the Soviet line." Stalin replied that "reform from the bottom would mean revolution"; see *FRUS, Tehran*, pp. 485–86. The President's remark should be seen as an expression of his populism and Americanism, rather than an endorsement of communism or proof of Roosevelt's naivete.

55. Moran, *Diaries*, pp. 144–45. Since Hopkins was not present at the Roosevelt-Stalin talks, what he passed on to Moran had to come via the President.

56. The Big Three discussions at Teheran are summarized in *FRUS, Tehran*, pp. 509–14, 552–55, 565–68. See also Hess, *The United States' Emergence as a Southeast Asian Power*, pp. 81–82; Louis, *Imperialism at Bay*, pp. 283–86; Iriye, *Power and Culture*, pp. 161–63.

Stalin's hint of an arrangement may have been what prompted Churchill to propose Soviet access to warm water ports, a long-standing Russian objective. To counter Churchill's gambit, Roosevelt returned to his theme of internationalization. This time he called for an international free zone for the former Hanseatic cities of Bremen, Hamburg, and Lubeck, as well as international control for the

Kiel Canal. When Stalin wondered what could be done similarly in the Far East, the President replied that a free port could be created there also, and mentioned Darien as the likely port city. Stalin expressed doubt that the Chinese would accept the proposal, but Roosevelt, perhaps kidding himself, gave assurance that Chiang would favor such a move.

57. Hess, *The United States' Emergence as a Southeast Asian Power*, pp. 89–90.

58. Minutes, 36th Pacific War Council meeting, 12 Jan. 1944, MR-FDRL; Hess, *The United States' Emergence as a Southeast Asian Power*, pp. 90–91; *FRUS, Tehran*, pp. 864, 868–70.

59. Roosevelt, *Press Conferences* 23, no. 931 [10–12].

60. Ibid., no. 933, [30–35].

61. Louis and Robinson in their essay "The United States and the Liquidation of the British Empire in Tropical Africa, 1941–1951," in Gifford and Louis, *The Transfer of Power in Africa*, pp. 31–55, work from the assumption that Roosevelt lumped India and Africa together in his thinking on colonialism. See also Hollis R. Lynch, "Pan-African Responses in the United States to British Colonial Rule in Africa in the 1940s," Prosser and Louis, eds., *Transfer of Power in Africa*, pp. 61–62. Roosevelt did tell the Pacific War Council that the Moroccans did not want to remain under French control, although they did want to benefit from French administration until Morocco could shift for itself; minutes, 27th Pacific War Council meeting, 3 Feb. 1943, MR-FDRL.

62. Welles to Roosevelt, 13 April 1942, attached to minutes, 3d Pacific War Council meeting, 15 Apr. 1942, MR-FDRL; reprinted in *FRUS, 1942*, I, pp. 870–72; William W. Stueck, Jr., *The Road to Confrontation: American Policy Toward China and Korea, 1947–1950* (Chapel Hill: Univ. of North Carolina Press, 1981), pp. 19–21; Hong-Kyu Park, "From Pearl Harbor to Cairo: America's Korean Diplomacy, 1941–43," *Diplomatic History* 13 (Summer 1989), pp. 343–58. Later in the war, Roosevelt's concern about Chinese expansionism may also have affected his thinking about Korea.

63. Quoted in Hess, *The United States' Emergence as a Southeast Asian Power*, p. 92.

64. Stettinius, *Diaries*, pp. 37–40.

65. After being warned by the Foreign Office, and then by William Phillips about Churchill's outbursts on India, the Americans did not bring up the subject of India or Indochina in their talks with the Prime Minister; ibid., p. 52. See Louis, *Imperialism at Bay*, chap. 20; Hess, *The United States' Emergence as a Southeast Asian Power*, pp. 102–3; Toynbee Memorandum, 14 April 1944, U2344, FO 371/4079; Minutes of Bowman meeting of 19 April 1944, U3409, FO 371/40690.

66. Hess, *America Encounters India*, pp. 141–49; Gardner, *Approaching Vietnam*, p. 43; John Morton Blum, *The Price of Vision: The Diary of Henry A. Wallace 1942–1946* (Boston: Houghton Mifflin Co., 1973), pp. 329, 352–54. Chiang Kai-shek and Wallace issued a joint press statement calling for the "recognition of the fundamental right of presently dependent Asiatic peoples . . . for self government within specified practical time limits." See also, *FRUS, 1944*, VI, pp. 216–46.

67. The report had been sent to Roosevelt in May 1943. The text of the Pearson column is printed in Mansergh, *Transfer of Power*, IV, doc. 603. See also docs. 602, 610, 617, 661, 664, 675; and ibid., V, docs. 2, 3, 5, 10, 14, 16, 23, 24, 37, 38, 53, 66, 216. Thorne, *Allies of a Kind*, p. 476, comments that Roosevelt and Hull suspected that Sumner Welles had leaked the report. Roosevelt "deplored" the leaks, but he seemed to have been more concerned about the existence of "leaks" than about the specific revelations.

68. Woodward, *British Foreign Policy*, V, pp. 312–13.

69. LaFeber, "Roosevelt, Churchill and Indochina," p. 1291; Hess, *The United States' Emergence as a Southeast Asian Power*, pp. 121–31; Gardner, *Approaching Vietnam*, pp. 42–48; on nonrecognition of de Gaulle's government, see Kimball, *Churchill & Roosevelt*, III, pp. 169–70, and C-707, C-798, C-801, C-803, R-631-draft A, R-631, R-633, C-822; on the SEAC controversy, C-913, R-724, C-943.

70. *FRUS, Quebec, 1944*, p. 327; See Hess, *The United States' Emergence as a Southeast Asian Power*, pp. 105–11. After his argument with Roosevelt about India, Churchill wrote to Halifax that he had not discussed the matter with the President; Mansergh, *Transfer of Power*, V, doc. 16. Roosevelt's suspicions of Churchill's intentions could only have been heightened by Hull's report, just prior to the conference, of various British schemes to expand their influence in Southeast Asia; *FRUS, Quebec, 1944*, pp. 261–65.

71. *FRUS, 1944*, III, pp. 777–80; the President's comment to Stettinius is in a memo of 1 Jan. 1945, ibid., *1945*, VI, p. 293. See also Gardner, *Approaching Vietnam*, pp. 49–50; Thorne, "Indochina and Anglo-American Relations," p. 83.

72. Halifax to F.O., 30 Dec. 1944 FO 371/40479, U8861; Churchill to Eden, 31 Dec. 1944, FO 371/50807; Eden to Churchill 8 Jan. 1945, FO 371/50807, U235/191/40. See also Louis, *Imperialism at Bay*, pp. 433–35.

73. *Stettinius Diaries*, 2 Jan. 1945, p. 212; Thorne, *Allies of a Kind*, p. 630. Neil Sheehan, *A Bright Shining Lie*, p. 150, concludes from all this that Roosevelt merely "wanted to be relieved of having to publicly approve of a French reoccupation" of Indochina. The issue was far more complicated than that conclusion suggests.

74. Louis, *Imperialism at Bay*, p. 437. Roosevelt's discussion with Stanley is summarized in ibid., pp. 436–40. See also Hess, *The United States' Emergence as a Southeast Asian Power*, p. 133.

75. *FRUS, 1945*, I, p. 141. In early 1942, the American and British governments agreed to establish the Anglo-American Caribbean Commission. With only advisory powers, the joint commission oversaw wartime social, political, and economic development in British possessions. Both governments believed that the commission could become a model for postwar trusteeships, although the British—in opposition to the Americans—insisted that international accountability not be part of any trusteeship scheme. The Anglo-American Caribbean Commission is discussed in Louis, *Imperialism at Bay*, esp. pp. 180–81. For additional detail, see Baptiste, *War, Cooperation, and Conflict*, pp. 215–17; and two articles by Howard Johnson, "The United States and the Establishment of the Anglo-American Caribbean Commission," *Journal of Caribbean History* 19 (1984), pp. 26–47, and "The Anglo-American Caribbean Commission and the Extension of

American Influence in the British Caribbean, 1942–1945," *Journal of Commonwealth and Comparative Politics* 22 (1984), pp. 180–203.

76. *FRUS, Yalta*, p. 769.

77. James F. Byrnes, *Speaking Frankly* (New York: Harper & Bros., 1947), p. x. Even the official conference record, understated as it is, caught Churchill's anger and outrage:

> The Prime Minister interrupted with great vigor to say that he did not agree with one single word of this report on trusteeships. He said that he had not been consulted nor had he heard of this subject up to now. He said that under no circumstances would he ever consent to forty or fifty nations thrusting interfering fingers into the life's existence of the British Empire. As long as he was minister, he would never yield one scrap of their heritage.

The less inflammatory State Department phrasing is in *FRUS, Yalta*, p. 844. Byrnes took shorthand notes, which suggests that his account may be more accurate.

78. Churchill was similarly "hasty" when he initialed the Morgenthau Plan concept during the 1944 Quebec Conference.

79. Louis, *Imperialism at Bay*, pp. 456–60; see also Hess, *The United States' Emergence as a Southeast Asian Power*, pp. 140–42; Gardner, *Approaching Vietnam*, pp. 49–51.

80. This is not an analysis of Dutch colonial policy or a claim that Roosevelt either appreciated or misunderstood Dutch intentions. At this point, his interest was the words spoken by the Dutch Queen, Wilhelmina, not the actuality.

81. Roosevelt, *Presidential Press Conferences 25*, no. 992 [70–73]; Hess, *The United States' Emergence as a Southeast Asian Power*, pp. 143–46; Gardner, *Approaching Vietnam*, pp. 51–52.

82. Thorne, *Allies of a Kind*, pp. 628–33, sets forth the details of both opposition to and confusion about Roosevelt's policy regarding Indochina.

83. Kimball, *Churchill & Roosevelt*, III, C-913, R-724, C-943; Short, *Origins of the Vietnam War*, pp. 38–39, esp. n. 28; Gardner, *Approaching Vietnam*, pp. 49–52; Hess, *The United States' Emergence as a Southeast Asian Power*, pp. 143–44.

84. Memorandum of conversation with Roosevelt by Charles Taussig, 15 March 1945, *FRUS, 1945*, I, p. 124; *Stettinius Diaries*, p. 305.

85. As quoted in Baptiste, *War, Cooperation, and Conflict*, p. 216 (from a British report of talks with Roosevelt, Oct.–Nov. 1942). See also ibid., p. 190 for a mention by Roosevelt of an inter-American trusteeship for the Vichy controlled French West Indies.

86. For the British Government debate on the implications of the trusteeship protocol, see Louis, *Imperialism at Bay*, chap. 30.

87. Stanley quoted in ibid., p. 468.

88. Ibid., p. 474; Churchill quoted in ibid., p. 509; *FRUS, 1945*, I, pp. 134–38.

During the early part of the war, Canada, Australia, and New Zealand came increasingly under American influence, as the United States replaced Great Britain as their protector. Under the American trusteeship plan, New Zealand and Australia were to become trustees of certain Pacific islands. Whatever their differences on the issue of international accountability, in April 1945, New Zealand and Australia were joined by Canada and India in supporting voluntary trusteeships for British possessions. The dispute between the dominions and Great Britain over the future of the British empire is covered in Louis, *Imperialism at Bay*, chap. 32. Australian dreams of a sphere of influence from New Caledonia into the Netherlands East Indies (now Indonesia) are discussed in David Day, *The Reluctant Warriors: The British Empire and the Pacific War*, forthcoming. Late in 1944, Roosevelt commented to one Australian diplomat that Britain should offer independence to Malay and Burma instead of trying to obtain the Netherlands East Indies. He went on to suggest that "the Americans and the Australians could work together on a liberal policy in these matters." Eggleston to Evatt, 21 Nov. 1944, quoted in Day, *Reluctant Warriors*.

89. *FRUS, 1945*, I, pp. 134–41, 194–95; LaFeber, "Roosevelt, Churchill and Indochina," p. 1294.

90. Roosevelt, *Presidential Press Conferences 25*, no. 998 [113–16]; *FRUS, 1945*, I, pp. 121–24; Hess, *The United States' Emergence as a Southeast Asian Power*, pp. 147–49; Louis, *Imperialism at Bay*, pp. 484–92; Foltos, "The New Pacific Barrier," pp. 317–42.

91. Berle diary, 10 Jan. 1944, in Berle and Jacobs, eds., *Navigating the Rapids*, p. 449.

92. The defection of Hopkins and Stimson, and the actions of Dunn and Stettinius are in Gardner, *Approaching Vietnam*, pp. 48–49, 58–59.

93. *FRUS, 1945*, I, p. 210; Louis, *Imperialism at Bay*, p. 492. Louis, in ibid., chaps. 30 and 32, provides additional detail.

94. Louis, *Imperialism at Bay*, pp. 553–54. Nor did Korean unanimity in opposition to trusteeship solve the knotty problem of which nationalist group to recognize.

95. This is the assertion of Lloyd Gardner, *Approaching Vietnam*, p. 354.

96. "General" Patrick Hurley angrily resigned his position as U.S. ambassador in China because he believed United States policy was too soft on both colonialism and communism; Watt, "American Anti-colonialist Policies," p. 98.

Chapter Eight
Naked Reverse Right

1. Kimball, *Churchill & Roosevelt*, III, R-624.

2. Ibid., C-790, 3 Oct. 1944; R-626, draft A, 4 Oct. 1944 (not sent).

3. Ibid., R-626, 4 Oct. 1944; C-791, 5 Oct. 1944.

4. Those records were filed in the British Public Record Office under the label TOLSTOY, their code name for the talks. For some reason—I do have a suspicious mind—that code name seems not to have been declassified until the general opening of those World War II files in 1972. Whether or not that was an intentional effort to make it a little harder to locate the records, it is clear that the TOLSTOY materials add a great deal to the account printed in Churchill's memoirs. I might also add that Churchill memoirs—which single-handedly established the accepted interpretations for Anglo-American diplomacy in the Second World War—need

to be reevaluated in the light of documentation made available since the early 1970s.

5. The quotations are from Robert Rhodes James, ed., *Winston S. Churchill: His Complete Speeches, 1897–1963* (New York: Chelsea House, 1974), 6, p. 6161; and Churchill, *The Gathering Storm*, pp. 448–49. See also Albert Resis, "Spheres of Influence in Soviet Wartime Diplomacy," *Journal of Modern History* 53 (Sept. 1981), pp. 422–24, 431–36.

British Prime Minister Neville Chamberlain likewise seemed willing to concede territory and influence in Eastern Europe to the Soviet Union. When asked to develop a statement on war aims, he suggested it might be best to avoid any commitment to expel the Soviets from their portion of eastern Poland. (Chamberlain to Lord Tweedsmuir, 25 Sept. 1939, Chamberlain Papers, Univ. of Birmingham, N.C. 7/11/32/288.) Joseph P. Kennedy, U.S. ambassador to Great Britain in 1939, may have heard Chamberlain express such sentiments since the two had maintained reasonably frequent contact, or Kennedy may have seen an advance copy of Churchill's speech. Whatever the source, Kennedy quickly recognized the thrust of British policy and on 30 September acidly warned Roosevelt that London was playing "power politics while talking in terms of philanthropy." Despite the claim that Britain had entered the war to protect Polish integrity, "the restoration of Poland—certainly Russian Poland—is being pushed gently but very firmly into obscurity." (PSF-Kennedy, FDRL.) Additional evidence on this point can be found in Martin Gilbert, *Finest Hour*, pp. 99–101. Even more intriguing is Churchill's 4 May 1939 statement to the House of Commons in support of a proposal that the Prime Minister take up Stalin's offer to discuss joint opposition to possible aggressors. After Chamberlain mocked the proposal, Churchill argued that the Soviet Union was needed to defeat Hitler and that "it should still be possible to range all the states and peoples from the Baltic to the Black Sea in one solid front against a new outrage or invasion." Surely Churchill recognized that only the Soviet Union could provide such "ranger" services and that the price would be an expansion of Soviet influence. Martin Gilbert, *Britain and Germany between the Wars* (London: Longman, 1964), p. 135, quotes the speech.

I am grateful to Lloyd C. Gardner for a number of items cited in this note. A look at his *A Covenant with Power*, pp. 567–69 and throughout, will reveal that our regular discussions have informed this essay on this and other points. The spheres-of-influence settlement in Rumania is discussed in various Churchill-Roosevelt exchanges; see Kimball, *Churchill & Roosevelt*, III, C-687, R-557, C-700, and R-560.

6. The Stalin-Roosevelt exchanges preliminary to the TOLSTOY talks are in *Stalin's Correspondence with Roosevelt*, nos. 230, 231. For Harriman's reports and the President's responses, see *FRUS, 1944*, IV, especially Harriman to Roosevelt, 10 Oct. 1944, p. 1006, and Roosevelt to Harriman, 11 Oct. 1944, p. 1009.

7. FO 800–302/7505 (PRO), p. 4.

8. Unless otherwise noted, the quotations in this summary of the TOLSTOY meeting are taken from the British minutes found in PREM 3/434/7 (PRO).

9. Kimball, *Churchill & Roosevelt*, III, C-799.

10. Ibid., C-801.

11. Ibid., R-632.

12. *Stalin's Correspondence with Roosevelt*, doc. 237.

13. Roosevelt to Stalin in R-635, Kimball, *Churchill & Roosevelt*, III.

14. See Churchill, *Triumph and Tragedy*, pp. 288–89. A recent secondary account is Lawrence Wittner, *American Intervention in Greece, 1943–1949* (New York: Columbia Univ. Press, 1982).

15. Kimball, *Churchill & Roosevelt*, C-845, 6 Dec. 1944.

16. Enclosure to C-850/1, Churchill to Hopkins, 11 Dec. 1944, ibid.

17. R-673, 13 Dec. 1944, ibid. The deleted phrase, indicated by brackets, was added to the State Department draft of this message, then deleted.

18. *Stalin's Correspondence with Churchill*, doc. 362. The Soviet concern about guerilla warfare was both real and justified. Allied intelligence was apparently unaware of the extensive activities of the Ukrainian Insurgent Army (UPA), estimated in 1944 to comprise about 100,000 men under arms. That army, some of which had resisted the Germans but saved it major efforts for the fight against the Soviets, operated in regiment-sized military formations in the western Ukraine until 1947. See "UPA in Light of German Documents," Taras Hunczak, ed., *Litopys UPA*, vols. 6 and 7 (Toronto: Litopys UPA, 1983).

19. Churchill, *Complete Speeches*, 7, p. 700.

20. *FRUS, Yalta Conf.*, pp. 218–19, 214–15.

21. Hopkins to Churchill, 16 Dec. 1944, Map Room papers (FDRL); Churchill, *Triumph and Tragedy*, p. 303.

22. Roosevelt to Stalin in R-675, 16 Dec. 1944 in Kimball, *Churchill & Roosevelt*, III.

23. See Eduard Mark, "Charles E. Bohlen and the Acceptable Limits of Soviet Hegemony in Eastern Europe," *Diplomatic History* 3 (Spring 1979), pp. 201–13; Watt, *Succeeding John Bull*, pp. 103–4.

24. Stettinius to Roosevelt, 31 Oct. 1944, PSF, box 66, "Poland, Sept.–Dec. 1944," FDRL.

25. Roosevelt to Stalin in R-684, 30 Dec. 1944, in Kimball, *Churchill & Roosevelt*, III.

26. Ibid., C-858, 26 Dec. 1944.

27. *FRUS, Yalta Conf.*, p. 508.

28. Ibid., p. 973. This discussion of the Yalta debates is taken primarily from this same source.

29. Hugh Dalton diary, vol. 32, p. 28, as quoted in David Reynolds, "Churchill, The Special Relationship, and the Debate about Post-War European Security, 1940–1945," delivered to the American Historical Association annual meeting, 28 Dec. 1983. Churchill was similarly optimistic in statements to the House of Commons and to the cabinet. His mood is captured in a 35mm film made by Soviet army photographers as he spoke to his Red Army bodyguard upon leaving the Crimea. With obvious enthusiasm, Churchill spoke about the long-term peace that the Yalta agreements would guarantee. (The film is in the Imperial War Museum Annex, Hayes, Middlesex, England.)

30. Quoted in Carlton, *Anthony Eden*, pp. 254, 255.

31. *FRUS, Yalta Conf.*, p. 729; Kimball, *Churchill & Roosevelt*, III, C-901, 28 Feb. 1945; Moran, *Diaries*, p. 240; Sherwood, *Roosevelt and Hopkins*, pp. 864, 852.

32. Foreign Office to Halifax, 5 Mar. 1945, as paraphrased in Woodward, *British Foreign Policy*, III, p. 496.

33. Kimball, *Churchill & Roosevelt*, III, C-905, 8 Mar. 1945.

34. Ibid., R-715, 12 Mar. 1945.

35. Ibid., C-910, 13 Mar. 1945.

36. Ibid., R-723, 21 Mar. 1945.

37. Ibid., C-932, 3 Apr. 1945.

38. Ibid., R-736, 6 Apr. 1945.

39. Ibid., R-742, 11 Apr. 1945.

40. Stettinius to Truman, 13 April 1945, Harry S Truman papers, Truman Library (Independence, Mo.).

41. Truman, *Memoirs*, I, p. 82; Harriman and Abel, *Special Envoy*, pp. 453–54. This is not to argue that Truman came to the White House seeking a confrontation with the Soviets; he did not. But his personal style and near total reliance on his advisers in foreign policy matters brought an abrupt, if unwitting, halt to Roosevelt's policies. See Watt, *Succeeding John Bull*, pp. 104–9.

42. Eduard Mark has examined the concept of spheres of influence in Eastern Europe as discussed within the State Department during the war. Although I disagree somewhat with his conclusions regarding the Truman administration, and I do not share his strident rejection of much of previous scholarship, we agree that the United States gave every indication to the Soviets that some type of spheres in Eastern Europe would be acceptable. And regardless of whether or not American policy shifted after Roosevelt's death, there remains the question of explaining the dramatic shift in British policy; Mark, "American Policy toward Eastern Europe and the Origins of the Cold War, 1941–1946: An Alternative Interpretation," *Journal of American History* 68 (1981), pp. 313–36.

43. Fraser J. Harbutt, "Cold War Origins: An Anglo-European Perspective," *Diplomatic History* 13 (Winter 1989), p. 125. Ellipses have been omitted for the sake of readability.

44. For example, Harbutt, *The Iron Curtain*. Stephanson, *Kennan and the Art of Diplomacy*, pp. 36–45, argues that Roosevelt failed to reconcile "maximalist" political and economic goals with "minimalist" diplomacy—which seems to mean Roosevelt's goals exceeded his efforts. The most strident of the recent publications is Nisbet, *Roosevelt and Stalin*, an attack on Roosevelt's "puerility" in dealing with the Soviet leader. Theodore Draper has exposed Nisbet's selective use of evidence in various issues of *The New York Review of Books* during a letters-to-the-editor debate between the two in 1987–88. See also Draper's *A Present of Things Past: Selected Essays* (New York: Hill & Wang, 1990). T. Michael Ruddy, *The Cautious Diplomat: Charles E. Bohlen and the Soviet Union* (Kent, Ohio: Kent State Univ. Press, 1986) presents Bohlen as a supporter of Roosevelt's concept of "open spheres" of influence. Eduard Mark, "October or Thermidor?" *American Historical Review*, pp. 937–62, suggests patterns of American thinking about the Soviet Union that support my interpretation. As in his other articles, already cited, he makes a clear distinction between a Soviet sphere of "domination" and a less threatening sphere of "influence"—what Roosevelt saw as a sphere of "responsibility." I should have originally cited Robert M. Hathaway, *Ambiguous Partnership* (New York: Columbia Univ.

Press, 1981), whose evidence supports my thesis; as does that of Albert Resis, "The Churchill-Stalin Secret 'Percentages' Agreement on the Balkans: Moscow, October 1944," *American Historical Review* 83 (1978), pp. 368–87; see also Keith Sainsbury, "Central and Eastern Europe at the Quebec Conference," and K.G.M. Ross, "The Moscow Conference of October 1944 (TOLSTOY)," both in *British Political and Military Strategy in Central, Eastern and Southern Europe in 1944*, William Deakin et al., eds. (New York: St. Martin's Press, 1988); Joseph Siracusa, "The Night Stalin and Churchill Divided Europe: The View from Washington," *The Review of Politics* 43 (July 1981), pp. 381–409, and "The Meaning of TOLSTOY: Churchill, Stalin, and the Balkans, Moscow, October 1944," *Diplomatic History* 3 (Fall 1979), pp. 443–63. The latter is a selection of excerpts from the Churchill-Stalin talks of October 1944. Terry H. Anderson, *The United States, Great Britain, and the Cold War, 1944–1947* (Columbia and London: Univ. of Missouri Press, 1981), pp. 28–51, accepts and argues for the speculation of Robert Dallek that "had he lived, Roosevelt would probably have moved more quickly than Truman to confront the Russians." Dallek, *Roosevelt and American Foreign Policy*, p. 534.

45. As quoted in Callahan, *Churchill: Retreat from Empire*, p. 185.

46. Sherwood, *Roosevelt and Hopkins*, p. 364. Paul Addison's excellent *The Road to 1945: British Politics and the Second World War* (London: Jonathan Cape, 1975), describes and explains the Conservative Party's decline during the war. Gilbert, *Road to Victory*, chronicles Churchill's forebodings about the 1945 general election. See the index entries under General Election, p. 1390.

47. Miner, *Between Churchill and Stalin*, p. 186; FRUS, *Tehran*, p. 512.

48. See " 'The Family Circle' " and " 'This Persistent Evangel of Americanism,' " elsewhere in this collection.

49. Berle and Jacobs, *Navigating the Rapids*, pp. 464, 466. The East European "quagmire" is discussed in " 'The Family Circle,' " elsewhere in this collection.

50. Dallek, *Roosevelt and American Foreign Policy*, pp. 436–37. "Be it as it may, the U.S. and Britain cannot fight the Russians," he reportedly told New York's staunchly anti-Soviet Francis Cardinal Spellman; as quoted in Eubank, *Summit at Teheran*, p. 361.

51. The latest discussions of this are in Hugh Phillips, "Mission to America: Maksim M. Litvinov in the United States, 1941–43," *Diplomatic History* 12 (Summer 1988), pp. 261–75; and Miner, *Between Churchill and Stalin*, pp. 213–25, and especially n. 63, p. 296. Phillips suggests that Roosevelt told the Soviet ambassador that a restoration of Czarist boundaries made sense, although Miner argues that the Soviet diplomat most likely misinterpreted the President's remarks, particularly since Roosevelt gave the British ambassador a different version of the conversation. Miner makes a persuasive case for British Foreign Secretary Anthony Eden, early in 1942, being even more eager than Roosevelt to convince Stalin that he could trust and work with the West. Miner points out that Sarah M. Terry, *Poland's Place in Europe* (Princeton: Princeton Univ. Press, 1983), shows how the Oder-Neisse line for Poland's western boundary was first suggested by the Poles, though not as part of a package deal ceding eastern Poland to the Soviet Union.

52. Kimball, *Churchill & Roosevelt*, I, R-50x, 14 July 1941. For more on

Roosevelt's support for plebiscites and his willingness to see continued Soviet rule over the Baltic states, see Sherwood, *Roosevelt and Hopkins*, pp. 709–15; Eden, *The Reckoning*, p. 432; *FRUS, 1943*, I, p. 542.

53. Statement made by President Bush at the close of his May–June 1989 trip to the NATO Conference in Brussels, reported on U.S. television.

54. This is the argument of Antony Polonsky in "Stalin and the Poles 1941–7," *European History Quarterly* 17 (1987), pp. 453–92. The Clark Kerr quotation is on p. 453 and is dated 20 Feb. 1944.

Chapter Nine
"This Persistent Evangel of Americanism"

1. There is the telling story that Roosevelt consistently refused to discipline his children, leaving that duty to Eleanor; Joseph Lash, *Eleanor and Franklin* (New York: Norton, 1971), p. 197; Gunther, *Roosevelt in Retrospect*, p. 196.

2. Edmonds, *Setting the Mould*, pp. 50–51.

3. Roosevelt's comment is paraphrased in Dallek, *Roosevelt and American Foreign Policy*, p. 441. Janeway, *The Struggle for Survival*, pp. 2–3. The critic quoted is Neumann, "Roosevelt's Options and Evasions," *Watershed of Empire*, p. 180.

4. Roosevelt repeatedly advocated the use of overwhelming force by the great powers to discipline aggressors; for examples see Sherwin, *A World Destroyed*, pp. 88–89.

5. David Reynolds summarizes the connections between American and British liberalism, particularly "Gladstonian" thinking, in foreign policy in "Rethinking Anglo-American Relations," *International Affairs* 65 (Winter 1988–89), pp. 99–104.

6. See Elliot A. Rosen, *Hoover, Roosevelt, and the Brains Trust* (New York: Columbia Univ. Press, 1977), pp. 362–64, 380; and Rosen, "The Possibilities for Peace: Hoover, Roosevelt, and the World Financial Crisis, 1933," an unpublished paper delivered at the Hoover Symposium VI, George Fox College, 24 Oct. 1987.

7. See, for example, Reynolds, *The Anglo-American Alliance*, esp. pp. 252–53; Kimball, *Churchill and Roosevelt*, I, pp. 14–15.

8. For examples see Elliot A. Rosen, "After Half A Century: The New Deal in Perspective" (unpublished). Whether or not the New Deal had an ideology or a philosophical stance that differed significantly from what had gone before is challenged, from three different points of view, by Rosen, *Hoover, Roosevelt, and the Brains Trust*; Karl, *The Uneasy State*; and Janeway, *Struggle for Survival*. The latter two question that the New Deal survived the war, but again, neither addresses the question of the internationalization of the New Deal.

9. Proving that Wilson's experiences played a conscious part in Roosevelt's thinking during the war is surprisingly difficult. It is invariably assumed by historians and Roosevelt's contemporaries, but is yet to be studied and systematically demonstrated. Sherwood, *Roosevelt and Hopkins*, makes just such assumptions but gives no evidence; see pp. 227, 263, 360, 697, 756–57, 855, 876. In each of those places, Sherwood resorts to spirits (and not one of FDR's martinis) claiming "Roosevelt was mindful of the ghost of Woodrow Wilson" or "haunted by the ghost of Woodrow Wilson." But he never quotes the President musing about

Wilson's "mistakes." Nor do other historians who profess not to "doubt that Roosevelt vividly remembered the tragic defeat of Woodrow Wilson"—the phrase of Herbert Feis (a contemporary turned historian), "Some Notes on Historical Record-keeping, the Role of Historians, and the Influence of Historical Memories During the Era of the Second World War," in *The Historian and the Diplomat* (New York: Harper & Row, 1967), p. 106; for similar examples, see Gunther, *Roosevelt in Retrospect*, pp. 10–13; May, *"Lessons" of the Past*, pp. 3–18. The two chroniclers of Roosevelt's foreign policy, Burns, *Roosevelt: The Soldier of Freedom*, and Dallek, *Roosevelt and American Foreign Policy* likewise rely largely on allusion and assumption (though see n. 3 above). Other historians continually draw parallels between the actions of Roosevelt and Wilson, but can only infer or speculate on the relationship. It is logical to assume Roosevelt thought of Wilson's "mistakes" and tried to avoid them, but the documentation, if it exists, has never been pulled together. Certainly Roosevelt was aware of the analogies. During the 1930s, historian Ray Stannard Baker, author of a biography of Wilson, wrote a number of letters to Roosevelt that pointed out similarities between the problems faced by Wilson and FDR. But that does not demonstrate that Roosevelt systematically or even consciously tried to learn from Wilson's "mistakes." The Baker-Roosevelt correspondence is in PPF-R. S. Baker (FDRL).

"Peace is indivisible" is a phrase attributed to Maxim Litvinov, Soviet ambassador to the United States in the 1930s.

10. *FRUS, Tehran*, pp. 485–86.

11. For a perceptive analysis and overview of American liberal assumptions in foreign policy, see Thomas G. Paterson, *On Every Front* (New York: Norton, 1979), chap. 4, "Abundance: The 'Fundamentals' of the United States." Lloyd C. Gardner's *Safe for Democracy: The Anglo-American Response to Revolution, 1913–1923* (New York: Oxford Univ. Press, 1984) has unwritten but clear implications for Roosevelt and his conception of the world. See also Donald Watt's useful analysis in "U.S. Globalism: The End of the Concert of Europe," in *For a Better World: The Legacy of World War II*, W. F. Kimball, ed. (Wilmington, Del.: SR Books, forthcoming); Robert A. Divine, *Roosevelt and World War II* (Baltimore: Johns Hopkins Univ. Press, 1969; Penguin ed., 1970); and Robert Dallek, *The American Style of Foreign Policy* (New York: Oxford Univ. Press, 1983), esp. pp. 150–53, wherein he argues that Roosevelt's public universalism was belied by his private realpolitik actions.

12. Samuel I. Rosenman, ed., *The Public Papers and Addresses of Franklin D. Roosevelt (PPA)* (13 vols.; New York: Harper & Bros., 1938–50), *1943*, press conf. of 28 Dec. 1943, p. 573. Eliot Janeway in *The Struggle for Survival*, p. 24, commented that the New Deal was never an ideology, but "a dollars-and-cents proposition." Roosevelt believed it was more than that.

13. The fourteen points are printed in Ruhl Bartlett, ed., *The Record of American Diplomacy* (4th ed.; New York: Alfred A. Knopf, 1964), p. 460. Besides the arguments made here and above in "Lend-Lease and the Open Door" and in " 'Baffled Virtue . . . Injured Innocence,' " see Kolko, *The Politics of War*, esp. pp. 242–313, which offers a persuasive case that Roosevelt and Hull shared a vision of ideal economic relationships.

14. The Tripartite (Anglo-French-American) Monetary Agreement was designed primarily to stabilize the French currency by guaranteeing its value in international trade. It was the kind of arrangement that Roosevelt had rejected in 1933 at the time of the London Economic Conference because it would not help solve American economic problems. In the short-term, that was still true in 1936, which suggests that, for Roosevelt, the agreement was more political than economic.

The agreement is discussed in Blum, *From the Morgenthau Diaries*, I, pp. 159–73; and Eckes, *A Search for Solvency*, pp. 26–27. Eckes calls the Tripartite Monetary Agreement "a giant stride toward Bretton Woods" by which "the United States acquired the dominant position in international monetary relations."

15. As quoted in Burns, *Roosevelt: The Soldier of Freedom*, p. 514.

16. Roosevelt's refusal to write collateral or other conditions into the Lend-Lease Act is discussed in my *"The Most Unsordid Act,"* passim, but esp. pp. 119–50. Reynolds, *Anglo-American Alliance*, pp. 145–68, adds material based on later British sources, but draws the same conclusions. An intriguing piece of documentary evidence is in a letter from Roosevelt to Hull, 11 Jan. 1941, printed in *F.D.R.: His Personal Letters*, II, pp. 1103–5.

17. Bartlett, ed., *Record of American Diplomacy*, p. 624. See Dobson, "Economic Diplomacy at the Atlantic Conference," *Review of International Studies* 10, pp. 143–63. Although Dobson argues that American diplomacy at the conference was inept, he illustrates that the Americans had a very clear economic agenda.

18. Robert Gilpin, *The Political Economy of International Relations* (Princeton: Princeton Univ. Press, 1987), pp. 131–42.

19. Roosevelt's thinking about Africa is difficult to pin down. His thoughts about the role of international pressure and accountability in decolonization are discussed in Louis, *Imperialism at Bay*, and above in " 'In Search of Monsters to Destroy.' " See also Louis and Robinson, "Liquidation of the British Empire in Tropical Africa," and Lynch, "Pan-African Responses," in Prosser and Louis, eds., *Transfer of Power in Africa*.

The British assumed that, except for the independent states like Egypt and the Union of South Africa, postwar Africa would be handled in conjunction with Europe; Woodward, *British Foreign Policy*, V, pp. 8, 12.

20. As quoted in Neumann, "Roosevelt's Options and Evasions," in *Watershed of Empire*, pp. 174, 175. In the same talk, Roosevelt condemned British colonial rule in the Gambia as "plain exploitation."

21. By 1944, Roosevelt was speaking of China taking fifty years to become a world power; Campbell and Herring, *Stettinius Diaries*, p. 53.

Thorne, *Allies of a Kind*; Louis, *Imperialism at Bay*; and Hess, *The United States' Emergence as a Southeast Asian Power*, each in their own way demonstrate and illustrate Roosevelt's conception of the Pacific/East Asian area as one that demanded direct American leadership and guidance. Roosevelt envisaged a trusteeship and postcolonial role in Southeast Asia for Australia.

Somehow, and perhaps for all the wrong reasons, Roosevelt's ideas remind one of Sukarno's rhetoric about "guided democracy" in Indonesia.

22. Roosevelt wrote George Norris of his "four-sheriffs" plan; see Green, *The Containment of Latin America*, p. 119.

23. See Kimball, *Churchill & Roosevelt*, II, R-457, for one example of Roosevelt's assumption that American forces would be quickly withdrawn from Europe. That assumption was shared by the U.S. military; see Kimball, *Swords or Ploughshares?* Even Churchill assumed that American forces would be quickly withdrawn from Europe; Reynolds, "Churchill, The Special Relationship and the Debate about Post-War European Security" (unpublished), p. 5. Stalin, presumably, made the same assumption.

24. Woodward, *British Foreign Policy*, V, pp. 33–34; Rosenman, ed., *PPA, 1944–45*, press conf. of 5 April 1945, p. 611. Roosevelt's attitude regarding the appropriate role for what became the General Assembly is made crystal clear in Divine, *Second Chance*. See also Kimball, *Churchill & Roosevelt*, II, p. 178; Sumner Welles, *Where Are We Heading?*, p. 4; Thomas M. Campbell, *Masquerade Peace: America's UN Policy, 1944–1945* (Tallahassee: Florida State Univ. Press, 1973), stresses the central role of the United Nations in Roosevelt's postwar system.

25. Richard Hofstadter, *The American Political Tradition and the Men Who Made It* (New York: Knopf, 1948). Burns in *The Soldier of Freedom*, reverts to his "Lion and the Fox" image of Roosevelt whenever such episodes occur. Dallek in *Roosevelt and American Foreign Policy*, sympathetic as it is to Roosevelt's difficulties, pictures his foreign policy largely as an attempt by the President to apply his domestic political style to foreign policy. The "Epilogue," however, is a perceptive portrait of the part of Roosevelt's persona that Dallek calls FDR's political realism-idealism.

26. *FRUS, 1942*, III, p. 594; Kimball, *Churchill & Roosevelt*, I, C-92, R-152; Sherwood, *Roosevelt and Hopkins*, p. 577. "Second Front diplomacy" is the phrase of Lloyd C. Gardner who sets forth the President's dilemma over the Second Front as symbol versus reality in *Architects of Illusion*, pp. 26–54. The entire matter is discussed in Stoler, *The Politics of the Second Front*.

27. With apologies to David Reynolds; but there are only so many ways to say the same thing.

28. The romanticized image of an Anglo-American "special relationship," particularly during the crisis atmosphere of the Second World War, has often been challenged, especially since the opening of the British and American archives in 1972–73. To say there is an "Anglo-American tension school" of interpretation is a bit too broad, but certainly historians have demonstrated that there were serious disagreements during the war between the two over a wide range of long- and short-term issues. David Reynolds has written extensively on this theme, beginning with his *The Anglo-American Alliance*, and summarizing his thoughts in "Roosevelt, Churchill, and the Wartime Anglo-American Alliance, 1939–1945: Towards a New Synthesis," in *The 'Special Relationship': Anglo-American Relations Since 1945*, Wm. Roger Louis and Hedley Bull, eds. (Oxford: Clarendon Press, 1986), pp. 17–41. Christopher Thorne's *Allies of a Kind* raises very fundamental questions about the relationship that go way beyond the East Asian arena that is the subject of the book. W. Roger Louis, in *Imperialism at Bay*, tracks the issue from the perspective of decolonization. For other and related arguments, see

Ryan, *The Vision of Anglo-America*; Hathaway, *Ambiguous Partnership*; Harbutt, *The Iron Curtain*; and my *Churchill & Roosevelt*, throughout, but esp. the introduction, I, pp. 3–20, and the other essays in this collection. A good historiographical survey for the World War II/postwar era is a review essay by Peter Boyle, "The Special Relationship: An Alliance of Convenience?" *Journal of American Studies* 22 (Dec. 1988), pp. 457–65. Reynolds and Dimbleby offer a twentieth-century overview in *An Ocean Apart*, and Reynolds looks at some of the broad historiographical issues in "Rethinking Anglo-American Relations," *International Affairs*, pp. 89–111.

29. The "balance wheel" concept is from Demaree Bess, "The Cost of Roosevelt's 'Great Design,' " *Saturday Evening Post* 116 (27 May 1944), p. 90, a piece very critical of Roosevelt. The *cordon sanitaire* analogy is from the Stimson Diary, 31 Dec. 1944, as quoted in Sherwin, *A World Destroyed*, p. 133. This is discussed more fully below in " 'The Family Circle' " and "Naked Reverse Right."

30. Roosevelt to Amb. Robert Bingham (London), quoted in Rock, *Chamberlain and Roosevelt*, p. 23.

31. Churchill speaking to the House of Commons, 20 Aug. 1940, as quoted in Reynolds, *The Anglo-American Alliance*, p. 169.

32. *The New York Times*, 22 Feb. 1988. This is taken from the Russian language version of Gromyko's memoirs. The English language edition, which was substantially edited, expresses similar sentiments about Roosevelt, but in quite different phrasing; Andrei Gromyko, *Memories*, trans. Harold Shukman (London: Hutchinson, 1989), pp. 39–42.

33. Roosevelt to Churchill, R-624, 28 Sept. 1944, Kimball, *Churchill & Roosevelt*, p. 339. Even if the "child" referred to by Roosevelt is obviously the postwar international organization, the President believed that the Russians had a good deal to "learn" about proper international behavior.

34. One analysis of Roosevelt's foreign policy, that of Divine in his *Roosevelt and World War II*, has essays on Roosevelt the isolationist, the interventionist, the realist, and the pragmatist. But there is none on Roosevelt the idealist. Or, for that matter, on Roosevelt the political economist.

35. As quoted in Larrabee, *Commander in Chief*, p. 187. See also Sherwood, *Roosevelt and Hopkins*, p. 417; Stoler, "Continentalism to Globalism," *Diplomatic History*.

36. This is the persuasive thesis of Sherwin, *A World Destroyed*. See also above, " 'The Family Circle.' "

37. Presidential Diary, 25 Aug. 1944, p. 1391, Henry Morgenthau, Jr., papers (FDRL). Roosevelt's preference for New York City as the location of the permanent U.N. secretariat is in Campbell and Herring, *Stettinius Diaries*, 24 Aug. 1944, p. 109.

38. For further discussion of this issue as it was discussed at the Teheran Conference, see above, " 'The Family Circle,' " especially notes 49, 55–56. Foreign Office and State Department officials conducted an ongoing debate that can be followed in the FO 371 files (U-/-/70) for 1943 through 1945 (PRO). For example, see the paper written by John Wheeler-Bennett, then in the Foreign Office Research Department, recommending a geopolitical, spheres-of-influence postwar system, since he assumed the United States would return to isolation and the

Soviet Union could not be trusted. He advocated the establishment of alliances and a Western European security system. The attached minutes agreed in principle; FO 371, U3704/180/70 of 29 April 1944. Churchill's comments about the United States of Europe is quoted in Sbrega, *Anglo-American Relations and Colonialism*, p. 173; his stormy reaction to suggestions for the internationalization of regional councils is in Campbell and Herring, *Stettinius Diaries*, 19 April 1944, pp. 59–60.

39. Memo to the secretary, 11 Jan. 1945, Campbell and Herring, *Stettinius Diaries*, p. 214. See also "Naked Reverse Right," above.

40. E.F.M.D. to Attlee, 12 April 1945, Piercy papers (BLPS), file 8/11.

41. Campbell, *Masquerade Peace*, p. 120.

42. Green, *The Containment of Latin America*, pp. 121–23; Campbell and Herring, *Stettinius Diaries*, pp. 272–77. Hull's fears were later borne out as proposals for regional security arrangements became a means of exempting certain areas or agreements from United Nations scrutiny; see, for example, ibid., 8 May 1945, pp. 354–56; Campbell, *Masquerade Peace*, pp. 111–21. The insertion into the U.N. Charter of articles 51–52, which recognized regional security organizations, is summarized on pp. 159–75.

The Bohlen memo is cited in Walter LaFeber, *Inevitable Revolutions: The United States in Central America* (New York: Norton, 1984), p. 89.

43. Marks, *Wind Over Sand*, pp. 55–56; Gellman, *Good Neighbor Diplomacy*, pp. 95–96.

44. Roosevelt's notion of establishing internationally controlled areas that would provide information free of censorship is discussed above in " 'The Family Circle.' " The plan for internationalized free ports for trade in places like Norway and the Persian Gulf, accessible to the USSR, is well described in Olav Riste, "Free Ports in North Norway, A Contribution to the Study of FDR's Wartime Policy Towards the USSR," *Journal of Contemporary History* 5 (1970), pp. 77–95. Stettinius to Roosevelt, 31 Oct. 1944, PSF, box 66, "Poland, Sept.–Dec. 1944," FDRL. See also "Naked Reverse Right" and " 'Baffled Virtue . . . Injured Innocence,' " above.

45. The Soviet government and Soviet historians in the Gorbachev-*glas'nost* period have consistently held up Soviet-American relations during World War II as an example of the practical ability of nations of differing ideological systems to work peacefully and productively with each other. See, for example, the joint protocol of the 1st US/USSR Symposium (Soviet Academy of Sciences/American Council of Learned Societies) on the History of World War II (Moscow, Oct. 1986) which uses just such language (in possession of the author and filed with the International Research and Exchange Board, Princeton, N.J.).

46. Kennan, *Russia and the West Under Lenin and Stalin* as quoted in Nisbet, *Roosevelt and Stalin*, pp. 5–6.

47. Welles, *Where Are We Heading?*, pp. 31–32. Welles wrote this in 1946, a time when he was bitterly attacking the Truman administration for betraying Roosevelt's principles. That may raise doubts about its accuracy. But the crude scale has the ring of one of Roosevelt's simplistic metaphors. Welles also wrote that the President premised the process on the Soviet Union's abandonment of "its doctrine of world revolution," a less likely sounding phrase for Roosevelt.

By 1951, Welles had nearly turned Roosevelt into a militant Cold Warrior, arguing that the President "believed communism would never prevail provided democracy became a living reality . . . [that would] strive for its supremacy with the same self-sacrificing fervour shown by the Marxists in fighting for their creed." *Seven Major Decisions*, p. 190.

Walter LaFeber has probed the question of revolution and American foreign policy, arguing that while the United States wanted a world shaped by open competition, that would not be done "by working with revolutionaries." See "The Evolution of the Monroe Doctrine from Monroe to Reagan," in *Redefining the Past*, Lloyd C. Gardner, ed. (Corvallis: Oregon State Univ. Press, 1986), p. 121.

48. Davis paraphrases the President in "Roosevelt's World Blueprint," *Saturday Evening Post*, p. 21.

49. Rosenman, *PPA, 1943*, 24 Dec. 1943. pp. 557–58 and *PPA, 1944–45*, 1 March 1945, p. 575. Unconditional surrender is discussed below in "The End of Romance." For Roosevelt's beliefs and comments about the Germans, see minutes, 25th Pacific War Council Meeting, 9 Dec. 1942, MR-FDRL, and my *Swords or Ploughshares?*, esp. pp. 25–34. His assumptions about race and genetics are treated by Thorne in *Allies of a Kind*, pp. 6–9, 158–59, 167–68n, 356, and on a broader canvas in his *The Issue of War*. Whatever the prevailing atmosphere and the pseudo-scientific basis for Roosevelt's racial theories, they are crude and disturbing. However, those notions must be considered within the context of the era. Late in 1942, he mused aloud to the Pacific War Council about underpopulated countries offering to accept surplus populations. When the minister from New Zealand asked if Roosevelt was suggesting "intermixture of the races," the President replied that, in the postwar world, racial prejudices would likely diminis¹ ɪn favor of a worldwide melting-pot; minutes of the 23d Pacific War Council meeting, 28 Oct. 1942, MR-FDRL.

50. See, for example, the sentiments of Gromyko, *Memories*, p. 114, where he writes of how Roosevelt consistently gave authority and respect to Stalin.

The Latin phrase is on the obverse of the Great Seal of the United States of America—an engraving of which is on the back of the U.S. one dollar bill.

51. Rosenman, *PPA*, 1 March 1945, pp. 585, 586.

52. Lippmann, *U.S. War Aims*, p. 22.

Bibliography

Archival Papers

Cadogan, Alexander. Diaries. Churchill College, Cambridge, England.

Citrine, Walter. Papers. British Library of Political and Economic Science (London School of Economics), London, England.

Cox, Oscar. Papers. Franklin D. Roosevelt Library, Hyde Park, N.Y.

Dalton, Hugh. Diary. British Library of Political and Economic Science (London School of Economics), London, England.

Great Britain, Foreign Office. Avon Papers (FO 954), Public Record Office PRO, Kew, England.

Great Britain, Cabinet Office. Cabinet Papers (CAB), Public Record Office, Kew, England.

Great Britain, Foreign Office. Foreign Office files (FO 371), PRO.

Great Britain, Prime Minister's Office. Premier 3 and 4 files, British Public Record Office, Kew, England.

Halifax, Lord. Papers (microfilm). Churchill College, Cambridge.

Hopkins, Harry L. Papers. Franklin D. Roosevelt Library, Hyde Park, N.Y.

Meade, James. Papers and diary. British Library of Political and Economic Science (London School of Economics), London, England.

Morgenthau, Henry, Jr. Diaries and papers. Franklin D. Roosevelt Library, Hyde Park, N.Y.

Piercy, William. Papers. British Library of Political and Economic Science (London School of Economics), London, England.

Roosevelt, Eleanor. Papers. Franklin D. Roosevelt Library.

Roosevelt, Franklin D. Papers. Franklin D. Roosevelt Library, Hyde Park, N.Y.

Stimson, Henry L. Diary. Sterling Memorial Library, Yale Univ., New Haven, Conn.

United States, Department of State. Decimal files. National Archives, Washington, D.C.

———. Leo Pasvolsky files. National Archives, Washington, D.C.

White, Harry Dexter. Papers. Princeton University, Princeton, N.J.

Published Sources, Diaries, and Memoirs

Acheson, Dean. *Present at the Creation: My Years in the State Department.* New York: Norton, 1969.

Baer, George W., ed. *A Question of Trust: The Origins of U.S.-Soviet Diplomatic Relations: The Memoirs of Loy W. Henderson.* Stanford, Calif.: Hoover Institution, 1986.

Barnes, John, and Nicholson, David, eds. *The Empire at Bay: The Leo Amery Diaries, 1929–1945.* London: Hutchinson and Co., 1988.

Berezhkov, Valentin. *History in the Making: Memoirs of World War II Diplomacy*. Moscow: Progress Publishers, 1983.

Berle, Beatrice Bishop, and Jacobs, Travis Beal, eds. *Navigating the Rapids, 1918–1971: From the Papers of Adolf A. Berle*. New York: Harcourt Brace Jovanovich, 1973.

Bland, Larry, et al., eds. *The Papers of George Catlett Marshall*. Vol. II; Baltimore: Johns Hopkins Univ. Press, 1986.

Blum, John M., ed. *The Price of Vision: The Diary of Henry A. Wallace 1942–1946*. Boston: Houghton Mifflin Co., 1973.

————. *Public Philosopher: Selected Letters of Walter Lippman*. New York: Ticknor & Fields, 1985.

Bohlen, Charles E. *Witness to History*. New York: Norton, 1973.

Bullitt, Orville H., ed. *For the President, Personal and Secret: Correspondence between Franklin D. Roosevelt and William C. Bullitt*. Boston: Houghton Mifflin Co., 1972.

Byrnes, James F. *Speaking Frankly*. New York: Harper & Bros., 1947.

Campbell, Thomas, and Herring, George, eds. *The Diaries of Edward R. Stettinius, Jr*. New York: New Viewpoints, 1975.

Chandler, Alfred, et al., eds. *The Papers of Dwight David Eisenhower: The War Years*. Vol. II; Baltimore: Johns Hopkins Univ. Press, 1970.

Chandos, Lord [Oliver Lyttelton]. *Memoirs*. London: Bodley Head, 1962.

Churchill, Winston S. *The Second World War*. 6 vols.; Boston: Houghton Mifflin Co., 1948–53.

Ciechanowski, Jan. *Defeat in Victory*. Garden City, N.Y.: Doubleday, 1947.

Colville, John. *The Fringes of Power: 10 Downing Street Diaries, 1939–1955*. New York: Norton, 1985.

Davies, John Patton. "Anglo-American Cooperation in East Asia," 15 November 1943, American Committee for the History of the Second World War *Newsletter* (Spring 1989), no. 41.

Dilks, David, ed. *The Diaries of Sir Alexander Cadogan*. New York: G. P. Putnam's Sons, 1972.

Eden, Anthony. *The Reckoning*. Boston: Houghton Mifflin Co., 1965.

Eisenhower, Dwight D. *Crusade in Europe*. New York: Doubleday, 1948.

Gaulle, Charles de. *The Complete War Memoirs of Charles de Gaulle*. New York: Clarion Book, Simon & Schuster, 1972.

Germany, Ministry of Foreign Affairs. *Documents on German Foreign Policy*. Series D, 12 vols.; Washington: USGPO, 1962.

Germany, Navy. *Führer Conferences on Matters Dealing with the German Navy*. Trans. and mimeographed by the Office of Naval Intelligence. Washington: Dept. of the Navy, ONI, 1947. [U.S. Naval Academy Library]

Great Britain. *The Transfer of Power, 1942–1947*. Nicholas Mansergh, ed. 12 vols; London: HMSO, 1970–1983.

Gromyko, Andrei. *Memories*. Harold Shukman, trans. London: Hutchinson, 1989.

Harvey, John, ed. *The War Diaries of Oliver Harvey*. London: Collins, 1978.

Hassett, William D. *Off the Record with F.D.R., 1942–1945*. New Brunswick: Rutgers Univ. Press, 1958.

Hooker, Nancy H., ed. *The Moffat Papers: Selections from the Diplomatic Journals of J. Pierrepont Moffat, 1919–1943.* Cambridge: Harvard Univ. Press, 1956.

Hull, Cordell. *The Memoirs of Cordell Hull.* 2 vols.; New York: Macmillan, 1948.

Iatrides, John, ed. *Ambassador MacVeagh Reports: Greece, 1933–1947.* Princeton: Princeton Univ. Press, 1980.

Ickes, Harold L. *The Secret Diary of Harold L. Ickes.* 2 vols.; New York: Simon & Schuster, 1953–54.

Israel, Fred L., ed. *The War Diary of Breckenridge Long: Selections from the Years 1939–1944.* Lincoln: Univ. of Nebraska Press, 1966.

James, Robert Rhodes, ed. *Winston S. Churchill: His Complete Speeches, 1897–1963.* 8 vols.; New York: Chelsea House, 1974.

Kennan, George F. *Memoirs, 1925–1950.* Boston: Little, Brown & Co., 1967.

Kimball, Warren F., ed. *Churchill & Roosevelt: The Complete Correspondence.* 3 vols.; Princeton: Princeton Univ. Press, 1984.

Leahy, William D. *I Was There.* New York: Whittlesey House, 1950.

Macmillan, Harold. *The Blast of War, 1939–1945.* New York: Harper & Row, 1968.

———. *War Diaries: Politics and War in the Mediterranean, January 1943–May 1945.* New York: St. Martin's Press, 1984.

Moran, Lord [Charles Wilson]. *Churchill: Taken From the Diaries of Lord Moran.* Boston: Houghton Mifflin Co., 1966.

Pendar, Kenneth. *Adventure In Diplomacy.* New York: Dodd, Mead, 1945.

Perkins, Frances. *The Roosevelt I Knew.* New York: Harper Colophon, 1964.

Phillips, William. *Ventures in Diplomacy.* North Beverly, Mass.: distributed by author, 1952.

Pickersgill, J. W., and Forster, D. F. *The Mackenzie King Record.* 3 vols.; Toronto: Univ. of Toronto Press, 1960–70.

Roosevelt, Archibald. *For Lust of Knowing.* Boston: Little, Brown & Co., 1988.

Roosevelt, Elliott. *As He Saw It.* New York: Duell, Sloan and Pearce, 1946.

Roosevelt, Franklin D. *Complete Presidential Press Conferences of Franklin D. Roosevelt.* 25 vols.; New York: DaCapo Press, 1972.

———. *F.D.R. His Personal Letters, 1928–1945.* Elliott Roosevelt, ed. 3 vols.; New York: Duell, Sloan and Pearce, 1950.

———. *The Public Papers and Addresses of Franklin D. Roosevelt.* Samuel I. Rosenman, ed. 13 vols.; New York: Harper & Bros., 1938–50.

Ross, Graham, ed. *The Foreign Office and the Kremlin: Documents on Anglo-Soviet Relations, 1941–45.* Cambridge: Cambridge Univ. Press, 1984.

Truman, Harry S. *Year of Decisions.* Vol. I of *Memoirs.* Garden City, N.Y.: Doubleday, 1955.

———. *Where the Buck Stops: The Personal and Private Writings of Harry S. Truman.* Margaret Truman, ed. New York: Warner Books, 1989.

United States, Dept. of Commerce, Bureau of Foreign and Domestic Commerce. *Economic series* (1937–1940).

United States, Dept. of State. *Bulletin.*

———. *The China White Paper.* Vol. 1; Stanford: Stanford Univ. Press, 1967.

United States, Dept. of State. *Foreign Relations of the United States*. Washington: USGPO, 1865–.

———. [Harley Notter]. *Postwar Foreign Policy Preparation, 1939–1945*. Washington: USGPO, 1950.

USSR, Ministry of Foreign Affairs. *Stalin's Correspondence with Churchill and Attlee, 1941–1945*. New York: Capricorn Books, 1965.

———. *Stalin's Correspondence with Roosevelt and Truman, 1941–1945*. New York: Capricorn Books, 1965.

———. *The Tehran, Yalta & Potsdam Conferences: Documents*. Moscow: Progress Publishers, 1969.

Welles, Sumner. *Seven Major Decisions*. London: Hamish Hamilton, 1951.

———. *Where Are We Heading?* London: Hamish Hamilton, 1947.

White, Theodore H., ed. *The Stilwell Papers*. New York: Schocken Books, 1972.

Willkie, Wendell. *One World*. New York: Simon & Schuster, 1943.

Zhukov, G. *Reminiscences and Reflections*. English trans.; Moscow: Progress Publishers, 1985.

Secondary Works

Books

Addison, Paul. *The Road to 1945: British Politics and the Second World War*. London: Jonathan Cape, 1975.

Ambrose, Stephen E. *Eisenhower and Berlin, 1945: The Decision to Halt at the Elbe*. New York: Norton, 1967.

———. *Rise to Globalism*. 5th rev. ed.; New York: Penguin, 1988.

Anderson, Terry H. *The United States, Great Britain, and the Cold War: 1944–1947*. Columbia and London: Univ. of Missouri Press, 1981.

Andrew, Christopher. *KGB: Foreign Operations* (forthcoming).

Baily, Samuel L. *Labor, Nationalism, and Politics in Argentina*. New Brunswick: Rutgers Univ. Press, 1967.

Baptiste, Fitzroy André. *War, Cooperation, and Conflict: The European Possessions in the Caribbean, 1939–1945*. Westport, Conn.: Greenwood Press, 1988.

Beaumont, Joan. *Comrades In Arms: British Aid to Russia 1941–45*. London: Davis Poynter, 1980.

Beard, Charles A. *American Foreign Policy in the Making, 1932–1940*. New Haven: Yale Univ. Press, 1946.

———. *President Roosevelt and the Coming of the War, 1941*. New Haven: Yale Univ. Press, 1948.

Bennett, Edward M. *Franklin D. Roosevelt and the Search for Security: American-Soviet Relations, 1933–1939*. Wilmington, Del.: SR Books, 1985.

———. *Franklin D. Roosevelt and the Search for Victory: American-Soviet Relations, 1939–1945*. Wilmington, Del.: SR Books, 1990.

Birkenhead, Earl of. *Halifax: The Life of Lord Halifax*. London: Hamish Hamilton, 1965.

Bishop, Jim. *FDR's Last Year*. New York: William Morrow, 1974.

Blum, John Morton. *From the Morgenthau Diaries*. 3 vols.; Boston: Houghton Mifflin Co., 1959–67.

Botti, Timothy J. *The Long Wait: The Forging of the Anglo-American Nuclear Alliance, 1945–1958*. Westport, Conn.: Greenwood Press, 1987.

Breitman, Richard, and Kraut, Alan M. *American Refugee Policy and European Jewry, 1933–1945*. Bloomington: Indiana Univ. Press, 1987.

Bryant, Arthur. *Triumph in the West*. Garden City, N.Y.: Doubleday, 1959.

———. *The Turn of the Tide*. Garden City, N.Y.: Doubleday, 1957.

Burns, James MacGregor. *Roosevelt: The Soldier of Freedom*. New York: Harcourt Brace Jovanovich, Harvest ed., 1970.

Callahan, Raymond A. *Churchill: Retreat From Empire*. Wilmington, Del.: SR Books, 1984.

Campbell, Thomas M. *Masquerade Peace: America's US Policy, 1944–1945*. Tallahassee: Florida State Univ. Press, 1973.

Carlton, David. *Anthony Eden*. London: Allen Lane, 1981.

———. *Britain and the Suez Crisis*. Oxford, Basil Blackwell, 1988.

Clark, Ian. *Reform and Resistance in the International Order*. Cambridge: Cambridge Univ. Press, 1980.

Cohen, Warren I. *The American Revisionists*. Chicago: Univ. of Chicago Press, 1967.

Cole, Wayne S. *Roosevelt and the Isolationists, 1932–45*. Lincoln and London: Univ. of Nebraska Press, 1983.

Conn, Stetson, and Fairchild, Byron. *The Framework of Hemisphere Defense*. (United States Army in World War II); Washington: OCMH, 1960.

Conn, Stetson; Engleman, Rose C.; and Fairchild, Byron. *Guarding the United States and Its Outposts*. (United States Army in World War II); Washington: OCMH, 1964.

Costello, John. *The Pacific War*. New York: William Morrow, 1981.

Craig, Gordon A., and George, Alexander L. *Force and Statecraft*. New York: Oxford Univ. Press, 1983.

Crispell, Kenneth R., and Gomez, Carlos F. *Hidden Illness in the White House*. Durham and London: Duke Univ. Press, 1988.

Cuff, R. D., and Granatstein, J. L. *Canadian-American Relations in Wartime: From the Great War to the Cold War*. Toronto: Hakkert, 1975.

Dallek, Robert. *Franklin D. Roosevelt and American Foreign Policy*. New York: Oxford Univ. Press, 1979.

Dawson, Raymond. *The Decision to Aid Russia*. Chapel Hill: Univ. of North Carolina Press, 1959.

Divine, Robert A. *Illusion of Neutrality*. Chicago: Univ. of Chicago Press, 1962.

———. *The Reluctant Belligerent*. New York: Wiley, 1965.

———. *Roosevelt and World War II*. Baltimore: Johns Hopkins Univ. Press; Penguin Edition, 1970.

———. *Second Chance: The Triumph of Internationalism in America During World War II*. New York: Atheneum, 1967.

Dobson, Alan. *The Politics of the Anglo-American Economic Special Relationship 1940–1987*. New York: St. Martin's Press, 1988.

————. *US Wartime Aid to Britain, 1940–1946.* London: Croom Helm, 1986.

Dougherty, James J. *The Politics of Wartime Aid.* Westport, Conn.: Greenwood Press, 1978.

Dower, John W. *War Without Mercy: Race and Power in the Pacific War.* New York: Pantheon, 1986.

Draper, Theodore. *A Present of Things Past: Selected Essays.* New York: Hill & Wang, 1990.

Eckes, Jr., Alfred E. *A Search for Solvency.* Austin: Univ. of Texas Press, 1975.

Edmonds, Robin. *Setting the Mould: The United States and Britain, 1945–1950.* New York: Norton, 1986.

Eisenhower, David. *Eisenhower At War, 1943–1945.* New York: Random House, 1986.

Erickson, John. *The Road to Berlin.* London: Weidenfeld and Nicolson, 1983.

Eubank, Keith. *Summit at Teheran.* New York: William Morrow, 1985.

Feis, Herbert. *Churchill, Roosevelt, Stalin.* Princeton: Princeton Univ. Press, 1957.

Funk, Arthur L. *Charles de Gaulle: The Crucial Years, 1943–1944.* Norman: Oklahoma Univ. Press, 1959.

————. *The Politics of TORCH.* Lawrence: Univ. Press of Kansas, 1974.

Gabriel, Jürg Martin. *The American Conception of Neutrality after 1941.* London: Macmillan, 1988.

Gaddis, John L. *The United States and the Origins of the Cold War.* New York: Columbia Univ. Press, 1972.

Gardner, Lloyd C. *A Covenant With Power.* New York: Oxford Univ. Press, 1984.

————. *Approaching Vietnam: From World War II through Dienbienphu, 1941–1954.* New York: W.W. Norton & Co., 1988.

————. *Architects of Illusion.* Chicago: Quadrangle, 1970.

————. *Economic Aspects of New Deal Diplomacy.* Madison: Univ. of Wisconsin Press, 1964.

Gardner, Richard N. *Sterling-Dollar Diplomacy.* Expanded ed.; New York: Oxford Univ. Press, 1969.

————. *Sterling-Dollar Diplomacy in Current Perspective.* New York: Columbia Univ. Press, 1980.

Gellman, Irwin F. *Good Neighbor Diplomacy: United States Policies in Latin America, 1933–1945.* Baltimore and London: Johns Hopkins Univ. Press, 1979.

Gifford, Prosser, and Louis, Wm. Roger, eds. *The Transfer of Power in Africa.* New Haven: Yale Univ. Press, 1982.

Gilbert, Martin. *Britain and Germany Between the Wars.* London: Longman, 1964.

————. *Winston S. Churchill: Finest Hour.* Boston: Houghton Mifflin Co., 1983.

————. *Winston S. Churchill: Road to Victory, 1941–1945.* Boston: Houghton Mifflin Co., 1986.

Gilpin, Robert. *The Political Economy of International Relations.* Princeton: Princeton Univ. Press, 1987.

Gorodetsky, Gabriel. *Stafford Cripps' Mission to Moscow, 1940–1942.* Cambridge: Cambridge Univ. Press, 1984.

Granatstein, J. L. *Canada's War: The Politics of the Mackenzie King Government, 1939–1945.* Toronto: Oxford Univ. Press, 1975.

Green, David. *The Containment of Latin America: A History of the Myths and Realities of the Good Neighbor Policy.* Chicago: Quadrangle, 1971.

Greenfield, Kent Roberts. *American Strategy in World War II: A Reconsideration.* Baltimore: Johns Hopkins Univ. Press, 1963.

Griswold, A. Whitney. *The Far Eastern Policy of the United States.* New York: Harcourt, Brace & Co., 1938.

Gromyko, A. A., and Ponomarev, B. N., eds. *Soviet Foreign Policy, 1917–1945.* 4th ed.; Moscow: Progress Publishers, 1981.

Gunther, John. *Roosevelt in Retrospect: A Profile in History.* New York: Harper & Bros., 1950.

Harbutt, Fraser J. *The Iron Curtain: Churchill, America, and the Origins of the Cold War.* New York: Oxford Univ. Press, 1986.

Harriman, W. Averell, and Abel, Elie. *Special Envoy to Churchill and Stalin, 1941–1946.* New York: Random House, 1975.

Harrod, Roy F. *The Life of John Maynard Keynes.* New York: Harcourt, Brace & Co., 1951.

Hathaway, Robert. *Ambiguous Partnership: Britain and America, 1944–1947.* New York: Columbia Univ. Press, 1981.

Hearden, Patrick J. *Roosevelt Confronts Hitler: America's Entry Into World War II.* DeKalb: Northern Illinois Univ. Press, 1987.

Heinrichs, Waldo. *Threshold of War: Franklin D. Roosevelt and American Entry Into World War II.* New York: Oxford Univ. Press, 1988.

Herring, George C., Jr. *Aid to Russia, 1941–1946.* New York: Columbia Univ. Press, 1973.

Hess, Gary. *America Encounters India 1941–1947.* Baltimore: Johns Hopkins Univ. Press, 1971.

———. *The United States' Emergence as a Southeast Asian Power, 1940–1950.* New York: Columbia Univ. Press, 1987.

Hilton, Stanley E. *Hitler's Secret War in South America.* Baton Rouge: Louisiana State Univ. Press, 1981.

Hinsley, F. H. *British Intelligence in the Second World War.* (British official History of the Second World War); 3 vols.; London: HMSO, 1979–88.

Holloway, David. *The Soviet Union and the Arms Race.* 2d ed.; New Haven: Yale Univ. Press, 1984.

Horne, Alistair. *Harold Macmillan, vol. I: 1894–1956.* New York: Viking, 1988.

Howard, Michael. *Grand Strategy, August 1942–September 1943.* (British official History of the Second World War); London: HMSO, 1970.

———. *War and the Liberal Conscience.* Oxford: Oxford Univ. Press, 1978.

Iriye, Akira. *Power and Culture: The Japanese-American War, 1941–1945.* Cambridge: Harvard Univ. Press, 1981.

Irving, David. *Churchill's War: The Struggle for Power.* Australia: Veritas Publishing Co. Pty., 1987.

Janeway, Eliot. *The Struggle for Survival.* New Haven: Yale Univ. Press, 1951.

Karl, Barry. *The Uneasy State.* Chicago: Univ. of Chicago Press, 1983.

Kennedy, Paul. *The Rise and Fall of the Great Powers.* New York: Random House-Vintage, 1989.

Kesaris, Paul L., ed. *The Rote Kapelle: The CIA's History of Soviet Intelligence and Espionage Networks in Western Europe, 1936–1945*. Washington: University Publications of America, 1979.

Kimball, Warren F. *"The Most Unsordid Act" Lend-Lease, 1939–1941*. Baltimore: Johns Hopkins Univ. Press, 1969.

———. *Swords or Ploughshares? The Morgenthau Plan for Defeated Nazi Germany*. Philadelphia: Lippincott, 1976.

Kolko, Gabriel. *The Politics of War*. Vintage ed.; New York: Random House, 1970.

Kottman, Richard N. *Reciprocity and the North Atlantic Triangle, 1932–1938*. Ithaca: Cornell Univ. Press, 1968.

LaFeber, Walter. *America, Russia, and the Cold War*. New York: John Wiley, 1967.

———. *Inevitable Revolutions: The United States in Central America*. New York: Norton, 1984.

Langer, William L., and Gleason, S. Everett. *The Challenge to Isolation*. New York: Harper & Bros., 1952.

———. *The Undeclared War, 1940–1941*. New York: Harper & Bros., 1953.

Larianov, V., et al., eds. *World War II: Decisive Battles of the Soviet Army*. Moscow: Progress Publishers, 1984.

Larrabee, Eric. *Commander in Chief: Franklin Delano Roosevelt, His Lieutenants and Their War*. New York: Harper & Row, 1987.

Lash, Joseph P. *Eleanor and Franklin*. New York: Norton, 1971.

———. *Roosevelt and Churchill, 1939–1941*. New York: Norton, 1976.

Layton, Edwin T., et al. *"And I Was There."* New York: William Morrow, 1985.

Leopold, Richard. *The Growth of American Foreign Policy: A History*. New York: Knopf, 1962.

Lingard, C. Cecil, and Trotter, Reginald C. *Canada in World Affairs, September 1941–May 1944*. Toronto: Oxford Univ. Press, 1950.

Lippmann, Walter. *U.S. Foreign Policy*. London: Hamish Hamilton, 1943.

———. *U.S. War Aims*. London: Hamish Hamilton, 1944.

Louis, Wm. Roger. *Imperialism at Bay*. New York: Oxford Univ. Press, 1977.

McJimsey, George. *Harry Hopkins*. Cambridge, Mass.: Harvard Univ. Press, 1987.

McMahon, Robert J. *Colonialism and Cold War: The United States and the Struggle for Indonesian Independence 1945–1949*. Ithaca: Cornell Univ. Press, 1981.

McNeill, William Hardy. *America, Britain, & Russia: Their Co-operation and Conflict, 1941–1946*. London, New York, Toronto: Oxford Univ. Press, 1953; Johnson reprint, 1970.

Manchester, William. *The Last Lion, Winston Spencer Churchill: Visions of Glory, 1874–1932*. Boston: Little, Brown & Co., 1983.

Marks, Frederick W., III. *Wind Over Sand*. Athens: Univ. of Georgia Press, 1988.

Martel, Leon. *Lend-Lease, Loans, and the Coming of the Cold War*. Boulder, Colo.: Westview Press, 1979.

Mastny, Vojtech. *Russia's Road to the Cold War*. New York: Columbia Univ. Press, 1979.

Matloff, Maurice. *Strategic Planning for Coalition Warfare, 1943–1944*. (United States Army in World War II); Washington: Office of the Chief of Military History, 1959.

May, Ernest R. *"Lessons" of the Past*. New York: Oxford Univ. Press, 1973.

Mayers, David. *George Kennan and the Dilemmas of US Foreign Policy*. New York: Oxford Univ. Press, 1986.

Mayle, Paul D. *Eureka Summit: Agreement in Principle and the Big Three at Tehran, 1943*. Newark: Univ. of Delaware Press, 1987.

Michel, Henri. *The Second World War*. New York: Praeger, 1975.

Miner, Steven M. *Between Churchill and Stalin: The Soviet Union, Great Britain, and the Origins of the Grand Alliance*. Chapel Hill: Univ. of North Carolina Press, 1988.

Moore, R. J. *Churchill, Cripps and India, 1939–1945*. Oxford: Oxford University Press, 1979.

Morgan, Ted. *FDR: A Biography*. London: Grafton Books, 1986.

Nisbet, Robert. *Roosevelt and Stalin: The Failed Courtship*. Washington: Regnery Gateway, 1988.

O'Connor, Raymond G. *Diplomacy For Victory: FDR and Unconditional Surrender*. New York: Norton, 1971.

Park, Bert E. *The Impact of Illness on World Leaders*. Philadelphia: Univ. of Pennsylvania Press, 1986.

Paterson, Thomas G. *On Every Front*. New York: Norton, 1979.

———. *Soviet-American Confrontation*. Baltimore: Johns Hopkins Univ. Press, 1973.

Pogue, Forrest C. *George C. Marshall: Organizer of Victory*. New York: Viking, 1973.

Range, Willard. *Franklin D. Roosevelt's World Order*. Athens: Univ. of Georgia Press, 1959.

Read, Anthony, and Fisher, David. *The Deadly Embrace: Hitler, Stalin, and the Nazi-Soviet Pact, 1939–1941*. New York: Norton, 1988.

Reynolds, David. *The Creation of the Anglo-American Alliance, 1937–1941: A Study in Competitive Co-operation*. London: Europa, 1982.

Reynolds, David, and Dimbleby, David. *An Ocean Apart: The Relationship between Britain and America in the Twentieth Century*. New York: Random House, 1988.

Rhodes, Richard. *The Making of the Atomic Bomb*. New York: Simon & Schuster, 1986.

Robertson, Terence. *The Ship With Two Captains*. New York: E. P. Dutton, 1950.

Rock, David. *Argentina, 1516–1987*. Berkeley: Univ. of California Press, 1987.

Rock, William R. *Chamberlain and Roosevelt*. Columbus: Ohio State Univ. Press, 1988.

Rosen, Elliot A. *Hoover, Roosevelt, and the Brains Trust*. New York: Columbia Univ. Press, 1977.

Ruddy, T. Michael. *The Cautious Diplomat: Charles E. Bohlen and the Soviet Union*. Kent, Ohio: Kent State Univ. Press, 1986.

Ryan, Henry B. *The Vision of Anglo-America*. Cambridge: Cambridge Univ. Press, 1987.

Rzheshevsky, Oleg. *World War II: Myths and the Realities.* Moscow: Progress Publishers, 1984.

Sainsbury, Keith. *The North African Landings, 1942.* Newark: Univ. of Delaware Press, 1976.

———. *The Turning Point: Roosevelt, Stalin, Churchill, and Chiang Kai-shek, 1943; The Moscow, Cairo, and Teheran Conferences.* New York: Oxford Univ. Press, 1985.

Sayers, R. S. *Financial Policy, 1939–1945.* (British official History of the Second World War); London: HMSO, 1956.

Sbrega, John J. *Anglo-American Relations and Colonialism in East Asia, 1941–1945.* New York: Garland, 1983.

Schaller, Michael. *The U.S. Crusade in China, 1938–1945.* New York: Columbia Univ. Press, 1979.

Schneider, James C. *Should America Go to War?* Chapel Hill: Univ. of North Carolina Press, 1989.

[Sevost'ianov, Grigory, ed.]. *Soviet-U.S. Relations, 1933–1942.* Moscow: Progress Publishers, 1989.

Sheehan, Neil. *A Bright Shining Lie: John Paul Vann and America in Vietnam.* New York: Random House-Vintage, 1989.

Sherwin, Martin J. *A World Destroyed: The Atomic Bomb and the Grand Alliance.* New York: Alfred A. Knopf, 1975.

Sherwood, Robert. *Roosevelt and Hopkins: An Intimate History.* Rev. ed.; New York: Grosset & Dunlap, Universal Library, 1950.

Short, Anthony. *The Origins of the Vietnam War.* London and New York: Longman, 1989.

Shtemenko, S. M. *The Soviet General Staff at War, 1941–1945.* Robert Daglish, trans.; Moscow: Progress Publishers, 1985.

Sipols, Vilnis. *The Road to Great Victory: Soviet Diplomacy, 1941–1945.* Moscow: Progress Publishers, 1985.

Smith, Arthur. *Churchill's German Army.* Beverly Hills and London: Sage, 1977.

Smith, Denis. *Diplomacy of Fear: Canada and the Cold War, 1941–1948.* Toronto, Buffalo, London: Univ. of Toronto Press, 1988.

Steel, Ronald. *Walter Lippmann and the American Century.* London: The Bodley Head, 1980.

Steele, Richard W. *Propaganda in an Open Society.* Westport, Conn.: Greenwood Press, 1985.

Stein, Harold, ed. *American Civil-Military Decisions.* Birmingham: Univ. of Alabama Press, 1963.

Steiner, George. *In Bluebeard's Castle.* London and Boston: Faber & Faber, 1971.

Stephanson, Anders. *Kennan and the Art of Diplomacy.* Cambridge: Harvard Univ. Press, 1989.

Steward, Dick. *Trade and Hemisphere: The Good Neighbor Policy and Reciprocal Trade.* Columbia: Univ. of Missouri Press, 1975.

Stiller, Jesse H. *George S. Messersmith: Diplomat of Democracy.* Chapel Hill and London: Univ. of North Carolina Press, 1987.

Stoler, Mark A. *George C. Marshall: Soldier-Statesman of the American Century.* Boston: Twayne, 1989.

————. *The Politics of the Second Front: American Military Planning and Diplomacy in Coalition Warfare, 1941–1943*. Westport, Conn.: Greenwood Press, 1977.

Stueck, William W., Jr. *The Road to Confrontation: American Policy Toward China and Korea, 1947–1950*. Chapel Hill: Univ. of North Carolina Press, 1981.

Tella, Guido di, and Watt, D. C., eds. *Argentina between the Great Powers, 1939–46*. Basingstoke: Macmillan/St. Antony's College, Oxford, 1989.

Thorne, Christopher. *Allies of a Kind*. New York: Oxford Univ. Press, 1978.

————. *Border Crossings*. Oxford: Basil Blackwell, 1988.

————. *The Issue of War: States, Societies, and the Far Eastern Conflict of 1941–1945*. New York: Oxford Univ. Press, 1985.

Tuttle, Dwight W. *Harry L. Hopkins and Anglo-American-Soviet Relations, 1941–1945*. New York: Garland, 1983.

Vigneras, Marcel. *Rearming the French*. (United States Army in World War II); Washington: OCMH, 1957.

Watt, Donald Cameron. *How War Came: The Immediate Origins of the Second World War, 1938–1939*. New York: Pantheon, 1989.

————. *Succeeding John Bull*. New York: Cambridge Univ. Press, 1984.

Whaley, Barton. *Codeword BARBAROSSA*. Cambridge: MIT Press, 1973.

Wheeler-Bennett, J., ed. *Action This Day*. London: Macmillan, 1968.

Williams, William A. *The Great Evasion*. Chicago: Quadrangle, 1964.

————. *The Tragedy of American Diplomacy*. New York: World Publishing Co., 1959.

Wilson, Theodore. *The First Summit*. Boston: Houghton Mifflin Co., 1969.

Winfield, Betty Houchins. *FDR and the News Media*. Urbana and Chicago: Univ. of Illinois Press, 1990.

Wittner, Lawrence S. *American Intervention in Greece, 1943– 1949*. New York: Columbia Univ. Press, 1982.

Wood, Bryce. *Dismantling the Good Neighbor Policy*. Austin: Univ. of Texas Press, 1985.

————. *The Making of the Good Neighbor Policy*. New York: Columbia Univ. Press, 1961; Norton ed., 1967.

Woods, Randall Bennett. *The Roosevelt Foreign-Policy Establishment and the "Good Neighbor": The United States and Argentina, 1941–1945*. Lawrence: The Regents Press of Kansas, 1979.

Woodward, Llewellyn. *British Foreign Policy During the Second World War*. (British official History of the Second World War); 5 vols.; London: HMSO, 1970–76.

Wyman, David. *Paper Walls*. Amherst, Mass.: Univ. of Massachusetts Press, 1968.

Articles

Allen, William R. "Cordell Hull and the Defense of the Trade Agreements Program, 1934–1940." In A. DeConde, ed., *Isolation and Security*. Durham: Duke Univ. Press, 1957.

————. "The International Trade Philosophy of Cordell Hull, 1907–1933." *American Economic Review* 43 (1953): 101–16.

Bess, Demaree. "The Cost of Roosevelt's 'Great Design.' " *Saturday Evening Post* 116 (27 May 1944).

Boyle, Peter. "The Special Relationship: An Alliance of Convenience?" *Journal of American Studies* 22 (Dec. 1988): 457–65.

Bratzel, James F., and Rout, Leslie B. "FDR and the 'Secret Map,' " *The Wilson Quarterly* 9 (New Year's 1985): 167–73.

Bruenn, Howard G. "Clinical Notes on the Illness and Death of President Franklin D. Roosevelt." *Annals of Internal Medicine* 72 (1970): 579–91.

Campbell, A. E. "Franklin D. Roosevelt and Unconditional Surrender." *Diplomacy and Intelligence during the Second World War*, Richard Langhorne, ed. (Cambridge: Cambridge Univ. Press, 1985).

Clifford, J. Garry. "Both Ends of the Telescope: New Perspectives on FDR and American Entry into World War II." *Diplomatic History* 13 (Spring 1989): 213–30.

Clymer, Kenton J. "The Education of William Phillips: Self Determination and American Policy toward India, 1942–1945." *Diplomatic History* 8 (Winter 1984): 13–25.

———. "Franklin D. Roosevelt, Louis Johnson, India and Anticolonialism: Another Look." *Pacific Historical Review* 57 (1988): 261–84.

Davis, Forrest. "Roosevelt's World Blueprint." *Saturday Evening Post* 115 (10 April 1943).

———. "What Really Happened at Teheran." *Saturday Evening Post* 116 (13 and 20 May 1944).

DeConde, Alexander. "Essay and Reflection: On the Nature of International History." *International History Review* 10 (May 1988): 282–301.

Dobson, Alan P. "Economic Diplomacy at the Atlantic Conference." *Review of International Studies* 10 (April 1984): 143–63.

Elsey, George. "Some White House Recollections, 1942–53." *Diplomatic History* 12 (Summer 1988): 357–64.

Emerson, William R. "Franklin Roosevelt as Commander-in-Chief in World War II." *Military Affairs* 22 (Winter 1958–59): 183–92.

Feis, Herbert. "Some Notes on Historical Record-keeping, the Role of Historians, and the Influence of Historical Memories During the Era of the Second World War." In *The Historian and the Diplomat*. New York: Harper & Row, 1967.

Fogelson, Nancy. "Greenland: Strategic Base on a Northern Defense Line." *Journal of Military History* 53 (January 1989): 51–63.

Foltos, Lester J. "The New Pacific Barrier: America's Search for Security in the Pacific, 1945–47." *Diplomatic History* 13 (Summer 1989): 317–42.

Funk, Arthur L. "The 'Anfa Memorandum': An Incident of the Casablanca Conference." *Journal of Modern History* 26 (Sept. 1954): 246–54.

Gardner, Lloyd C. "The Atomic Temptation, 1945–1954." In *Redefining the Past*, L. C. Gardner, ed. (Corvallis: Oregon State Univ. Press, 1986).

———. "The Role of the Commerce and Treasury Departments." In *Pearl Harbor As History*, Dorothy Borg and S. Okamoto, eds. (New York: Columbia Univ. Press, 1973), 261–85.

———. "A Tale of Three Cities: Tripartite Diplomacy and the Second Front,

1941–1942." In *Soviet-U.S. Relations, 1933–1942*. Moscow: Progress Publishers, 1989.

Gorodetsky, Gabriel. "Stalin und Hitlers Angriff auf die Sowjet Union." *Vierteljahrsheft für Zeitgeschichte* 4 (1989): 645–72.

Haines, Gerald K. "Under the Eagle's Wing: The Franklin Roosevelt Administration Forges an American Hemisphere." *Diplomatic History* 1 (Fall 1977): 373–88.

Harbutt, Fraser J. "Churchill, Hopkins, and the 'Other' Americans: An Alternative Perspective on Anglo-American Relations, 1941–1945." *International History Review* 8 (May 1986): 236–62.

———. "Cold War Origins: An Anglo-European Perspective." *Diplomatic History* 13 (Winter 1989).

Henrikson, Alan K. "The Map as an 'Idea': The Role of Cartographic Imagery During the Second World War." *The American Cartographer* 2 (1975): 19–53.

Herndon, James S. "British Perceptions of Soviet Military Capability, 1935–9." In *The Fascist Challenge and the Policy of Appeasement*, Wolfgang J. Mommsen and Lothar Kettenacker, eds. (London: George Allen & Unwin, 1983).

Herring, George C., Jr. "The Truman Administration and the Restoration of French Sovereignty in Indochina." *Diplomatic History* 1 (Spring 1977): 97–117.

———. "The United States and British Bankruptcy, 1944–1945: Responsibilities Deferred." *Political Science Quarterly* 86 (June 1971): 260–80.

Hess, Gary. "Franklin Roosevelt and Indochina." *Journal of American History* 59 (1972): 353–68.

Iriye, Akira. "The Internationalization of History." *American Historical Review* 94 (Feb. 1989): 1–10.

Johnson, Howard. "The Anglo-American Caribbean Commission and the Extension of American Influence in the British Caribbean, 1942–1945." *Journal of Commonwealth and Comparative Politics* 22 (1984): 180–203.

———. "The United States and the Establishment of the Anglo-American Caribbean Commission." *Journal of Caribbean History* 19 (1984): 26–47.

Jukes, Geoff. "More on the Soviets and ULTRA." *Intelligence and National Security* (forthcoming).

———. "The Soviets and ULTRA." *Intelligence and National Security* (April 1988): 233–47.

Kaplan, Lawrence S. "The Cold War and European Revisionism." *Diplomatic History* 11 (Spring 1987): 143–56.

Kimball, Warren F. " 'Beggar My Neighbor': America and the British Interim Finance Crisis, 1940–1941." *The Journal of Economic History* 29 (1969): 758–72.

Koch, H. W. "Hitler's 'Programme' and the Genesis of Operation 'BARBAROSSA.' " *The Historical Journal* 26 (1983).

LaFeber, Walter. "American Empire, American Raj." In *America Unbound: World War II and the Making of a Superpower*, W. F. Kimball, ed. New York: St. Martin's Press, 1992.

LaFeber, Walter. "The Evolution of the Monroe Doctrine from Monroe to Reagan." In *Redefining the Past*, Lloyd C. Gardner, ed. Corvallis: Oregon State Univ. Press, 1986.

———. "Roosevelt, Churchill, and Indochina: 1942–45," *American Historical Review* 80 (Dec. 1985): 1277–95.

Langer, John D. "The Harriman-Beaverbrook Mission and the Debate Over Unconditional Aid for the Soviet Union, 1941." In Walter Laquer, ed., *The Second World War: Essays in Military and Political History* (London and Beverly Hills: Sage, 1982).

Lawlor, Sheila. "Britain and the Russian Entry into the War." In *Diplomacy and Intelligence during the Second World War*, Richard Langhorne, ed. (Cambridge: Cambridge Univ. Press, 1985).

Lees, Lorraine M. "National Security and Ethnicity: Contrasting Views During World War II." *Diplomatic History* 11 (Spring 1987): 113–25.

Leitenberg, Milton. "The Soviet Union and the Lessons of World War II." *SHAFR Newsletter* 19, no. 2 (June 1988): 11.

Leuchtenburg, William E. "The Pertinence of Political History: Reflections on the Significance of the State in America." *Journal of American History* 73 (Dec. 1986).

Louis, Wm. Roger, and Robinson, Ronald. "The United States and the Liquidation of the British Empire in Tropical Africa, 1941–1951." In *The Transfer of Power in Africa*, Prosser Gifford and Wm. Roger Louis, eds. New Haven: Yale Univ. Press, 1982.

Lynch, Hollis R. "Pan-African Responses in the United States to British Colonial Rule in Africa in the 1940s." In *The Transfer of Power in Africa*, Prosser Gifford and Wm. Roger Louis, eds. New Haven: Yale Univ. Press, 1982.

MacLean, Elizabeth Kimball. "Joseph Davies and Soviet-American Relations, 1941–1943." *Diplomatic History* 4 (Winter 1980): 73–93.

Maddux, Thomas R. "Watching Stalin Maneuver between Hitler and the West: American Diplomats and Soviet Diplomacy, 1934–1939." *Diplomatic History* 1 (Spring 1977): 140–54.

Maier, Charles S. "The Politics of Productivity: Foundations of American International Economic Foreign Policy after World War II." *International Organization* 31 (Autumn 1977): 607–33.

Major, John. "F.D.R. and Panama." *The Historical Journal* 28, no. 2 (1985): 357–77.

Mark, Eduard. "American Policy Toward Eastern Europe and the Origins of the Cold War, 1941–1946: An Alternative Explanation." *Journal of American History* 68 (1981): 313–36.

———. "Charles E. Bohlen and the Acceptable Limits of Soviet Hegemony in Eastern Europe." *Diplomatic History* 3 (Spring 1979): 201–13.

———. "October or Thermidor? Interpretations of Stalinism and the Perception of Soviet Foreign Policy in the United States, 1927–1947." *American Historical Review* 94 (October 1989): 937–62.

Najafov, Janghir. "German Invasion of the U.S.S.R. and the U.S. Position." *Soviet-U.S. Relations, 1933–1942*. Moscow: Progress Publishers, 1989.

Neumann, William L. "Roosevelt's Foreign Policy Decisions, 1940–1945." *Modern Age* (Summer 1975).

———. "Roosevelt's Options and Evasions in Foreign Policy Decisions, 1940–1945." In *Watershed of Empire*, L. Liggio and J. Martin, eds. Colorado Springs: Ralph Myles, 1976.

Ninkovich, Frank. "Interests and Discourse in Diplomatic History." *Diplomatic History* 13 (Spring 1989): 135–61.

Park, Hong-Kyu. "From Pearl Harbor to Cairo: America's Korean Diplomacy, 1941–43." *Diplomatic History* 13 (Summer 1989): 343–58.

Patterson, James T. "Robert A. Taft and American Foreign Policy, 1939–1945." In *Watershed of Empire: Essays on New Deal Foreign Policy*, L. Liggio and J. Martin, eds. Colorado Springs: Ralph Myles, 1976.

Phillips, Hugh. "Mission to America: Maksim M. Litvinov in the United States, 1941–43." *Diplomatic History* 12 (Summer 1988): 261–75.

Pietz, William. "The 'Post-Colonialism' of Cold War Discourse." *Social Text* 19/20 (Fall 1988).

Pollock, Fred E. "Roosevelt, the Ogdensburg Agreement, and the British Fleet: All Done With Mirrors." *Diplomatic History* 5 (Summer 1981): 203–19.

Polonsky, Antony. "Stalin and the Poles 1941–7." *European History Quarterly* 17 (1987): 453–92.

Resis, Albert. "The Churchill-Stalin Secret 'Percentages' Agreement on the Balkans: Moscow, October 1944." *American Historical Review* 83 (1978): 368–87.

———. "Spheres of Influence in Soviet Wartime Diplomacy." *Journal of Modern History* 53 (1981): 422–36.

Reynolds, David. "Churchill and the British 'Decision' to Fight on in 1940: Right Policy, Wrong Reasons." In *Diplomacy and Intelligence during the Second World War*, Richard Langhorne, ed. Cambridge: Cambridge Univ. Press, 1985.

———. "Rethinking Anglo-American Relations." *International Affairs* 65 (Winter 1988–89): 99–104.

———"Roosevelt, Churchill, and the Wartime Anglo-American Alliance, 1939–1945: Towards a New Synthesis." In *The 'Special Relationship': Anglo-American Relations Since 1945*, Wm. Roger Louis and Hedley Bull, eds. Oxford: Clarendon Press, 1986.

Riste, Olav. "Free Ports in North Norway, A Contribution to the Study of FDR's Wartime Policy Towards the USSR." *Journal of Contemporary History* 5 (1970): 77–95.

Ross, K.G.M. "The Moscow Conference of October 1944 (TOLSTOY)." In *British Political and Military Strategy in Central, Eastern and Southern Europe in 1944*, William Deakin et al., eds. New York: St. Martin's Press, 1988.

Rotundo, Louis. "Stalin and the Outbreak of War in 1941." *Journal of Contemporary History* 24 (April 1989): 277–99.

Sainsbury, Keith. "Central and Eastern Europe at the Quebec Conference." In *British Political and Military Strategy in Central, Eastern and Southern Europe in 1944*, William Deakin et al., eds. New York: St. Martin's Press, 1988.

Schatz, Arthur W. "The Anglo-American Trade Agreement and Cordell Hull's

Search for Peace, 1936–1938." *Journal of American History* 57 (1970): 85–103.

Schlesinger, Arthur, Jr. "The Origins of the Cold War." In *The Origins of the Cold War.* Boston: Ginn & Co., 1970, orig. pub. in *Foreign Affairs* 46 (Oct. 1967).

———. "War and the Constitution: Abraham Lincoln and Franklin D. Roosevelt." Fortenbaugh Memorial Lecture (Gettysburg: Gettysburg College, 1988).

Schroeder, Paul. "The Nineteenth Century System: Balance of Power or Political Equilibrium?" *Review of International Studies* 15 (April 1989): 135–53.

Siracusa, Joseph. "The Meaning of TOLSTOY: Churchill, Stalin, and the Balkans, Moscow, October 1944." *Diplomatic History* 3 (Fall 1979): 443–63.

———. "The Night Stalin and Churchill Divided Europe: The View from Washington." *The Review of Politics* 43 (July 1981): 381–409.

Smith, Bradley. "Sharing ULTRA in World War II." *International Journal of Intelligence and Counterintelligence* 2 (Spring 1988): 59–72.

Stoler, Mark A. "From Continentalism to Globalism: General Stanley D. Embick, the Joint Strategic Survey Committee, and the Military View of American National Policy during the Second World War." *Diplomatic History* 6 (Summer 1982): 303–21.

———. "The 'Pacific-First' Alternative in American World War II Strategy." *The International History Review* 2 (July 1980): 432–52.

Stolfi, Russel H. S. "BARBAROSSA: German Grand Deception and the Achievement of Strategic and Tactical Surprise Against the Soviet Union, 1940–1941." In *Strategic Military Deception*, D. C. Daniel and K. L. Herbig, eds. New York: Pergamon, 1982.

Thorne, Christopher. "Indochina and Anglo-American Relations, 1942–1945." *Pacific Historical Review* 45 (1976): 73–96.

Unterberger, Betty Miller. "American Views of Mohammad Ali Jinnah and the Pakistan Liberation Movement." *Diplomatic History* 5 (Fall 1981): 313–36.

Walker, J. Samuel. "The Decision to Use the Bomb." *Diplomatic History* 14 (Winter 1990): 97–114.

Watt, Donald Cameron. "American Anti-colonialist Policies at the End of the European Colonial Empires, 1941–1962." In *Contagious Conflict: The Impact of American Dissent on European Life*, A.N.J. Hollander, ed. Leiden: E. J. Brill, 1973.

———. "Britain and the Historiography of the Yalta Conference and the Cold War." *Diplomatic History* 13 (Winter 1989): 67–98.

———. "Every War Must End." *Transactions of the Royal Historical Society*, 5th ser., 28 (1978).

———. "U.S. Globalism: The End of the Concert of Europe." In *America Unbound: World War II and the Making of a Superpower*, W. F. Kimball, ed. New York: St. Martin's Press, 1992.

Wilson, Theodore. "In Aid of America's Interests: The Provision of Lend-Lease to the Soviet Union, 1941–1942." In *Soviet U.S. Relations, 1933–1942*. Moscow: Progress Publishers, 1989.

Unpublished Essays and Manuscripts

Andrew, Christopher. "Intelligence Collaboration between Britain and the United States during the Second World War." Paper (1st draft).

Day, David. "The Reluctant Warriors: The British Empire and the Pacific War." Manuscript (in press).

Gardner, Lloyd C. "The Riddle of the Sphinx: Russia and Reconstruction." Paper presented to the 3d Symposium of the US/USSR Project on the History of World War II (Moscow, Oct. 1988).

Kennan, George F. Comment delivered on 17 April 1974, at the annual meeting of the Organization of American Historians, Denver, Colorado.

Miner, Stephen M. " 'The Other Side of the Hill': Soviet Sources on the Teheran Conference." Paper presented at the 3d Symposium of the US/USSR Project on the History of World War II (Moscow, Oct. 1988).

Paterson, Thomas G. "Toward Spheres of Influence: United States Postwar Planning and Soviet-American Relations." Revised version of a paper written for the US/USSR Symposium on Soviet-American Relations in the Cold War (Moscow 1987).

Resis, Albert. "Allied Policy Toward the Future Germany, 1942–43." Paper presented to the 3d Symposium of the US/USSR Project on the History of World War II (Moscow, Oct. 1988).

Reynolds, David. "Churchill, The Special Relationship and the Debate about Post-War European Security, 1940–1945." Paper delivered at the American Historical Association meeting, 29 Dec. 1983 (San Francisco, Calif.).

Rosen, Elliot A. "After Half A Century: The New Deal in Perspective."

———. "The Possibilities for Peace: Hoover, Roosevelt, and the World Financial Crisis, 1933." Paper delivered at the Hoover Symposium 6 (George Fox College, 24 Oct. 1987).

Schomburk, Sir Evelyn. Remarks at the conference, "Argentina Between the Great Powers, 1939–1946," St. Antony's College, Oxford, 3–5 July 1986.

Index